The Knowledge Argument

Frank Jackson's knowledge argument imagines a super-smart scientist, Mary, forced to investigate the mysteries of human colour vision using only black and white resources. Can she work out what it is like to see red from brain-science and physics alone? The argument says no: Mary will only really learn what red looks like when she actually sees it. Something is therefore missing from the science of the mind, and from the 'physicalist' picture of the world based on science. This powerful and controversial argument remains as pivotal as when it was first created in 1982, and this volume provides a thorough and incisive examination of its relevance in philosophy of mind today. The cutting-edge essays featured here break new ground in the debate, and also comprehensively set out the developments in the story of the knowledge argument so far, tracing its impact, past, present, and future.

Sam Coleman is Reader in Philosophy at the University of Hertfordshire and is the author of various articles on philosophy of mind.

Classic Philosophical Arguments

Over the centuries, a number of individual arguments have formed a crucial part of philosophical enquiry. The volumes in this series examine these arguments, looking at the ramifications and applications which they have come to have, the challenges which they have encountered, and the ways in which they have stood the test of time.

Titles in the series

The Knowledge Argument

Edited by

Sam Coleman

University of Hertfordshire

CAMBRIDGE
UNIVERSITY PRESS

CAMBRIDGE
UNIVERSITY PRESS

University Printing House, Cambridge CB2 8BS, United Kingdom

One Liberty Plaza, 20th Floor, New York, NY 10006, USA

477 Williamstown Road, Port Melbourne, VIC 3207, Australia

314–321, 3rd Floor, Plot 3, Splendor Forum, Jasola District Centre, New Delhi – 110025, India

79 Anson Road, #06-04/06, Singapore 079906

Cambridge University Press is part of the University of Cambridge.

It furthers the University's mission by disseminating knowledge in the pursuit of education, learning, and research at the highest international levels of excellence.

www.cambridge.org
Information on this title: www.cambridge.org/9781107141995
DOI: 10.1017/9781316494134

© Cambridge University Press 2019

First published 2019

Printed in the United Kingdom by TJ International Ltd, Padstow Cornwall

A catalogue record for this publication is available from the British Library.

Library of Congress Cataloging-in-Publication Data
Names: Coleman, Sam (Senior lecturer), editor.
Title: The knowledge argument / edited by Sam Coleman, University of Hertfordshire.
Description: New York: Cambridge University Press, 2019. |
Series: Classic philosophical arguments |
Includes bibliographical references and index.
Identifiers: LCCN 2019019729 | ISBN 9781107141995 (hardback) |
ISBN 9781316506981 (paperback)
Subjects: LCSH: Philosophy of mind. | Knowledge, Theory of. |
Jackson, Frank, 1943– | Materialism.
Classification: LCC BD418.3 .K59 2019 | DDC 128/.2–dc23
LC record available at https://lccn.loc.gov/2019019729

ISBN 978-1-107-14199-5 Hardback
ISBN 978-1-316-50698-1 Paperback

Contents

Contributors

Torin Alter is Professor of Philosophy at the University of Alabama.

Tim Crane is Professor of Philosophy at the Central European University.

Brie Gertler is Commonwealth Professor in the Corcoran Department of Philosophy at the University of Virginia.

Philip Goff is Assistant Professor at Durham University.

Robert J. Howell is Professor of Philosophy at Southern Methodist University.

Frank Jackson is Emeritus Professor at the Australian National University.

Amy Kind is Professor of Philosophy at Claremont McKenna College.

Tom McClelland is Leverhulme Trust Early Career Research Fellow at Warwick University.

Hedda Hassel Mørch is a Post-Doctoral Researcher at the University of Oslo.

David Pitt is Professor of Philosophy at California State University, Los Angeles.

David Rosenthal is Professor of Philosophy and Coordinator of the Interdisciplinary Concentration in Cognitive Science at the Graduate Center, City University of New York.

Galen Strawson is Professor of Philosophy at the University of Texas at Austin.

Michael Tye is Professor of Philosophy at the University of Texas at Austin.

Introduction: The Enduring Significance of Jackson's Knowledge Argument

Sam Coleman

I.1

In 1982 Frank Jackson published 'Epiphenomenal Qualia', in which he imagined the near-future scenario of a researcher into colour vision who is confined to a monochrome environment. Because it is the imaginary near future, she is able to compile *all* the scientific information about the physical goings-on that underpin colour vision. He describes her situation thus:

> [A] Mary is a brilliant scientist who is, for whatever reason, forced to inves-
> tigate the world from a black and white room *via* a black and white televi-
> sion monitor. She specializes in the neurophysiology of vision and acquires,
> let us suppose, all the physical information there is to obtain about what
> goes on when we see ripe tomatoes, or the sky, and use terms like 'red', 'blue',
> and so on. She discovers, for example, just which wavelength combinations
> from the sky stimulate the retina, and exactly how this produces *via* the
> central nervous system the contraction of the vocal chords and expulsion
> of air from the lungs that results in the uttering of the sentence 'The sky
> is blue'.

> [B] What will happen when Mary is released from her black and white
> room or is given a color television monitor? Will she *learn* anything or not?
> It seems just obvious that she will learn something about the world and our
> visual experience of it. (Jackson 1982: 130)

In a later paper Jackson envisages that on leaving the black-and-white room Mary 'will learn what it is like to see something red, say',[1] and philosophers

---

[1] Jackson 1986: 291.

have associated Mary with learning what red is like ever since. Given that Mary does learn, Jackson next infers:

> [C] [I]t is inescapable that her previous knowledge was incomplete. But she had *all* the physical information. *Ergo* there is more to have than that, and Physicalism is false. (Jackson 1982: 130)

In this way Mary's story is used to deploy an argument against *physicalism*, roughly the view that the world is wholly physical. The argument moves from considerations about Mary's knowledge to the conclusion of physicalism's falsity. Hence Jackson dubbed it 'the knowledge argument'. Generalising the knowledge argument's purport, he continued:

> Clearly the same style of Knowledge argument could be deployed for taste, hearing, the bodily sensations and generally speaking for the various mental states which are said to have (as it is variously put) raw feels, phenomenal features or qualia. The conclusion in each case is that the qualia are left out of the physicalist story ... the polemical strength of the Knowledge argument is that it is so hard to deny the central claim that one can have all the physical information without having all the information there is to have. (Jackson 1982: 130)

We can put the knowledge argument more formally by compressing the passages [A], [B], and [C] into two premises and a conclusion:

Premise 1   Mary before her release knows everything physical there is to know about people.

Premise 2   Mary before her release does not know everything there is to know about people, because on her release she learns what it is like for them to visually experience red.

Conclusion   There are things to know about people that escape the physicalist story, so physicalism is false.

This formulation is slightly adapted from Jackson (1986: 294). There Jackson's premises talk of Mary knowing everything physical about *other* people; but the conclusion is that there are truths about other people *and herself* that escape the physicalist story. It is clear enough that there is something Mary does not know about herself pre-release: she may know what physical brain state she will come to have when she sees red, but she does not know what her associated visual experience will be like. So I talk here simply of 'people', to include other people and herself. Jackson also omits mention of the sort of thing Mary will learn, in premise 2, so I have made that explicit. Moreover, Jackson's original conclusion does not say openly that physicalism's falsity follows, though this inference is clear from the rest of his exposition – so I have again spelt that out. Finally, his conclusion talks of truths, not knowledge. But the sense of 'knowledge' intended throughout must be of truths (or facts) for the argument to work (a point objectors focus on – see below), and *knowledge about* is plausibly of this sort (more on this point below).

A great deal has been written about Jackson's knowledge argument in the nearly forty years since its publication; so much, indeed, that if one keeps up with the literature one is apt to start to feel – a bit like Mary herself – that one knows all that can possibly be written down on the subject. Still, it seems the way with philosophy that there is always more to say. New decades bring fresh ideas, or at least a freshening of approaches to existing ideas, and that recurrent, curlicuing, self-updating process is the main manner by which large-scale progress is achieved in philosophy, when it is achieved at all. Therefore it is worth while to revisit this classic argument now – in order to witness how the years have affected it, to understand how the argument has affected us in those years, and to anticipate where it might lead us henceforth. Herein is a new set of essays on the knowledge argument, embodying major trends of thought at the present time. This volume is a record of the argument's relevance to and impact upon the present, and a pointer to its enduring significance in the future.

The knowledge argument shares those virtues characteristic of the very greatest arguments in the history of philosophy, possessing an overt formal simplicity of presentation, and invoking intuitively accessible ideas, but combining this with a depth of reach into complex fundamental issues. One thinks also of Descartes's *Cogito* and Anselm's ontological argument in this bracket, to name but two. Jackson's argument is additionally notable for being doubly influential. A horde of philosophers have been impelled to react to its *content*, either by defending or debunking its reasoning and the claims Jackson took to follow from this. (Interestingly, Jackson himself is now a debunker, having undergone a doctrinal turnaround every bit as dramatic, philosophically speaking, as Asoka's conversion to Buddhism. Nowadays a physicalist, his chapter in this collection presents his latest thoughts on where earlier Jackson went wrong.) But philosophers have also been influenced by the knowledge argument's *form*, proceeding to adapt the scenario of an apparently all-knowing subject who nonetheless learns in order to demonstrate conclusions not necessarily directly related to claims about consciousness and physicalism. Essays of the two kinds feature in this collection. In both ways, the knowledge argument's circle of influence is far from completed. It remains as timelessly timely as ever: a mirror of perennial concerns about mind, consciousness, and matter, as well as a crucible for the forming and testing of new philosophies – still a key resource in our endeavour to understand our place as minded creatures in a world of matter.

1.2

The ostensible target of Jackson's argument is *physicalism*, roughly the thesis that every concrete existent in our world is wholly physical in nature – i.e. all properties are physical properties, and these are the only properties possessed by the things that bear properties. Mary's situation seems to show that one could know all about the world's physical nature and yet learn still more about it, specifically as regards the visual colour experiences people routinely undergo.

The physicalist thesis can be put somewhat more precisely by saying that a duplicate of our world that featured only its physical ingredients would be its duplicate in every way – with all the aesthetic, moral, meteorological, and, most notably, psychological richness of actuality.[2] What does 'physical' mean? Without facing the myriad complications of pinning down this term,[3] the ruling idea in the literature on consciousness and the knowledge argument is that the physicalist looks to science, especially the hardest science, physics, for the catalogue of basic physical existents and a description of their characters and the events they participate in. The controversial physicalist claim when it comes to the mind, then, is that it ultimately involves nothing but physical goings-on in this sense.

The knowledge argument is important in part because physicalism is such a large target. Though it has never totally dominated philosophical opinion, it certainly represents the orthodoxy in the philosophy of mind over the last century or so (the thesis that the mind is material of course has a long history).[4] How did physicalism become prevalent? A prominent motivation, which acquired its full strength with the physical, biological, and neuroscientific advances of the last century,[5] derives from the 'causal

---

[2] See Jackson (1993) for the first formulation of this idea, but further complications are discussed in Stoljar (2015a) and references contained therein. See also Montero (2012).

[3] See e.g. Crane and Mellor (1990); Spurrett and Papineau (1999); Wilson (2006).

[4] For twentieth- and twenty-first-century physicalism see Smart (1959); Armstrong (1968); Lewis (1996); Melnyk (2003). For historical proponents see e.g. Democritus; Hobbes (1655).

[5] See Papineau (2002) for an account of this development in connection with the causal argument.

argument' for physicalism, centred on the empirical premises that physical events always have purely physical causal histories, and that conscious mental states routinely have physical effects, e.g. bodily motions. From this it follows, with a little more reasoning,[6] that the relevant conscious mental states are themselves physical. There are many ways of resisting this argument,[7] but it has doubtless been, as much implicitly as explicitly, an influential driver to physicalism.

As stated, physicalism is an *ontological* creed: about the nature of what there is. Yet Jackson's case against it turns on considerations concerning *knowledge*.[8] These facts are especially evident in the conclusion as I framed it, which contains an inference – the first part summarising the knowledge claims made in the premises, and the second part drawing the metaphysical moral of physicalism's falsity. Philosophers of the present era are deeply wary of deriving metaphysical consequences from epistemic claims.[9] In order to generate his metaphysical conclusion, Jackson must therefore attribute to physicalism an epistemological thesis as a corollary to its metaphysical claim. This thesis is evidently that the physical truths are the only truths one need know – science can tell us all the facts about the world, in other words. More strictly put, the content of any apparently non-physical truths (truths in non-scientific vocabulary) can be derived *a priori* given full physical knowledge and relevant empirical premises. If physicalism is committed to this thesis, and yet Mary can learn more about the world on seeing red, despite knowing all the scientific facts, then physicalism's falsity as a metaphysical doctrine plausibly

---

[6] A 'no systematic overdetermination' premise is also usually inserted, to rule out the possibility that a non-physical mental and a physical event are always sufficient but independent causes of the physical effects of conscious mental states.

[7] Popular among these are arguments that the physical completeness premise is as a matter of fact false, or begs the question when formulated precisely (see Gibb (2014) for a survey). 'Russellian monism' is another way out, for those who consider it a form of physicalism – see e.g. Chalmers (2015); Montero (2015); Goff (2017) and this volume.

[8] The 'knowledge intuition', that someone can know all physical or scientific truths and yet learn about experience is, as has often been noted, of great vintage, and Jackson's version has antecedents in Broad (1925); Dunne (1927); Russell (1927a); Nagel (1974); Robinson (1982), and others. See the excellent introduction to Ludlow, Nagasawa, and Stoljar (2004) for further sources of historical arguments of the same style, as well as discussion of the ways that Jackson's argument improves upon them, and Strawson (this volume) for erudite and entertaining exposition of several more. Jackson's influential revisiting of the knowledge intuition in 1982 is an example of philosophy's self-updating process, as mentioned in I.1 above.

[9] Kripke (1972) was influential in this separation of matters epistemic from matters metaphysical.

follows. Jackson has expended much energy, especially since his conversion to physicalism, in defending this epistemological corollary to physicalism.[10]

The knowledge argument has a deceptively smooth philosophical hide, but this appearance conceals a complicated set of interlocking theoretical vertebrae, and physicalists (and others) have been quick to attack each joint in the attempt to break the argument's back. Some points of attack: (1) Need Mary learn at all, given the (for us) unimaginable richness of her physical knowledge? (the *no-new-knowledge response* – also known as the *ignorance response*[11]). (2) Indeed, might the intuition that Mary learns be based upon subtle misconceptions about the nature of colour experience? (*the representationalist response*[12]). (3) Assuming that she does learn, is it so obvious that she learns a *truth* or *fact* about the world, or might she just gain a set of *skills* or *abilities* which come only with experiences, e.g. to remember and recognise the novel visual experience of red? (*the ability hypothesis*[13]). In that case, the physicalist need not concede that the scientific account of the world is incomplete. (4) And even if she learns a truth or fact, must it concern a new subject matter – some non-physical property of consciousness, as Jackson holds – rather than being in some sense a mere re-phrasing or re-conceptualising of knowledge already in her possession under a scientific guise? (*conceptual dualism*, aka *the phenomenal concept strategy*[14]). In that case physicalism is not guilty of a lack of metaphysical coverage, even if alternative vocabularies also exist for expressing some of the physical facts. (5) Or, then again, might Mary's gain in knowledge consist merely in a hitherto-unavailable, and peculiarly *direct*, sort of cognitive grasp of visual redness, a grasp comporting by itself no new factual content? (*the acquaintance response*[15]). (6) For that matter, is it even so clear that physicalists must hold that all physical truths can be known via the relatively remote means at Mary's disposal within her room? (*subjective*

---

[10] See e.g. Jackson (1998a), (2005a). His present position, roughly, is that Mary can work out what it is like to see red ahead of time, on pain of physicalism's falsity – see his contribution to this volume.

[11] For example Churchland (1985); Dennett (1991); Stoljar (2006). See McClelland's contribution to this volume.

[12] Jackson (2003), this volume.

[13] See e.g. Nemirow (1980); Lewis (1990); Mellor (1993); Jackson (2003). Objections: Jackson (1986); Stanley and Williamson (2001); Coleman (2009b). See Kind's chapter in this volume.

[14] Loar (1997); Papineau (2002); Levin (2007a); Balog (2012). Objections: Chalmers (2006); Levine (2007); Goff (2017). Defence: Diaz-Leon (2010). Anti-physicalist versions: Gertler (2001); Chalmers (2003). See Goff's chapter in this volume.

[15] Conee (1994); Tye (2009). Gertler objects (this volume) that acquaintance is unhelpful to physicalists. See also Goff 2015a; Pitt (this volume).

physicalism[16]). These questions, and combinations thereof, are among the major issues in the vast debate around the knowledge argument, and they all surface in one or another way in the following chapters.

I.3

Tim Crane (Chapter 1, 'The Knowledge Argument Is an Argument about Knowledge') argues that the knowledge argument has an exclusively *epistemic* payoff – in fact nothing metaphysical follows from it. Therefore, it does not threaten physicalism after all. What it shows, Crane maintains, is only that there is some factual knowledge that one cannot have without undergoing specific kinds of experience. Criticising prominent physicalist objections to Jackson's argument, Crane makes the case that it is nonetheless an ineffective tool in the hands of anti-physicalists. One benefit of Crane's exposition is his bringing to the surface a premise often left tacit in presentations of the knowledge argument, including Jackson's own: that Mary learns a fact. Still, the notion of fact is ambiguous between a metaphysical and a purely epistemic sense, and Crane gives reasons for favouring an epistemic reading. But this reading does not threaten physicalism, for, according to Crane, physicalists should not hold that all pieces of knowledge are knowable through science. Crane's chapter heads the collection not least due to its clear and full account both of the knowledge argument and of some major physicalist objections, features that make it ideal for orienting, or re-orienting, oneself in the debate.

David Rosenthal (Chapter 2, 'There's Nothing about Mary') reveals a tension among the claims that Mary's knowledge is new, and that it is factual. Through a critique of existing treatments of the knowledge argument, notably the phenomenal concepts response,[17] the ability hypothesis,[18] and the acquaintance response,[19] Rosenthal argues that Mary's knowledge, if factual, must be available to her within her black-and-white room. Alternatively, if she encounters a genuine epistemic novelty, this cannot involve factual knowledge (only something like acquaintance). Either way the knowledge argument's conclusion,

---

[16] See e.g. Searle (1992); Crane (2003, this volume); Van Gulick (2004); Howell (2009a); Goff (2017). I include here 'Russellian monism' as a response to anti-physicalist arguments including the knowledge argument. See Goff's chapter in this volume for Russellian monism, and the summary of it below, as well as Alter and Nagasawa (2012) and Chalmers (2015). Russellian monism need not be construed as physicalism, but proponents often do so construe it, and it is certainly physicalism in the sense of subjective physicalism.

[17] See n. 14 for references.

[18] See n. 13 for references.

[19] See n. 15 for references.

that Mary learns a new truth about people, fails to be secured. Rosenthal further criticises a consciousness-based way of construing the subjective content of conscious experiences, and offers an alternative based on his 'quality-space theory'. This approach has interesting consequences for Mary's first experience of red: it may be far less rich and far less like any conscious experience of ours than commentators have assumed.

Brie Gertler (Chapter 3, 'Acquaintance, Parsimony, and Epiphenomenalism') explores the implications of the acquaintance response, the suggestion that Mary cannot know what red is like without experiencing it because knowledge of experiential properties requires a special kind of direct cognition – known as acquaintance.[20] This response takes physicalist as well as dualist forms, but Gertler argues that embracing acquaintance reduces physicalism's appeal with respect to dualism. That causes a problem for physicalism, she suggests, because invoking acquaintance is an attractive way of analysing what happens to Mary. Not only is acquaintance problematic for physicalism in itself, Gertler argues, but positing it also bolsters the epiphenomenalist variety of dualism, on which experiential properties are causally inert with respect to the physical.[21] Since acquaintance does not present experiential properties *as* physical – for otherwise science would tell Mary what red is like – Gertler finds acquaintance physicalists to be deeply pessimistic about our conceptualisations of experience: such conceptualisations, they must hold, are deceptive about the real nature of experiential properties. On the other hand, acquaintance physicalists are highly *optimistic* about scientific conceptualisations of the world. Since physicalism's claim to greater parsimony than dualism rests on this optimistic attitude about scientific concepts coupled with pessimism about experiential concepts, Gertler observes that this apparent double standard requires justification independent of physicalism's truth. Having issued this challenge to physicalists she follows up by wielding acquaintance to deflect several important objections to epiphenomenalism.

David Pitt (Chapter 4, 'Acquaintance and Phenomenal Concepts') argues that knowing what an experience is like is pure acquaintance knowledge, not to be construed as at all propositional or conceptual. Rather, Pitt claims, knowing what an experience is like is to be identified simply with *having* that experience. It follows that when Mary learns what red is like, that knowledge involves no propositional epistemic gain. This view is similar to Conee's,[22] but

---

[20] For references see n. 15.

[21] This is the position originally embraced by Jackson (1982) in his work, hence the title 'Epiphenomenal Qualia'.

[22] Conee (1994).

Pitt motivates it via an original critique of the phenomenal concept strategy.[23] He argues that there is no principled way of making out the constitutive role that experiences are supposed to play in providing the contents of phenomenal concepts – hence there are no such concepts. It follows that there are no thoughts about experiences that one can think only having had the relevant experiences. As Pitt puts it, the difference between Mary and someone who has seen red is *perceptual*, not *conceptual*. Pitt maintains that his account is neutral about the nature of the property Mary encounters when she experiences red, and about experiential properties in general. But as a way of overturning physicalism, his reasoning implies that the knowledge argument fails.

Frank Jackson (Chapter 5, 'The Knowledge Argument Meets Representationalism about Colour Experience') further develops his response to the knowledge argument based on representationalism about perceptual experience.[24] He thereby rejects not only his earlier argument for dualism, but his even earlier arguments for a sense-datum theory.[25] Jackson now defends a 'possible worlds'-based account of the content of visual experience, analysing the vaunted 'feel' of visual experience as comprising the conjunction of a certain seamless richness, 'pig-headedness' (even when we know we are witnessing an illusion the illusory appearance persists), its nagging quality (the illusory appearance insists that it represents how things are), and a striking immediacy. On this account, Mary should be able to deduce the content of her experience of red given her physical knowledge. For a physicalist account of the representational content of experience should be possible, Jackson observes – and if it is not, the knowledge argument is not needed in order to refute physicalism. He concedes a sense in which Mary cannot know what red is like, but explains away this residue in terms of the ability hypothesis,[26] and ends by offering an analysis of the content of Mary's new visual state, as representing that there is a property of surfaces standing in the resemblance relationships characteristic of red as captured by the colour solid. Breaking with previous work, he defends the thesis that such properties are genuinely instantiated.

Galen Strawson (Chapter 6, 'The Mary-Go-Round') argues that though the descriptive reach of physical science is not sufficiently extensive to include what it is like to have visual colour experience, this supports a broadening in our conception of physicalism, rather than the inference that physicalism is false.

---

[23] See n. 14 for references.
[24] Jackson (2003).
[25] Jackson (1977). It is a superlative career indeed wherein one can successively, and influentially, repudiate various pieces of one's own finest work.
[26] See n. 13 for references.

In Strawson's view the moral of Mary's story is that physicalism should not be conflated with 'physics-alism', on which the physicalist ontology is restricted to those things and properties that physics – and the physical sciences more generally – can comprehensively characterise. He diagnoses this conflation as at fault for mistakes on both sides of the 'Mary-go-round': namely, a physicalist tendency to deny that Mary learns about the world when she experiences red, and the equally culpable propensity of anti-physicalists to take the Mary story as refuting physicalism. Mary, thus, is no problem for physicalism, properly understood. The quasi-Kantian lesson Strawson draws is humility about the nature of the physical, excepting that part of the physical present in our experiences.

Though it was once a popular thesis that Mary's learning consists at least in part in gaining a new 'phenomenal concept' – a concept directly picking out the experiential character of visual redness,[27] a widespread view nowadays is that the relevant concept is not beyond Mary's reach within her black-and-white room. For Mary can acquire the term RED, or even PHENOMENAL RED, from her books, or community, and use it to refer to what other people refer to with it. This constitutes an objection both to the physicalist phenomenal concept strategy, and to the knowledge argument itself, on the assumption that the argument implies that Mary gains a new concept. In response, the move has been to say that although Mary may possess this concept, she cannot *fully* possess, or master, it without experiencing red. Torin Alter (Chapter 7, 'Concept Mastery, Social Externalism, and Mary's New Knowledge') defends the thesis that Mary's epistemic progress consists at least partly in gaining mastery of the phenomenal concept RED against objections by Ball and Rabin. What those objections show, he argues, is that Mary's original story might have to be modified if purveyors of phenomenal concepts are to establish the existence of a gap between the physical and conscious experience. Specifically, proponents of the knowledge argument might have to consider a Mary who is in full possession of the phenomenal concept of red. But such methodological concessions do nothing to blunt the force of the knowledge argument, so Alter maintains.

Amy Kind (Chapter 8, 'Mary's Powers of Imagination') takes issue with the ability hypothesis – the proposal that rather than learning factually about people, Mary's new knowledge of what red is like is best analysed as a gain of abilities: to recognise, remember, and imagine red.[28] Kind

---

[27] See n. 14 for references.

[28] For references see n. 13.

argues that the debate around the ability hypothesis, wherein proponents and opponents agree that pre-release Mary lacks the ability to imagine red, fosters a misleading conception of the imagination. For, in the relevant sense, Mary could already imagine red before leaving her black-and-white room. In Kind's analysis, the thesis that Mary cannot imagine red depends on the claim that she cannot imagine it *correctly*. Kind makes the case that *imagining x* is not like *remembering x*, in that one can perfectly well imagine x even if x is not really how one imagines it to be. The consequence is that though Mary can imagine red before seeing it, this will not teach her what red is like (the ability hypothesis thus errs doubly). Kind argues that proponents of the ability hypothesis face a dilemma. If the notion of being able to imagine correctly is restrictive enough that pre-release Mary lacks the relevant ability with respect to redness, this risks ruling out cases where people have plausibly achieved accurate imagining of experiences distant from their own. But if the notion is left suitably lax, then Mary may not need to see red to have the ability. So, either the analysis of imagination fails to capture real-world cases, or, if accurate, does not serve the ability hypothesis's purposes. Thus, Kind concludes, the notion of imagination is of no use to the ability hypothesis, and has been widely mishandled by commentators. Her parting shot is that philosophers have obscured the imagination's role in *providing* us with knowledge, by using the notion in an *analysis* of knowledge. She does not take her argument to have decisive consequences for the knowledge argument's success, nor does she take a stand over physicalism's truth. But if her argument is correct it poses a challenge to at least one physicalist way of responding to Mary, which Jackson, notably, has come to embrace (see his chapter in this volume).

Tom McClelland's contribution (Chapter 9, 'The Knowledge Argument Is Either Indefensible or Redundant') develops the ignorance response to the knowledge argument into a dilemma argument. On the ignorance response the knowledge argument is inconclusive, since we cannot predict the content of completed physical science sufficiently well to be sure that Mary in her ideal epistemic situation will not be able to work out what red is like.[29] Jackson's argument therefore requires 'future-proofing': some account is called for of the kind of truth physical truths are, such that it will be plausible that no amount of knowledge of that sort, even in completed future science, will suffice to deduce the character of visual experiences. Chalmers's proposal that physical truths are structural-dynamic truths could be seen as one attempt at

[29] See n. 11 for references.

future-proofing.[30] But McClelland points out that if we are given in this way good reason to believe that physical truths do not entail truths about experience, then we do not need the knowledge argument to make the case against physicalism. On the other hand, if we cannot provide the required substantive characterisation of physical truths, then the knowledge argument remains vulnerable to the ignorance objection. Thus, McClelland concludes, the knowledge argument is either redundant or it is indefensible.

Philip Goff (Chapter 10, 'Grounding, Analysis, and Russellian Monism') investigates the prospects of 'Russellian monism',[31] an increasingly popular response to anti-physicalist arguments such as the knowledge argument. He makes the case that even if Russellian monism is a plausible response to the knowledge argument, a related argument seems to refute it – the 'phenomenal analysis argument'. Roughly, Russellian monism posits a 'deep' nature to the physical, which metaphysical thesis is accompanied by the epistemological thesis that physical science does not tell us about this nature. The deep nature of the physical, in addition, is posited as being directly relevant to the generation of consciousness. In the context of the knowledge argument, the Russellian monist suggestion is that Mary knows only about the shallow nature of the physical, those physical truths that concern, say, its dispositional as opposed to 'categorical' character, since this is the sort of truth physical science exclusively reveals.[32] What Mary needs in order to know the deep truth about the physical state of experiencing red is to see red for herself. This plausibly makes Russellian monism a form of subjective physicalism.[33] Goff's novel argument against Russellian monism focuses on the fact that Russellian monists see facts about experiences as susceptible of a certain form of analysis: into facts about the experiences of things other than the subject (such as facts about her microphysical parts, for panpsychists), or into facts about protoexperiences (for panprotopsychists). But Goff argues that phenomenal facts are not plausibly analysable in either of these ways. He builds the phenomenal analysis argument on certain key premises of the conceivability argument against physicalism,[34] but notes that his argument, if sound, refutes Russellian monism,

---

[30] Chalmers (2010a). For further discussion of the notion of structure and dynamics, and of the 'structure and dynamics' argument Chalmers builds on this basis, as well as its relation to the knowledge argument, see also Stoljar (2015a) and Alter (2016).

[31] Alter and Nagasawa (2012); Chalmers (2013).

[32] An analysis of science deeply influenced by Russell (1927a), hence the name 'Russellian monism'.

[33] Though this issue depends on whether physicalism is defined so as to include or to exclude the alleged deep nature of the physical – see Goff (2017) for discussion.

[34] See e.g. Chalmers (1996).

whereas the conceivability argument, together with the knowledge argument, leaves Russellian monism open. Goff's argument, if successful, enhances the prospects of dualist, emergentist, and *a posteriori* physicalist responses to Mary.

Hedda Hassel Mørch (Chapter 11, 'Phenomenal Knowledge *Why*: The Explanatory Knowledge Argument against Physicalism') develops a novel form of knowledge argument against physicalism, the *explanatory knowledge argument*. She focuses on what might be learnt in one's first experience of pain given complete physical factual knowledge, and argues that one key new piece of knowledge concerns the basis of regularities involving pain behaviour: i.e. why people avoid pain. Once one experiences pain, this regularity is explained in an ultimate way, Mørch claims. Given that pain feels as it does, it does not make sense, she argues, to ask why people try to avoid it. That it necessitates such behaviour can be grasped from pain's nature. But this is not true, she maintains, of any physical explanations: for even when we hit the laws of physics we can always ask why they are the way they are. Since only factual knowledge is capable of explaining facts about regularities, Mørch concludes that pained Mary (or her protagonist Maya) learns a new fact. That this fact is non-physical follows from the inadequacy of her physical knowledge to supply this sort of explanation. Thus not all facts are physical facts. One way of seeing this argument is as adding to the set of facts a Mary-style character would supposedly learn. There is much dispute about the status of alleged facts about the sheer qualitative character of experiences,[35] but if Mørch is right about the explanatory power of knowledge of experiences concerning behavioural regularities, this might provide a more robust case in support of factual learning by the protagonist of a knowledge argument.

Robert J. Howell (Chapter 12, 'The Knowledge Argument and the Self') proposes a new version of the knowledge argument, concerning the *self*. He suggests that his argument is a corollary of Jackson's argument, the upshot of which he takes to be that there are facts about people, specifically about the qualitative character of their experiences, that escape the objective picture of the world. The conclusion of Howell's new knowledge argument is that the self is also absent from this objective picture. One can see this argument as harking back to concerns prominent in Nagel's 'What Is It Like to Be a Bat?',[36] where it is not just the qualitative character of experiences (e.g. visual redness) that is taken to be elusive to science, but also the fact that subjects have a 'point

---

[35] Witness the disagreement among authors in this volume over whether Mary learns a fact, abilities, or merely becomes acquainted with visual redness.

[36] Nagel (1974).

of view' or conscious perspective on the world. A conceptual distinction is often drawn in the literature between awareness, which is present equally in all conscious episodes, and qualities, that feature wherein experiences differ. It is perhaps natural to view Jackson's argument as focusing on the latter aspect of experience, and Howell's as focussing on the former. If Howell is correct then there is an underexplored difficulty associated with the objective explanation of subjectivity. Though cautious about whether his argument might support a metaphysical conclusion, as Jackson's is intended to do, Howell concludes that even if the world is wholly physical the self should be added to the list of items that elude the physical, objective point of view. This suggests a deep tie between consciousness and selfhood worthy of further investigation.

Michael Tye (Chapter 13, 'What Uninformed Mary Can Teach Us') uses a Mary-style scenario as a departure point for a new sort of argument concerning what experience reveals about colour properties. His protagonist is *uninformed Mary*, who, like her Jacksonian namesake, has been imprisoned in a colourless room hitherto. Unlike the first Mary, 'U-Mary' also lacks complete physical knowledge. She is then subjected to a hallucination, of a set of red, green, and orange patches. According to Tye U-Mary can come to know, on the basis of this hallucination, the fact that red is more similar to orange than to green. Yet there are, Tye supposes, no real colours instantiated in this scenario. Tye infers that U-Mary must be directly aware of the items that the novel fact concerns, i.e. the colours red, green, and orange, from which the provocative and interesting conclusion follows that there exist such things as uninstantiated colours.[37] He replies to a range of objections, including the suggestion that Mary is aware of colourful sense-data, not uninstantiated colours. In that case, Tye wryly observes, she is not hallucinating after all!

---

[37] As Tye acknowledges, other authors have argued for the same conclusion, notably Johnston (2004). But Tye's argument has an attractive simplicity, derived in part from its formal resemblance to Jackson's Mary scenario.

1 The Knowledge Argument Is an Argument about Knowledge

Tim Crane

1.1 Introduction

The knowledge argument is something that is both an ideal for philosophy and yet surprisingly rare: a simple, valid argument for an interesting and important conclusion, with plausible premises.[1] From a compelling thought experiment and a few apparently innocuous assumptions, the argument seems to give us the conclusion, a priori, that physicalism is false. Given the apparent power of this apparently simple argument, it is not surprising that philosophers have worried over the argument and its proper diagnosis: physicalists have disputed its validity, or soundness or both; in response, non-physicalists have attempted to reformulate the argument to show its real anti-physicalist lesson.

I disagree with both groups of philosophers: I think the argument is sound, but that it does not show that physicalism is false. What the argument shows is that there is some propositional or factual knowledge which you can only have if you have certain experiences. This is an important, interesting and fairly controversial conclusion, but it is consistent with both physicalism and dualism. The knowledge argument, I claim, is an argument about knowledge, not about the metaphysics of the mind.

I first expound the knowledge argument in its least contentious, controversial version, and give a little historical background. I then show why the standard (physicalist) critiques of the argument miss their mark, why the argument does not establish dualism, what the real lesson of the argument is,

[1] This chapter develops and corrects some of the ideas about the knowledge argument first put forward in Crane (2001 ch. 3 and 2003). Thanks to Sam Coleman, Kati Farkas, Lizzie Fricker, Philip Goff, Henry Taylor and especially Howard Robinson for discussion of this argument, and to participants at a 2016 workshop in Cambridge on Robinson's latest book (Robinson 2016), and at the 2017 Midwest Epistemology Workshop in St. Louis. The chapter was written with the help of a grant from the John Templeton Foundation, 'New Directions in the Study of the Mind'.

and why the dualists' required developments of the argument lack suasive or dialectical force. But first, the argument itself.

1.2 The Knowledge Argument Summarised

Many things have been called the knowledge argument, but the essence of the argument is a thought experiment where someone is imagined to have complete knowledge of a certain kind A, but lacks knowledge of another kind B. Scenarios are then sometimes envisaged in which they gain genuine knowledge of kind B, or it is tacitly assumed that they have it anyway. So the knowledge they had of the kind A cannot be all there is to know. Of course, the case which we are interested in is where A knowledge is 'physical' and B knowledge is 'phenomenal'; and the conclusion of interest is the one where the fact that not all knowledge is 'physical' is supposed to entail that physicalism is false.

The scenario envisaged by Frank Jackson (1982) is the thought experiment of Mary the omniscient scientist who lives in a black-and-white room, and then sees something red for the first time. Nothing of great significance depends on the specific details of this particular version of the thought experiment. For example, if someone finds the scenario of someone learning physics in Mary's predicament hard to imagine – maybe because her physics books cannot all be in black and white – then they should imagine instead Mary being blind, and then recovering her sight. Physics can be in braille (Maddox 2007). By the same token, the argument does not depend on anything specific to vision – it could be formulated in terms of the knowledge given in hearing, smell or taste.

Given the basic assumptions of the thought experiment, we can express the argument in terms of the following three premises and a conclusion:

Premise 1: Mary knows all the physical facts about seeing red in the black-and-white room.

Premise 2: Mary learns something new when she leaves the room and sees red for the first time.

Premise 3: What Mary learns is a fact.

Conclusion: Not all facts are physical facts.

If physicalism is the doctrine that not all facts are physical facts, then the conclusion is the negation of physicalism.

A few brief clarifications about the dialectical role of the premises. The first premise is simply a stipulation of one of the features of the thought experiment.

Accepting this premise and accepting the thought experiment are basically the same thing. Of course, one might reject the thought experiment on broadly methodological grounds, as Daniel Dennett (1991) famously did; if one does this, there is no need to discuss the rest of the argument. After all, one can hardly say 'Oh yes the thought experiment is fine, it's just that Mary wouldn't know *all* the physical facts in that situation' – for the thought experiment is, by definition, a supposedly possible situation in which Mary knows all the physical facts.

The second premise, unlike the first, is not simply a stipulation involved in the thought experiment; it is rather something we are invited to conclude after being told the story of Mary leaving the room and seeing red for the first time. It would be a coherent reaction to the argument to accept the first premise and deny the second, for example; or to put it another way, to accept the coherence or intelligibility of the thought experiment and yet reject premise 2. In this way, premise 2 is a distinct claim from the mere coherence of the thought experiment.

Premise 3 makes explicit what is needed in order for the argument to be valid. Given the widely held view that there are at least three kinds of knowledge – knowing that, knowing how and knowing things – it could be claimed that the argument equivocates if it just involves premises 1 and 2. For it may be that premise 1 is about knowing that, but for all the thought experiment says, premise 2 might be about knowing how (or 'ability' knowledge) or knowing things ('acquaintance' knowledge). The point of premise 3 is to explicitly rule out those options. So those who adopt the ability response (Lewis 1999; Mellor 1992; Nemirow 1990) or the acquaintance response (Churchland 1985; Conee 1994; Tye 2009) can accept premise 2 and reject premise 3.

The story of Mary and the black-and-white room comes, of course, from Frank Jackson's articles 'Epiphenomenal Qualia' (1982) and 'What Mary Didn't Know' (1986). Because of the catchiness of the Mary story, the knowledge argument has sometimes been attributed to Jackson, although he himself has been generous in acknowledging influences and independent presentations of the argument. Of these presentations, attention must be drawn to Howard Robinson's concise statement at the opening of his *Matter and Sense*, published in the same year as Jackson's 'Epiphenomenal Qualia':

> Imagine that a deaf scientist should become the world's leading expert on the neurology of hearing. Thus, if we suppose neurology to be more advanced than present, we can imagine that he knows everything there is to

know about the physical processes involved in hearing, from the ear-drum in. It remains intuitively obvious that there is something which this scientist will not know, namely *what it is like* to hear. (Robinson 1982: 4)

In his recent reflections on the knowledge argument, Robinson comments that he 'did not then treat this as a refutation of physicalism, but rather as a way of setting up the problem that faced the physicalist' (Robinson 2016). But it is easy to see how this brief vignette contains almost the entire argument as represented above – all it lacks is the claim that knowledge of what it is like to hear is knowledge of a fact. With this added, Robinson's argument is as clear a statement of the knowledge argument as any.

As a number of writers (e.g. Nida-Rümelin 2009) have pointed out, something like the knowledge argument is present in C. D. Broad's *The Mind and its Place in Nature* (1925), Herbert Feigl's 'The "Mental" and the "Physical"' (1958), and Thomas Nagel's 'What Is It Like to Be a Bat?' (1974). To these precursors of the argument, I would add my own favourite statement of its basic idea, by Bertrand Russell:

> It is obvious that a man who can see knows things which a blind man cannot know; but a blind man can know the whole of physics. Thus the knowledge which other men have and he has not is not a part of physics. (Russell 1927a: 389)

However, the relationship between these precursors and the arguments of Jackson and Robinson is not straightforward. Robinson and Jackson in 1982 were opposing physicalism, as was Broad (in the name of 'mechanism'); but Russell draws no explicit conclusion about physicalism. Nor did Feigl and Nagel (at least in 1974) take their own 'knowledge arguments' to tell against the truth of physicalism. Feigl was defending a version of the identity theory, combined with the view that there are two kinds of knowledge of the mind-brain. Nagel's conclusion was that even though physicalism (materialism) is true, it is in a certain sense unintelligible to us.

The arguments of Jackson and Robinson, therefore, do add something new and clear which was not explicitly there in these predecessors: the use of these considerations about knowledge to undermine the doctrine of physicalism. Physicalists quickly rose to the challenge and over the past few decades have offered various criticisms of the argument. These have been effectively discussed in great detail in many places, and my aim here is not to present a full survey of these discussions. Rather, what I want to do is to identify what seem to me to be the essential features of the most common physicalist responses.

1.3 The Usual Physicalist Responses

Making premise 3 explicit enables us to treat physicalists as objecting to the argument as unsound, rather than invalid. This useful simplification allows us to group physicalist responses to the argument into those which deny premise 2 or those which deny premise 3. Less common, in my experience, is the response mentioned above which denies the coherence of the thought experiment – in other words, which denies premise 1. Here I will ignore this less popular response. It may be that it deserves a detailed treatment, but I will not give this here.

The denial of premise 3 can be dealt with quickly here; what a physicalist should say about premise 2 will take a little more unravelling. Those who deny premise 3 do so because they think either that Mary acquires only ability knowledge, or that she acquires only acquaintance knowledge. The existence and nature of ability knowledge and acquaintance knowledge has been intensely discussed in the last decade (e.g. Bengson and Moffett 2011; Tye 2009). It is true that if there were no such thing as ability knowledge or acquaintance knowledge, then these responses to premise 3 would fail. But this does not mean that if there were such things, the responses would succeed. To deny premise 3 you have to deny that what Mary learns is a fact; but it is plain that acquiring ability knowledge or acquaintance knowledge is compatible with learning a fact. What these physicalists have to show, then, is that Mary *only* acquires ability knowledge or acquaintance knowledge, and no propositional knowledge. There is a lot that can be said here, but I will rest with the significant observation that most physicalists make no explicit attempt to do this. An exception is David Lewis, who bases his critique of the argument on the assumption that 'phenomenal information' (i.e. the objects of propositional knowledge of phenomenal states) must be rejected by physicalists (Lewis 1999: 285). I will argue below that physicalists can accept this kind of information – at least in one sense of the word – with impunity.

This brings us to premise 2. On the face of it, it is hard to deny that Mary learns something, as the story is usually told. In general, it seems that having new experiences gives us new knowledge – at the very least, it gives us some knowledge of what it is like, in a perfectly ordinary sense, to have such experiences. How could the experience of seeing red for the first time fail to give knowledge? One could, of course, reject the coherence of the whole scenario, but in the way I am setting the argument up, this is a denial of premise 1, not premise 2.

In his more recent guise as a physicalist, Frank Jackson has defended a denial of premise 2 which deserves mention, not least because of Jackson's role in setting up the original argument. Jackson's way of denying (2) appeals to the representational theory of experience: the phenomenal character of experience is exhausted by its representational content. So when Mary experiences something red she comes to be in a state which represents a property – phenomenal red – which does not exist:

> Physicalists can allow that people are sometimes in states that represent that things have a nonphysical property. Examples are people who believe that there are fairies. What physicalists must deny is that such properties are instantiated. (Jackson 2003)

Jackson's response to the knowledge argument would make sense if the argument assumed or entailed that what Mary learns about are 'qualia' conceived of as non-physical, non-intentional property. Then his response would be: Mary's experience is a representation of something which does not exist, a non-physical quale. But there are no such things as qualia. Therefore Mary's experience is an illusion and cannot be the basis of any new knowledge of the world. Mary learns nothing new.

Of course every theory of mind must allow that some conscious experiences are illusions. But the experience of colour is just one kind of conscious experience, and nothing in the general structure of the knowledge argument requires either a realist theory of colours, or a commitment to qualia (conceived of as non-intentional properties of experience). The knowledge argument is compatible with a Galilean theory of colours, and also with intentionalism or representationalism about experience. For a Galilean about colour, the argument would just need to be formulated in terms of some experienced phenomenal property other than colour (taste, smell, pain …). And the argument only needs one case to make its point. So Jackson's response will only work in general if all these kinds of features of conscious experience are illusions. But this is barely credible. It is barely credible, for example, that pain is an illusion. But Jackson needs to make this claim if his argument is to work.

There is little to be gained for a physicalist, I think, by digging in their heels and simply insisting that Mary gains no knowledge. It's not that this position is incoherent, but rather that it lacks any plausibility, given our normal views about the relationship between knowledge and experience. And, as we shall see, it is completely unnecessary for a physicalist to insist on this, when a far more plausible response to the argument is available.

This far more plausible response is simple, and has been around in the literature at least since Terence Horgan's 1984 response to Jackson's original paper.

The essence of it is this: the fact that Mary gains new knowledge does not in itself show that it is knowledge of something non-physical. In Mary's case, as in many everyday cases, we learn something new about the world even though the things we are learning facts about are things we already knew about in some other way. When we are experientially representing a thing or property which we have previously represented in some other way, this does not mean one has no new knowledge of this thing or property. This point has sometimes been explicated in terms of the idea of the intensionality of (propositional) knowledge (Chalmers 1996: 141), and sometimes in terms of the comparison with Frege's famous discussion of the Morning Star and the Evening Star (Frege 1892). Two modes of presentation of something does not imply two things presented.

This response is clearly a way of *accepting* premise 2, since it acknowledges that Mary learns something new. So it would muddy the waters to describe the response as saying that Mary does not *really* learn anything new, but only learns 'an old fact in a new way' (I take the phrase from Chalmers 'Phenomenal Concepts and the Knowledge Argument' (2004: §1); in her useful survey, Nida-Rümelin (2009) calls this the 'Old Fact/New Knowledge' response). If Mary does learn a new fact, then it cannot be the same fact as something she already knew. Should we say that the ancient astronomers who discovered that Hesperus is Phosphorus merely learned that Hesperus is Hesperus in a new way? Of course not: learning that Hesperus is Phosphorus is in no sense whatsoever a 'way' of learning that Hesperus is Hesperus. The 'old fact in a new way' talk is a convoluted formulation of a much simpler idea: that Mary learns something new and this does not imply that the entities about which she gains this knowledge are distinct from the entities she knew all about in the black-and-white room.

It may be replied to this that, in philosophy at least, 'fact' is ambiguous: facts can be constituents of reality ('the world is the totality of facts': Wittgenstein 1922) or they can be objects of knowledge ('a fact is a thought which is true': Frege 1918–1919). So perhaps premise 3 is ambiguous and the 'old fact in a new way' talk is just supposed to make this explicit: Mary learns a new (Frege-style) fact which is a mode of presentation of an old (Wittgenstein-style) fact.

It's true of course that these two notions of fact have been used in twentieth-century philosophy, and they are both perfectly legitimate notions which have their different uses. But this does not mean that the knowledge argument, as I stated it above, equivocates. The argument talks about *learning* facts and *knowing* facts – where the knowledge in question is clearly propositional. But it is only facts in Frege's sense which can be the objects of propositional knowledge: what you know is true, it is something that can be learned, and something that can be conveyed to others. Being true, learned and conveyed to others – these are not features of facts in the Wittgensteinian 'constituent-of-reality' sense. Constituents of reality are not true, and you cannot learn or convey them (as opposed to learning or conveying truths about them). There is a sense in which you can know constituents of reality – you can know people, for example – but this is not propositional knowledge, since propositional knowledge is knowledge of truths and truths are not constituents of reality in the relevant sense. And the knowledge argument is explicitly about propositional knowledge. (The debate about the existence of propositions is not relevant to this point: no one should think that whether physicalism is true turns on whether propositions exist.)

For this reason, then, it is a mistake to say that the argument equivocates: it's perfectly clear which notion of fact is involved in the argument, and the physicalist should have no objection to this notion of fact, so long as they accept the idea of objects (or contents) of propositional knowledge.

Many of those who respond to the argument in this way have put it in terms of Mary's gaining a new kind of concept, a 'phenomenal concept', which she did not have in the black-and-white room (Balog 2009; Papineau 2002). If concepts are in some way the constituents of states of knowledge, then this new concept would indeed explain why the knowledge is also new. However, phenomenal concepts are somewhat controversial (Crane 2005; Sundström 2011), and it would be better not to rest the defence of premise 2 on such controversial ideas. After all, the truth of premise 2 seems more obvious than any complex theoretical claims about concepts. And maybe Edouard Machery (2009) is right, and the idea of a concept will play no role in a future science of the mind. But this should not undermine the idea that Mary would gain new knowledge in the scenario described.

Fortunately, it is not necessary to adopt any novel theory of concepts in order to maintain premise 2. Mary could simply employ a demonstrative concept – '*that* is what red looks like!' – which is a kind of concept she also could employ when in the black-and-white room. A new experience can provide the opportunity for new knowledge – knowledge of a new truth or proposition – using concepts one had before. Just as one might express one's new knowledge of a person by saying 'That is the same person I met in Albuquerque last year', so Mary can use a demonstrative to express her new knowledge deriving from her new experience (Crane 2003). It is a further step, and not obligatory, to explain the truth of this demonstrative judgement in terms of phenomenal concepts in Balog's or Papineau's senses.

Howard Robinson (2016) has combined the idea that Mary gains factual knowledge with the idea that she gains knowledge by acquaintance. In laying out the options in response to the knowledge argument, Robinson says that 'Mary lacked and later acquired some factual knowledge concerning the nature of phenomenal colour' (2016: 21). I agree this is the right response to the argument. But I disagree with his further gloss on this:

> The information in question will not be propositional, but be a form of know-ledge by acquaintance, but it will still be factual information concerning the nature of colour and colour experience. (2016: 21)

I see no difference between factual knowledge and propositional know-ledge – factual knowledge is knowledge of Frege-facts or true propositions. I don't think there is another viable sense of factual knowledge, though there is a viable sense of 'fact': the Wittgensteinian sense. But for the reasons given above, Wittgensteinian facts are not the objects of factual knowledge. And knowledge by acquaintance – if it exists as a distinctive kind at all – is compatible with physicalism and its negation. So in his defence of the knowledge argument Robinson should only appeal to factual knowledge. (I will return to Robinson's views in 1.5 below.)

The lesson I want to draw here is that the overwhelmingly plausible physicalist response to the argument – that the same things can be known about in different ways – is compatible with accepting all three premises of the argument. Those who make this response should not dispute the claim that Mary learns something new, and (if they want to maintain the analogy with other cases of the intensionality of knowledge ascriptions) they should not deny that Mary learns a fact. The standard response, then, should not dispute the premises of the argument as I have presented them above.

And since the conclusion follows from the premises, the standard response should not dispute the conclusion either. So defenders of this response should say that not all facts are physical facts. This might look like a strange thing for a physicalist to say, until we take into account what the knowledge argument means (and must mean, if it is to be intelligible) by 'physical fact'. This is really the key to understanding the argument, as we shall see.

1.4 Physicalism and Physical Truths

As we have seen, the knowledge argument employs the notion of a fact as an object of knowledge, so spelled out literally the conclusion says that not all objects of knowledge are physical objects of knowledge. I am arguing that physicalism should be unworried by this conclusion: someone can be a physicalist and accept that not all objects of knowledge are physical. To defend this position requires answering two questions: what is physicalism? And second, what makes an object of knowledge physical in the relevant sense?

There has been an extensive debate about the content of physicalism over the last few decades (Melnyck 2003; Montero 2013; Ney 2008a; Papineau 2001; Poland 1994; Stoljar 2010). Most of these details – e.g. what counts as physics, 'Hempel's dilemma', the precise statement of the causal closure principle, etc. – need not concern us here. What should be uncontroversial about physicalism, these days at least, is that it is a thesis about the world, about reality, about what there is. It is an ontological thesis. Physicalists might say, for example, that all objects and events are physical (sometimes called 'token physicalism') or they might say that all properties are physical (sometimes called 'type physicalism'). Or they might say that all states of affairs in D. M. Armstrong's sense ('facts' in the Wittgensteinian sense) are physical. Or they might say that everything is determined by its physical nature, or that everything supervenes on physical reality. However they think 'physical' should be defined, physicalists these days tend to treat physicalism as an ontological doctrine, a doctrine about what reality contains.

It wasn't always like this. In his essay, 'Psychology in Physical Language' Rudolf Carnap described the thesis of physicalism as 'physical language is a universal language, that is, a language into which every sentence may be translated' (Carnap 1932–1933: 107). It was characteristic of the logical empiricist philosophy of the day (and the later philosophy which it influenced) to formulate ontological doctrines in linguistic terms. This practice survived into, for example, Chisholm's (1957) attempts to find linguistic criteria of intentionality, which is supposed to distinguish the mental from the physical (see also Dennett 1969, ch. 1). But these days physicalism is not formulated as a doctrine about sentences.

The upshot is this. Given that there can be genuinely different facts in the 'object of knowledge' sense (Frege facts), without this difference corresponding to any ontological difference, it follows that physicalism as an ontological thesis is not a thesis about facts in the 'object of knowledge' sense. So the pre-physicalist Jackson was therefore quite wrong when he said that 'if physicalism is true, Mary knows all there is to know' (1986: 291). Physicalism can be true and yet Mary in the room can be ignorant of certain facts. The knowledge argument as stated in 1.2 above does not refute physicalism.

This brings us to the second question: what makes an object of knowledge (or true proposition) 'physical' in the sense employed by the knowledge argument? This is not the same question as what 'physical' means for physicalists. For that latter question is about how to make an ontological classification; but the former question is about how to classify objects of propositional knowledge. The 'physical facts' according to the knowledge argument are all those true propositions that Mary could learn within the black-and-white room scenario. So let's ask what kinds of propositions Mary *could* learn within this scenario. Obviously she can learn the truths of physics. But what else? The pre-physicalist Jackson says that what Mary learns is knowledge that is part of physics, 'in a wide sense of "physical" that includes everything in completed physics, chemistry and neurophysiology' (Jackson 1986: 291). He is surely right that it clearly makes no difference to the story whether Mary learns facts about the physiology of the brain in addition to facts about fundamental physics. But the same could be said about the facts of theoretical psychology. It's in the spirit of the knowledge argument to say that Mary could learn everything in a completed scientific psychology in the room. And she would still not know what it was like to see red. Similarly, a blind person could learn a 'completed' psychology of vision and not know what it was like to see.

Pushing this idea a bit further, let's suppose that some kind of dualism is true, but it is a scientific dualism: a dualism which appeals to irreducible psychological laws which talk about or quantify over irreducible mental properties, which do not necessarily supervene on physical properties. Not all forms of dualism are like this of course; some forms of dualism are explicit that there cannot be a science of the mental at all. But it serves my purpose if there merely *could* be a form of dualism like this – indeed, Chalmers (1996) speculates about such a naturalistic dualism. Now if Mary were to learn such a theory in the black-and-white room, would it help her to know what it was like to see red? In so far as we have a grip on what this science might be, the answer seems to me clearly no.

What lesson should we draw from this? What do all these propositions have in common? It is misleading to say that anything that Mary can learn inside the room is physical, given that this word has an independent sense, the sense employed in the ontological debates about physicalism. So let's not introduce a second sense of 'physical' to go along with the second sense of 'fact'. What we should say instead is that the facts that Mary can learn in the back-and-white room scenario are the kind of facts that do not require any specific kind of experience. You may need some kind of experience in general in order to learn the full scientific theory of colour vision – you have to get the information somehow – but it is plausible that you don't need full chromatic colour vision. Similarly, you may need some kind of experience or other to learn the full scientific theory of taste and olfaction; but you don't need the experience of all the tastes. This is the point Russell is making when he says that a blind man can learn the whole of physics.

In an earlier paper (Crane 2003), I called the kind of knowledge Mary can acquire in the black-and-white room 'book-learning'. This was inspired by David Lewis's remark that our 'intuitive starting point wasn't just that *physics* lessons couldn't help the inexperienced to know what it is like. It was that *lessons* couldn't help' (Lewis 1999: 281). The idea of something that can be learned in a book is vivid, but it is hard to make wholly explicit. What sorts of things can be learned in books, and what cannot? What the knowledge argument shows, at the very least, is that this is an important question for epistemology. The argument shows that the distinction between book-learning and non-book-learning is not the same as that between propositional and non-propositional knowledge, since Mary's new knowledge is, as I have argued, propositional. This is a significant result for epistemology.

John Perry (2001) has argued that Mary's new knowledge is just a special case of indexical knowledge. When Perry, following a trail of sugar in the supermarket in order to alert the person making the mess, discovers that the leak is coming from his own bag, he gains the knowledge that *he* is making a mess. This is new propositional knowledge, but it is not book-learning: in order to acquire it, Perry had to recognise something about his position in the world at that moment. He had to occupy a specific position in the world; his knowledge was not available without occupying that position. Perry claims that Mary's position is comparable to this. And just as Perry the shopper's predicament has no ontological consequences, Mary's predicament does not either.

The analogy is plausible, but does it give an account the kind of knowledge Mary gains? I myself once thought something like this (Crane 2003), but now I think things cannot be that simple. Consider a Laplacean demon who has a complete theoretical, third-personal, objective knowledge of all the facts before Perry's shopper's discovery. The demon would be able to deduce that Perry's shopper will be able to know that *he* is the shopper making the mess. The demon would not, of course, be able to know that she herself, the Laplacean demon, was making a mess, because it is not true – she cannot truly think the proposition that Perry is thinking. But despite this, she knows – without remainder, I want to say – which proposition it is that Perry comes to know.

The situation is different when it comes to Mary's predicament. Given that she has total knowledge of physics, psychology, linguistics, etc., the demon would be able to predict that Mary will think 'this is what red looks like' after she sees red for the first time. But if the demon herself had not seen red, then there would still be something significant lacking from her knowledge: what red looks like. This is a more substantial lack than in the Perry case. There the demon knew exactly what was going on, but in the case of seeing red, she was genuinely lacking something. For this reason, I don't think Perry is right that Mary's predicament is explained simply by the theory of indexicality. Something else is going on.

The conclusion of the knowledge argument is not simply that some knowledge requires experience; it is that there is some specific kind of knowledge which requires a specific kind of experience, and that this cannot be obtained in another way. Mary's knowledge of what red looks like is knowledge of this kind. It is expressible in a proposition – *red looks like this* or *this is what red looks like* – but this proposition requires specific kind of visual experience in order to be learned. The idea that there might be knowledge of this kind is not trivial, but the knowledge argument provides one plausible reason for believing in it. Exactly how this species or kind of knowledge should be characterised, it seems to me, is a substantial question for epistemology.

1.5 How to Get the Dualist Conclusion

In my interpretation of the argument, then, dualism does not follow from the conclusion of the knowledge argument. I disagree therefore with Robinson when he says, 'if the contrast between Mary and others, or between Mary before and after is a genuine one, then property dualism is established and one must adjust one's views accordingly' (Robinson 2016: 59). I reject this inference, not because I reject property dualism, but because one can accept that there is a genuine contrast, and still be a property monist. The contrast lies purely in Mary's experience and in her knowledge of the situation.

It is worth asking, then, why some philosophers think that the argument or something like it does establish dualism. In the final section of this chapter I will venture a hypothesis about this, by way of a discussion of Robinson's version of the argument in his recent book, *From the Knowledge Argument to Mental Substance* (2016).

Robinson presents the argument in a slightly different way from the way I present it above. Here is his version:

(1) Mary knows all those facts about the perception of chromatic colour which can in principle be expressed in the vocabulary of physical science.

(2) Unlike those who have normal visual experiences, Mary does not know the phenomenal nature of chromatic colour (what it is like to perceive chromatic colour).

Therefore

(3) The phenomenal nature of chromatic colour in principle cannot be characterised using the vocabulary of physical science.

(4) The nature of any physical thing, state or property can be expressed in the vocabulary of physical science.

Therefore

(5) The phenomenal nature of chromatic colour is not a physical thing, state or property. (Robinson 2016: 16–17)

One obvious difference between my version of the argument and Robinson's is that Robinson focuses on Mary's predicament inside the room, rather than on the change after the new experience. Robinson takes it for granted at this stage that Mary will gain new knowledge after seeing red, and of course I am happy to follow him in this.

What about the rest of his argument? Robinson's premise (1) is weaker than my premise (1) (it is a consequence of the latter) but otherwise his version introduces some somewhat different ideas. Premise (2) talks about knowing 'the phenomenal nature' of a property, which I take to be equivalent to knowing what it is like to experience that property. To show that (3) follows from (1) and (2) we need two things. First, we need to show that the knowledge in (1) is the same kind as that in (2) – i.e. propositional or factual knowledge – to avoid equivocation (as explained in 1.2 above). Robinson should adopt something like the reasoning I gave in 1.2 for the univocality of the knowledge claims here. And second, we should stipulate that 'expressed' and 'characterised' mean the same thing in this context. Given these two points, (3) will follow from (1) and (2). Premise (1) says Mary knows all the facts that can in principle be expressed by physics, and (2) says that she does not know the facts about what it's like. So the facts about what it's like to experience the property cannot be something in principle expressed by physics.

(It would be possible to question the equation of 'expressed' and 'characterised', on the grounds that physics can characterise an experience without expressing it – a scientific description of a brain state, for a physicalist, can be a way of characterising something which is as a matter of fact an experience, but the scientific description does not in any plausible way 'express' the experience. However, I don't think Robinson is relying on any significant distinction between expressing and characterising, so I will not pursue this criticism of his argument.)

So far, Robinson's argument is fairly similar to the argument as I presented it above. But premise (4) is an additional premise. It says that the nature of a physical thing can be expressed in the vocabulary of physical science. This is unobjectionable in itself, but if the conclusion (5) is to follow, then premise (4) should say 'the *entire* nature of any physical thing can be expressed in the vocabulary of physical science'. If we do not add 'entire' (or some synonym), then it would be possible for a physicalist to say that physical science can express or characterise the nature of experiences (which are, as a matter of fact, identical with brain states), but that other aspects of their nature can also be expressed using other descriptive materials. But this fact does not entail that this other aspect is not, ontologically speaking, a physical thing. On this view, although physical science can give a characterisation of the state, it would not give a full characterisation. Full characterisations can only be given when one employs all the concepts available; and some of these concepts are only available to those who have had the experience. But the experience can be a physical state for all that. In fact, this seems to me the essence of the 'phenomenal concept' response to the argument, stripped of the confused idea of an 'old fact in a new way'. I myself am sceptical about the specific idea of phenomenal concepts employed by Papineau, Balog, and others. But this is not relevant to the dialectical point here against Robinson.

It may be objected that once it is accepted that there are 'aspects' of things which cannot be described in physical terms, then physicalism has conceded the point. But this is not so; physicalists can allow such aspects, so long as they are conceived of epistemologically. The physicalism I have in mind has been helpfully labelled by Robert Howell 'inclusive subjective physicalism', according to which 'a complete physics will refer to every property and event that there is. There are simply ways of understanding those properties that will not be imparted by an understanding of the theoretical descriptions of physics' (Howell 2009a: 316).

How can this kind of physicalist accept these aspects? Physicalists accept experiences, and (I would argue) they should accept that you don't know what it's like to have a kind of experience unless you have had one of that kind. So they should say that experiences have the following aspect, feature or property: *they are such that you cannot know what they are like without having had them.* Therefore you cannot know what they are like through book-learning alone (as Einstein is supposed to have said, 'science cannot give you the taste of chicken soup'). But this is just another way of distinguishing between the knowledge you get from books (whatever books are exactly) and the know-ledge you get from tasting something. And that distinction itself is just a con-sequence of the sort of thing that tastes (etc.) are.

So Robinson's argument will get its dualist conclusion if premise (4) is modi-fied to include the word 'entire': 'the entire nature of any physical thing, state or property can be expressed in the vocabulary of physical science'. But this is not something a physicalist has to accept. That was the upshot of my discussion in this section and 1.3.

Other versions of the knowledge employ the idea of knowing something in its entirety – but in the mirror image, so to speak, of the claim that Robinson needs. They use instead the idea that experiencing something enables you to know its *phenomenal nature* in its entirety. Reflection on an experience there-fore enables you to know, *ipso facto*, that it is not also a physical phenomenon. As Nida-Rümelin comments:

> The intuitive idea … has been expressed in different ways. Some say that qualia 'have no hidden sides'. Others say that qualia are not natural kinds in that it is not up to the sciences to tell us what having an experience of a particular kind amounts to (we know what it amounts to by having them and attending to the quality at issue). It is quite clear that an account of this intuitive idea has to be one of the ingredients of a dualist defense of the knowledge argument. (Nida-Rümelin 2009)

What Nida-Rümelin here calls the intuitive idea is not just one of the ingredients of a dualist knowledge argument – it is, arguably, *the* active ingredient in a wholly different argument from the one discussed above (1.2–1.3). For if you accept the idea that experience allows you to know an experienced property in its entirety, then you need little else to get the dualist conclusion. For it is plain that you cannot learn that an experience is a physical state merely by having that experience and reflecting upon it. So if the experience is supposed to give you knowledge of the entire nature of phenomenal properties, you could refute the identity theory simply by reflecting on your experience.

Philip Goff has recently put this point by saying that concepts of phe-nomenal states are 'transparent' – they reveal the nature of those states (2017: 74). Although he himself thinks that phenomenal concepts are trans-parent, Goff argues plausibly that 'the knowledge argument does not have the resources to establish' this claim, 'without which Mary's knowledge is no threat to physicalism' (2017: 75). This is, in effect, one of the lessons of the present chapter.

There are two substantial assumptions, then, that can be used to derive dualist conclusions when added to the knowledge argument's premises. One is the assumption Robinson needs: that the entire nature of any physical thing, state or property can be expressed in the vocabulary of physical science. The other is what Nida-Rümelin calls the 'intuitive idea', and what Goff calls 'transparency': that the entire nature of a phenomenal property can be known from experiencing it. The first assumption can be used when you concentrate, as Robinson does, on what Mary doesn't know in the black-and-white room; the second assumption can be used when you concentrate on what Mary comes to know in having the relevant new experience.

These are both very strong assumptions. And although it is possible to build arguments against physicalism using one or both of them (see Goff 2017; Nida-Rümelin 2007), it should be clear that they cannot be derived from the uncontroversial premises of the original 1982 knowledge arguments of Jackson and Robinson. But without these additional assumptions, physicalism is untouched by the argument.

1.6 Conclusion

In this chapter, I have not disputed the significance of the knowledge argument itself, but only its usual interpretations. I have disputed both the dualist interpretation, and the usual physicalist interpretations. Although not a physicalist myself, I argued above that the argument is not effective against physicalism. But this is not because the argument itself, considered in terms of the most plausible reading of its premises and conclusion, is invalid or unsound. It is because the real target of the argument is not physicalism, but a certain conception of knowledge. So instead of an unsound argument against physicalism, we have a sound argument which identifies a particularly important form of knowledge. The precise nature of that knowledge is a matter for further epistemological investigation.

One final point. Physicalists and non-physicalists have commented on the fact that the knowledge argument moves from epistemological premises to metaphysical conclusions, and some have wondered how this is possible. The answer is that in the case of what I think of as the core of the knowledge argument, it is not. Whether or not such metaphysical conclusions can be drawn from other epistemological premises I will not discuss; I restrict myself to the conclusion that the knowledge argument itself does not yield any significant metaphysical conclusions.

2   There's Nothing about Mary

David Rosenthal

2.1 Introduction

Frank Jackson's (1986) Mary is confined in a room in which the visual stimuli are all grayscale, so that her visual experiences have all been achromatic. Nonetheless, from books and television lectures, she has gotten all factual knowledge one can get from any source that pertains to the having of conscious visual experiences. It could indeed be "everything [factual] there is to know about the physical nature of the world," based on "*completed*" science. But, Jackson writes, "[i]t seems ... that Mary does not know all there is to know. For when she is let out of the black-and-white room or given a color television, she will learn what it is like to see something red, say" (1986, 291; emphasis Jackson's).

Jackson presents this as an argument against physicalism. Though Mary has "complete physical knowledge" (291) about the world before first seeing red, she nonetheless learns something new on being presented with a red stimulus. And that new knowledge is factual; it's the fact that this is what it's like to see red. Since Mary learns a new fact and already knew all the physical facts, the new fact must be nonphysical. This is the so-called knowledge argument against mind–body physicalism.[1]

My focus here will not be on physicalism, though the implications for the anti-physicalist argument will be plain. Rather, my concern is how to understand the case Jackson describes and whether standard descriptions (e.g., in Ludlow, Nagasawa, and Stoljar 2004) are correct. Careful focus on that case, I'll argue, shows that though Mary is plainly in a mental state that is new to her

---

[1] Jackson (1982). The basic argument is not new; "A blind man could know the whole of physics, but he could not know what things look like to people who can see, nor what is the difference between red and blue as seen" (Russell 1927a, 182). I am grateful to Galen Strawson for this reference. See also Robinson (1982, 4–5).

on first seeing something red, the factual knowledge that this is what it's like to see red would not be new to her. It would have been contained in her books.

2.2 What Mary Learns

Jackson describes what Mary learns simply as "what it is like to see something red." What it's like to see something red is, for these purposes, the conscious qualitative character of the relevant state of seeing. So we can equivalently describe Mary as learning what the conscious qualitative character of seeing red is.

Both descriptions describe Mary's new knowledge not by way of a "that" clause, but rather as coming to know "wh."[2] To describe somebody as knowing "wh" is to describe their knowledge in an incomplete way. If I describe you as knowing where the treasure is buried or what's behind the door, I'm saying that you know the answer to the question where the treasure is buried or what's behind the door. But knowing those answers is knowing that something is the case. My description in terms of knowing "wh" abstracts from the knowledge "that" I take you to have, knowledge that something is the case.[3]

Since knowing "wh" is knowing the answer to the question expressed by the "wh" clause and that the answer can be expressed by a "that" clause, there is an important connection between knowing "wh" and knowing "that." One knows "wh" only if one knows that something relevant is the case (e.g., Vendler 1972). If one knows what's behind the door, one can in some way describe what's behind the door, even if in incomplete terms, and that would express knowledge that something is the case. Without some relevant knowledge that something is the case, there's nothing in virtue of which one knows "wh."

So when Mary knows what it's like to see something red or what the conscious qualitative character is that's characteristic of seeing red, she must have at least some knowledge that something is the case, something relevant to her knowledge "wh." And if her knowing "wh" is new to her, that factual, descriptive knowledge must be as well.

---

[2] Cf. Daniel Stoljar's (2016) subtle and penetrating semantic account of "what it's like" statements, on which, to a first approximation, "There is something it is like to have a toothache" means that there is a way that having a toothache affects one. So knowing what it's like to have a toothache is knowing what that way is (1171–2). The "wh" construal is preserved for knowing what it's like.

[3] Some (e.g., Higginbotham 1996) have urged that knowing "wh" is definable in terms of knowing that something is the case; but it is doubtful that actual definability is possible (e.g., Farkas 2015 and George 2013).

But Jackson tells us nothing about what that new factual knowledge might be. What is it that Mary comes to know to be the case on first seeing something red? What is the new factual knowledge that underwrites her new knowledge "wh?"

The natural candidate is that Mary comes to know that *this* is an example of what it's like to see red or of the conscious qualitative character of seeing red, where "this"[4] refers to her new experience. These seem to be clear cases of knowing that something is the case, which could underwrite Mary's coming to know "wh" – what it's like to see red and what the qualitative character of seeing red is.

Mary's new knowledge is that whatever "this" refers to is an example of seeing red. So the foregoing account of Mary's knowledge requires that we be able to tell which experience "this" refers to independent of its being an example of seeing red. Mental pointing is unlikely to help here; without an independent account such an appeal simply labels the need to fix the reference of "this."

But mental pointing isn't needed. We can fix the reference of "this" descriptively, by the location of the experience in Mary's visual field relative to other describable items also present in that field. So one way to capture the factual knowledge Mary is supposed to gain on first seeing something red is that her new experience is an example of what it's like to see something red or, equivalently, an example of the conscious qualitative character of seeing red.[5]

---

[4] More precisely, the mental analogue of "this," though I'll typically take that as understood.

[5] Indeed, it is arguable that all pointing and all demonstratives in thought or speech can be fully cashed out in descriptive terms. Zenon Pylyshyn (2007, ch. 2, esp. 2.1) has contested this, arguing that some mental demonstratives are ineliminable. His argument appeals to his ingenious and highly influential experimental work in multiple-object tracking, in which subjects can visually track roughly four moving targets when presented with four moving distractors. This, he writes, "make[s] it very unlikely that objects are tracked by regularly updating a description that uniquely picks out the objects" (17).

But that is not obvious. Subjects cannot consciously report descriptively how they track roughly four objects, but that does not show that the tracking is not achieved by descriptive information that either is unconscious or conscious for just a moment until no longer needed. Consider tracking just a single object with a single distractor, or perhaps two. In that case, most subjects could doubtless report in descriptive terms how they track. Adding objects to the limit of subjects' ability to track imposes substantial additional attentional load (e.g., Lavie 1995, 2010), diminishing other cognitive abilities, including conscious awareness (Lavie et al. 2014). So the failure to report in descriptive terms the tracking of all four might well be just a casualty of attentional load, even if tracking is actually achieved by descriptive processing. One test might be to freeze the movement of tracked items from time to time and ask subjects to give whatever descriptive information about tracking they can, perhaps for just one or two items.

Subjects are of course visually acquainted with the items, though as argued in the next section such acquaintance does not figure in any operative conceptual content. And we have so far no reason, even in this ingenious experimental paradigm, to think that an irreducible

But this way of capturing the factual knowledge Mary is supposed to gain does not, as Jackson notes, result in a problem for physicalism. Mary's experience of seeing red is by hypothesis new to her. So the knowledge simply that her new experience is an example of what it's like to see red is also new to her; Mary's books could not have covered facts about a token state of Mary's that had not yet occurred when those books were written. As Jackson puts it, "physicalist and nonphysicalist alike can agree" that Mary "could not have known facts about her [novel] experience of red, for there were no such facts to know" (1986, 292).

But that has no bearing on Jackson's anti-physicalist argument. The problem for physicalism, he urges, is not that on first seeing something red, Mary learns that her new experience is an example of what it's like to see something red. It's that she learns that the property her new experience exemplifies is also what it's like for others to see something red. She learns that the conscious qualitative character exemplified by her new experience is exemplified generally by people's experiences on seeing something red.[6]

And others had seen red before Mary did, and her books would have described the neurophysiology and behavioral consequences of their doing so. But the books could not, according to Jackson, have included the fact that Mary's new conscious qualitative character is that of experiences that people generally have on seeing something red. So that's something new Mary learns that could not have been in her books.

This raises two questions. One is whether, on Mary's learning that her new experience exemplifies what it's like to see something red, she does also learn what it's like for others to see something red. The other is whether Mary's books could have contained descriptive knowledge of the conscious qualitative character of seeing something red, the qualitative property that characterizes others' past experiences of seeing red. To answer these two questions we must get clear about what that conscious qualitative character consists in, that is, what the property is that Mary has knowledge about.

---

demonstrative component figures in the tracking, as against purely descriptive information. This in turn casts serious doubt on any appeal to demonstratives in capturing the cognitive content of new factual knowledge Mary allegedly gains.

[6] It's unclear that all discussions of the knowledge argument cast the problem in this way. Some seem to proceed on the assumption that the problem for physicalism might be simply learning what the conscious qualitative character is of Mary's new experience. But I'll follow Jackson's treatment on this. In casting things this way Jackson must be tacitly assuming that undetectable inversion of conscious mental qualities cannot occur, since if it could, Mary could not know what it's like for others just by knowing what it's like for her. I won't pursue that issue here.

2.3 Phenomenal Concepts

To sustain Jackson's argument, Mary must on first seeing something red have knowledge that is both factual and new to her. We need to know what properties that new factual knowledge would be about. And a promising way to become clear about the properties a particular type of factual knowledge is about is by appeal to the conceptual content of that knowledge. And it has seemed to many that the relevant concepts here are so-called phenomenal concepts.

There are many accounts of phenomenal concepts (Alter and Walter 2007; Nida-Rümelin 2009). But they have in common that one can have and deploy a particular phenomenal concept only if one has had the relevant qualitative experience. That's because the qualitative experience itself is the mode of presentation in virtue of which the phenomenal concept applies to a conscious qualitative state.

Accounts of phenomenal concepts vary in respect of how the conscious qualitative property serves as the mode of presentation in virtue of which phenomenal concepts apply to those conscious qualitative properties. But I'll focus here on this pivotal common feature. Mary comes to know that this is what it's like to see something red, where the concept in her knowing that applies to the property of what it's like to see something red is a phenomenal concept.

If Mary's knowledge involves phenomenal concepts so construed, her knowledge is plainly new to her on first seeing something red. Knowledge cast in terms of phenomenal concepts could not have been in any books, since one cannot have phenomenal concepts at all without having the relevant qualitative experiences. We need know nothing more about conscious qualitative character to conclude that knowledge about it could not be in Mary's books. And since phenomenal concepts are concepts, knowledge cast in terms of them should be expressible by "that" clauses. So Mary's knowledge should be genuinely factual, descriptive knowledge, as Jackson's argument requires.

One might have some concern about the appeal concepts so perfectly tailored to deliver the results Jackson's argument requires.[7] Since phenomenal concepts are exactly what the argument calls for, we should want some reason to think such concepts actually occur, a reason that's independent of a desire to

---

[7] A point of clarification: Phenomenal concepts are typically invoked to explain how Mary can gain new factual knowledge without thereby undermining mind–body physicalism. My concern here is only tangentially about mind–body physicalism; I am primarily concerned to contest that Mary does get new factual knowledge. And it is that claim that the positing of phenomenal concepts is so perfectly tailored to fit with Jackson's account.

see Jackson's argument as sound. We cannot dispel this concern simply by providing an account of what phenomenal concepts are. We must have an independent reason to think there are any such concepts, and that they actually occur in one's thinking about one's own conscious qualitative states.

But set that methodological concern aside. There is a wholly distinct challenge about whether phenomenal concepts could be genuinely conceptual at all. The defining characteristic of phenomenal concepts is their tie to qualitative experiences. But the standard test for whether a mental item is conceptual is whether it has distinctively conceptual connections to other mental items that are themselves plainly conceptual.

If there are phenomenal concepts that occur in an individual's thinking or knowledge, they apply to the qualitative experiences of that individual, as they are conscious for that individual. So we could expect such phenomenal concepts to have distinctively conceptual ties with concepts that apply to qualitative experiences independent of whether one has had the experiences, concepts one could apply indifferently to oneself and to others. An example would be the concepts that a blind person could apply to the visual experiences of others.

As noted above, Jackson himself assumes that on coming to know that her new experience exemplifies the qualitative character of seeing red, Mary also comes to know that the experiences others have on seeing red have the same qualitative character that her new experience exhibits. "[T]he knowledge Mary lacked which is of particular point for the knowledge argument against physicalism is *knowledge about the experiences of others*, not about her own" (1986, 292; emphasis Jackson's). For that to be so, Mary's new knowledge must be cast in concepts that apply indifferently to herself and to others or, if not, then at least in concepts with robust conceptual ties to concepts that do apply indifferently to oneself and to others.

But phenomenal concepts cannot satisfy this condition. The mode of presentation in virtue of which phenomenal concepts apply to qualitative experiences ineliminably involves the very qualitative experiences to which they apply. So phenomenal concepts cannot themselves apply to others' qualitative experiences. If they did, one could have phenomenal concepts without having any relevant qualitative experiences, undermining the type of mode of presentation phenomenal concepts are said to have.

So the only way phenomenal concepts can function as concepts at all is for robust conceptual ties to hold between the phenomenal concepts, in terms of which Mary's knowledge is cast, and other, nonphenomenal concepts that apply to others' qualitative experiences. Such concepts would apply to others' qualitative experiences at least in part on the basis of third-person considerations.

But it's far from clear that any clearly conceptual connection can hold between a concept of seeing red that applies independently of whether one has seen anything red and a putative concept that applies only to oneself and only if one has seen something red, and indeed in virtue of one's having done so. Conceptual connections obtain in virtue of the application conditions of the relevant concepts, and the requirement that phenomenal concepts apply only to the individual that has the concepts makes connections with concepts that apply independent of that constraint unlikely. And the connection must be uncontroversially conceptual, since that's the key to whether a mental item is conceptual. This is the main challenge for any appeal to phenomenal concepts.

Ordinary concepts operate descriptively, by applying to a tolerably well-defined range of items. So there's typically no difficulty in articulating distinctively conceptual connections among them. But an advocate of phenomenal concepts might contest the use of such connections to test whether phenomenal concepts are genuinely conceptual. Phenomenal concepts are by hypothesis a special case.

But the knowledge argument requires that Mary's new knowledge be factual; so the knowledge must be expressible in conceptual terms. Without some way to show that phenomenal concepts are genuinely conceptual, we have no reason to hold that positing them can sustain the claim that Mary does gain new factual knowledge. And there seems no way to show that phenomenal concepts are genuinely conceptual except by appeal to conceptual connections with other concepts.

The issue about conceptual ties between phenomenal concepts and other concepts reflects a deeper difficulty that often arises in discussions of mental phenomena. Plainly we have first-person access to our own mental states, access independent of observing ourselves and independent of conscious inference. But we also have access to others' mental states, and that third-person access does rest on observation and inference. And though our first-person access is only to our own states, the states of others to which we have third-person access are states of the very same sort as those to which we have first-person access. If I say I'm in pain and you deny that I am, we are not talking past one another; we are talking about states of the very same sort (see Rosenthal, in press).

This gives us compelling reason to hold that whatever concepts apply to our own experiential states must have distinctively conceptual connections with concepts that apply indifferently to experiential states of ourselves and others. The problem with phenomenal concepts is the stricture that one cannot have them at all without having had the relevant experiential states.

This makes it difficult to see how conceptual ties might hold between them and nonphenomenal concepts of experiential states, and so casts doubt on whether so-called phenomenal concepts are genuinely conceptual at all.

An advocate of phenomenal concepts might urge that they can, after all, apply to others' qualitative experiences. But it is unclear how that can fit with such concepts' having modes of presentation always inextricably tied to qualitative experiences of one's own. And if phenomenal concepts aren't inextricably tied to one's own qualitative experiences, it's unclear how they can sustain Jackson's claim that Mary comes to have new factual knowledge. Simply claiming that one can extrapolate from the application of phenomenal concepts to oneself to applying them to others does nothing but ignore the challenge.

The most influential account of phenomenal concepts is due to Brian Loar (1997), and that deserves special attention. Phenomenal concepts, according to Loar, are recognitional; they apply in virtue of one's ability to recognize things of some relevant type. There are two worries about this. One is that, as with knowing "wh," it's doubtful that one has the ability to recognize anything that one cannot describe in some way, even if that description is by itself often not precise enough to enable recognition of the relevant thing.

Loar considers recognizing a type of cactus. As he notes, one might typically have that ability without being able to describe the type of cactus sufficiently well to enable such recognition. Still, it's hard to imagine a case in which one could recognize a type of cactus and yet be unable to say anything descriptive that could help individuate that type.[8]

So having the ability to recognize a case of one's seeing red should similarly require that one be able to describe, even if in some minimal way, what it is to be a case of seeing red. And if we understand phenomenal concepts as applying in virtue of a recognitional ability, applying the phenomenal concept of seeing red will require being able to describe, using ordinary, nonphenomenal

---

[8] One might construe an ability to recognize as one's knowing how to recognize. And then knowing how to recognize something would require that one have some relevant descriptive knowledge about that type of thing. Still, that does not imply the controversial claim of Stanley and Williamson (2001) that knowing how is itself a kind of knowing that. See in the present context their discussion of the Mary case (443–4), as well as their discussion of Mary in terms of gaining a new skill (Stanley and Williamson, in press).

It is in any case unclear that an ability to recognize is accurately seen in general either as a skill or as knowing how to recognize. One might be able to recognize something without there being any skill involved in doing so. And many abilities resist being described as cases of knowing how to do something; it's at best misleading to describe one's ability to look off to the left as one's knowing how to look off to the left. Similarly, if you can recognize somebody, it's also arguably at best misleading to describe that as your knowing how to recognize that person.

concepts, a case of seeing red. Construing phenomenal concepts in terms of recognitional abilities does not avoid the demand to specify what it is for one to see red in ordinary, nonphenomenal, descriptive terms.

And there is a second difficulty. Mary's seeing red might very well enable her to recognize subsequent cases of seeing red, but there can be no guarantee. Seeing a sample of a particular type of cactus might enable one to recognize future cases of that type, but it might not. Similarly, Mary's knowing that she is in a particular token state cannot ensure that she would be able to recognize future instances of that type, or even that she has any grasp, recognitional or otherwise, of what type that particular token belongs to.

Seeing red is so familiar to us that it's tempting to think that it's unmistakable; if one has seen red, surely one will recognize any future case. But extrapolating from our situation to Mary's is unwarranted; her first experience of seeing red might be so overwhelming in its novelty as to result in its being unclear whether future chromatic experiences are of the same type. And if Mary were to see red without gaining the ability to recognize future cases, she would not have a phenomenal concept of seeing red construed in recognitional terms. I'll return to and expand on this point in 2.4, along with other issues that arise in connection with the appeal to phenomenal concepts.

2.4 Ability and Acquaintance

It is unlikely that phenomenal concepts, however construed, will help provide an account of the conceptual content of the new factual knowledge that Mary is supposed to gain on first seeing something red. This is especially so if phenomenal concepts are understood in terms of a recognitional ability, since there might be nothing conceptual at all in the mere gaining of an ability.

This invites consideration of a proposal by Lawrence Nemirow (1980, 1990, 2007) and David Lewis (1983a, 1999) that what is new to Mary is not factual knowledge at all, but rather just an ability to recognize, imagine, or remember the relevant type of experience.[9] And there is on this account no new type of concept that results from gaining the relevant ability.

This ability hypothesis seeks to accommodate the idea that Mary comes to have knowledge not covered in her books, but unlike the appeal to phenomenal concepts it denies that this new knowledge is factual. Since the new knowledge doesn't show there are nonphysical facts, it can't undermine physicalism.

---

[9] Nemirow relies principally on the ability to imagine (1990, 495).

But the considerations that caused difficulty for Loar's proposal apply equally to the ability hypothesis. For one thing, Mary might on first seeing red simply not gain any of the relevant abilities. One can have an experience of a new type but be unable to recall its nature or imagine or recognize another instance of its type.

But even if Mary did gain the relevant recognitional ability, she would also gain factual knowledge about the kind of state she comes to be able to recognize. This is clear from the foregoing discussion of recognitional concepts; it is difficult to believe that one could come to be able to recognize something and yet be unable to say anything descriptive, howsoever general, about the thing one comes to be able to recognize. And such descriptive information would be factual.

One might suppose that this factual knowledge would be new to Mary, since it accompanies her new recognitional ability. But we cannot simply assume that; the recognitional ability might be new but the factual knowledge that new ability elicits might have been covered in her books. To assess whether the factual knowledge that accompanies Mary's new recognitional ability could have been in her books, we would have to get clear about the descriptive content of that factual knowledge.

Whatever factual knowledge accompanies a new recognitional ability that Mary gains will describe the things Mary has come to be able to recognize, namely, the conscious qualitative character of her experiences. Though the ability hypothesis denies that gaining a recognitional ability involves gaining factual knowledge, there is compelling reason to hold that it does. So we need an independent account of the nature of the qualitative character of experiences to determine what factual knowledge might accompany Mary's first seeing something red or gaining the ability to recognize such an experience. Only then can we assess whether such factual knowledge could have been in Mary's books.

There is another proposal that, like the ability hypothesis, seeks to accommodate Mary's gaining new knowledge but deny that the new knowledge is factual. On that proposal, the new knowledge is a type of acquaintance; "learning what an experience is like is identical to becoming acquainted with the experience" (Conee 1994, 140). Following Bertrand Russell's famed distinction between descriptive knowledge and knowledge by acquaintance (1912, ch. 12), Mary might then gain new knowledge by becoming newly acquainted with an experiential property, but not thereby gaining any new factual knowledge. In the same spirit, Paul Churchland urges that Mary's new knowledge might just be "knowledge by acquaintance" (1985, 24), and hence not factual.

But as with the proposal that the knowledge Mary gains is an ability to recognize, it's doubtful that one can become acquainted with something without having some descriptive knowledge relevant to that thing. Being acquainted with something in the ordinary case involves perceiving it, and that in turn must involve some descriptive knowledge about it. Acquaintance with an experience is due in some way to consciousness, not perception. But there is no reason to think that the same doesn't hold there. Being acquainted with a conscious experience always enables one to say something informative about that experience, because being acquainted with it rests on some measure of descriptive information about it. Some descriptive knowledge is always built into acquaintance.[10] What we need to know is whether that could have been in Mary's books.

One might suppose that consciousness results in acquaintance with our experiences in some direct way that precludes any descriptive knowledge. Indeed, some such picture very likely underlies the appeal to phenomenal concepts. I'll turn to that idea in the next section. But that picture aside, there is no reason to suppose that acquaintance with anything, even with conscious qualitative experiences, can occur without one's being able to describe what one is acquainted with, if not precisely and in detail, at least in general terms.

The ability and acquaintance hypotheses are proposals for seeing Mary as gaining new knowledge, but not descriptive knowledge and so not knowledge that could be covered in her books. But in both cases, the new nondescriptive knowledge would be accompanied by some relevant descriptive knowledge. Only when we know exactly what content that descriptive knowledge would have can we assess whether it could have been in Mary's books.

2.5 What Consciousness Tells Us

The appeal to phenomenal concepts is intended to ensure that on first seeing something red Mary comes to have knowledge that is both new to her and factual. That the knowledge would be new is built into what phenomenal concepts are; one cannot have them without having a token of the relevant type of qualitative experience. The difficulty is in ensuring that the so-called phenomenal concepts are genuinely conceptual, since unless they are the new knowledge won't be factual.

---

[10] This goes beyond Russell's mild concession that "it would be rash to assume that human beings ever, in fact, have acquaintance with things without at the same time knowing some truth about them" (1912, 46), and explains why what he says is so.

Still, it may continue to seem inviting that one does get new factual know-ledge of some sort when one has a qualitative experience of a new type, know-ledge that is not merely one's acquiring a new ability or one's coming to be acquainted with an experience of that type. Consciousness, it may seem, tells one something new when one has a qualitative experience of a type new to one. And what consciousness tells us, it may seem, is factual; one comes to have factual information that one didn't have before.

On this picture, consciousness tells one, without mediation or help from any other source, what it's like for one to have each conscious experience, what the qualitative character is of any experience one has. It must be without help from any other source to ensure that the factual knowledge consciousness delivers will not be in Mary's books. Consciousness on its own gives one fac-tual knowledge about the qualitative character of each experience.

But it's by no means obvious what factual information that could be. Consciousness plainly does often provide one with an experience of a type new to one. But that by itself does not show that consciousness also by itself provides one with factual knowledge about those new experiences. Simply providing a conscious experience of a type new to one will not sustain the knowledge argument.

And the new factual information one gains cannot simply be that *this*, refer-ring to the new experience, is what it's like to see something red. The know-ledge that *this* is what it's like to see something red refers, by hypothesis, to an experience that's new to one. But it does so demonstratively or by picking the experience out in relation to other current experiential states one can describe. Though the experience referred to is of a type new to one, the refer-ring does not by itself constitute new informational content. The referring in one's knowledge that this is what it's like to see something red does not provide new conceptual content.

The factual knowledge that this is what it's like to see something red does not simply refer to an experience of a type new to one; it also predicates a property of that experience. But it's not obvious that that property that factual knowledge predicates of the experience referred to could not have been described in Mary's books. The factual knowledge says that the experience in question is a case of what it's like to see something red. Why couldn't that property be in Mary's books?

It's tempting to say it couldn't be in Mary's books because the property of being what it's like to see something red is ineffable. So that property is not subject to being described in any articulate way at all. Consciousness in effect shows us the property, so that we know from consciousness what that property is. But it simply is not the sort of property that could have been in Mary's books, because it is not the sort of property that lends itself to being described in any way at all. This is reflected in Ned Block's colorful appeal, in saying what qualitative mental states are, to Louis Armstrong's remark about jazz: "If you gotta ask, you ain't never gonna get to know" (Block 1978, 281).

This is why the appeal to phenomenal concepts is so inviting. If the knowledge that this is what it's like to see something red involves applying a phenomenal concept of the experience that knowledge refers to, then the first time one has an experience of the sort that phenomenal concept applies to there will be conceptual content that is new to one. So the factual knowledge will itself be new to one. The appeal to phenomenal concepts is a way of capturing the idea that though consciousness does tell us something about our qualitative experiences, what it tells us cannot be put in words; it does not allow for any articulate description.

This fits with the earlier discussion of a problem for phenomenal concepts. The difficulty was in establishing that phenomenal concepts so called are genuinely conceptual, that they contribute to the conceptual content of the new factual knowledge Mary is supposed to gain. Absent any conceptual connections that phenomenal concepts would have with other relevant concepts, there is reason to doubt that phenomenal concepts are concepts at all. And the lack of such conceptual connections goes hand in hand with the apparent ineffability of what consciousness is supposed to tell us about our qualitative experiences. If the so-called phenomenal concepts lack ties to ordinary concepts, there will be no way to articulate the content of the alleged phenomenal concepts.

This, to reiterate, is because phenomenal concepts have as modes of presentations one's own qualitative experiences, the very experiences that the phenomenal concepts are posited to apply to in a distinctively first-person way. But it is difficult to see how such concepts could have robust conceptual ties with any other concepts, and without such robust ties phenomenal concepts cannot figure in any articulate or informative remarks even about one's own qualitative experiences. Hence the ineffability.

Those who posit phenomenal concepts may be tempted to urge that they operate only partly as ordinary nonphenomenal concepts do, and that the demand that they connect conceptually with other concepts is accordingly unreasonable. But the advocate of phenomenal concepts must then ensure that the nonstandard nature of phenomenal concepts not only allows them to qualify as a kind of concept at all, but also and more important that their nonstandard nature as concepts will permit them to do the job the advocates have in mind. It is far from clear that either demand can be met.

It might seem, however, that consciousness does somehow give us articulate information about our qualitative experiences after all. Consider an experience of seeing something red; doesn't consciousness tell us that this experience is more like an experience of seeing something orange than like an experience of seeing something blue? Doesn't consciousness tell us countless other comparative things about the various types of qualitative experience we have?

In general, comparing things requires being able to identify and individuate those things independently of the comparison. If one compares two objects in respect of their size or shape or color, one must be able to pick those things out independently of the comparison. So for consciousness to deliver comparative information about qualitative experiences, we must be able, relying exclusively on what consciousness tells us, to identity and individuate the experiences being compared independently of the comparisons. So such comparisons tell us nothing about the nature of the individual mental qualities that we wouldn't already have known from what consciousness had told us about each mental quality on its own. At least this is so if consciousness is to deliver comparative information without help from any other source. And if consciousness gets help from another source, whatever information that other source contributes might well be in Mary's books.

Consciousness can compare qualitative experiences only if it has some way to identify and individuate each experience on its own. But it's unclear how consciousness might do that. Consciousness by itself seems to have nothing informative to say about individual experiences; whatever consciousness might tell us about them is ineffable, incapable of being described. So consciousness by itself cannot deliver comparative information about our qualitative experiences. Nothing that consciousness by itself could tell us about our qualitative experiences could appear in Mary's books. But that is not because consciousness gives us information of some special sort. It's because consciousness tells us nothing about our qualitative experiences that could figure in any factual knowledge about them.[11]

---

[11] Thomas Nagel (1974) has famously urged that conscious experience requires to be treated in subjective terms, and that subjectivity drives out any objective treatment. This is a natural conclusion if a treatment is subjective only if it relies solely on consciousness. But one need not so construe subjectivity; one can construe it in a way that both does justice to the contrast between subjective and objective and also leaves open the possibility of an objective treatment of conscious experience (Rosenthal 1983).

2.6 Qualitative Experience

The idea that we can learn what the nature of qualitative experiences is solely from what consciousness tells us is basic to the knowledge argument and to the positing of phenomenal concepts. Phenomenal concepts are consciousness-based concepts, whose possession and application rest solely on how consciousness presents the relevant qualitative character. It's this feature of phenomenal concepts that seals them off from conceptual ties with any other concepts.

The idea that we can learn what the nature of qualitative experiences is solely from what consciousness tells us is often simply taken for granted in the current philosophical literature, as though it's so obvious that no argument or assessment is called for. But without some articulate account of what information consciousness provides us about qualitative experiences, it's hard to avoid the conclusion that consciousness, by itself, doesn't provide any information at all. The fallback claim that what consciousness tells us is ineffable doesn't help; if it's ineffable, it isn't information. It certainly isn't anything that could underwrite the idea that Mary on first seeing something red gains new factual knowledge. If it's factual, it can be expressed descriptively. One might contest that connection, but it is difficult to see what being factual could amount to otherwise.

Still, it may seem that there is no alternative to this consciousness-based picture, that there simply is no source of information about the nature of qualitative experience other than consciousness.[12] So it's important to assess whether there is an alternative to the exclusive reliance on consciousness that underlies the knowledge argument. Is there a way to tell about the nature of qualitative experience and about specific types of qualitative experience other than from the inside?

The widespread reliance on first-person access may blind us to the crucial tie that qualitative experiences have with perception, a tie that we can exploit to construct an alternative to the consciousness-first approach. Our having qualitative experiences is intimately tied to our ability to discriminate among stimuli of various sorts; indeed, it is in virtue of our having qualitative experiences of different types that we are able to discriminate perceptible stimuli at all. One discriminates stimuli with distinct shades of red by having different qualitative experiences of the relevant stimuli, and similarly with all perceptual discrimination.

---

[12] This conviction reflects the influence of Nagel (1974), and is nicely epitomized in Adam Pautz's evocative slogan, "consciousness first" (2013, 195). It is also reflected in David Chalmers's claim that "there is nothing we know more directly than" mental qualities, that qualitative character "is the most vivid of phenomena; nothing is more real to us" (1996, 3).

Since qualitative experiences are the states that enable us to discriminate perceptible stimuli, we should be able to use the tie between qualitative experiences and perceptual discrimination to understand both the nature of qualitative experiences and how to characterize the various types of qualitative experience. Whenever two stimuli are discriminable by an individual, that individual will have qualitative experiences that themselves differ in a way that corresponds to the relative difference among the stimuli.

This correspondence of differences between stimuli and qualitative experiences can be made precise. We can begin with the most minimal case of perceptual discrimination, so-called just noticeable differences (JNDs), where an individual is able to discriminate two stimuli that would be indistinguishable were they physically any closer. Experimentally, display to an individual two stimuli that are physically identical; the individual will report that they're the same. Then adjust one of the stimuli to be slightly different from the other in its physical nature by successive minimal steps until the individual reports that now they're different. Those two stimuli are now JND.[13]

Having established JNDs among all stimuli accessible by a particular modality, we can then use these minimal discriminable differences among stimuli to construct a space that represents the distance in respect of JNDs between any two stimuli thus accessible. Since differences in qualitative experiences enable these discriminations, we have a space that also represents the qualitative distance between any two experiences. So the space of JNDs among discriminable stimuli also provides us with an account of the mental qualities of experiences that are responsible for such discriminability (Rosenthal 1991, 1999, 2001, 2005, chs. 5–7, 2010).[14]

---

[13] There are various methodological issues in this procedure that aren't relevant for present purposes. Experimental subjects tend to be conservative, so that they may continue to report no difference even when they can discriminate the stimuli; this can be controlled by interspersing irrelevant displays. And noise in the perceptual channels may yield inconsistent reports, requiring statistical techniques to get a definite result. There are also issues about how to handle the well-known intransitivity of JNDs; see Goodman (1951, 256–8). JNDs must be tested individual by individual, but the results can be averaged to get discriminability for a species or other group.

It is crucial for present purposes that what is just noticeably different are the perceptible stimuli and not, as some discussions in psychophysics assume, the subjective assessments of differences in mental quality between distinct experiences. That's because the present proposal is to explain qualitative experiences by appeal to their role in the perceptual discrimination of stimuli.

[14] For more on quality spaces generally, see Clark (1993) and Kuehni (2010).

This quality-space account of mental qualities can be extended to provide a way of individuating the perceptual modalities themselves; two mental qualities belong to the same

This quality-space theory of qualitative character and of its various types makes no appeal to what consciousness might tell one about qualitative experiences generally or about particular types. It relies exclusively on testing the ability to discriminate various stimuli and the tie between discriminative ability and types of qualitative experiences. It's plain that if on being presented with two stimuli the qualitative experiences that result are the same in type, one will be unable to perceive any difference between them. Only when qualitative experiences differ can we distinguish the stimuli that give rise to them.

The quality space of mental qualities derives from the quality space of discriminations that an individual can make among various stimulus properties. Constructing that quality space relies on testing what discriminations are possible, which won't always follow the physical nature of those stimulus properties. This is as it should be; types of qualitative character don't reflect the physical nature of stimuli, but the discriminative abilities an individual has in respect of those stimuli.[15] Differences among qualitative characters are what enable perceptual discriminations of stimuli.

The connection between experience and perceptual discrimination is fundamental to our conception of what a qualitative experience is. Quality-space theory simply capitalizes on that connection, and constructs a way to assess and calibrate the discriminable differences among stimuli with differences among mental qualities. And because the quality-space account of qualitative character makes no appeal to what consciousness might tell one, it provides a robust alternative to the consciousness-first approach, which at best delivers ineffable pronouncements devoid of articulable, factual information.

2.7 Consciousness vs. Perceptual Role

Quality-space theory, which appeals to the role qualitative states have in perception, offers a clear, articulate account of what qualitative character is and how the various types of qualitative character are individuated. Exclusive reliance on consciousness to learn about qualitative character, by contrast, provides no descriptive knowledge, and so nothing that could sustain the idea that Mary gets new knowledge about what it's like for one to see something red simply by having a new conscious experience of seeing something red.

---

modality if there is a chain of JNDs that leads from one to the other (Rosenthal 2015; Young, Keller, and Rosenthal 2014).

[15] So quality-space theory differs crucially from Churchland (2007), which relies on the physical nature of the relevant stimuli.

Still, the exclusive reliance on consciousness is so entrenched in current discussions of qualitative character that it's worth addressing objections that those who endorse that reliance may raise for quality-space theory, as well as considering several additional ways that quality-space theory has advantages over a consciousness-based approach.

One concern a consciousness-first theorist will immediately raise is the neutrality of quality-space theory about whether the mental qualities in question are conscious. Perceptual discrimination occurs without being conscious; indeed unconscious perception can yield very accurate discriminations; forced-choice guesses in subliminal perception of various types, for example, in masked priming (Breitmeyer and Öğmen 2006; Cheesman and Merikle 1986; Marcel 1983), are typically highly accurate. And change detection can occur in the absence of subjective awareness (Fernandez-Duque and Thornton 2000; Laloyaux et al. 2003).[16] If mental qualities are, as quality-space theory hypothesizes, the mental properties responsible for perceptual discrimination, then mental qualities occur in these cases without being conscious.

Unconscious qualitative character is anathema to a consciousness-based approach, on which we learn about qualitative character exclusively from consciousness. And many discussions simply identify qualitative character with what Block (1995) calls phenomenal consciousness, in effect building consciousness into qualitative character by terminological stipulation. But absent some substantive reason to insist that qualitative character cannot occur without being conscious, we should resist that stipulation.[17]

One might take the term "mental quality" as simply implying consciousness; it is likely that the term "quale" does carry that implication, as does Block's (1995) term, "phenomenal consciousness." But even if one so construed "mental quality," one can always adopt another term that is neutral between being conscious and not. And construing the term as implying consciousness would in any case beg the substantive question of whether the mental

---

[16] Indeed, unconscious discrimination is sometimes more accurate than conscious discrimination (Scott and Dienes 2010).

[17] A traditional way to differentiate perception from nonperceptual cognition is that perception involves mental qualitative character, whereas cognition on its own does not (cf. Firestone and Scholl 2016, 1). But this relies on conscious perception, and so cannot work if qualitative character cannot occur without being conscious but perception can. This is doubtless responsible for the rejection by many today of that traditional line between perception and cognition, and the search for an alternative that does not appeal to qualitative character at all (e.g., Block 2016). Accommodation of qualitative character that need not be conscious would obviate the need for that search.

properties we refer to in the conscious case as mental qualities can also occur without being conscious.

An advocate of that approach might insist that the insistence that qualitative character cannot occur without being conscious is not mere stipulation, but reflects compelling pretheoretic intuition. But pretheoretic intuition would be unable to access unconscious qualitative states if they did occur; intuition can at best tell only about those mental phenomena that are conscious. So the appeal here to pretheoretic intuition at best merely channels the consciousness-based approach.

In any case, so-called intuitions often serve simply as cover for undefended theoretical assumptions, for getting others to accept theoretical claims without having to defend them.[18] And relying on intuition here seems an especially vivid case of that, since whether qualitative states can fail to be conscious is a theoretical, not a commonsense issue. We cannot settle the question by appeal to intuition, but must appeal to relevant theoretical considerations.

And many considerations, both theoretical and commonsense, favor quality-space theory and its appeal to the role qualitative character plays in perceptual discrimination. Suppose you see an object of a particular shade of red and I ask you to tell me about your conscious visual experience. One way you might reply would be to tell me your experience is more like that of seeing a red tomato than that of seeing a fire engine or the like. These objects needn't be present when one sees the target object; they are objects whose characteristic colors we readily remember and so can compare with the shade under consideration.

Such a reply is along the lines of quality-space theory; you're describing the relative location your visual experience has in a space that is fixed, in turn, by a range of discriminable red stimuli, stimuli that typically exhibit characteristic shades of red. Such a reply can't sustain an appeal to consciousness. You're not telling me something you learn from consciousness, but about how your experience compares with other experiences you might have of objects known to us both.

There is another possible reply to such a question. If there are several red objects visible in the current scene, you might instead tell me how your experience of the target red object compares to your experiences of those others.

[18] As what we might call theory pumps, inverting Daniel Dennett's inviting idea of an intuition pump (1980, 429; 1991, 282, 397). The consciousness-based approach has notable historical precedents, e.g., among British empiricists and among logical empiricists. But the view was advanced by those writers as a theoretical claim, to be defended by overall theoretical considerations, not by appeal to allegedly pretheoretic intuition.

That is again in keeping with quality-space theory; you're locating the target experience within a space of experiences fixed in turn by stimuli we can independently pick out. This second reply does not rely just on something consciousness tells us about the nature of the target experience. In commonsense contexts we describe our qualitative experiences comparatively, by how they compare to other experiences that we can pick out by appeal to independently identifiable stimuli.

It might seem that terms like "red," "green," and "blue," which readily anchor types of visual experience, are not comparative after all. And if they are not, perhaps their use rests on some intrinsic qualitative character as revealed by consciousness. But that impression is misleading. If we describe the qualitative character of seeing red to somebody who is red–green color-blind, we would explain those ostensibly noncomparative terms comparatively. The experience of seeing something red, for example, is typically more like an experience of seeing yellow than like one of seeing blue. Even ostensibly noncomparative terms, such as "red" and "green," get cashed out comparatively when we can't rely on shared experience. Our pretheoretic, commonsense ways of describing mental qualities are comparative, relying on relevant similarities and differences.

Indeed, the way color input is processed neurally itself fixes the color mental qualities comparatively, and not one by one, even for colors that figure dominantly in our classification of things, such as red, green, and blue. Information about levels of excitation of rods and cones in the retina is passed on to cells that process that information comparatively, comparing the strength of red stimulation with that of green stimulation, blue with yellow, and white with black. This so-called opponent processing results in the neural signals that result in mental qualities of color. Mental qualities of color are produced by comparisons that serve in effect to locate those mental qualities within a space of possible qualities fixed by opponent-processing comparisons. Mental qualities of color are not produced atomistically, using a distinct process for each type of mental quality.

Our commonsense practice of describing qualitative experiences by appeal to comparisons with experiences that result from a currently accessible or remembered range of stimuli undermines the idea that we know about qualitative experiences by what consciousness tells us about them. We know about them comparatively, by what types of stimulus they reflect. And if what we know about our qualitative experiences is not from consciousness, we no longer have any reason to reject the idea that qualitative character can occur without being conscious.

A striking aspect of our qualitative experiences is that we can identify and distinguish them in a far more fine-grained way when they occur simultaneously than when they occur in succession. If one has several experiences of shades of red that are very close to one another, they may seem indistinguishable if they occur in succession but clearly different if they occur together (Halsey and Chapanis 1951; Pérez-Carpinell et al. 1998). Indeed, we are aware of such qualitative experiences as indistinguishable when they occur in succession and as plainly distinct when they occur simultaneously. Consciousness relies on comparisons to individuate our qualitative experiences. This holds not only for color experiences, but also for the qualitative character distinctive of other modalities (e.g., Burns and Ward 1982). What consciousness tells us about our qualitative experiences is itself comparative.

Because consciousness presents shades in respect of more fine-grained differences when simultaneous than when in succession, some have claimed that the effect is due simply to limitations of memory, limitations that prevent one from comparing successive experiences (e.g., Raffman 1995). But whatever explains the effect, being presented with a red stimulus of a particular shade results in a different subjective experience when presented together with other stimuli with closely related shades as against being presented with no such stimuli. The availability of comparison with closely related stimuli changes the subjective character of the experiences that result. Consciousness presents the qualitative character of those experiences comparatively. Consciousness does not reveal intrinsic properties of experiences, which would be independent of any such comparisons.

The comparative way we ordinarily think about qualitative character, which reflects the way consciousness presents those experiences, gives reason to question the currently fashionable idea that the mental qualities of our experiences cannot diverge from the way consciousness presents them.[19] Being presented with a particular color stimulus results in a different subjective experience depending on whether that stimulus is accompanied by others closely related to it. Imagine seeing a particular sample of red by itself, and then the same sample accompanied by one only very slightly different. Consciousness presents the two cases differently; the comparison available in seeing the two slightly different reds results in fine-grained subjective experience of each.

But the stimulus is the same in either case. So apart from subjective appearances, we have no reason to think each stimulus results in the same

---

[19]   Thus Nagel: "The idea of moving from appearance to reality seems to make no sense" in connection with conscious experience (1974, 444; cf. 448). Cf. Kripke on pain (1980, 151–2).

mental quality, regardless of whether the stimulus is accompanied by another. Consciousness accordingly presents us with subjective mental appearances that diverge from the underlying mental reality.[20] Subjective awareness can be wrong about the mental qualities that figure in perceptual discrimination (Peels 2016; Rosenthal 2011).

A particularly nice demonstration is Raffman's (2011) finding that when adjacent hues differ by less than just-noticeable differences, though subjects of course judge two to be indistinguishable, they adjust a third hue to match only one of the hues in a systematic way. Visual processing is more fine-grained when it relies on manual matching than on subjective awareness. In a different context, Scott and Dienes (2010) have shown, as noted above (n. 16) that unconscious perceptual processing can be more accurate than conscious processing.

The denial that experiential states can subjectively appear differently from the way they actually are, which is seldom if ever argued, is simply a reflection of the adoption of a first-order theory of consciousness, since on such a theory there is no second factor that can diverge from the first-order experience.

It is possible that commonsense and ordinary usage stress first-person access in ways that seem to support the view that mental qualities cannot occur without being conscious. But the emphasis in ordinary conversational interactions on the first person likely reflects nothing more than the social impropriety of challenging first-person pronouncements about a person's mental states, which downplays our third-person access to others' states. This has no bearing on whether the distinguishing mental properties of conscious qualitative states can also occur without being conscious, and cannot outweigh the theoretical considerations adduced above.

Since mental qualities are the mental properties responsible for perceptual discriminations, the space of mental qualities mirrors that of discriminable stimulus properties. So we can take each mental quality to represent the stimulus property whose relative location in its quality space corresponds to the relative location of that mental quality in its quality space.

Representationalism is the view that the only qualitative character one is ever aware of in perceiving are properties one perceives something to have (Byrne 2001; Harman 1990). The only qualitative character that occurs in consciously seeing a green object, for example, is the green color one sees that object to have. There is no qualitative character in perceiving except the properties that perceiving represents perceived objects as having.

---

[20] For additional considerations in support of that distinction, see Rosenthal (in press).

Quality-space theory defines a representational role for mental qualities. But quality-space theory is not a type of representationalism. Mental qualities are the distinguishing mental properties of perceptual states, and are independent of any representational role. We taxonomize and individuate qualitative states and explain their nature not by appeal to their representational role,[21] but their role in perceptual discrimination. Indeed, the only sound reason for taking mental qualities to represent stimulus properties is the role they play in perceptual discrimination. Discriminative role forges the tie mental qualities have to stimulus properties, and mental qualities represent only because of that tie.

Because representationalism sees conscious qualitative character as solely a matter of the properties we perceive things to have, it rejects the compelling folk view that what it's like for one in conscious perceiving is a matter of the type of psychological state one is in. Quality-space theory does justice to that folk view by construing qualitative character as a matter of the perceptual mental states themselves.

Representationalism is appealing in part because it sidesteps mental qualities altogether, and so can avoid quandaries that mental qualities allegedly lead to. But quality-space theory can retain mental qualities and still dispel those quandaries by allowing mental qualities to occur without being conscious. Representationalism also trades on the inviting idea that the properties one perceives are in some way relevant to the nature of perceptual states. Quality-space theory has a richer explanation of how the properties we perceive figure in the nature of perceptual states, again without jettisoning mental qualities; mental qualities are individuated by discriminability relations among the stimulus properties.

Since quality-space theory relies on perceptual role for an account of qualitative character, it's neutral as regards whether states with qualitative character are conscious. So we need additional resources to explain why some qualitative states are conscious and others not. It's useful to begin with the commonsense observation that if we have good reason to conclude that an individual is in some qualitative state but that individual is wholly unaware of being in it, that state is not a conscious state. And since being wholly unaware of a mental state that one is actually in is sufficient for that state not to be conscious, a necessary condition for a state to be conscious is that one be aware of being in it (Rosenthal 2005; cf. Dienes 2004 for relevant empirical tests).

---

[21] As Jacob Berger (2018) in effect urges we do, in developing and arguing for an ingenious and novel form of representationalism. My thanks to Berger for suggesting the title for this chapter.

Being aware of a state requires being in some state in virtue of which one is aware of that target state.[22] But that higher-order state need not itself be conscious. The qualitative state does not inherit its being conscious from the higher-order state's being conscious; rather one's being aware of oneself as being in the qualitative state itself constitutes that state's being conscious. Since the way we're aware of our conscious states seems subjectively to be unmediated, it must not seem subjectively that this higher-order awareness relies on inference or observation. I have argued elsewhere that the way one is aware of a mental state that is conscious is by having a thought to the effect that one is in that state (e.g., Rosenthal 2005). That fits well with our ability to report being in states that are conscious; those verbal reports express the relevant higher-order thoughts. But for present purposes, we can stick in more generic terms simply with an appeal to some suitable higher-order awareness.[23]

Still, what's crucial for present purposes is that this account of what it is for mental states to be conscious explains how subjective awareness presents states as having different mental qualities. When a qualitative state is conscious, one is aware of oneself as being in a state with some particular type of mental quality. But what it is for a mental quality to be of a particular type is for it to have a particular relative location in a quality space.

So one's being aware of being in a state with a particular type of mental quality simply is being aware of oneself as being in a state with a mental quality that occupies a particular location in the relevant quality space. Consciousness presents mental qualities comparatively, in respect of their relative quality-space location. This explains why consciousness presents states resulting from closely related stimuli as indistinguishable if they occur successively but different if they occur simultaneously; consciousness presents the states in respect of relative location in a quality space. It is unlikely that any other

---

[22] One might posit that the target state makes one aware of itself (e.g., Kriegel 2009), but that makes for unnecessary complications in accommodating qualitative states that aren't conscious. Also, there is evidence that the onset of qualitative states precedes their becoming conscious (Libet 2004, ch. 2). And there are other disadvantages of a theory that builds the higher-order awareness into the state (Phillips 2014; Rosenthal 2004, §5).

We cannot construe one's being conscious of one's conscious states as simply a cognate accusative, as with one's smiling one's smiles (Sosa 2003, 276), since that would preclude cases in which one fails to be conscious of one's mental states.

[23] So a state is conscious if one is aware of it and not otherwise. So being conscious is dichotomous in that way, not graded (contra Overgaard et al. 2006). Nonetheless, the higher-order awareness in virtue of which a state is conscious can itself be more or less vivid or compelling. And that suggests that states that are conscious can be conscious to different degrees.

account can explain this effect as well. Consciousness does not present mental qualities in respect of some intrinsic property of the qualitative state.

It may seem that an account of the nature of conscious qualitative character in terms of relative location in a quality space, supplemented by a higher-order awareness of being in a state with such a relative location, is overly intellectual and in that way does not comport with our pretheoretic intuitions about qualitative experiences. It may be thought that since those intuitions proceed at a commonsense level, a highly theoretical account cannot conform to them.

But that's a mistake. The desire for an account that does nothing but conform to our pretheoretic intuitions stems from assuming that consciousness is our only source of knowledge about qualitative experiences. If we know about qualitative experiences in other ways, as I've argued we must, we have to expect that those other ways will involve a measure of theorizing.

The correct constraint is that the theorizing conforms to our commonsense way of describing qualitative experiences, even if it also goes well beyond it. And quality-space theory and a higher-order theory of consciousness satisfy that demand. We describe qualitative experiences in comparative terms, and we describe what it's like to have a particular experience by being aware of ourselves as having particular experiences and comparing them with others we can independently identify by appeal to characteristic or currently present stimuli.

2.8 Mary's Knowledge

The knowledge argument requires that Mary, on first seeing something red, come to have knowledge about what it's like that is both factual and new. And the foregoing discussion poses difficulties for Mary's having knowledge that is not only new but also factual.

Mary does come to know that she is having an experience unlike any she has had before. That is new factual knowledge, but it's not the knowledge needed for Jackson's argument. And it is plainly comparative knowledge, comparing her new experience with experiences she has had before. By itself, it is knowledge only that her new experience differs from previous ones; it is not even knowledge of how it compares with those she's had before.

Suppose, following most discussions, that one adopts a consciousness-based approach to how one learns about one's qualitative experiences; consciousness tells one directly all one can know about the nature of those experiences. It's compelling, on such an approach, that Mary does get new knowledge. The trouble is that there seems to be no way to cast that new knowledge as factual.

We cannot express descriptively what we learn on a consciousness-based approach. The new knowledge is ineffable.

This is why many have pursued the possibility that the new knowledge is either a matter of acquaintance or a matter of gaining a recognitional or imaginative capacity. Even if one opts for phenomenal concepts to capture Mary's new knowledge, the most influential version of that hypothesis (Loar 1997) itself appeals to recognitional abilities. And it's likely that this version tacitly underlies other attempts to formulate Mary's new knowledge by appeal to phenomenal concepts.

A consciousness-based approach encourages us to think that Mary's knowledge on first seeing something red is new but causes difficulty in construing that knowledge as factual. But we have seen that a perceptual-role approach, such as quality-space theory, has advantages over a consciousness-based approach. How does Mary's knowledge fare on that kind of view?

Mary sees something red for the first time, and she says, "This is what it's like to see something red." That statement expresses knowledge about her new experience; she is characterizing that experience in respect of its conscious qualitative character. Quality-space theory provides a straightforward factual account of exactly what Mary's conscious qualitative character consists in. It is qualitative character that occupies a particular relative location in the quality space of mental color qualities.

And Mary is also aware of being in a state with qualitative character specified in respect of that relative location, a higher-order awareness of the first-order qualitative state. On quality-space theory, Mary's knowledge of what it's like to have an experience of seeing red has clear descriptive content. When she says or thinks, "This is what it's like to see something red," the descriptive content of her statement or thought is that her experience compares to other color experiences in such-and-such a way.[24]

But Mary is a special case. Before first seeing something red, her visual experiences had all been grayscale. So the range of color experiences she has available to compare her new experience with is vastly more limited than the experiences with which we could compare such a new experience. The quality space in terms of which one could describe the comparisons available to Mary would be far smaller than the quality space that normal individuals operate with.

---

[24] Churchland suggests a similar view when he writes, rather in passing, that Mary's knowledge about sensations and their properties might "be a matter of being able to *make* certain sensory discriminations, or something along these lines" (1985, 23; emphasis Churchland's).

So what it would be like for Mary to have her new experience would not be what it's like for us to see red. Indeed, since the quality space in terms of which Mary can compare conscious experiences is vastly smaller than ours, it is unclear that we can form any accurate picture of what it would be like for her. Mary would not learn what it's like to see red, in general; she would not even learn what it's like simply for her to see red, since that too would change with exposure to stimuli of various versions. If she does learn what it's like at all, it would at best be what it's like for her to see red having previously been confined to grayscale stimuli.

One might urge that Mary does, after all, have a normal quality space. Mental qualities are fixed by the discriminations among stimuli that an individual is capable of making. And if presented with a range of chromatic hues, perhaps Mary could discriminate among them much as we do. Construing Mary's discriminative ability to include new stimuli she could be presented with would reflect her potential discriminative ability. And it would yield a quality space much like ours, not limited to those she has already seen.

On this more liberal construal of discriminative ability, Mary would have mental qualities corresponding to all the discriminations she could make if presented with the relevant stimuli. This seems theoretically extravagant. Mary's visual apparatus has the potential to generate those mental qualities, but in advance of being presented with the relevant stimuli she doesn't yet have them.[25] The quality space that figures in what it's like for Mary is a matter of experiences she has had, not those she could have if presented with the relevant stimuli.

But even if Mary did have all those latent mental qualities awaiting suitable stimuli, there would still be nothing that it's like for her to be in states with the unactivated mental qualities. Mary would never be aware of herself as being in such states until she is actually in such states. The latent mental qualities are simply mental qualities her perceptual apparatus provides her with the potential to have; they are not actual mental qualities. So Mary would be unable subjectively to compare her new experience with those she would have if presented with novel stimuli. So far as conscious subjectivity is concerned, Mary is restricted to comparing her new experience with others she has actually had.

Since the subjective color comparisons available to Mary are far fewer than ours, the descriptive content of her thought or remark, "This is what it's like to

---

[25] Indeed, the operative areas of visual cortex will likely have been recruited for other functions. That may be reversible, but likely not immediately. See, e.g., Kauffmann et al. 2002.

see red," will be different from the content of anything we might say or think. Mary's content will be roughly that the new experience is very different from anything she has ever seen, along with some comparisons with various gray-scale shades.[26]

By contrast, when we see something red and say or think, "This is what it's like to see red," our descriptive content involves locating our experience among a dramatically greater range of colors. Mary's first experience of seeing red will be subjectively very different from ours and likely very different from ours even independent of subjective considerations. It may be difficult, if possible at all, for us to imagine subjectively what her experience would be like, though there is no difficulty at all in describing it.

It's useful to consider an argument of Lewis's against a particular type of appeal to resemblance relations. "A literalist," he writes, "might see the phrase 'know what it's like' and take that to mean: 'know what it resembles'. Then he might ask: … Why can't you just be told which experiences resemble one another? You needn't have had the experiences – all you need … is some way of referring to them." But as Lewis notes, " 'know what it's like' does not mean 'know what it resembles.'" He concludes: "If you are taught that experience A resembles B and C closely, D less, E not at all, that will help you know what A is like – if you know already what B and C and D and E are like. Otherwise, it helps you not at all" (1999, 265–6).

When Mary first sees something red, she has a new experience. And we can colloquially say that in having that experience she knows what it's like to have it. The phrase, "know what it's like," can refer in this minimalist way to one's simply having the relevant experience. So understood, knowing what it's like is not a kind of knowing at all. So on that minimalist construal, it's overly literalist to see the phrase, "know what it's like," as involving any kind of knowing at all.

But knowing what it's like can also, more generously, mean actually having knowledge about what kind of experience one has. And on that construal, resemblance relations do help. The only factual knowledge[27] available to Mary or to anybody about the kind of experience Mary comes to have is knowledge about the resemblance relations that define the relative location of that experience in Mary's color quality space. This is not because of some literalist reading

---

[26] This is not an artifact of Mary's prior limitation to grayscale stimuli. The point would hold equally if she has previously had grayscale and green stimuli available.

[27] Lewis, as noted in 2.4, above, urges that we understand this knowledge not as factual, but in terms of a recognitional ability. But as argued there, recognitional abilities bring with them factual knowledge, knowledge, expressible in sentential form.

of "like" in the phrase, "what it's like." It's simply because there is no other way to give a genuinely informative description of any type of experience. There are no other terms in which one can express factual knowledge about the kind of qualitative experience anybody has.

Jackson's argument rests on Mary's coming to have new factual knowledge, knowledge that could not have been in Mary's books. A consciousness-based approach permits thinking that Mary does get new knowledge, though it's hard to see how it could be factual. Quality-space theory, by contrast, casts Mary as having knowledge that is plainly factual. The issue is whether that knowledge is new, whether it could have been in Mary's books.

What it's like for one to see something red is a matter of one's being aware of oneself as having an experience of a particular type. On quality-space theory, one is aware of oneself as having an experience with a particular relative location in a suitable quality space. Mary's awareness of that relative location will be limited to color experiences she's already had. Still, there's no difficulty in constructing the quality space that her subjective comparisons rely on; it's all the grayscale shades plus the new shade of red.

And that quality space could readily be in Mary's books, along with color quality spaces for normal individuals and those with various deficits, such as one or another type of color blindness. And since what it's like for Mary to see something red for the first time is a matter of the qualitative comparisons she could be subjectively aware of, what it's like for her could itself readily be in Mary's books, as well as what it's like for the rest of us.

Jackson holds that Mary's books, not being historical accounts, would not contain knowledge of what it's like for Mary to see red for the first time, but insists that she would, on first seeing something red, gain new factual knowledge of what it's like for people in general to see something red. But there's no difficulty in Mary's books containing both types of factual knowledge. And reading Jackson's article would doubtless have motivated the authors of Mary's books to be sure to include both types of factual knowledge. Neither type of factual knowledge would be new to Mary.

I've argued that quality-space theory is preferable on many counts to a consciousness-based approach. But the core difficulty for Jackson's argument is a dilemma that doesn't require choosing between the two approaches. On a consciousness-based approach, the knowledge Mary has on first seeing something red is new, but not factual. On quality-space theory, whatever knowledge Mary has is factual, but not new; it would be in Mary's books.

There is of course something new to Mary when she first sees something red; she has her first conscious experience of seeing something red. But what is new is not factual knowledge. An account that relies on perceptual-role, such as quality-space theory, provides that Mary can have knowledge that is factual about the kind of experience she comes to have, but that factual knowledge will be in her books and so not new. A consciousness-based approach may encourage the idea that Mary comes to have knowledge of some sort that would not be in her books, but on such an approach it is unclear what such knowledge could be. There is in any case no reason to see Mary as coming to have any knowledge that is both new and factual.

The idea that Mary gains new factual knowledge likely derives from running together these two incompatible ways of understanding the nature of qualitative experience. On one way of understanding the nature of qualitative experience, Mary has knowledge that's factual about her new experience. On the other, that knowledge is new to her. But it's only the experience that's new to Mary; she gains no factual knowledge about the experience that is also new to her.

Mary has mastered all the factual knowledge in her books. So she has factual knowledge about what it's like for somebody whose previous color experiences are all achromatic to see something red for the first time. Would her first seeing something red elicit that factual knowledge?

It might well. Compare having factual information about what somebody looks like. Seeing that person for the first time might elicit the factual knowledge one had. But it also might not. One's factual knowledge about what the person looks like might not be sufficiently detailed for the experience to elicit that knowledge. Or that knowledge might simply not come to mind.

Similarly, Mary's books can contain factual knowledge about what it's like for somebody whose previous color experiences are all grayscale to see something with a particular shade of red. But that experience might not, for whatever reason, elicit the factual knowledge from Mary's books. It is natural to expect that it might well not. Mary might simply be at a loss as to just what kind of new experience she is having.

But the knowledge that concerns Jackson is knowledge of what it's like for people in general to see something red. That's knowledge about the type of experience it is. If that knowledge is factual, it will be in Mary's books. Mary comes to have no new factual knowledge on first seeing something red, and hence none that causes any problem for physicalism.[28]

---

[28] My thanks to Sam Coleman for numerous comments, which led to many significant clarifications.

3 Acquaintance, Parsimony, and Epiphenomenalism

Brie Gertler

Why does Mary learn something when she leaves the room? One answer, endorsed by some physicalists as well as most dualists, is as follows. Mary learns something because phenomenal knowledge requires direct acquaintance with phenomenal properties. For this reason, there is an epistemic gap between the physical and the phenomenal: phenomenal facts cannot be deduced from physical facts. This is *the acquaintance response* to the Knowledge Argument. The physicalist and dualist versions of the acquaintance response diverge as to whether this epistemic gap reveals an ontological gap between the physical and the phenomenal.

The acquaintance response is, I believe, an especially promising way to make sense of the Mary case. I will not argue for the acquaintance response here, although I do hope to make its appeal clear. My focus will be on teasing out its implications for the debate between physicalism and dualism. Specifically, I will argue that the acquaintance response casts doubt on two claims often made on behalf of physicalism: that physicalism is more parsimonious than dualism, and that no plausible view about mental causation is compatible with dualism.

The chapter has three sections. Section 3.1 explicates the acquaintance response to the Knowledge Argument and outlines Acquaintance Physicalism, the position that combines the acquaintance response with physicalism. In 3.2, I argue that physicalism's claim to greater parsimony is less straightforward than usually assumed, and that the commitments of Acquaintance Physicalism present special obstacles to invoking parsimony in an argument for physicalism. And I show that on an alternative interpretation of parsimony (Sober 2015), physicalism is not more parsimonious than dualism *per se*. Section 3.3 shows how acknowledging the phenomenon of acquaintance can ease the dualist's problems with mental causation, by dispelling three key objections to epiphenomenalism. The most challenging of these objections is that epiphenomenalism blocks an evolutionary explanation of the fact that events beneficial to the organism are generally pleasurable, while harmful events are generally painful. In response, I draw on the relation of acquaintance to describe how pleasures and pains, while themselves epiphenomenal, might nonetheless explain positive and negative associations with stimuli. Because these associations affect behavior, they can contribute to fitness. I close by arguing that epiphenomenalism does not threaten human agency.

3.1 Acquaintance Physicalism

3.1.1 The Acquaintance Response to the Knowledge Argument

The Phenomenal Concept Strategy (PCS) attempts to block the Knowledge Argument's anti-physicalist implications by claiming that, when Mary is released from the room and sees something red, she merely acquires a new way of conceptualizing phenomenal redness. She does not gain knowledge of a previously unknown *property*. The PCS allows that Mary learns something upon her release, but blocks the inference to dualism by drawing on the idea that our ways of conceptualizing reality are more fine-grained than the reality we represent.

On one version of the PCS, what Mary gains is simply a new way of *referring to* phenomenal redness, perhaps via an introspective demonstrative such as *this* color (Papineau 2002; Levin 2007a). This way of cashing out Mary's new phenomenal concept is what Chalmers calls a "thin" account, as it implies that Mary's new knowledge does not constitute a substantial epistemic advance. (Compare: it is only by visiting the Vatican that I can refer to the Pope's residence by pointing at it. Yet the fact that I can now knowledgeably say "The Pope lives *there*" does not mark a substantial epistemic advance.) The chief worry about thin versions of the PCS is that they cannot accommodate the epistemic intuitions that drive anti-physicalist arguments, such as the intuition that Mary acquires substantial new knowledge when she is released and learns what it's like to see red (Chalmers 2006).

My current concern is not with thin accounts of phenomenal concepts. It is instead with the acquaintance response to the Knowledge Argument, which construes phenomenal concepts as epistemically substantial or "thick." According to the acquaintance response, Mary's new knowledge is a genuine epistemic advance. Phenomenal knowledge – knowledge of what it's like – requires a grasp of the phenomenal property that can be achieved only through direct acquaintance with that property. It therefore requires that the target property is instantiated in one's own experience. This is why Mary gains phenomenal knowledge of redness only by experiencing redness herself;

she cannot deduce this from the knowledge she has about redness before her release.

The claim that phenomenal knowledge requires acquaintance explains why there is something that Mary doesn't know about "seeing red" experiences until she is released from her room. Before her release, she can conceptualize phenomenal redness in physical terms – e.g., as *the phenomenal property that ordinary persons experience when their retinas are struck by light with a wavelength of 620–780 nanometers*, and perhaps as *the phenomenal property correlated with neural state N*. But she cannot conceptualize it phenomenally. It is only upon her release, when she is acquainted with an instance of phenomenal redness (seeing a stop sign, perhaps), that she is in a position to conceptualize this property phenomenally.

Generalizing from this case, we get the following principle:

Phenomenal Acquaintance. One conceptualizes a phenomenal property *phenomenally* – i.e., in terms of what it's like – only when one is acquainted with the property, which in turn requires having the relevant phenomenal experience. Phenomenal conceptualization provides for *phenomenal knowledge*: epistemically substantial knowledge of what it's like. Phenomenal knowledge cannot be achieved by deductive inference from non-phenomenal knowledge, e.g., from knowledge involving only physical concepts.

This principle is part of the acquaintance response to the Knowledge Argument. That response is endorsed by most dualists (Nida-Rümelin 1995; Chalmers 2003; Gertler 2012; Goff 2015a). It is also accepted by some physicalists (Balog 2012; Howell 2013). I'll call these positions *Acquaintance Dualism* and *Acquaintance Physicalism*, respectively.

3.1.2 Acquaintance Physicalism: The View

Chalmers argues that the acquaintance response to the Knowledge Argument cannot be reconciled with physicalism, since "crucial explanatory elements in the account will not be physically explainable" (Chalmers 2006, 183). In particular, he thinks that the notion of *acquaintance* resists physical explanation. Levine nicely illuminates why simply invoking acquaintance will not resolve explanatory gap worries. He considers a standard view, on which acquaintance involves an instance of the phenomenal property being contained within the physical structure that realizes the phenomenal concept of that property.

Acquaintance, or cognitive presence, or whatever it is that is supposed to constitute the especially immediate and intimate cognitive relation between phenomenal concepts and their objects, is just that: a *cognitive* relation. It is not at all clear why, or how, *physical* presence [an instantiation of the phenomenal property] translates into *cognitive* presence. (Levine 2007, 162)

The transition from physical containment to awareness – the special kind allegedly afforded by phenomenal concepts – is still an inexplicable transition. It is subject to its own explanatory gap, just as much as is the original relation between phenomenal properties and their physical correlates. (Levine 2007, 163)

Acquaintance Physicalists concede this point but deny that it threatens physicalism. For example, Balog grants that physical theory will not bridge the gap between Mary's way of conceptualizing phenomenal redness before her release – viz., in physical terms – and the conceptualization made possible by acquaintance with that property. But, she argues, the remaining epistemic gap between physical and phenomenal conceptualizations does not threaten physicalism unless it is assumed that "epistemic gaps always indicate ontological gaps" (Balog 2012, 18). And she thinks physicalists should reject that assumption.

Howell shares this outlook. He acknowledges the force of the Chalmers–Levine worry: "There appear to be truths about acquaintance that cannot be deduced from the complete physical truth" (Howell 2013, 147). And he notes that this non-deducibility is itself an explanatory gap: physical theory cannot explain the relevant facts about acquaintance. But since explanation is itself an epistemic notion, he says, the remaining gap is only epistemic. So it is compatible with physicalism, which is after all an ontological thesis.

The Knowledge Argument uses an epistemic divide – that phenomenal knowledge cannot be achieved by deduction from physical knowledge – to establish an ontological divide between the phenomenal and the physical. Acquaintance Physicalists recognize the epistemic divide but reject the inference to ontological dualism. Acquaintance Physicalism is therefore a version of *a posteriori* physicalism. But whereas most *a posteriori* physicalists assimilate the phenomenal-physical epistemic gap to the epistemic gaps that allegedly characterize other cases of *a posteriori* necessities or identities, Acquaintance Physicalists invoke the distinctive metaphysics of the acquaintance relation to explain what is epistemically special about acquaintance. In acquaintance, a "token of a phenomenal concept applied to current experience is (partly) constituted by that token experience" (Balog

2012, 7). Or "acquaintance imports phenomenal states into propositions" (Howell 2013, 123).

Acquaintance Physicalism contests, and thereby reveals, deep-seated presumptions about the relation between the epistemic and the ontological. These presumptions are operative in Chalmers' (2006) claim that PCS strategists face a dilemma: *thin* accounts of phenomenal concepts may be explainable in physical terms, but will not do justice to the explanatory gap; *thick* accounts of phenomenal concepts may do justice to the explanatory gap, but will not be explainable in physical terms. The second horn of this dilemma is premised on the idea that physicalism, an ontological thesis, would be undermined if the epistemic significance of acquaintance were physicalistically inexplicable – an epistemic shortcoming.

Strikingly, these deep-seated presumptions about the relation between the epistemic and the ontological are also present in arguments that favor physicalism. In a recent paper, Veillet presents a dilemma that is in some respects similar to Chalmers' (Veillet 2015). But while Chalmers intends his dilemma to show that physicalists cannot answer the challenge presented by the epistemic gap between the physical and the phenomenal, Veillet intends her dilemma to show that they *need not* answer it.

The first horn of Veillet's dilemma is that knowledge (or the concepts exercised therein) is individuated more finely than its objects (or the properties conceptualized). In that case, Veillet says, the fact that Mary gains new knowledge upon her release poses no threat to physicalism: "the challenge [to physicalism] simply dissolves" (2964). The second horn is that knowledge is individuated coarsely. Veillet argues that the only reasonable way to make sense of the idea that phenomenal and physical knowledge differ, *when knowledge is individuated coarsely,* is to say that they are knowledge of different properties. But on this reading of the epistemic gap between physical and phenomenal knowledge, she contends, the claim that there is such a gap begs the question against physicalism. So Mary's new knowledge is either too insubstantial to present a challenge to physicalism, or too substantial to avoid begging the question against physicalism.

Acquaintance Physicalists maintain that knowledge of phenomenal properties is individuated at a finer grain than those properties; in this sense, they endorse the first horn of Veillet's dilemma. But they allow that the Mary case poses a genuine and powerful challenge to physicalism. And while they ultimately deny that the challenge succeeds, they maintain that answering the challenge is a significant task. It ultimately requires commitment to *acquaintance* as an epistemically and metaphysically distinctive phenomenon, to explain why there remains, in Howell's terms, an "epistemological rift" between the physical and the phenomenal. Howell says that by adopting his view,

> we have staved off a metaphysical rift in the world, but that comes at the cost of an epistemological rift. There is a sense in which we cannot fully grasp the physicality of conscious states. It is my view that this is a rather significant admission. (Howell 2013, 173)

Chalmers and Veillet, who disagree on the question of physicalism, agree on how epistemic matters bear on ontological matters in this context. They agree that if Mary's new knowledge is epistemically substantial, then physicalism is in jeopardy. (Their disagreement concerns whether this link between the epistemic and the ontological threatens physicalism or, rather, shows that epistemic arguments such as the Knowledge Argument beg the question.)

Acquaintance Physicalists reject this shared outlook. They claim that Mary's new knowledge is epistemically substantial, and that what explains why phenomenal knowledge cannot be achieved by deduction from physical facts – namely, that some epistemically substantial knowledge requires acquaintance – itself resists physicalistic explanation. So Mary's new knowledge is epistemically substantial enough to pose a real challenge to physicalism. But physicalism can meet this challenge, by invoking the notion of acquaintance to explain the fundamental epistemic gap between the physical and the phenomenal.

3.1.3 Acquaintance Physicalism As an Error Theory

The acquaintance response is an appealing way to make sense of the Mary case. As I mentioned above, most dualists accept the acquaintance response. The Acquaintance Dualist construes Mary's epistemic advance as discovering that certain genuine metaphysical possibilities, e.g., that a different phenomenal property correlates with the physical features she associates with *seeing red*, are non-actual.

But Acquaintance Physicalists deny that what Mary learns is that certain metaphysical possibilities are non-actual. They maintain that the possibilities ruled out by her new knowledge – e.g., that the physical features associated with *seeing red* are correlated with phenomenal greenness – are only epistemic or conceptual possibilities, not metaphysical possibilities. On their view phenomenal properties are metaphysically necessitated by (or identical to) physical properties, despite the fact that phenomenal facts cannot be deduced from physical facts. So Acquaintance Physicalism is an error theory. The phenomenon of acquaintance, with its distinctive epistemic and metaphysical characteristics, is invoked to explain why a necessary link between the phenomenal and the physical *seems* contingent.

> There is a sort of cognitive block that prevents us, and will always prevent us, from deducing conscious states from physical states. (Howell 2013, 170)

> Of course, physicalism would remain puzzling and downright incomprehensible if a perspicuous physicalist explanation of the epistemic gaps themselves was not possible. The crucial element of [my account] is that it provides just such an explanation. It offers the next best thing to a perspicuous explanation of Q [the phenomenal facts] in terms of P [the physical facts], namely, it offers a perspicuous explanation of why we can't have one. (Balog 2012, 20)

Acquaintance Physicalists are driven to an error theory about the apparent contingency of the phenomenal-physical relation by their antecedent commitment to physicalism. This brings us to the motivations for physicalism. Physicalism is thought to possess at least two important advantages over dualism: it is thought to be theoretically preferable to dualism on grounds of parsimony, and it is believed to provide for a more plausible view about mental causation.[1] I address these two alleged advantages in the next two sections, respectively. (*Note to the reader*: Sections 3.2 and 3.3 are largely independent. Those interested primarily in the issue of mental causation can proceed directly to 3.3.)

3.2 Acquaintance Physicalism and the Question of Parsimony

3.2.1 Is Physicalism Obviously More Parsimonious Than Dualism?

One factor that seems to favor physicalism is that it is ontologically more parsimonious than dualism. It's not clear how much weight parsimony considerations carry in the current debate. They are sometimes mentioned,[2] but

---

[1] These are general considerations that drive the preference for physicalism. Since Acquaintance Physicalism is a position about how to reconcile physicalism with the relevant anti-physicalist intuitions, Acquaintance Physicalism is neutral as to the various arguments for physicalism. Howell rests his case for physicalism largely on concerns about mental causation.

[2] "The identity theory should be favored for broadly theoretical reasons. Whether simplicity and parsimony are the best reasons to favor the theory is another matter. They may be. But they are at least examples of such reasons" (Polger 2011, 15). Papineau (2002) and Melnyk (2003) also appeal to parsimony in their arguments for physicalism.

physicalists more frequently cite concerns about mental causation. Still, it often seems that parsimony concerns are working behind the scenes, fueling the sense that dualists bear the initial burden of proof because they posit kinds of properties beyond those recognized by the physicalist.

It seems hard to deny that physicalism is more parsimonious than dualism. After all, physicalism is the thesis that all of concrete reality is, or is metaphysically necessitated by, entities that belong to a single kind: the physical. (I will use the term "entity" liberally, to cover properties, events, and things.) Dualism rejects this monism, taking the mental to be an additional basic kind. So physicalism seems clearly more parsimonious: it recognizes fewer basic kinds of entities.[3]

However, the situation is not as clear as it seems. Physicalism is a genuine monism only if "the physical" names a single kind. But it is far from obvious that there is a principled (non *ad hoc*) way of individuating kinds so that all physical entities belong to a single kind. And if "the physical" comprises numerous fundamental kinds, physicalism may not be significantly more parsimonious than dualism. If the set of "physical" kinds is highly heterogeneous, then dualism may be just as parsimonious as physicalism. For example, accommodating the relevant data in a way that avoids dualism could require positing a *sui generis* basic physical kind. If "the physical" is a heterogeneous motley, then this *sui generis* kind may not be more similar to other physical kinds than a non-physical kind would be. In that case, physicalism and dualism could be equally parsimonious.

3.2.2 The Epistemic Optimism of the "Greater Parsimony" Claim

Physicalism is standardly regarded as more parsimonious than dualism because "the physical" is taken to name a single kind, or to encompass a relatively homogeneous set of kinds. The claim that physicalism is more parsimonious than dualism seems to me to rest on highly optimistic assumptions about how we conceptualize physical reality. These assumptions fit uneasily with Acquaintance Physicalism's claim that our way of conceptualizing the

---

[3] Dualism incurs additional complexity in explaining the relations between these two basic kinds, e.g., by positing psychophysical laws in addition to the physical laws accepted by both physicalists and dualists (Chalmers 1996). Now if physical entities are individuated by their causal features, then the number of laws may not vary independently of the number of kinds of entities. So the number and complexity of laws will be connected to the issues raised in this section, concerning the degree of heterogeneity among physical entities. In any case, my discussion here is limited to the question of ontological parsimony, namely, the number of basic kinds recognized by a theory.

phenomenal is fundamentally misleading. I'll make this case in reference to one formulation of physicalism, though as we will see, the point can be generalized to at least some other leading formulations.

How should we understand physicalism? Some philosophers argue that the point at issue between physicalists and dualists is whether mentality appears at the fundamental level of ontology (Montero 2001). This may be a reasonable way to interpret the debate. But it does not imply that physicalism is monistic, or even that it is more parsimonious than dualism. The "no fundamental mentality" thesis associated with physicalism simply says that there is a particular kind, the mental, that is not part of fundamental ontology. It says nothing about how many kinds of entity are fundamental. More to the point, that a theory denies that a particular kind is ontologically basic does little to support the claim that it is more parsimonious than a theory that includes that kind in its basic ontology. For as just mentioned, it might be that excluding that kind requires recognizing additional kinds.

A reasonable formulation of physicalism should be linked with our empirically informed conception of the physical. To deal with Hempel's dilemma, a formulation of physicalism must be liberal enough to allow that physical theory may advance in unanticipated directions, yet restrictive enough to avoid rendering physicalism trivially true or equivalent to naturalism. The formulation I will adopt begins from the idea that physical theory interprets concrete reality as having a spatiotemporal structure, and individuates entities by their causal powers and relations.

The version of this approach I will use is Howell's. Ignoring some complications, Howell's basic conception of physicalism is as follows (the label "Spatiotemporal-Causal Physicalism" is my own).[4]

> Spatiotemporal-Causal Physicalism: [T]he concrete properties and things in this world [metaphysically] supervene upon the properties in this world that are exhausted by their implications for the distribution of things over space and time. (Howell 2013, 53)

Let's call this thesis "STC Physicalism." And let's use the term "STC entities" for the concrete entities it recognizes: that is, for entities that are "exhausted by their implications for the distribution of things over space and time," or

---

[4] Howell later qualifies this formulation, to allow categorical properties not exhausted by causal or dispositional implications. On his view, such properties are *physical* only if they are *individuated by* their dispositional implications, relative to a world (Howell 2013, 25–30).

metaphysically supervene on properties meeting that description. This conception of physicalism construes phenomenal property dualism as the claim that phenomenal properties are not STC entities. This is a plausible construal. Even those dualists who take the phenomenal to have causal powers will deny that phenomenal properties are causally analyzable, or metaphysically supervene on properties amenable to causal analysis.

How parsimonious is STC Physicalism? This depends on whether "STC entities" names a single kind; or, if not, whether STC entities form a relatively homogeneous set. I don't know how to begin to answer that question. Physicists now suspect that positing novel kinds of fundamental (presumably STC) entities will be needed to solve remaining mysteries, such as the nature of dark matter and how it exerts gravitational force. Arguably, then, no one is currently in a good position to determine whether the basic kinds of STC entities form a homogeneous set.

Of course, the real issue is comparative: whether STC Physicalism is more parsimonious than dualism. The claim that STC Physicalism is more parsimonious than dualism depends on the assumption that the distinction between STC entities and non-STC entities carves nature at a real joint, one that is comparatively deep. This assumption is needed to exclude possibilities like the following. The class of STC entities comprises a heterogeneous mix of dozens of different basic kinds, and the differences between these kinds are just as deep as the difference between STC and (perhaps merely possible) non-STC entities. In that case, STC Physicalism would be only marginally more parsimonious than dualism. And if STC Physicalism required positing a basic physical kind beyond the physical kinds recognized by dualism, then these theories could conceivably be on a par as regards parsimony. So the parsimony question rests on whether the STC/non-STC distinction carves nature at a particularly deep joint.

Let's grant that the sciences generally conceptualize physical entities in terms of their STC features. This approach to conceptualization is informed, it seems, by how we detect physical entities: namely, through their spatiotemporal effects (broadly speaking). It's hard to deny that this way of conceptualizing physical entities has proven amazingly effective in navigating physical reality. STC Physicalism ambitiously claims that this understanding is not only useful, but captures the nature of concrete reality in itself, and does so comprehensively. And the claim that STC Physicalism's ontology is significantly more parsimonious than an ontology that recognizes non-STC entities puts even more stock in our conceptualization practices. For it implies that our way of conceptualizing physical reality, in spatiotemporal-causal terms, reflects an especially deep ontological division, between STC and (possible) non-STC entities.

My purpose is not to deny that physicalism is more parsimonious than dualism. It is only to expose an epistemically optimistic assumption required to establish that thesis, at least on the STC construal of physicalism. This assumption is that our conceptualization of physical entities, itself derived from our means of observation, reflects genuine and significant divisions in nature. With this assumption in mind, let's return to the acquaintance response to the Knowledge Argument.

3.2.3 The Epistemic Pessimism of Acquaintance Physicalism

According to the acquaintance response, our phenomenal conceptualization of the property *phenomenal redness* is derived from a particular means of apprehending this property, namely, through direct acquaintance with it. This conceptualization is as a non-STC property: it does not represent phenomenal redness as exhausted by its causal implications for spatiotemporal entities. If it did represent phenomenal redness that way, this conceptualization would be available to Mary before her release. For the same reason, phenomenal facts (facts under a phenomenal conception) are not conceptualized *as* necessitated by physical facts (or facts involving entities at the STC base, viz., those exhausted by their STC implications). To conceptualize Q as necessitated by P is to conceptualize Q in a way that makes it seem deducible from P.

The Acquaintance Dualist allows that the conceptualization afforded by acquaintance captures a truth about phenomenal properties: that they are non-STC entities. By contrast, the Acquaintance Physicalist regards our means of achieving phenomenal knowledge, namely through acquaintance, as fundamentally misleading about the nature of concrete reality.

Acquaintance Physicalism thus rests on two sharply diverging assessments of how we conceptualize concrete reality, as follows. On the one hand, our means of understanding the physical, through detecting effects (and inferences therefrom), shapes our conceptualization of the physical as STC entities. This conceptualization is broadly accurate. And it is comprehensive, in that it encompasses all of concrete reality. On the other hand, our means of understanding the phenomenal, through acquaintance, shapes our conceptualization of phenomenal properties as non-STC properties. This conceptualization is fundamentally mistaken, and coming to terms with it requires an elaborate error theory.

The rationale for these differing verdicts is of course the commitment to physicalism. But if my argument above is correct, one advantage claimed for physicalism – its comparative parsimony – requires a high degree of confidence in our physical conceptualization of concrete reality. Reason to think that STC Physicalism is more parsimonious than dualism rests on the assumption that our conceptualization of concrete reality – in particular, our distinction between STC and non-STC entities – reflects not only a real onto-logical difference, but one that is especially significant, relative to differences between kinds of STC entities. So an appeal to parsimony puts even more stock in our conceptualization of the physical. An appeal to parsimony would thus increase the already sharp disparity between Acquaintance Physicalism's high confidence in our (perceptually derived) physical conceptualization of concrete reality, and that view's error theory about our (acquaintance-derived) phenomenal conceptualization of it. Justifying these sharply diver-ging assessments of our conceptualization practices, in a way that is not *ad hoc*, is a substantial task.

The claim that STC Physicalism is more parsimonious than dualism relies on the assumption that our conceptualization practices track genuine, signifi-cant divisions in concrete reality. This is true of parsimony claims concerning physicalism on at least some other formulations as well. To avoid portraying physicalism as trivially true, or equivalent to naturalism, an adequate formu-lation of physicalism must include some restrictions on "the physical." These restrictions standardly involve some way of conceptualizing the physical that derives from the basic methods or commitments of physical science. And for the reasons just given, physicalism thus construed has a claim to parsimony only if these conceptualizations track genuine, significant divisions in concrete reality.

Parsimony claims on behalf of physicalism are highly optimistic about one dimension of our conceptualization practices. Acquaintance Physicalism is committed to an error theory about another dimension of our conceptualiza-tion practices. The need to provide a principled justification for this disparity constitutes a hurdle for an Acquaintance Physicalist who wishes to invoke parsimony.

3.2.4 Parsimony and Predictive Accuracy

Might the case for physicalism's greater parsimony be made in a way that doesn't rely on the accuracy of our conceptualization practices? Sober presents such a case, using a model selection framework. But this argument may not help the physicalist. For the framework Sober advances does not associate a theory's greater parsimony with a greater likelihood of truth; it instead associates parsimony with a theory's predictive accuracy. Sober expresses skepticism about the association of parsimony with truth, as regards mental ontology.

> Placing the mind/body identity theory and dualism within the context of model selection theory requires one to think of the contending theories in terms of their predictive accuracy, not their truth. Metaphysicians may balk at this, proclaiming that they don't care about predictive accuracy and want only to figure out what is true. I am not arguing against that preference. Rather, my point is that the parsimony argument for the identity theory finds a natural home in the model selection framework. If there is another treatment of the argument that establishes its connection with truth, I do not know what that treatment is. (Sober 2009, 137)

Insofar as our concern is with the truth of physicalism, the results of the model selection framework may not be directly relevant to our discussion.

Still, it's worth noting that those results do not straightforwardly favor physicalism over dualism. In the model selection framework, models are selected by their Akaike Information Criterion score, a mark of predictive accuracy in which parsimony yields greater predictive accuracy (all else being equal). This framework ties a model's parsimony to the number of "adjustable parameters" it allows, where this number derives from the number of possibilities compatible with the model. Consider the four logical possibilities represented in a table provided by Sober (2015).

	The brain monitor says "c-fibers are firing."	The brain monitor says "no c-fibers are firing."
S pushes the button that says "pain."	f_1	f_2
S pushes the button that says "no pain."	f_3	f_4

Versions of physicalism that allow for multiple realizability are compatible with three possibilities – f_1, f_2, and f_4. Of course, these physicalist views do not deny that f_3 is possible; they merely imply that any occurrence of f_3 is due to measuring error. But precisely the same is true of leading versions of dualism, which take the phenomenal to be nomologically linked with the physical. If c-fiber firing nomologically suffices for pain (and these are synchronous), then f_1, f_2, and f_4 could occur. And f_3 will not occur unless there is measuring error. So nomological supervenience dualism has precisely the same adjustable parameters as multiple realization physicalism. And so these theories have the same number of adjustable parameters, the measure of parsimony that factors into their predictive accuracy scores.[5]

This result comes about because the model selection framework is insensitive to mere (non-actual) possibilities. It therefore will not distinguish between the metaphysically necessary supervenience associated with versions of physicalism that allow for multiple realizability, and the nomological supervenience associated with leading versions of dualism.[6] For the same reason, the identity theory's predictive accuracy score will be shared by a version of dualism according to which c-fiber firing is nomologically necessary as well as nomologically sufficient for pain. These theories are both compatible with f_1 and f_4, and they will count f_2 and f_3 as due to measuring error. So the identity theory is more parsimonious than a theory allowing multiple realization, and the dualist theory just described is more parsimonious than one on which c-fiber firing is nomologically sufficient but not necessary for pain. The model selection framework enables these comparisons, but it does not imply that physicalism is more parsimonious than dualism *per se*.

3.2.5 Summing Up: Acquaintance Physicalism and the Question of Parsimony

The parsimony case for physicalism depends on an especially high degree of confidence in our conceptualization practices. Acquaintance Physicalism's skepticism about our conceptualization of the phenomenal is therefore an obstacle to the parsimony case for physicalism. An alternative approach to parsimony, model selection theory, evaluates parsimony in terms of empirical possibilities recognized by the theory. But because it is not sensitive to merely modal differences, it does not imply that physicalism is more parsimonious than dualism *per se*.

---

[5] Since each allows for three possibilities, they each have two adjustable parameters: the number of adjustable parameters corresponds to the variables needed to fix the remaining probabilities, once an initial probability has been fixed.

[6] Sober makes a similar point, about nomological supervenience preventing the generation of AIC scores, in another context (Sober 2015, 262–63, esp. n. 18). Sober says that on the model selection framework, dualism is less parsimonious than either the identity theory or physicalist functionalism. But the version of dualism he considers allows phenomenal properties to vary independently of physical properties: that version of dualism thus has an additional adjustable parameter, corresponding to f_3.

3.3 Acquaintance and Epiphenomenalism

3.3.1 Worries about Epiphenomenalism

The most frequently cited motivation for physicalism concerns mental causation. The positions compatible with dualism – interactionism, parallelism, and
(bottom-up) epiphenomenalism – are generally thought to be unappealing.
I will focus on epiphenomenalism, the position that Jackson defended in
his 1982 paper. Philosophers famously express dismay at the prospect of
epiphenomenalism. At best it's "repugnant to good sense" (Lewis 1999, 285);
at worst, it's "the end of the world" (Fodor 1989, 79).

But *why* this prospect should trouble us is unclear. The worry does
not seem to be that epiphenomenalism is patently false. The falsity of
epiphenomenalism is not an introspective datum. For familiar Humean
reasons, no amount of introspective observation could reveal the mental's
causal powers. And Jackson provides a plausible explanation for why phenomenal states seem causally efficacious. So long as physical states with
causal potency nomologically suffice for – or, on Jackson's version, cause –
phenomenal states, it will seem that phenomenal states have causal potency.
If the firing of c-fibers both nomologically suffices for pain and causes the
subject to yell "ouch!", it might easily seem that the pain causes the yelling.
The general point is similar to that just made, about the limitations of model
selection theory. Observation of regularities will not distinguish between
being (necessitated by or identical to) the cause and merely being nomologically linked with the cause.

In this section, I show how recognizing the role of acquaintance in phenomenal knowledge can mitigate three key objections to epiphenomenalism.
The first objection, which others have addressed, is that epiphenomenal states
would not be observable. The second objection is that epiphenomenalism
amounts to an unpalatable exceptionalism about phenomenal properties or
states, and so commitment to epiphenomenalism would compromise the simplicity of a theory. The third objection is, to my mind, the most challenging.
It is that epiphenomenalism blocks evolutionary explanations of the fact that
events harmful to the organism tend to be painful, while beneficial events tend
to be pleasurable. I suggest that acquaintance can help to neutralize this objection as well.

These three objections are broadly epistemic: they concern apparent evidence against epiphenomenalism. I conclude this section by briefly addressing
a non-epistemic but serious concern, namely that epiphenomenalism would
deprive us of agency.

3.3.2 Epiphenomenalism and Knowledge of Phenomenal Properties

Watkins worries that "on Jackson's epiphenomenalism we cannot know of our own qualitative experiences … If qualia are not causally efficacious, then my beliefs and memories would be just as they are whether there were qualia or not" (Watkins 1989, 160). This is known as the *self-stultification* objection. It challenges the Knowledge Argument itself, since it suggests that if epiphenomenalism were true then Mary couldn't know what it's like to see red even after her release (Campbell 2003).

The acquaintance thesis provides for a response to the self-stultification objection (Nagasawa 2010), since knowledge by acquaintance is achieved through a non-causal route. As Balog says, in acquaintance an instance of the property serves as a mode of presentation of the property itself. So the relation between the thought about the property – "*this* is what it's like to see red" – and the property instance is direct and non-causal. This constitution relation enables the subject to directly (non-causally) grasp the experience's phenomenal character. The experience needn't cause the awareness of it, since it partly constitutes that awareness. When one grasps a phenomenal property by acquaintance, one's judgment regarding that experience is tied to reality directly: an instance of the phenomenal property is part of the judgment, which expresses how that reality epistemically seems to the subject. (For details and defense of this claim, see Gertler 2012.)

De Brigard expresses a worry related to the self-stultification objection. He worries that epiphenomenalists cannot explain "how the content of a mental state … can refer to a particular sensation" (De Brigard 2014, 125). He reasons that such reference must be causal or, at the very least, nomological. This worry can also be assuaged by the claim that we can grasp phenomenal properties through acquaintance. In knowledge by acquaintance, the phenomenal properties serve as the mode of presentation for their referents. Because reference is grounded in a *constitution* relation, it is more direct and epistemically secure than a causal relation.

Another worry, also related to the self-stultification objection, concerns knowledge of other minds. Jackson's response to this worry implicitly relies on the assumption that I can be aware of my own phenomenal states. He argues that one can know that someone else is in pain by inferring from a behavioral effect back to its cause (a neural event, say), and then inferring the occurrence of another standard effect of that neural event (a phenomenal state). For example, if I hear you yell "ouch!", I can infer that you are undergoing a neural event of the type that standardly causes pain. Jackson does not explain how the association between the behavior and the phenomenal state is originally established, but presumably this can be established only by using my own phenomenal states: I know that I yell "ouch!" only when I feel pain. So this response to the worry about other minds implicitly assumes the capacity for self-knowledge. Fortunately for this account, one can make this association without accepting epiphenomenalism. One may mistakenly believe that the association between yelling "ouch!" and pain is between an effect and its cause, when in fact it's between two effects of a single cause.

3.3.3 Epiphenomenalism and Simplicity

Papineau suggests that accepting epiphenomenalism would violate simplicity considerations.

> If epiphenomenalism [about conscious states] were true, then the relation between mind and brain would be like nothing else in nature. After all, science recognizes no other examples of "causal danglers," ontologically independent states with causes but no effects. So, given the choice between epiphenomenalism and materialism, standing principles of scientific theory choice would seem to favour materialism. (Papineau 2002, 23)

This argument relies on an inference, from the fact that science doesn't recognize non-mental epiphenomena, to the conclusion that there aren't any. But that inference is unjustified. After all, standard scientific methods detect entities by their effects. Indeed, it is the idea that all events are detected by their effects that motivates the previous worry about self-knowledge. So standard scientific methods couldn't detect epiphenomena even if they were present. In such cases, where the evidence is insensitive to the phenomenon in question, Occam's Razor does not prescribe denying that the phenomenon occurs. To use Sober's terms, what applies in this case is not the "razor of denial" but instead the "razor of silence" (Sober 2015).

3.3.4 Epiphenomenalism and Natural Selection

To my mind, the most serious objection to epiphenomenalism is the explanatory challenge raised by William James (among others). If phenomenal properties are epiphenomenal, then the "match" between a condition's consequences for the organism, and the phenomenal properties associated with it, would seem to be a matter of mere coincidence.

[I]f pleasures and pains have no efficacy, one does not see … why the most noxious acts, such as burning, might not give thrills of delight, and the most necessary ones, such as breathing, cause agony. (James 1890, 144)

Robinson aptly refers to this fact, that beneficial events are generally pleasurable while harmful events are generally painful, as "the hedonic/utility match" (Robinson 2007). The natural explanation of this match is an evolutionary one: a creature that feels pain on encountering harmful stimuli will be more likely to withdraw and, hence, more likely to survive long enough to reproduce. But if phenomenal properties are not causally efficacious – e.g., if pain cannot cause a creature to withdraw from a harmful stimulus – then the fact that an experience's hedonic value matches its utility, for a particular creature, will not affect that creature's chance of surviving to reproduce. So epiphenomenalism blocks this natural explanation of the hedonic/utility match.

Jackson (1982) responds to a different objection concerning evolution. This is the objection that epiphenomenal properties, of any sort, would not be present in a species that evolved through natural selection. Jackson argues that epiphenomenal properties could be a by-product of something that *is* selected for, just as the heaviness of a polar bear's coat is a by-product of the coat's warmth. This response shows that the presence of epiphenomenal properties is compatible with evolution. But it doesn't explain the hedonic/utility match.

In fact, the idea that epiphenomenal properties are merely by-products of something that is selected for strengthens James's objection. Jackson uses the example of the polar bear's coat because, from a fitness perspective, having a heavy coat is disadvantageous; hence, it is not a property that would be selected for. This disadvantage is presumably outweighed (as it were) by the more significant benefit of added warmth. The argument that epiphenomenal qualia may be mere by-products is intended to explain why they could be present, consistent with not being selected for. If the polar bear's heavy coat can yield to an evolutionary explanation despite this property's having a negative effect on fitness, surely qualia can yield to an evolutionary explanation despite having *no* effect on fitness. But if qualia have no effect on fitness, then the hedonic/utility match would appear to be a sheer coincidence.[7]

---

[7] Robinson (2007) argues that an evolutionary explanation of the hedonic/utility match need only make sense of the idea that sensations with hedonic value, such as pleasure, could be correlated with certain kinds of behavior (e.g., pursuit of certain stimuli). And this is accomplished with the hypothesis that pleasure is causally linked with neural events that produce the behavioral effects in question. But as Corabi (2008) observes, Robinson's

Adequately dealing with James's objection requires showing how the hedonic/utility match can improve fitness, and hence be selected for, even if phenomenal properties are epiphenomenal. I propose that the fact that an experience has a certain hedonic value can help to explain a creature's behavior even if the phenomenal properties constituting the experience are causally inert. My proposal, which is admittedly speculative, rests on the idea that the subject's acquaintance with causally inert phenomenal states can give rise to attitudes or associations with causal efficacy.

Let's begin with a mundane case in which the hedonic value of an experience helps to explain what someone does.

> Alexis tries cilantro for the first time and discovers that, alas, she belongs to the sizeable minority of people for whom cilantro tastes like soap. She says "yuck!" and vows never to eat cilantro again.

It's tempting to say that the phenomenology involved – the yuckiness – *causes* Alexis to say "yuck!" and to subsequently avoid eating cilantro. But epiphenomenalism is incompatible with this claim. This is the nub of the current puzzle. Epiphenomenalism blocks a natural explanation of our avoidance of unpleasant stimuli, and thereby blocks a natural explanation of why the hedonic/utility match increases the odds that a creature will survive long enough to reproduce.

Here is my proposal. Acquaintance with the yucky taste leads Alexis to realize that cilantro tastes terrible. Her judgment to this effect incorporates an instance of the yucky phenomenal property, which serves as the property's mode of presentation.[8] It is structured as follows:

> *Eating cilantro causes <u>this</u>* <yucky gustatory phenomenology> *sensation, which is unpleasant.*

The gustatory phenomenology does not *cause* Alexis to judge that this sensation is unpleasant. She registers its unpleasantness directly, through her (non-causal) acquaintance with the phenomenology. So the phenomenology – the

proposal leaves a crucial puzzle unresolved: why it would be more likely for events benefiting the organism to cause pleasure than to cause pain.

[8] In other words, how the experience seems to Alexis *epistemically* is constituted by its qualitative nature, that is, its phenomenal reality. This is not to say that how the property epistemically seems to Alexis *exhausts* its phenomenal reality. As the famous case of the speckled hen demonstrates, phenomenal appearances outstrip epistemic appearances. (I discuss these issues, and the metaphysics of the acquaintance relation, in Gertler 2012.)

yuckiness – can help to explain why she judges that the taste is unpleasant, without causing that judgment.

With the judgment *eating cilantro causes this unpleasant sensation*, Alexis associates eating cilantro with a phenomenal property, roughly *this* (yucky) *taste*. But she also classifies it in a more general way, as *unpleasant*. This more general association abstracts away from the specific way in which eating cilantro is unpleasant – that is, its particular phenomenology. It is a relatively generic negative association, signaling that eating cilantro is to be avoided.

I suggest that this negative association is causally responsible for Alexis's decision to avoid cilantro and her future cilantro-avoidance behavior. The gustatory phenomenology helps to explain why Alexis judges that eating cilantro is unpleasant, and hence to explain her negative association with eating cilantro. But as just outlined, the phenomenology's contribution to explaining these things is non-causal. And what causally contributes to Alexis's cilantro-avoidance behavior is only the negative association, not the phenomenology that explains it.

In order for this proposal to remain compatible with epiphenomenalism, the negative association cannot owe its causal efficacy to phenomenology. And this seems plausible. After all, associations often operate unconsciously, as simple behavioral dispositions; and such dispositions can persist beyond any memory of their basis. Alexis need not be aware of the reason she avoids cilantro. When asked why she does this, she may be unable to say more than "I don't like it" – where this is not tied to any phenomenological memory. In fact, Alexis's belief that she dislikes cilantro may itself be inferred from her disposition to avoid it. The habit of avoiding cilantro may be so ingrained that she supposes, reasonably enough, that she must have once tried it and disliked it.

But negative associations, when triggered, often do involve phenomenology. For example, when Alexis sees a cilantro-flavored dish listed on a restaurant menu, she may remember the yucky taste. The presence of that memory can easily make it seem, to Alexis, that the phenomenology causally contributes to her avoidance of cilantro. But on my proposal this is a mistake. The phenomenological memory may contribute to non-causally explaining her aversion, just as the gustatory phenomenology helps to explain her judgment in the original case. But what causes Alexis to avoid cilantro is only the negative association with cilantro, an association that abstracts away from the phenomenological details.

So I propose that an experience's hedonic value can contribute to explaining the subject's behavior, compatibly with epiphenomenalism. The subject can register an experience's hedonic value by acquaintance with the phenomenal properties involved. In registering an experience's hedonic value, the subject associates the relevant stimulus (such as eating cilantro) with a hedonic value (in this case, negative). Crucially, the phenomenal properties of the experience do not *cause* the association with a hedonic value: rather, those properties are *experienced as* having a certain value, and so in grasping those properties through acquaintance the stimulus is associated with that value. This association, which may initially take the form of a judgment, is causally efficacious. It causally contributes to current behavior, e.g., deciding never to eat cilantro again. And it generates a disposition to avoid cilantro in the future.

In this way, acquaintance provides a bridge from the phenomenal properties of experience – instances of which partly constitute judgments about them – to causally efficacious associations or attitudes that are not phenomenological (or, at least, do not owe their causal powers to their phenomenology).[9]

Now to the heart of James's challenge. The hedonic/utility match, in humans, would be a remarkable coincidence unless this match contributed to fitness in our more primitive ancestors. Consider a primitive creature with the kind of hedonic/utility match we've been discussing. Let's call this creature Match. Match experiences pleasure when (to use other examples from James) filling an empty stomach or resting after fatigue, and pain when undergoing starvation or incurring tissue damage.

Suppose that Match moves close to a flame and experiences a painful burning sensation. Crucially, the phenomenal quality of the burning sensation does not *cause* it to be experienced as painful; it *constitutes* that way of experiencing it. The phenomenology thereby helps to explain, but does not cause, Match's association of proximity to flame with *unpleasant* or *to be avoided*. This negative association abstracts away from the specific kind of unpleasant phenomenology linked with proximity to flame – that it's a burning sensation rather than, say, a stabbing sensation. And it causes Match to avoid flames in

---

[9] This claim, that Alexis's negative association with eating cilantro is causally efficacious, faces an objection. The association at issue seems initially to be a kind of judgment, to the effect that *eating cilantro causes something unpleasant*. (This judgment presumably yields a dispositional belief with this content and a disposition to avoid cilantro.) Some have argued that judgments have phenomenal character. And given the assumption of epiphenomenalism, Alexis's negative association with eating cilantro cannot owe its causal powers to phenomenology. However, epiphenomenalism implies only that any phenomenology tied to the judgment is irrelevant to its causal powers. So long as judgments do not owe their efficacy to their causal powers, they can both have phenomenal character – even what Pitt (2004) calls "proprietary phenomenology" – and be causally efficacious, compatibly with epiphenomenalism.

Still, my proposal is incompatible with some stronger claims on behalf of cognitive phenomenology. For example, if the judgments or associations I describe have their causal powers in virtue of their intentional contents, then (on the assumption of epiphenomenalism) intentional content cannot be exhaustively constituted by phenomenology. (I return to this issue in the next subsection.)

the future: Match maintains a safe distance from flames. Seeing a flame may trigger a memory of the burning sensation. But just as with Alexis's memory of the yucky taste, the phenomenology involved in this memory does not cause Match's avoidance behavior. At most it contributes (non-causally) to explaining this behavior, in the way outlined earlier.

This case illustrates how an experience's hedonic value can contribute to explaining a primitive creature's behavior, compatibly with epiphenomenalism. The creature registers the event's hedonic value by experiencing it *as* pleasant (positive) or unpleasant (negative). The creature associates the relevant stimulus with this hedonic value. Crucially, the phenomenology of the experience does not *cause* the association with a hedonic value. Rather, the creature registers the experience *as* pleasant or unpleasant directly, through acquaintance with the relevant phenomenal properties. Associating a stimulus with phenomenal properties *experienced as* having a certain hedonic value thus means associating the stimulus with that value. This association can causally contribute to current behavior, e.g., Match's withdrawing from the flame. And it can generate dispositions, such as the disposition to avoid proximity to flames in the future.

The explanation of the hedonic/utility match is then straightforward. The negative association with flames causally contributes to Match's avoiding close proximity to flames, and thereby to Match's survival. Things are different for Mismatch, a primitive creature in which the hedonic/utility relation is reversed. Mismatch experiences a pleasant sensation when close to flames. Mismatch thus develops a positive association with proximity to flames, and does not avoid or withdraw from them. As compared with Match, Mismatch will be less likely to survive long enough to reproduce. (But we needn't feel too badly: Mismatch presumably dies a blissful death.)

3.3.5 Does Epiphenomenalism Deprive Us of Agency?

I have argued that recognizing the role of acquaintance in grasping phenomenal properties undercuts the epistemic arguments against epiphenomenalism. But I doubt that it is epistemic considerations that cause such dismay among philosophers like Fodor and Lewis. It's instructive to consider the context of Fodor's "end of the world" lament.

> [I]f it isn't literally true that my wanting is causally responsible for my reaching, and my itching is causally responsible for my scratching, and my believing is causally responsible for my saying … [ellipsis in original] if

> none of that is literally true, then practically everything I believe about any-
> thing is false and it's the end of the world. (Fodor 1989, 79)

Fodor worries that epiphenomenalism would overturn some of his deeply held and cherished beliefs; and the beliefs in jeopardy concern *action*. I suspect that his dismay stems from the idea that, if epiphenomenalism is true, then in a real sense we lack agency.

The relationship between agency and epiphenomenalism is a weighty topic, and I cannot hope to do it justice here. But I will make a few brief points.

First, because the Knowledge Argument aims to establish dualism only about the phenomenal, the epiphenomenalism at issue concerns only the phenom-enal. But some of Fodor's worries concern the causal efficacy of states that, on most accounts, are not phenomenal. Even if desires and beliefs have associated and proprietary phenomenology, on most accounts they are not exhausted by their phenomenology. So long as my desires, beliefs, and intentions do not owe their causal powers to their phenomenal character, epiphenomenalism about the phenomenal does not threaten most ordinary agency. It does not threaten the idea that my desire for water, and my belief that the cup contains water, causally contribute to my reaching for the cup.

Fodor also mentions itching. Epiphenomenalism implies that the phe-nomenal character of the itch cannot cause the scratching. However, the kind of proposal sketched in the previous section might explain how, con-sistently with epiphenomenalism, "I scratched because of an itch" could be true. I grasp the feeling through acquaintance, and think "*this <itchy>* feeling would be relieved by scratching"; that thought is a way of thinking "I have a feeling that would be relieved by scratching." That description is very intellectualized, and so dubious – especially considering that my dog seems to scratch when feeling an itch. But as before, a primitive analogue is available. In the primitive case, the sensation is brutely associated (either innately or through experience) with relief that comes from scratching or just the urge to scratch. So as with the previous cases, a non-causal rela-tion of acquaintance provides a bridge from the *itching* sensation to causally efficacious attitudes or associations that do not owe their causal efficacy to phenomenal character.

Even putting aside that proposal, I confess that I am not very troubled by the idea that some of my scratching is not caused by my itching. What I have in mind is scratching that is *unreflective*, unmediated by deliberation – e.g., about whether scratching might inflame a mosquito bite. Suppose that unre-flective scratching is a non-agential reflex directly triggered by the neural basis of itching, rather than by (the feel of) the itch itself. The comparison with my dog suggests, to me at least, that that possibility isn't cause for deep dismay.

What would be dismaying is the idea that we lack a deeper kind of agency, the kind associated with the capacity to act on intentions formed through reflective deliberation about our values and goals. Most contemporary accounts of agency, both compatibilist and libertarian, locate our agency in a capacity of that sort. But the causal factors at issue in those accounts are not phenomenal states, or at least are not states exhausted by phenomenal character. They are largely attitudes: beliefs, desires, (attitudes towards) values, intentions, hopes, etc. Deliberation may involve conscious attitudes of these types, and conscious attitudes may have associated – even proprietary – phenomenology. But since the epiphenomenalism under consideration is only epiphenomenalism about the phenomenal, it does not imply that conscious attitudes are causally inefficacious. It implies only that such attitudes derive their causal powers from something other than their phenomenal character.

Even those who emphasize the importance of consciousness to agency generally deny that it is *phenomenal* consciousness that matters. For example, in arguing that responsibility for action requires consciousness of one's reasons, Levy makes it clear that what he has in mind is *access* consciousness rather than *phenomenal* consciousness. "What is at issue is the availability of certain kinds of representations to the agent, not whether they experience qualia" (Levy 2013, 213). And the issues raised by the Libet cases and others, about whether the time lag of conscious intentions threatens agency, also concern access consciousness – that is, consciousness *of* intentions (Holton 2004).

3.3.6 Summing Up: How Acquaintance Quiets Worries about Epiphenomenalism

I have argued that invoking acquaintance can defuse apparent evidence against epiphenomenalism. Those dismayed by the prospect of epiphenomenalism may find solace in my proposal that acquaintance can forge a bridge between phenomenal properties and causally efficacious attitudes. Even if my itching doesn't cause my scratching, it may well be that my itching *explains* my scratching. And epiphenomenalism poses no threat to standard models of agency, which require at most that my decisions are the product of values of which I am aware, or are formed on the basis of accessible reasons.

3.4 Conclusion

Many philosophers share the intuition that Mary makes a substantial epistemic advance the first time she sees something she knows to be red. The acquaintance response is an appealing way to make sense of this intuition. I have suggested that the acquaintance response weakens the case for physicalism in two ways. First, the acquaintance response commits physicalists to an error theory about how we conceptualize the phenomenal. This commitment fits uneasily with the robust confidence in our conceptualization practices required to justify the claim that physicalism is more parsimonious than dualism. Second, the idea that we can grasp phenomenal properties through acquaintance goes a long way in neutralizing concerns about epiphenomenalism. It thereby eases the worry that dualism is not compatible with any plausible view about mental causation. This worry is further eased by coming to appreciate that epiphenomenalism does not threaten standard models of agency.

That some physicalists have recently embraced the acquaintance response is strong evidence of its appeal. If my arguments here succeed, the acquaintance response lessens the appeal of physicalism in ways not previously recognized.[10]

[10] For valuable comments on drafts of this chapter, I'm indebted to Robert Howell, Walter Ott, and especially Sam Coleman.

4   Acquaintance and Phenomenal Concepts

David Pitt

In this chapter I defend the view that to know *what it is like* to experience a phenomenal property is just to be consciously acquainted with it, to experience it.[1] Knowledge of what it is like is not knowledge *that*. It is not conceptual/propositional at all. It does not require thought, or the deployment of concepts. Nor is it knowledge-*what* in the sense of, for example, knowing what time it is, or knowing what the positive square root of 169 is, which is also conceptual. And it is not some kind of know-*how*. It is, I will argue, simple *acquaintance with*, being *familiar with*, a phenomenal property. To know what a particular kind of experience is like is to be familiar with the phenomenal property or properties that characterize it; and to be familiar with such properties is just to experience them. Acquaintance is the fundamental mode of knowledge of phenomenal properties instantiated in experience, it *is* knowing what it is like; and all it requires is the experience itself.[2]

I will call this kind of knowledge "acquaintance-knowledge" (Conee calls it "phenomenal knowledge"). It is not the same as, and cannot be explained in terms of, knowledge *by* acquaintance. Perhaps acquaintance-knowledge is what Russell meant by 'knowledge by acquaintance' (or what he meant when he said that "there is a sense of 'knowing' in which, when you have an experience, there is no difference between the experience and knowing that you have it" [Russell 1940: 49]). Nonetheless, there is an important distinction to be made between

---

[1] To my knowledge, this view of knowing what it is like was first proposed as a response to Jackson's thought experiment by Earl Conee (Conee 1994). Much of what I have to say echoes what Conee says; and I reach some of the same conclusions about Jackson's argument. But I have different motivations and arguments. In particular, I think the view is inevitable given certain facts about the nature of concepts and the nature of qualitative experience, and given my views about the nature of thought and thinking. Moreover, I specifically address the "phenomenal concept strategy," which Conee does not do.

[2] It might require *attentive* experience, or experience *for more than a millisecond*. I will set these complications aside for the time being.

propositional knowledge *based upon* acquaintance and the acquaintance it is based upon. The former involves thought and the deployment of concepts, whereas the latter consists merely in conscious experience. As I will use the phrase, knowledge *by* acquaintance with a phenomenal property Q has the general form of knowing that *Q is like this* (or that *this is what Q is like*), where the demonstrative refers to the instance of Q with which one is acquainted.

Knowledge by acquaintance that *this is what Q is like* must in turn be distinguished from non-acquaintance-based knowledge that *this is what Q is like*. Thoughts about phenomenal qualities one is not acquainted with can have the form *this is what Q is like*, but such thoughts cannot ground knowledge by acquaintance. Since one cannot be acquainted with the experiences of others, one cannot gain knowledge by acquaintance of phenomenal properties their experiences instantiate. One may succeed in referring to an instance of Q in experience not one's own, and one's thought that *Q is like this* may be true. And it may count as knowledge. But it will not be knowledge by *acquaintance*, since acquaintance is lacking. Indeed, supposing there could be unconscious experience, and, hence, that there could be phenomenal properties instantiated in one's *own* experience with which one is unacquainted, one could think such a thought truly about one's own experience. And such a thought might count as knowledge. But, again, it would not count as knowledge by acquaintance, since acquaintance requires conscious experience.

Knowing *what Q is like* is not knowing by acquaintance that *Q is like this*, since it does not involve conceptualization or propositional thought at all. It is, as I said, constituted merely by acquaintance, by conscious experience. To know what uni tastes like, for example, is to experience the taste of uni. The most obvious way to do this is to taste some uni, though there are of course other ways – e.g., tasting something that is not uni but tastes *just like it*. Not knowing what uni tastes like requires never having tasted it (or something that tastes just like it), or having tasted it but being unable to remember it. But one can know what uni tastes like without knowing it is uni that tastes like that – that is, without knowing by acquaintance the proposition *this is what uni tastes like*. This kind of knowledge requires having the concept UNI; but one need not have that concept (or indeed any concepts at all) in order to taste uni and, thereby, to know what it tastes like. Hence, knowing what uni tastes like is not knowledge by acquaintance that *uni tastes like this*.

Nor is knowing *what Q is like* knowing-what, in the sense of knowing what the positive square root of 169 is. To know this is to know that the positive square root of 169 is 13, and that requires understanding and deploying the concept THIRTEEN. But there is no *conceptual* knowledge of what uni tastes like (just try explaining it to someone who has never tasted anything). The concept THE TASTE OF UNI is not like the concept THIRTEEN: grasping it does *not* enable one to know the nature of its referent.

Nor, finally, is knowing *what Q is like* know-how, as proponents of the Ability Hypothesis have claimed. Though knowledge of what it is like may *enable* certain capacities to recognize, imagine and remember, it is obviously not the same thing. The Ability Hypothesis is, to my mind, a prime example of one of the worst proclivities of twentieth-century analytic philosophy – viz., the attempt to reduce phenomena to their effects, in an effort to avoid facing up to difficult facts (*especially* the difficult fact of conscious qualitative experience). It is simply *perverse*. I will not discuss it further.

Knowing what Q is like is simply being acquainted with it – experiencing it.

The consequences of this for Mary are obvious. When she leaves the black-and-white room (the Room) and sees puce for the first time, she knows *what puce looks like* simply by visually experiencing it. She becomes acquainted with something she had not been acquainted with before; and this acquaintance counts as knowledge all by itself. She does not gain propositional knowledge by acquaintance. What she comes to know does not depend upon her coming to be able to think that *this is what puce looks like*, or that *puce looks like this*. (These are thoughts she was able to think while in her drab captivity.) It does not require that she *think* anything at all. She can know what puce looks like without knowing that it is *puce* that looks like that – as she might if she were, like Nida-Rümelin's (1995) Mariana, released into a colorful antechamber, with no identifiable objects. She can know this without having the concept PUCE at all. Nor is Mary's new knowledge knowledge-*what*, in the sense identified above, since there are no *concepts* the grasp of which enables Mary to know what she knows when she sees puce. And, though she becomes able to do things she could not do before her release, the knowledge she gains cannot be *identified with* any form of knowledge-how. Thus, the only way to substantiate the intuitively correct claim that she gains new knowledge is to recognize that acquaintance *per se*, conscious experience, is its own kind of knowledge: knowing what it is like.

My argument for this will hinge on the rejection of "phenomenal concepts" (as that term is used by defenders of physicalism in response to Jackson's argument) and the phenomenal thoughts they would be constituents of, if they existed. None of the attempts to account for the change in Mary's epistemic situation by appeal to such special concepts and thoughts can succeed.

4.1 Phenomenal Concepts

A phenomenal concept, as I will use the term in this discussion, is a concept of a phenomenal property whose content is determined by the experience of the property, and which cannot therefore be possessed in the absence of experience of the property it is the concept of. There can be concepts *of* qualitative experiences – e.g., RED, DARK, SWEET; but the *contents* of such concepts are (I maintain) not individuated by the properties they are concepts of. If there are no phenomenal concepts in this sense – concepts the *grasp* of which requires *experience of* the properties they are concepts of – then there is no special *conceptual* knowledge of what it is like, no phenomenal *thought*. There is nothing one can *think* once one has experienced red that one could not *think* before experiencing it.

There are several ways in which the content of a concept could be individuated by experience of a phenomenal property. The experience could be taken to *be* a concept; it could be taken to be a *constituent* of the concept; the content of the concept could be individuated in virtue of *referring* to it; and the occurrence of the concept could be essentially tied to (caused by) experiences of the property. I have non-tendentious and tendentious reasons for thinking that none of these can work.

There are intuitively good reasons for thinking that concepts could not *be* percepts (or images). These are fundamentally distinct kinds of mental items. For one thing, we can think about, and have concepts for, things that cannot in principle be perceived (and, hence, not *imaged*), such as transfinite ordinals, ten-dimensional spaces, and (non-actual) possible worlds.

We can also think about, and have concepts for, things that can be perceived, but which cannot be imagined (*imaged*), such as chiliagons and ten-thousand-six-speckled hens. If we can think about things that cannot be perceived or imagined, then we have concepts of those things. But if we cannot perceive or imagine them, we do not have percepts or images of them. Hence, our concepts of them cannot be percepts or images of them.

Moreover, it seems obvious that perceiving and imagining are possible without thinking – as, for example, when one absentmindedly takes in one's perceivable environment, enjoys one's phosphenes, or listens to Bartók in one's head. These are, apparently, activities one can engage in without deploying concepts at all. And it certainly seems possible that there could be non-human creatures capable of perceiving and imagining but not of conceptualizing (and even vice versa), as well as that there could be (maybe there are) humans who can do one but not the other.

A deeper, but still, I think, intuitive reason for thinking that concepts are not percepts or images is that concepts (i.e., conceptual *contents*) must be *thinkable*, while percepts and images are not. It is nonsense – a category mistake – to say that *what I was thinking* (or *part of* what I was thinking) was *the smell of lavender* or *the sound of a distant trumpet*, or that the concept I was entertaining was *painful* or *amused*. It is true that I can think about these things, but only in the sense that I can have otherwise-content-individuated concepts that can *refer to* them. Concepts (their contents) must be things capable of being *thought* – in the course of thinking a complete thought of which they are constituents, or merely *entertained* – simply had in mind or considered.

I have a tendentious explanation for all of this. It is that thinking is a distinctive kind of *experience*, and that distinct *kinds* of experience are distinguished by distinct kinds of phenomenology. Thinking is *not the same as* seeing, hearing, smelling, tasting … So thinking must have its very own brand of phenomenology – a phenomenology which I have elsewhere (Pitt 2004) characterized as *proprietary*, *distinctive*, and *individuative*. Thinking is a *mode* of experience, and (I take this to be untendentious) experiential modes in general are distinguished phenomenally. Vision, audition, olfaction, gustation, etc., are modes of experiencing, and each is constituted by its own proprietary kind of determinable phenomenology (visual, auditory, olfactory, gustatory …). Hence, there is a proprietary determinable phenomenology for thought – what I called (Pitt 2004) *cognitive* phenomenology (though the terms *conceptual* and *propositional* phenomenology will do as well).

I have both epistemic and metaphysical reasons for believing that there is a proprietary, distinctive and individuative phenomenology of thought (that is, of thought *content*). Briefly, the epistemic reason (Pitt 2004) is that there is available to us a mode of access to the contents of our conscious occurrent thoughts – viz., introspective and non-inferential – that would not be available to us if occurrent conscious thought contents were not distinctively presented to us in conscious experience. In general, discriminatory non-inferential introspective awareness of occurrent conscious mental states requires that the states accessed be differentiated *in consciousness* – that is, they must be introspectively *distinguishable* and *identifiable* as the states they are. (This is analogous to the role that distinguishability and identifiability of objective properties plays in purely perceptual discrimination.) But differentiation in consciousness is entirely a matter of difference of phenomenology. Thus, we can be non-inferentially introspectively aware that we are experiencing a pain, and not a smell or a sound, that the pain is burning, and not achy or slashing, and that it has gotten worse, because pain experiences have proprietary, distinctive, individuative phenomenologies. And we can be non-inferentially introspectively aware *that* we are thinking, and not feeling pain or hearing a sound or smelling a smell, and that we are thinking about mathematics, and not about ice cream or international trade agreements. But if conscious thoughts can be thus discriminated from other conscious states (or events) and identified as the thoughts they are, introspectively and non-inferentially, they too must have proprietary, distinctive, individuative phenomenologies.

This is a *transcendental* argument: a certain kind of access to conscious occurrent thought content is possible; but it would not be possible if there were no proprietary, distinctive, individuative phenomenology of thought; hence, there is such phenomenology.

The metaphysical reason (Pitt 2011) focuses on the fact that conscious states in general are, *qua conscious*, phenomenally individuated. What distinguishes, for example, conscious smells from conscious sounds is their distinctive kinds of phenomenologies (olfactory and auditory). Hence, if conscious thoughts are not conscious sights, smells, sounds … then they must have their own kind of phenomenology that constitutes their determinable phenomenal kind.

If this is correct (and I assure you, it is), then one could no more *think* sounds or colors or smells than one could *smell* sounds or colors or thoughts. These kinds of experiencing are constituted by the instantiation of metaphysically *radically* distinct sorts of phenomenal properties. There can be no *cross-modal* experiences. One cannot experience olfactory percepts or images in the *way* one experiences colors, or experience colors the way one experiences sounds. Seeing is not smelling or hearing. Confused interpretations of the phenomenon of synesthesia aside, it is *absolutely impossible* to smell colors, hear flavors, etc. If thinking is a distinctive fundamental kind of experience, one cannot *think* any of these things either. Just as one can only hear sounds and smell smells, one can only think – i.e., cognitively experience – thoughts (and their constituent concepts).[3]

In light of this, my claim that there are no phenomenal concepts – i.e., that no concepts are individuated by phenomenology – must be refined to apply only to *non-cognitive* phenomenology: there are no concepts whose content is individuated by non-cognitive phenomenology. The crux of the claim is that conceptual contents are not *extensionally* individuated. And this is true in the

---

[3] The same reasoning can be used to show that external objects cannot *be* conceptual contents either. One could no more *think* a set of possible worlds, or water, or one's refrigerator, than one could think a smell or a sound. These are things of the wrong kinds; they are not phenomenal properties.

case of higher-order concepts, as well (it is possible to introspectively misidentify a concept).

4.2 Phenomenal Immiscibility

I also think it is untendentious and intuitively clear that experiences of different phenomenal modalities cannot *mix*. Not only can one not smell colors or taste thoughts, there cannot be conscious states of any of these phenomenal kinds partially consisting of instantiations of different kinds of phenomenology. That is, there cannot be a sound a *part of which* is a smell, or a sight *a part of which* is a taste. There may be experiences that have sounds, smells, sights, and tastes as constituents (as for example one's *total* experience at a given moment). But the constituents remain metaphysically independent. Experiences of different modalities cannot *combine* the way experiences of the same modality can – for example, in the synergistic way the taste of chocolate and taste of orange combine, or the way the sound of middle C on a trumpet followed by the sound of a drumroll can be temporal parts of a single auditory experience. The orange-chocolate taste is still a *taste*; and the trumpet-drum sound sequence is still a *sound*. There can be no orange-trumpet *taste* (or *sound*), or chocolate-drumroll sound (or *taste*).

I call this general fact the *Principle of Phenomenal Immiscibility*.[4]

4.3 The Phenomenal Concept Strategy

The phenomenal concept strategy in defense of physicalism is to claim that though Mary gains new concepts, and, hence, new knowledge upon her release, she does not learn any new *facts*. What happens is that she relearns old facts in new ways. On one account, the new concepts she gains are content-individuated by percepts or images of the previously unperceived/unimagined properties she nonetheless had complete scientific knowledge of in the Room. These might be "quotational" phenomenal concepts in the style of Balog (2012), Block (2006), and Papineau (2002), which in some way "contain" samples of the phenomenal properties they are concepts of. Or they might be concepts whose contents are individuated by broadly referential relations to the properties they are concepts of, as on Sainsbury and Tye's (2011) "originalist" view,

---

[4] The same reasoning can be used to show that external objects cannot be *constituents of* conceptual contents either. One's thought could no more *contain* Mont Blanc as a constituent than it could the sound of a trumpet. The Principle of Phenomenal Immiscibility is thus in the spirit of Frege's principle that only senses can be constituents of senses.

or Evans's (1982) and McDowell's (1984) object-dependent sense view. On another account, Mary acquires what Loar (1997) calls *recognitional* concepts, which bear a special relation to experiences one has had, in virtue of which they are "triggered" by subsequent experiences of the same kind. These would be analogous to, say, the concepts of middle C and the B-flat below it that people with perfect pitch have: they hear the pitch; they automatically token the MIDDLE C or B-FLAT BELOW MIDDLE C, and on the basis of this come to know what the pitch is.

Beyond the obvious problem that all of these accounts build in more or less intimate relations to *conscious qualitative properties* that Mary had not experienced before her release, and so still face the problem they were supposed to finesse (i.e., the metaphysical status of those properties), these strategies are all ruled out by the facts about experience, concepts, and thought detailed above.

The Principle of Phenomenal Immiscibility rules out quotational phenomenal concepts. Concepts are cognitive-phenomenal experiences; colors (sounds, smells …) are not. So colors cannot be constituents of concepts. There is no special puce-percept-or-image-containing concept that Mary acquires upon experiencing puce for the first time. It is impossible for such things to exist. What is not impossible is for there to be a phenomenal sample (a percept or an image) that one is thinking *about* – applying a concept to. But the *content* of the concept cannot involve non-cognitive phenomenology, any more than a Fregean *sense* could contain a mountain, or a color, or the sound of a distant trumpet. These are the wrong kinds of things to be thought constituents. For me, senses (thought contents) are cognitive phenomenal types (see Pitt 2009), and they (their tokens) can only be composed of (tokens of) cognitive phenomenal types.

Such concepts are also ruled out because their contents, not being cognitive phenomenal, cannot be *thought* – i.e., *cognitively* experienced.

For essentially the same reasons, I deny that there are concepts whose contents are individuated by their referential relations to percepts or images (or to anything else, for that matter), whether these be Kaplanian indexical concepts, Evans–McDowellian referentially-individuated-sense concepts or Sainsbury–Tye "originalist" concepts. Anything non-cognitive-phenomenal is the wrong kind of thing to be a conceptual content individuator. Conceptual contents are cognitive phenomenal types, individuated entirely phenomenally, and phenomenal properties in general are not individuated relationally. The pain of a sunburn is not *per se* different from the pain of a windburn or an iceburn because it was caused by the sun and not by the wind or ice. The same holds for cognitive experiences. The demonstrative concept THIS PAIN does

not change its cognitive content depending upon its referent, or its origin. THIS
PAIN applied to a burning pain is the same concept as THIS PAIN applied to an
ache. And the thoughts I DO NOT LIKE THIS PAIN thought of the burning and
the aching are the same thought. They are the same thought, thought about
different things.

In fact, I do not think that *any* indexical concepts are content-individuated
referentially. If you and I both think I HATE THAT IDIOT, we are thinking
the same thought, even if the referents of our concepts I and THAT IDIOT
are different. We deploy the *same* concepts, I and THAT IDIOT. The fact that
my token of I *must* refer to something different from your token, or that our
tokens of THAT IDIOT in fact refer to different idiots, does not make them
different concepts. (Any more than my hat is a different hat when it is on your
head.) It is not in general true that possible difference in truth value entails
difference in content. The expression "the democratic presidential nominee"
(and the concept it expresses) had a different referent in 2016 than it did in
2012, and the expression "the democratic presidential nominee in 2016" has
a different referent in other worlds. But it does not follow that it changed its
meaning in 2016, or that it means something different in other worlds. I do
not think there is any good reason to think that there is a principled difference
between such expressions and indexicals. They differ only in the scope of the
context with respect to which their referents are determined.[5]

Also for these reasons, I reject Loar's recognitional concept strategy. I do
not think that a person with perfect pitch has a different *concept* of MIDDLE C
from me. The fact that he instantly identifies the pitch when he hears it does
not make his concept different from mine. What is different between us is his
automatic and infallibly correct application of it. His concept of MIDDLE C
is like my concept RED. I recognize red on sight. But I do not think I have a
different *concept* from someone who is color blind, or *totally* blind.

Concepts are constituents of *thoughts*. Thinking is a metaphysically distinct
kind of experience from seeing. Hence it is possible for one to occur without
the other. So it is possible for the congenitally blind to *think* THIS IS RED of
something they are touching. And what they think is *exactly the same as* what
I think when I think THIS IS RED of something I see. When it comes to *saying*
what red is, Mary is as conceptually competent as I am. If you ask Mary to *tell
you* about red, she will tell you exactly what you would tell her if she asked you
to tell her about red. The differences between us are not *conceptual*, they are

---

[5] This view of indexical (including demonstrative) concepts is defended in Pitt 2013. It is
further developed in my forthcoming book *The Quality of Thought.*

perceptual. Blind people can have exactly the same concept of red as sighted people. The fact that sighted people know how red things look and blind people do not does not entail that they have different *concepts*.

If one recognizes thinking as a fundamental kind of experience, irreducible to and immiscible with any other fundamental kind of experience, it becomes very clear that not everything that is happening in the conscious mind can be treated as part of what one is consciously *thinking*. I may have visual experiences Mary does not have, but it does not follow that I have *cognitive* experiences she does not have. To be sure, I know propositions she cannot know. But, as I have been arguing, this is not because I can think things she cannot think. I may be able to think things *truly* that she cannot think truly – as, for example, that *this thing* is puce.

In *this* sense I may be capable of knowing things Mary cannot know. But it is not in virtue of my being able to deploy concepts she cannot deploy. It is simply a mistake to assimilate the perceptual differences between us to differences in what we can think. It is a mistake to assimilate all knowledge to knowledge *that*. The various kinds of experiencing must be kept strictly apart in our theories of mental content.

The knowledge that I can have that Mary cannot have is knowledge of what it is like to see chromatic colors – acquaintance-knowledge of particular phenomenal properties.

4.4 An Objection: Tye on Knowing What It Is Like

Michael Tye (2011) argues that being acquainted with a phenomenal property (which I assume is what he means by "know[ing] the phenomenal or subjective character of an experience") *cannot* be the same as knowing what the property (the experience) is like, because of the logic of knowledge-*wh* statements. For example, according to Tye the following argument is invalid:

1. Mary knows the phenomenal character of the experience of seeing puce.
2. The phenomenal character of the experience of seeing puce is what it is like to see puce.

Therefore,

3. Mary knows what it is like to see puce.

It is invalid because it has the same form as the following obviously invalid arguments:

1a. Samantha knows the color red.
1b. The color red is what my favorite color is.

Therefore,

1c. Samantha knows what my favorite color is.

2a. Paul knows Ann.
2b. Ann is who Sebastian loves.
Therefore,
2c. Paul knows whom Sebastian loves.

His explanation of the invalidity of these arguments is that it is in general not true that *wh-* expressions can be replaced with co-referring expressions in intensional contexts, *salva veritate*.

But Tye's arguments are invalid because they equivocate, not because *wh-* expressions cannot be replaced with co-referring expressions within the scope of an intensional verb. The word "know" is being used in different senses in their first premises and their conclusions. In the premise-sense, to "know" is *to be acquainted with* (to bear a certain relation to a property); in the predicate-sense, to "know" is *to know that* (to bear a certain relation to a proposition). It is easy to see why these arguments are invalid if we disambiguate:

1a′. Samantha is acquainted with the color red.
1b. The color red is what my favorite color is.
Therefore,
1c*. Samantha knows what my favorite color is.

That is,

Samantha knows that my favorite color is red.

2a′. Paul is acquainted with Ann.
2b. Ann is who Sebastian loves.
Therefore,
2c*. Paul knows who Sebastian loves.

That is,

Paul knows that Sebastian loves Ann.

If we read "know" in the conclusion in the acquaintance sense, the arguments are valid:

1a′. Samantha is acquainted with the color red.
1b. The color red is what my favorite color is.
Therefore,
1c′. Samantha is acquainted with what my favorite color is.

2a′. Paul is acquainted with Ann.

2b. Ann is who Sebastian loves.

Therefore,

2c′. Paul is acquainted with who Sebastian loves.

These arguments are valid because "acquaintance" contexts are *extensional*.

If 1c′ and 2c′ are a bit awkward, it is because 1b and 2b are a bit awkward. They are awkward ways of saying, respectively, that red is my favorite color and that Ann is the person Sebastian loves. (Perhaps they are best thought of as employing *focus* or *topicalization*.) If we adopt the less awkward phrasing, it is even clearer that the arguments are valid:

1a′. Samantha is acquainted with the color red.

1b′. Red is my favorite color.

1c′. Samantha is acquainted with my favorite color.

2a′. Paul is acquainted with Ann.

2b′. Ann is the person Sebastian loves.

2c′. Paul is acquainted with the person Sebastian loves.

Of course "acquainted with" can be used to describe a relation one stands in to propositions, as in "I am acquainted with the continuum hypothesis" (I know what it is; I know that it is that there are no numbers between $\aleph_0$ and $2^{\aleph_0}$) or "I am acquainted with your dietary restrictions" (I know what they are; I know that they are that you detest celery). But to interpret the conclusions in this way is to equivocate on the two senses of this phrase, for surely it is not being used in this sense in the first premises. It does not follow from 1a′ and 1b′ that Samantha is acquainted with the fact that my favorite color is red, or from 2a′ and 2b′ that Paul is acquainted with the fact that Sebastian loves Ann.

I conclude that there is no logical reason not to identify acquaintance-knowing with knowing what it is like.

4.5 Physicalism

The account of Mary's epistemic situation that I am promoting is neutral with respect to the ontological status of the properties she becomes acquainted with upon her release.[6]

Nothing I have said entails anything about the metaphysical nature of the experiential properties Mary becomes acquainted with.

---

[6] Conee (1994: 147) draws the same conclusion.

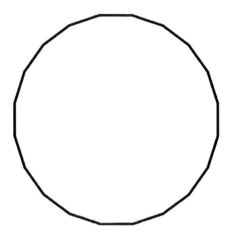

Figure 4.1 An icosagon.

Though I have argued that acquaintance-knowledge is knowledge of the intrinsic properties of experiences, nothing follows about the nature of those properties. Acquaintance-knowledge is a mode of knowing a phenomenal property that requires that the property be directly experienced. Mary does not have this kind of knowledge of phenomenal puce, because she has never experienced it. Acquaintance-knowledge is the fundamental kind of knowledge for phenomenal properties. Without it there can be no knowledge of the nature of phenomenal properties, no knowledge of what it is like to experience them, and no knowledge *by* acquaintance of them, knowledge that *this* is what Q is like.

However, there can be acquaintance-knowledge of *non*-phenomenal properties as well. In such cases acquaintance is not the *only* way to come to know the nature of the properties; but it still constitutes a different mode of knowing. For example, one may have complete theoretical knowledge of what an icosagon is (see Figure 4.1), but not be *acquainted with* the property of icosagonality, because one has never perceptually encountered an instance of it.

Suppose Mary is in such a situation. Though she is *theoretically* geometrically omniscient, there are no instances of icosagonality in the Room. There are no icosagonal objects, and she has never bothered to draw an icosagon. So she has never perceived icosagonality.

Moreover, she, like the rest of us, cannot construct one in her imagination.

Though she knows what icosagonality *is* (twenty-sidedness), she is not *acquainted with* it. If one day she draws an icosagon, or Googles "icosagon," she will become perceptually acquainted with the property of icosagonality. But we cannot conclude from this that icosagonality is not a physical property (i.e., a property that physical objects can instantiate). Surely it is. What she lacked before she drew an icosagon was acquaintance-knowledge of the shape. Nothing follows about the nature of the property she has gained acquaintance-knowledge of.

The same is true of acquaintance with physical *objects*. If Mary has never seen Lake Balaton, she is not perceptually acquainted with it, in spite of her physical omniscience. Even if she has seen pictures of Lake Balaton, or imagined it, if she has never *been there*, she is not perceptually acquainted with it. She is not in a position to think, truly, *this* is Lake Balaton. If, when she is released, she goes to Hungary and visits Lake Balaton, she will gain something she could not have had in the Room – acquaintance-knowledge of Lake Balaton. And she will thereby become capable of knowledge *by* acquaintance of it. It does not follow that Lake Balaton is not a physical object.

From the fact that theoretically physically omniscient Mary cannot have a particular kind of knowledge while in the Room, we cannot conclude that any knowledge she gains upon her release is knowledge of non-physical facts. She gains a new *mode* of knowing certain things, which may themselves be either physical or not.

4.6 Retaining Acquaintance-Knowledge

When Mary leaves the Room, she gains acquaintance-knowledge of chromatic colors – even if she cannot apply her color concepts to them or identify them by name. Visually experiencing them counts as knowing them, in the only way in which it is possible to know the nature of phenomenal properties, what they are like. At the instant Mary sees a color, she knows what it is like to see it. And as long as she is looking at it, she retains this knowledge. When she is not experiencing a color (perceptually or imaginatively), I maintain, she does *not* know what it looks like. If she is not seeing it or imagining it, she does not acquaintance-know it (and, hence, she does not by-acquaintance know it). Retention of the capacity to imagine or recognize a phenomenal property is not retention of knowledge of what the property is like. It is retention of the *capacity* to know what it is like. The capacity to know is not knowing, any more than the capacity to whistle is whistling. We may *say* that Mary continues to know what puce looks like while she is not experiencing it, just as we say that someone continues to believe that 5 + 7 = 12, or to be a good whistler, while asleep. But it is not literally true.[7]

---

[7] I develop this point a bit more in Pitt 2016.

Suppose Mary, still in the Room, has never tried to imagine puce, but, through some neurological fluke, could do so if she tried. If she tries, she will come to know what puce looks like. But before she imagines it, she does not know what it looks like, because she has never been acquainted with it. Hence, having the capacity to imagine puce is not knowledge of what it is like. Moreover, having the capacity to (imaginatively) *remember* what puce looks like does not count as knowing what it is like either. For this is just the *non-flukish* capacity to imagine it. Having the capacity to remember a phenomenal property does not count as knowing what it is like any more than having the capacity to non-memorially imagine it. Again, the capacity to know what it is like – the capacity to experience it – is not the same as experiencing it. If Mary is asked if she knows what puce looks like, she will not be able to give a positive answer unless she can re-experience it. She may *think* she does, because she *thinks* she can; but if she *cannot*, then she *does not* know. If she tries and fails, she must admit that though she *once* knew what puce looks like, she no longer does. And this is because to know it is just to experience it, to be acquainted with it. She would have to remind herself what it looks like by looking at a sample of it. Acquaintance-knowledge of phenomenal properties (like all genuinely *mental* states[8]) exists only in the conscious moment. If you know what puce looks like, it is not because you can imagine it. You know what puce looks like when you imagine it (or see it). If you *can* imagine it, then you *can* know it. But "can" does not imply "is." Being able to know what it is like does not imply that you do know it what it is like.

---

[8]   I realize saying this is like announcing to your therapist that you're from another planet as you're leaving your session. I do have reasons for believing this controversial claim. They are discussed in detail in my forthcoming book.

5   The Knowledge Argument Meets Representationalism about Colour Experience

Frank Jackson

Mary has new kinds of experiences when she leaves the black and white room. The change is akin to the difference between seeing black and white films and seeing films in colour. That much is common ground in the debate over the knowledge argument. This suggests that an ultimately satisfying reply to the argument on behalf of physicalism should base itself on a plausible view about the nature of the experiences she has for the first time on leaving the black and white room. It is, after all, the nature of these experiences that lies at the heart of the argument's intuitive appeal. In this chapter, I offer an account of colour experiences and explain how it tells us physicalists what is wrong with the knowledge argument.[1]

The account is a version of representationalism. Representationalism about colour experiences is part of a representationalism about perceptual experiences in general, although we will focus on visual experiences.[2] The version I favour has three parts: one concerns the content of perceptual experiences; the second concerns the attitude to the content; the third concerns how the first two parts, suitably supplemented, explain the phenomenal nature of perceptual experiences. We will walk through these parts in turn. With this as background, I will then explain where (according to me) the

---

[1] What I will be saying is broadly consistent with but substantially extends and, I trust, improves on Jackson (2003 and 2005a).

[2] I have many debts. The biggest is to Armstrong (1961, chs. 9 and 14), despite the fact he does not talk in terms of representation. There are also debts to many others, especially Tye (2000), who does talk in terms of representation. All the same, I take responsibility for the particular version of representationalism defended here. I am also indebted to the many who have discussed these issues with me over the years. I cannot name all of them, but must name David Braddon-Mitchell, David Lewis, Victoria McGeer, Philip Pettit, Michael Smith and Daniel Stoljar. Finally, I am indebted to the editor of this volume for excellent feedback and for encouraging me to undertake this exercise.

knowledge argument goes wrong. Although this explanation draws on representationalism about colour experiences, it does not draw on any particular view about the precise nature of their contents. We will conclude with a short discussion of that more particular question and why physicalists should concern themselves with it.

5.1 Reflections on the Content of Visual Experiences

Although we talk about colour experiences and contrast them with, for example, shape experiences and experiences of visual depth, this is potentially misleading. When an object looks to be a certain colour, that object also looks to be a certain shape and distance away. But there aren't three experiences, one of shape, one of distance away and one of colour. Rather, there is a single experience whose content concerns *inter alia* the object's colour, shape and distance away.

I have just slipped the word 'content' into the conversation. This is common enough but is it justified? Yes, if one thinks of content in the right way. It is undeniable that there is a distinction between veridical perceptions, illusions and hallucinations. We might disagree about details, but that there is an important distinction here is a Moorean fact. What is more, the question as to whether a given perceptual experience is veridical, illusory or hallucinatory turns on the extent to which it does or does not correspond to how things in fact are. This means that it makes sense to compare and contrast perceptual experiences with how things are. The content of a perceptual experience is that feature of the experience that allows us to make sense of comparing and contrasting the experience with how things are. To this extent, we can think of perceptual experiences as representational states, meaning by this that they have content in the just explained sense. And in this sense, desire is also a representational state. A desire is or is not satisfied to one extent or another, and that is a matter of the extent to which what is desired does or does not match how things in fact are. The case for holding that desires have content parallels the case for holding that visual experiences have content. However, we will see shortly that it is plausible that perceptual experiences are representational states in a stronger sense, a sense in which desires are not representational states.

We now have an obvious question. What ways of thinking of the contents of visual experiences allow us to make sense of comparing and contrasting them with how things are? There are three answers on the market: as items that those who have the experiences stand in some kind of direct awareness relation to; as propositions; and as sets of possible worlds (the position I will be supporting, with an important amendment).

The first answer is sometimes called the relational picture of experience and is, in essence, the traditional sense datum view. On this view, the difference between veridical perceptions, illusions and hallucinations lies in the correspondences or lack of correspondences between the relevant sense data – the items subjects are posited as being directly aware of – and how things in fact are, along with matters to do with the causal origins of the sense data. Although it seems to be undergoing something of a revival, I will take it for granted, in much company, that the sense datum answer was an interesting mistake.[3]

A more popular answer is propositions. Consider a case where a natural way to report my visual experience is with the sentence 'I see that that cup is white'. The content is then said, on one version of the propositional view, to be the ordered couple consisting of the cup and the property of being white (provided the cup exists and has the right causal connection to the experience).[4] And the perception is an illusion, for example, if the cup exists but is not white. On other versions, the content is said to be that there exists a white cup at so and so a distance in front of me, causally interacting with me in such and such a way, etc. And whether the experience is veridical, illusory or is a hallucination turns, in one way or another, on the extent to which how things in fact agree with or differ from that existential content.

I think there are three problems for the propositional view, problems which have nothing in particular to do with the issue just canvassed. First, as usually presented anyway, it wrongly identifies the content of a visual experience with the content of some sentence one might naturally use to report on the experience. The content of a visual experience is rich and seamless. Take the point about richness first. When an object looks to be a certain way to one, it looks to be a certain colour, shape, distance away, to be moving or not moving, to be related in various ways to other nearby objects, etc. The best we can do using words is to capture some aspect or other of that rich content. What do I mean by saying that the content is seamless? A passage of prose can say a lot about how things are, but different parts of the passage will relate more especially to one or another aspect of how things are being said to be. This is because the words for shapes, for example, are different from those for colours and motion. But, as we said at the beginning of this section, a single visual experience speaks to all of colour, shape, distance away, motion, relations to

---

[3] Made by Jackson (1977), among many. Incidentally, some do not count the relational or sense datum view as a kind of representationalism. We are doing so in order to make having content the marker for being a representational state.

[4] See, e. g., Tye (2009, ch. 4), for a view of this kind.

nearby objects, etc. It does not have parts that relate more especially to, say, shape and extension than to colour. Indeed, an experience says something about, for example, colour and extension by saying something about shape, and conversely. For in order to represent that some item has a certain colour, a visual experience needs to represent something about shape and extension – the shape and extension of the item that is represented as having the colour. Conversely, in order to represent that some item has a certain shape and exten- sion, a visual experience has also to represent something about colour – the colour difference between the item and the background.

The second problem is that propositions have truth conditions in the classical sense: a proposition is either true or false, whereas the contents of experiences have location conditions – they are true or false *of* one location or other. When something looks thus and so to you, your experience represents how things are vis-à-vis where you are located at the time of having the experi- ence, but without saying anything about where you are located other than that things are thus and so vis-à-vis that location. This is connected with what is sometimes called the ego-centricity of perceptual content, and the idea that the contents of perceptual experiences are positioned scenarios.[5] An experi- ence partitions possible locations into those which do and those which do not conform to it.[6]

The final problem for the propositional view is that it lacks a signal virtue of the possible worlds view, or, better, a signal virtue of the possible locations view, given the point just made, but we will talk in terms of worlds to start with and introduce the complication later. The signal virtue relates to the fact that the content of visual experience is indeterminate in a highly distinctive way. When an experience represents how things are in front of you, locations, colours and shapes are not represented absolutely precisely. There is no abso- lutely precise hue or shape that is represented as being instantiated. What is more, the degree of indeterminacy rises sharply as one moves outwards and away from the region you are focusing on. The distance away, colour and shape of a nearby object directly in front of you is represented reasonably precisely, but objects off to the side go 'vague' very quickly, and the same is true for objects seen in the distance. An account of the content of experi- ence needs to model all this, and the possible worlds account does so set- theoretically. For any experience, there is a set of worlds which conform to that experience. The indeterminacy of the content of the experience is then

---

[5] On the latter, see Peacocke (1992).
[6] An experience *token* is then veridical just if the conforming locations in the actual world include the actual location of the subject having the experience.

reflected in variations across the conforming worlds. In each conforming world, there is a region where the shapes, colours, etc., of the objects are pretty much alike across the conforming worlds – this corresponds to the region in front of you towards which your gaze is directed – but as one moves away from that region in each conforming world, the amount of variation rises sharply. For example, the shapes and colours of objects to, say, the left of that region in conforming world w_1 may be very different from those in some other conforming world w_2.

A side benefit of the possible worlds treatment of the indeterminacy of experiential content just outlined is the way it handles a famous tricky case for representationalism in, e. g., Peacocke (2002). Symmetrical, six-by-six arrays of dots can be seen as six rows of six evenly spaced dots, or as six columns of six evenly spaced dots. Let A be such an array. Seeing A as six rows is a different experience from seeing A as six columns. The challenge for representationalism is that how A is being represented to be is, it might be thought, one and the same in both cases. However, when you see A as six rows, the rows will be more precisely represented than the columns, and when you see A as six columns, the columns will be more precisely represented than the rows. That is why, in the first case, the rows 'jump out' at one, whereas, in the second, the columns jump out at one. But this means that the set of worlds that is the content (the conforming worlds) when A is seen as six rows is *not* the same as the set of worlds that is the content when A is seen as six columns. The worlds in the first set will vary less in where the rows are located than in where the columns are located; those in the second set will vary less in where the columns are located than in where the rows are located. On the possible worlds account of the content of experience, it is false that seeing A as six rows has the same content as seeing A as six columns. The relevant sets overlap but are distinct.

Now for the complication mentioned earlier. We should, strictly speaking, be talking about conforming locations rather than conforming worlds, in terms, that is, of a function from a location in a world to truth just when the location is the right way – that is, conforms to the experience – in that world; or, equivalently, in terms of centred worlds, where each centre conforms in its world to the experience.[7] Degree of indeterminacy is then captured in

---

[7] Our appeal to centred worlds here should be distinguished from its use to express a kind of relativism according to which some perceived properties are relative, in one way or another, to perceivers. For detail on this, see Brogaard (2011), and for a paper that gives centring double duty – to capture relativist thoughts and for the ego-centric aspect we are concerned with – see Egan (2006).

terms of the extent of variation between conforming locations. Well, not quite. Perceptual experiences typically represent that things are thus and so in front of you or off to the left, say, at the time of having the experience, and what 'in front of' and 'off to the left' come to is a matter of how things are relative to your body.[8] So, strictly, the location conditions are the locations of people with bodies, where things are the right, conforming way in relation to their bodies.

There is a second reason for making explicit mention of bodies. Plausibly, there is a causal element in the content of experience. The point is obvious in the case of painfully loud sounds and dazzling lights, but, as many have noted, there is reason to think it is ubiquitous. And the causal impacts are represented as being on the perceiver's body.

I have just outlined two advantages of the possible worlds – or, better, possible locations of persons with bodies in worlds – account of the content of experience. But, it seems to me, the decisive reason for favouring the account is that it makes good sense of how we establish whether an experience is veridical, illusory or hallucinatory. We investigate the world the experiencer occupies, and the verdict on whether some experience is veridical, illusory or hallucinatory is driven by what the investigation reveals about the nature of the location the experiencer's body occupies and the body's causal relationships with that nature. Take me at the time of writing these words: an investigation will reveal that the experience I am now having is veridical just if it reveals that my body occupies a location with a desk, computer, etc., in front of me, with the desk, etc., having the right properties and standing in the right causal relationships to my body. The details are famously controversial but the basic picture is not.

Finally, the possible locations of persons with bodies account of content handles the rich, seamless nature of perceptual content in the obvious way. For any given experience, the conforming locations will be alike in ways that reflect the rich, seamless nature of that content – conforming locations will be alike to varying degrees in their spatial, temporal and causal relations to objects which have *all* of colour, shape and extension, and are or are not moving.

5.2 The Attitude to the Content

We noted earlier that the case for saying that perceptual experience has content is akin to that for saying that desire has content. But there is a big difference

---

[8] As Peacocke (1992) notes.

in the relationship to the content. Desires represent how a subject would like things to be but do not 'say' that the world is in fact that way. By contrast, experiences are strongly representational in that they are a kind of constantly renewed account of how things are. You come home late and have forgotten to leave the porch light on. In consequence, you have trouble getting your key in the lock. When someone turns the light on, what was hard becomes easy. And what happens isn't that you get a one-off piece of information as to where the lock is in relation to the key in your hand. For as long as the experience lasts, you are in receipt of a constantly refreshed and updated account of where the lock is in relation to the key in your hand. On this picture, experience is an active state. It is the issuing and continual renewing of an account of how things are. Of course you do not have to accept the account. Typically, you do, and do so without a second thought, but everyone knows about illusions and hallucinations. What is true is that the account delivered by experience is the default account. It is the account you accept absent good reason to the contrary.

In sum, the perceptual experiences of a subject are states of the subject that are the issuings and continual refreshings of an account of how things are, an account which is, for the subject, a default account of how things are. I should emphasise that the experiences are the issuings of the account. They are not something separate on which the subject bases an account. When an object looks to be a certain distance in front of one, its so looking *is* the issuing of the account. The experience in and of itself says that that is how things are. This is why the description of experience collapses into the description of what's putatively experienced.

We can now make sense of the intuitively attractive idea that the nature of an experience is the nature of what's experienced – the transparency or diaphanousness of experience.[9] We know it isn't correct read literally. The natural way to describe the experience one has when subject to, say, the Hering Illusion is in terms of curved vertical lines on the page in front of one, and there are no curved vertical lines on the page in front of one. Rather, that there are curved vertical lines on the page in front of one is an integral part of the account one's visual system is issuing of how things are. The truth in the thesis that experience is diaphanous is that the phenomenology of experience lies in the nature of the account experience issues about how things are. In striving to describe an experience, one can only describe the account of how things are that the experience is issuing.

---

[9] See, e. g., Harman (1990); Moore (1922).

5.3 Have I Left Out the Phenomenology?

I have plenty of company in thinking that the key to understanding the phenomenology of experience lies in understanding aright the diaphanousness of experience, and I have just explained how the version of representationalism I like tells us how to do this. How then could I have left out the feel? All the same, many will insist that I have done exactly that. The sort of example that often motivates this thought runs as follows. You are looking at a hedge. Your experience delivers an account of how things are (in the sense of being the delivering of that account), including how far away the hedge is, how green its leaves are, that it is not moving, and so on. You are confident that you are not under illusion and so believe that the hedge is a certain distance away, has leaves of such and such a colour and so on. You then close your eyes. You have every reason to think that nothing much changed on closing your eyes, and so believe that the hedge is as it was a moment ago. This means, runs the objection, that how you represent the hedge to be remains the same, but there is a big change in the nature of your experience. It follows that all the talk about representation leaves out the feel. Maybe experiences are essentially representational, but there's more to feel than representation plus some kind of affirmation of the content of the representation.

I think this objection overlooks the implications of the highly distinctive way that experiences deliver default accounts of how things are. Let's spell this out, and here we will be referring back to some of what is said in previous sections. First, the account of how things are delivered by experience is essentially rich. There is no such thing as a visual experience that says that there is a hedge in front of one without saying anything at all about how far in front of one it is, what colour it is, how large it is and how things are between it and oneself, etc. What's more, the way an experience urges on one an account of how things are is seamless. A single visual experience says something about colour by saying something about shape, about shape by saying something about extension, about extension by saying something about distance away, about motion by saying something about colour differences, and so on. Further, the account delivered by experience, in addition to being a default account, is pigheaded. It survives a subject's being certain that they are under an illusion or even that they are hallucinating. That's the message of, for example, the Hering Illusion. Everyone reading this chapter will be sure that the vertical lines are not curved. All the same, their experience when subject to the Hering Illusion will be saying to them that the lines are curved. Also, experience nags. As we note above, experience is an active state that continually issues and refreshes its account of how things are. This is why if someone asks you whether the leaves in the middle of the hedge are greener than those near the top, you will have no trouble answering the question while your eyes are open. It is, however, much harder to answer the question when your eyes are shut. In that case, you need to rely on memory and the belief that things have not changed since you closed your eyes. As we might put it, the drip feed of information ceases the moment you close your eyes. Finally, plausibly causal origin is part of what is being drip-fed. When you see the hedge as a certain distance away and a certain shape, part of the account that is being continually issued to you is that the distance away and the shape are, here and now, casually active in producing the account that says that the hedge is a certain distance away and a certain shape. But when you remember the colour and location of the hedge, what you remember is not that the hedge's nature is here and now urging you to accept that its location and colour are thus and so. At most, you remember that the hedge's nature in the recent past urged you to accept that its location and colour were thus and so. In sum, it isn't true that how things are being represented to be can remain the same in the absence of having the visual experience.

I think the 'feel' in visual experience lies in the combination of the fact that the account experience delivers is rich and seamlessly so, is pig-headed, nags, and concerns the current causal role of the relevant features of what's putatively seen. When you shut your eyes in front of that hedge, what happens is that you lose detail immediately, you enter a state that is able to say something about, for example, colour without saying anything about shape, you are no longer in a state that is pig-headed, the nagging stops, and the account being urged on you no longer concerns what the relevant properties are doing to you here and now. Wouldn't being in a state that by its very nature continually urges on one a rich, seamless account of how things are in front of you in terms of shape, colour, distance away, etc., an account that asserts itself even when you are sure it is mistaken, and has as a part that the relevant properties are impacting on you here and now, seem awfully like being in an acquaintance relation with something that has the very features in question? And isn't that the essence of the feel? And isn't that what explains why the sense datum theory was so beguiling?

5.4 How Representationalism Undermines the Knowledge Argument

The short answer is by undermining the fundamental intuition that drives the argument, but, as we will see, there is more to say.

The intuition that drives the knowledge argument is that when Mary leaves the black and white room, she becomes related to instances of properties that are distinct from any she knew about, or could have known about, while in the black and white room. This is the 'she won't say "Ho hum" intuition', if you like.[10] Perhaps the most natural way to express the intuition is by saying that when she leaves the room, she will see something as, say, red for the first time, and seeing something as red is entering the seeing-something-as-having relation to an instance of redness, and it is this very redness that she did not know about before. One philosopher or other may argue that 'seeing as' is not the right term for the relation. Perhaps we need a special notion of direct acquaintance, spelt out in some way or other, or maybe argued to be indefinable. Our philosopher may also say that 'red' isn't the right word for the property. What Mary becomes acquainted with is an instance of some property that bears one or another systematic relationship to being red, a property we might use 'red*' for. But these are points of detail in the present context. What is important in the present context is that the intuition that drives the argument is a *relational* way of thinking about the experience of seeing something as red, and about visual experience more generally. But if representationalism about experience is correct, the relational picture is a tempting but fundamental mistake. The right way to characterise the relation and the right words to use for the property instances are side issues. In the Hering Illusion, the fact that the vertical lines look curved is not to be accounted for in terms of a relationship to an instance of being curved or an instance of being curved*. It is instead a matter of being in a state that is constantly issuing an account of how the lines are that has them as curved. And being in such a state does not require being in a relation to an instance of being curved or of being curved*, any more than believing in the devil requires being in a relation to the devil or to the devil*.

I know from experience that friends of the knowledge argument may concede that the intuition that drives the knowledge argument is mistaken – sometimes in the full-blooded sense of 'concede', and sometimes in the 'for the sake of the argument' sense – but insist that the reply in the previous paragraph leaves untouched another way of thinking of the challenge posed by the knowledge argument.[11] On this way of thinking of the challenge, what matters is the fact that the experiences Mary has on leaving the black and white room are very different from those she has while in the black and white room. This means that her experiences instantiate new properties. This is the case independently

---

[10] Jackson (1986).
[11] And some who are not friends of the argument make a similar point. See, e. g., Byrne (2006).

of whether or not these new properties are properties of something Mary is related to, the issue of the previous paragraph. And, needless to say, the friends go on to point out that Mary did not know what the new experiences were like while in the black and white room, from which it follows, they argue, that the new properties are additions to the kinds of properties envisioned in the physicalist story and so serve to refute physicalism.

It is at this point that we need to be a little forensic about what knowing what it is like comes to. Knowing what X is like can mean knowing the properties of X. That is the obvious meaning to give the phrase when discussing the knowledge argument, for the contention of friends of the argument is that Mary, while in the black and white room, is ignorant of some of the properties of the experiences she will undergo when she leaves the room. However, in that sense, if a representationalism of the kind outlined here is true, it is false that Mary does not know what it is like to see something as, say, red. Or, more precisely, it is false provided physicalism can give an account of what it takes to be in the kinds of representational states we have been talking about, and if physicalism cannot do that, we have no need of the knowledge argument in order to bury physicalism. And, in the broad, we know what physicalism says about representation: to be in such and such a representational state is to be in a state that is sensitive to, and putatively carries information about, features of our world and which helps us achieve our desires.[12] There are many additions and modifications that may be made to this skeleton. Some will talk of design, with perhaps a nod to selectional history; some will talk of isomorphisms between the states that carry the information and the features tracked; some will tell the story in a way that allows brains in vats to represent alike with you and me, others will do the opposite; some will talk of inner maps; some of the language of thought and causal connections between its words and the world; and so it goes. What is more, the account will need to take into account the special features we have urged are distinctive of the way in which perceptual experiences represent. However, all this, and any at all plausible developments of it, are available to Mary while in the black and white room. She will know that people outside the room are in states that play distinctive roles with respect to the surface properties of, for example, ripe tomatoes, and that she herself is never in such a state, and she will know the selectional history of these states, how they allow the people outside the room to group objects together reliably, to detect when fruit is ripe, etc. She will also know, or can know given how smart she is and how much science she knows, that when she leaves the room,

---

[12]   And, of course, this kind of account is attractive regardless of where one stands on physicalism.

she herself will be in such a state. The upshot is that if representationalism about experience is true, physicalists can and should insist that Mary knows what it is like to experience red, in the relevant sense of knowing what it is like.

It is, however, true that there is another sense of knowing what it is like in which she will not know what it is like to be in the kind of representational state that representationalism affirms is having something's looking red to one. This is the sense that Laurence Nemirow and David Lewis talk about, and is the sense in which physicalists can happily grant that Mary, while in the black and white room, does not know what it is like to see something as red.[13] When Mary sees something as red for the first time, she will acquire the ability to recognise being in that state and to imagine and remember being in that state. But before she leaves the black and white room – before, that is, she herself is in that state – she lacks those abilities, despite knowing (or being able to know) what state it is. There is, I should perhaps add, nothing mysterious about this fact. Many abilities require the right causal history – being able to play the piano, for example.

Here is a way to think about it. Some people suffer from face-blindness, prosopagnosia. There is a sense in which these people know what it is like to recognise faces, and a sense in which they do not. They know what it is like in the sense that they know the properties of the state that most of us are in from time to time but they themselves are never in. This explains why they regret the fact that they suffer from prosopagnosia. But they do not know what it is like in the ability sense. They cannot recognise being in that state and cannot imagine or seem to remember being in that state (and words from us who do not suffer from prosopagnosia will not remedy matters).

5.5 The Question That Remains[14]

I might stop here. My remit was to explain how representationalism provides physicalists with a reply to the knowledge argument. There is, however, a question that arises when we ask exactly what the content of colour experience might be, a question that bears directly on an important issue for physicalists concerning what happens to Mary when she leaves the black and white room. If representationalism is true, perceptual experiences are putative sources of information about how things are, with the putative information corresponding to their contents. Indeed, most grant this be they representationalists or not,

---

[13] Lewis (1999); Nemirow (1980).

[14] What happens to the question that remains if one is not a representationalist? It does not go away, or so I argue in Jackson (2016).

though we representationalists insist that we have the best explanation of it.[15] A good question, therefore, is what putative information about how things are is provided by seeing something as being a certain colour. And, of course, this is the putative information that Mary gets when she exits the black and white room. What is more, physicalists have to hold either that Mary gets old information, albeit from new kinds of experiences, or else that she gets mis-information. They cannot afford to say that she gets new information (information proper) about how things are when she sees things as having one or another colour. To say that would contradict their physicalism.

Which way should physicalists jump? To answer this question, we need to ask after the content of colour experiences, because the information – information proper or merely putative – that Mary gets when she leaves the room is given by that content. Now one might be tempted to hold that the right answer to this question, for representationalists anyway, depends on what optical science tells us. Leaving out the frills, the answer will be given by which physical properties of objects typically causally co-vary with colour experiences, and that's a question for science. But, in the sense of 'representation' on which representationalism is a plausible account of the nature of perceptual experience in general and colour experience in particular, the answer does not depend on what science tells us. The key idea behind representationalism about experience, or anyway the kind defended here, is that the phenomenology of experience lies in the nature of the account the experience continually issues and urges on one about how things are. This could hardly be true if the account in question waited on science. The folk know the difference between seeing something as red and seeing it as blue without knowing the relevant science. If representationalism is to give phenomenology its due, the contents it talks about have to be, as it is sometimes put, personal-level contents or available contents. And, to reinforce the point, think of the way, long before the rise of modern science, we were able to acquire a great deal of information via our senses. This reminds us that the ways our perceptual experiences represent things to be – their contents – are available to the folk. Someone might perhaps seek to undermine this last consideration by drawing a sharp contrast between the way experiences represent, for example, shape and distance away, on the one hand, and colour, on the other, arguing that shape and distance away content is available to the folk without their having to read science journals, whereas colour content is not. But this is hard to believe given the already emphasised

---

[15] Part of Armstrong's reason for embracing representationalism (under another name) goes back to this claim, see Armstrong (1961, chs. 7 and 9).

rich, seamless nature of perceptual experience. The way visual experiences represent colour, motion, distance away and shape is all of a piece.

What then is the (available) content of colour experience? I think the answer to this question is provided by the colour solid. The colour solid is a three-dimensional object that represents relationships between colours along the dimensions of hue, brightness (lightness) and saturation. What is more, the relationships are available to the folk. The folk do not need to read science journals to see that the solid gets the relationships between hue, saturation and brightness correct. Reasonable colour vision is enough.[16] Accordingly, the representational contents of colour experiences are, I submit, that seen objects have surface properties standing in the difference and similarity relations represented by the colour solid.[17] That is to say, the account of the nature of the objects we see that colour experiences continually issue is that the objects have surface properties standing in a certain network of similarity and difference relations, along with a metric (the colour solid represents not just difference and similarity but also degree of difference and similarity). Call this network **N**. Look at any given point in the colour solid. What property does the experience you are having represent that point as having? Having the property that stands in that very place in **N**. What then does it take to be a certain colour – that is, to be a colour of such and such a hue, saturation and brightness – it is to have the property, whatever it is, that stands in the relevant place in **N**.

This account of the content of colour experience is inspired by something David Armstrong said many years ago. He said that the concept of colour was the concept of properties of a nature unknown to the perceiver, standing in various difference and similarity relationships. He then went on to argue that the properties that stand in these relationships will turn out to be physical properties, and held that we should identify colours with the physical properties that stand in these relationships, whatever they turn out to be.[18] But having a property that stands in such and such a set of relationships is itself a property. I am suggesting that we should instead identify the colours with *having* the properties that stand in the relationships, not with the properties that in fact stand in the relationships. In a familiar jargon, I am suggesting that the colours are the role properties and not the realiser properties. Instead of saying that redness, for example, is the property that stands in a certain place in **N**, I am

---

[16] Of course, reasonable colour vision does not, *by itself*, allow one to express all this in words.

[17] We are restricting the discussion to surface colour. What to say about, e.g., stained glass and coloured light is being set to one side.

[18] Armstrong (1968, 275).

suggesting that redness is the property of having the property that stands in that certain place.

Why do I resist following Armstrong all the way? It seems to me that anyone sympathetic to representationalism about experience has no choice but to hold that redness, to stick with this example, is the property that seeing an object as red represents it to have. What other property could it be? The property corresponds, therefore, to the content of the experience of seeing something as red. This means that if we identified redness with the property that in fact stands in the complex set of relationships, we would violate the availability requirement on the content of seeing something as red. This is because which property it is that stands in the 'red' place in the complex set of relationships specified by **N** is a matter for science, not something available to the folk.

Any account that specifies a property in terms of a place in a complex set of relationships faces the 'husband–wife' question. It is not enough to specify a husband as someone with a wife, and a wife as someone with a husband. One has, in addition, to point to a feature that differentiates husbands from wives. For some marriages, one can use gender; for some, role in the relationship. For some marriages, there is no suitable differentiating feature, in which case there is, for those marriages, no distinction between husbands and wives. What does the differentiating in the case of the complex relationships between the colours? The answer, I suggest, lies in the fact that the colour solid is asymmetrical.[19] One cannot permute the 'entries' in the colour solid and preserve truth. There is no inverted spectrum exercise that preserves the relationships. That is to say, the differentiation is done by a colour's place in the network (colour in the wide sense, not in the hue sense of course). One might also appeal to familiar facts about which objects have which colours.[20] What differentiates red from green are the familiar, known to the folk, differences in which objects are which colour. However, making this part of the content threatens the connection between representational content and phenomenology. Surely, which objects in our world have one or another colour might have been very different – blood might have been green, the sky might have been yellow, and so on – without there having to be a difference in the nature of seeing something as red or seeing something as blue. By contrast, it is very plausible that one cannot 'shift' a colour's location in the colour solid without changing its colour. Move it further from the core and you increase the saturation, and that's a change in colour (again, in the wide sense of colour, not

---

[19] See Harrison (1967); Hazen (1999).
[20] See, e. g., Lewis (1997).

the hue sense), move it down and you darken it and that's a change in colour, and so on.

We can now tackle the question of whether physicalists should hold that Mary gets old information, or instead that she gets misinformation when she leaves the black and white room. For physicalists, the question is one and the same as the question as to whether or not objects have surface, physical properties that stand in the similarity and difference relations specified in **N**. There are two possibilities. One is that there are no such properties. In that case, Mary gets misinformation when she leaves the black and white room. Colour is an illusion. The other possibility is that there are such properties. In that case, she gets old information. Old information because, while in the black and white room, she will be able to discover all there is to know about the kinds of similarities and differences that obtain between the properties of objects' surfaces. No doubt she will focus on similarities and differences creatures like us are causally sensitive to. For although the similarities and differences themselves are not a function of the way our sense organs work, *which* similarities and differences we are sensitive to is a function of the way our sense organs work.

I am nowadays a supporter of the old information answer. I think the survival and navigational value of having colour experiences make it unlikely that the way colour experiences represent similarities and differences is sufficiently out of kilter with the way things actually are to justify going eliminativist about colour. I also observe, as have many, that the colours objects look to have remain much the same over large variations in viewing conditions – the phenomenon known as colour constancy. This suggests that we are latching onto objective features of the surfaces we are seeing. But, of course, there is a hostage to fortune here.

5.6 Coda

Suppose the surface similarities and differences exist, and that Mary knows this and knows people outside the room have a way of latching on to these similarities and differences akin to the way she herself latches on to the facial patterns that underlie face recognition. She will realise that she stands to people outside the room regarding these similarities and differences somewhat as someone who cannot recognise faces stands to someone like herself who can. Won't she have the 'I do not know what it is like' thought, but in the sense that does not imply ignorance of which properties are instantiated in our world?

6   The Mary-Go-Round

> As it is easier for a theorist to struggle with the most stubborn
> discrepancy than to abandon a favourite system, he has recourse
> to circumstances, which, though they leave precisely the same
> difficulty as before, are at least more complicated, and therefore
> better fitted to hide an inconsistency from the author himself, as
> well as from those whom he addresses.
>
> (Brown 1806: 119–20)

6.1

Frank Jackson's Mary

> is a brilliant scientist who is, for whatever reason, forced to investigate
> the world from a black and white room via a black and white television
> monitor. She specializes in the neurophysiology of vision and acquires, let
> us suppose, all the physical information there is to obtain about what goes
> on when we see ripe tomatoes, or the sky, and use terms like 'red', 'blue', and
> so on. She discovers, for example, just which wave-length combinations
> from the sky stimulate the retina, and exactly how this produces via the
> central nervous system the contraction of the vocal chords and expulsion
> of air from the lungs that results in the uttering of the sentence 'The sky is
> blue' (Jackson 1982: 130).

Now, however, she crosses the threshold of the odourless black and white
room – after a teetotal lifetime nourished on tasteless pap. She passes grace-
fully into a well-lit white windowless room containing a black table. It's quite a
moment. The first thing she sees is a large Bloody Mary on the table. She picks it
up and drinks it down. Then she sees and smells Emil Du Bois-Reymond's rose:

> what conceivable connection is there between specific movements of spe-
> cific atoms in my brain, on the one hand, and on the other hand such

(for me) primordial, indefinable, undeniable facts as these: 'I feel pain, or pleasure; I experience a sweet taste, or smell a rose, or hear an organ, or see something red'. (1874: 28)[1]

She smells a vial of ammonia thoughtfully supplied by C. D. Broad, who observed in 1925 that an 'archangel' with perfect scientific knowledge

> would know exactly what the microscopic structure of ammonia must be; but he would be totally unable to predict that a substance with this structure must smell as ammonia does when it gets into the human nose. The utmost that he could predict on this subject would be that certain changes would take place in the mucous membrane, the olfactory nerves and so on. But he could not possibly know that these changes would be accompanied by the appearance of a smell in general or of the peculiar smell of ammonia in particular, unless someone told him so or he had smelled it for himself (1925: 71).

Plainly Mary learns many new things about the nature of reality, concrete reality, although she's already omniscient when it comes to current physics and neurophysiology. For she learns what it is like, experientially, for someone like her to see red, taste a mixture of vodka and tomato juice, smell ammonia and a rose, feel drunk. She learns that a Bloody Mary looks like *this* (colourwise) and tastes like *this* to someone with her physical constitution who is in the physical state she is in when she drinks it (the first 'this' denotes the experiential-qualitative character of the colour-experience she has on looking at the Bloody Mary, the second denotes the experiential-qualitative character of the taste-experience she has on drinking it). She learns that it makes her feel like *this* (drunk) twenty minutes later. There is as al-Ghazālī says

> a great difference between your knowing the definition of drunkenness – viz., that it is a term denoting a state resulting from the predominance of vapors which rise from the stomach to the centres of thought – and your actually being drunk. (*c.* 1106: §82)

And the difference is – of course – a difference in what you know about concrete reality. For these feelings are indubitably concretely real features of an indubitably concretely real entity – herself. It appears that the only way to avoid the conclusion is to beg the question by simply assuming that experience is not part of concrete reality.

---

[1] When I cite a work I give the date of first publication, or sometimes the date of composition, while the page reference is to the edition listed in the bibliography. In the case of quotations from languages other than English I give a reference to a standard translation but do not always use precisely that translation.

6.2

Mary's existence until now has been painless. We hope that this will continue. We spare her William James's toothache, and grant her a vision of his cloudless sky as she steps now into the open air:

> a blind man may know all *about* the sky's blueness, and I may know all *about* your toothache, conceptually … but so long as he has not felt the blueness, nor I the toothache, our knowledge, wide as it is, of these realities, will be hollow and inadequate. Somebody must *feel* blueness, somebody must *have* toothache, to make human knowledge of these matters real. (1890: 2.7)

We may also spare her Jacobs's headache, and leave childbirth for later:

> consider a doctor who has been lucky enough never to have suffered a headache in his life. [According to] the materialists … such a fortunate physician would not only know more than his patients about headaches, i.e., the relational contexts in which headaches are set; *he could know all there was to know about headaches without ever having had one.* Take another case … a male physician could know all there was to know about [childbirth]. It would be difficult to convince two mothers of this. (1937: 604, my emphasis)

Many have made the point. Russell made it in 1927:

> it is obvious that a man who can see knows things which a blind man cannot know; but a blind man can know the whole of physics. Thus the knowledge which other men have and he has not is not a part of physics. (1927a: 389)

It's a one-sentence point, or at best a one-paragraph point, a point to be made in passing, a starting datum. Here is Thomas Huxley:

> take the … feeling of redness. Physical science tells us that it commonly arises as a consequence of molecular changes propagated from the eye to a certain part of the substance of the brain … Let us suppose the process of physical analysis pushed so far that one could view the last link of this chain of molecules … and know all that is physically knowable about them. Well, even in that case, we should be just as far from being able to include the resulting phenomenon of consciousness, the feel of redness, within the bounds of physical science, as we are at present. (1886/1892: 166–7)

Schrödinger put it (somewhat wordily) as follows:

> the sensation of colour cannot be accounted for by the physicist's objective picture of light-waves. Could the physiologist account for it, if he had fuller knowledge than he has of the processes in the retina and the nervous processes set up by them in the optical nerve bundles and in the brain? I do not think so. We could at best attain to an objective knowledge of what nerve fibres are excited and in what proportion, perhaps even to know exactly the processes they produce in certain brain cells – whenever your mind registers the sensation of yellow in a particular direction or domain of our field of vision. But even such intimate knowledge would not tell us anything about the sensation of colour, more particularly of yellow in this direction – the same physiological processes might conceivably result in a sensation of sweet taste, or anything else. (1956/ 1967: 154–5)[2]

Eddington might have had Mary in mind in 1939, when, talking of the physical sciences, he noted that

> ideally all our knowledge of the physical universe could have been reached by visual sensation alone – in fact, by the simplest form of visual sensation, colourless and non-stereoscopic. (1939: 197)

---

[2] Feigl agrees: 'in the case of the congenitally blind who by a cataract operation suddenly attain eyesight, the experience of colors and (visual) shapes is a complete novelty. Suppose that all of mankind had been completely blind up to a certain point in history, and then acquired vision. Presupposing physical determinism we should … in principle be able to predict the relevant neural and behavioral processes, and thus to foretell all the discriminatory and linguistic behavior which depends upon the new cortical processes (which correspond to the emergent, novel qualities of experience). What is it then that we would not or could not know at the time of the original prediction? I think the answer is obvious. We would not and could not know (then) the color experiences by acquaintance; i.e., (1) we would not have them; (2) we could not imagine them; (3) we could not recognize (or label) them as "red", "green", etc., even if by some miracle we suddenly had them, except by completely new stipulations of designation rules' (1958/1967: 49). 'A congenitally blind scientist equipped with modern electronic instruments … could establish the (behavioristic) psychology of vision for subjects endowed with eyesight. The blind scientist could thus confirm all sorts of statements about visual sensations and qualities – which in his knowledge would be represented by "hypothetical constructs." But if *ex hypothesi* all connections of the subjective raw feels with the intersubjectively accessible facts are radically severed, then such raw feels are, I should say by definition, excluded from the scope of science' (18).

Locke in 1689 imagined 'a child … kept in a place, where he never saw any other but black and white, till he were a man' and had, in consequence, 'no ideas of scarlet or green' (1689/1975: 2.1.6).

6.3

So Mary learns something completely new about concrete reality. If you doubt it, ask her. 'Is there something you know now about reality as a whole – about the human animal that you are yourself, and other such animals – that you didn't know before you left the black and white room?' She will quite certainly say Yes. (She is not, I take it, a philosopher. Even if she were, she'd have to be a very special kind of post-1960 analytic philosopher of mind, fatally precommitted to a philosophical view that required her to say No, in order to say No.)

> When she is let out of the black-and-white room or given a color television, she will learn what it is like to see something red … This is rightly described as *learning* – she will not say 'ho, hum'. (Jackson 1986: 291)

How may we characterize the new things she learns about the nature of concrete reality? We can say if we like (1) that she acquires completely new knowledge about certain features of concrete reality about which she already knew a great deal: certain specific sorts of neural states. Alternatively, we can replace 'certain specific sorts of neural states' in the last sentence with 'conscious experience', and say (2) that she acquires completely new knowledge about a feature of concrete reality about which she already knew a lot: conscious experience, and in particular visual experience. (She already knew about black-grey-white visual experience, now she learns about red visual experience.) Alternatively, we can say (3) that she acquires knowledge about the nature of certain features of concrete reality about which she knew nothing at all: the experiential-qualitative character, considered just as such, of the (concretely real) occurrence that consists in her seeing something red, or something blue.[3]

---

[3] Strictly speaking one should say the experiential-qualitative character *for her*, because – on the hugely plausible assumption that different human beings standing together may have different colour experiences on seeing something they all agree to be red – there is simply no such thing as *the* experiential-qualitative character of seeing something red, even if we add 'in standard lighting conditions'. By the same token, the expressions 'red-experience' can't be supposed to name a single particular qualitative type of experience. I will put this complication aside (see Strawson 1989).

All these three remarks are true, suitably interpreted. None of them is seriously in question. Philosophers question them, but nothing follows from this, because philosophers constantly question things that aren't seriously in question. The claim that something is controversial has zero dialectical force in philosophy, although it's often made by referees rejecting papers submitted to learned journals. This is because there is as Louise Antony says 'no banality so banal that no philosopher will deny it' (2007: 114). Even when we put this point aside, everything is controversial in philosophy.

6.4

Let me now set out the central issue as I see it. I take it, to begin, that materialism or physicalism is the view that

[1] Everything that concretely exists is wholly physical.[4]

The Mary-carousel rotates round a mistake shared on both sides.[5] The mistake consists in the endorsement of a highly substantive thesis about physics, the thesis that

[2] Physics can (in principle) give a full or exhaustive characterization of the nature of the physical.

[1] and [2] entail the view I call *physics-alism*: 'the view – the faith – that

[3] the nature or essence of all concrete reality can in principle be fully captured in the terms of physics'.[6]

  One can re-express [3] in a way that matches the wording of [2]

[3] physics can in principle give a full or exhaustive characterization of the nature of everything that concretely exists.

The mistake, on both sides of the Mary-go-round, is to turn materialism/physicalism into physics-alism by adding [2] to [1] to produce [3]. Endorsement of [2] leads to the false identification of [1] physicalism with [3] physics-alism.

---

[4] I follow Lewis (1996) in using 'materialism' and 'physicalism' interchangeably, although there is more to the physical than matter.

[5] This is not to say that the mistake is made by all participants in the debate (my exposition doesn't directly track the actual debate).

[6] Strawson 2006/2008: 54; cf. Strawson 2004: 292. The 'in principle' licenses us to look beyond current physics to 'completed physics', understood as the best physics that human beings can possibly come up with.

On one side of the roundabout we confront the adamantine truth, already recorded, that on leaving the black and white room

[4] Mary learns something new about the nature of concrete reality

in having a red-experience (an indubitably real concrete phenomenon) that has the experiential-qualitative character (an indubitably real concrete phenomenon) it does have. (If you doubt this, ask her.) This couples with the widely agreed fact that

[5] physics cannot characterize the nature of red-experience (colour experience in general)

to produce the mistaken conclusion that

[6] Mary raises a difficult and seemingly insoluble problem for physicalism

by showing that there is an undeniably real part of concrete reality that physics can't characterize.

On the other side of the roundabout, [2] couples with the endorsement of the truth of [1], physicalism, to produce the mistaken conclusion that (in some sense or another) [4] is false – that Mary does not learn something new about concrete reality when she leaves the black and white room.

Two mistakes. The solution is simple. Give up [2]. Nothing in [1], physicalism, requires any attachment to [2], a thesis about the descriptive reach of physics. It's vital for physicalists to give up [2] because it is certainly false if physicalism is true. It's equally vital for those who reject physicalism to give up [2], because their rejection of physicalism can have no real force if it relies on [2]. If it relies on [2] it begs the question: it defines physicalism/materialism in such a way that it can't be true.

What if we replace 'physics' by 'the physical sciences' in [2], to get

[2] the *physical sciences* can (in principle) give a full or exhaustive characterization of the nature of the physical?

I will argue later (in 6.10) that the fundamental point remains untouched, and continue for the moment to focus on physics.

6.5

The tragedy of the debate is that the mistake is locked into large parts of it by a tendency (either covert or overtly acknowledged) to think of [2] as something like a thesis about meaning, something like

[7] '*x* is physical' entails '*x*'s nature is (in principle) fully characterizable in the terms of physics'.

The tragedy is that such an extraordinary amount of time has been wasted. [7] is provably false (see 6.11), and the fact that Mary learns something new about concrete reality when she leaves the black and white room (she learns what it is for her red-experience to have the experiential-qualitative character it does have) is, as remarked, a one-sentence point to be noted in passing, not something to be argued over for decades.

Papineau's proposal that we 'understand *physical* as simply meaning *nonmental*' (2001: 12) is a striking instance of the malaise in the debate. It's a peculiar proposal to make when one is trying to work out whether – or argue that – the mental is in fact physical, and it's notable that Papineau doesn't flinch from the consequence, claiming that if we make this move we can reach 'the worthwhile conclusion that the mental must be identical with the non-mental' (12) – i.e. conclude to the truth of a contradiction. The malaise also gives rise to the worst sort of casuistry, and a terminological morass. A terminological morass always develops when people are unable to give up treasured but indefensible positions.

6.6

If this line of thought is right, the mistake on both sides is – to repeat – to confuse materialism or physicalism with physics-alism. The mistake is a mistake whether it leads materialists to deny a certain truth (that on leaving the room, Mary learns something completely new about the nature of concrete reality, and hence, if materialism is true, about the nature of physical reality) or whether it leads those who reject materialism to beg the question against materialism. It is a distinctively twentieth- and twenty-first-century mistake.[7]

On one side of the merry-go-round we find the younger Jackson on a shining steed. The younger Jackson is initially disposed in favour of the view that [1] materialism is true, but he takes the case of Mary to show that it's false. This is because he accepts [2]. His problem arises because he also quite rightly accepts that

[8] colour experience (as ordinarily conceived) is real, a concretely existing phenomenon

---

[7] If Mary were God and souls were brains, we might implicate the seventeenth century: 'THEODORE: Oh, oh, Aristes! God knows pain, pleasure and the rest. But he does not feel these things. He knows pain, *since he knows what that modification of the soul is in which pain consists* … But he does not feel it … To know pain … is not to feel it. ARISTES: … But to feel it is to know it, is it not? THEODORE: No indeed, since God does not feel it in the least, and yet he knows it perfectly' (Malebranche 1688/1997: 34).

– which together with [1] entails that

[9] colour experience (as ordinarily conceived) is wholly physical –

and he is rightly clear on the point that [5] physics cannot characterize the nature of colour experience (as ordinarily conceived); from which it follows that [2] is false: physics cannot after all give an exhaustive characterization of the nature of the physical. His mistake, on these terms, and as remarked, is to

[1] *Materialism* or *physicalism*: everything that concretely exists is wholly physical in nature.

[2] Physics can give an exhaustive characterization of the nature of the physical.

[3] Physics can give an exhaustive characterization of the nature of everything that concretely exists.

[4] Mary learns something new about concrete reality when she leaves the black and white room.

[5] Physics cannot characterize the nature of colour experience.

[6] Mary raises a difficult and perhaps insoluble problem for physicalism.

[7] 'x is physical' entails 'x's nature is in principle fully characterizable in the terms of physics'.

[8] Colour experience is real, a concretely existing phenomenon.

[9] Colour experience is wholly physical.

[10] Physicalism doesn't entail physics-alism.

accept [2]. [8], [9] and [5] entail the falsity of [1] only given [2]. Younger – earlier – Jackson needs to give up [2], which is certainly false if materialism is true. He can then reject [6], the idea that Mary raises a problem for physicalism, while continuing to accept both [1] and [8]: while continuing to be both a materialist (and in any case a genuine monist) and a genuine realist about colour experience. He can also accept [9] and [5], which entail the falsity of [2]. All will then be well. It will be apparent that [6] is false – that Mary doesn't pose a difficult problem for materialism/physicalism, let alone an insoluble one. All will be well because [6] is false: [1] doesn't entail [2], and [2] is certainly false if [1] is true. We can express the point with a new numbered proposition.

[10] Physicalism isn't – doesn't entail – physics-alism.

There is of course a sense in which younger Jackson isn't making a mistake. He isn't making a mistake insofar as his argument is directed against a certain conception of physicalism (quite widespread among analytic philosophers of mind) according to which true physicalism is physics-alism (or entails it). If physicalism *were* physics-alism, Jackson would be right that [6] Mary raises a difficult and seemingly insoluble problem for physicalism. This is the Mary-go-round – unless it's a see-saw.

6.7

Let me make a clarificatory remark about [8] (it should be unnecessary, but these are troubled times). It is that [8] incorporates *genuine* realism about colour experience – *real* realism about colour experience, and indeed conscious experience in general. I call this 'real realism about conscious experience' because some philosophers who claim to be realists about conscious experience are really no such thing.

What is it to be a real realist about conscious experience? One simple way to convey it is to say that it's to take colour experience, or taste experience, or experience of pain, considered generally and just as such, i.e. just as subjective feeling, to be exactly what one took it to be – knew it to be in having it – before one did any philosophy: when one was six, for example, or ten, or fifteen. (Perhaps one was as a child given food whose taste one didn't like, or asked a friend what something tasted like, or whether they liked the taste. Perhaps one looked at a bright light with one's eyes closed and experienced reddish-orange, and then covered one's eyes with one's hands and watched the reddish-orange dim to black. Perhaps one wondered, as children often do, vividly aware as they are of the sense in which experience is essentially private, whether one's brother, sister, or friend saw colours just as one did oneself.)[8]

I think this is a sufficient characterization of real realism about conscious experience, but it may also help to characterize it as the view of conscious experience that is shared in all essentials by (to take a small sample) Block, Chalmers, Chomsky, Fodor, Kripke, Levine, Lockwood, McGinn, Nagel, Parfit and Searle; not to mention all philosophers prior to about 1915, and almost all

---

[8] See e.g. Strawson 2015: 218–19. Children make many experiments with experience, squeezing their eyeballs to see double, rubbing their closed eyes to 'see stars', blocking and unblocking their ears, spinning round until they're dizzy, then stopping and watching the world swirling, fully aware that it's their experience, not the world, that is swirling. They're well aware that objects that have a constant colour appear to be different colours in different lights. They know that their faces and the faces of their friends look a different colour in daylight and under a neon light in a bathroom mirror. They're fully competent with the general conception of experience that appreciation of these phenomena involves (the only conception of experience that concerns us at present) whether or not they can be said to possess this conception in any linguistically expressible form.

philosophers today who are not analytic philosophers of mind. Scientifically informed real realists about conscious experience learn many remarkable facts from psychologists, facts about the neurophysiology of conscious experience, for example, or the 'filling-in' that characterizes visual experience, or 'change blindness', or 'inattentional blindness'. They also learn that physical objects aren't coloured in the way we standardly suppose them to be; and so on. But their basic *general* understanding of what colour experience or pain experience (etc.), considered as subjective experience, remains exactly the same as it was before they did any philosophy. It remains, in other words, wholly correct, grounded in the fundamental respect in which to have experience is already to know what it is – however little one reflects about it. There is a fundamental respect in which *the having is the knowing*. This is because the knowing is just – just is – the having. It's (non-discursive) knowledge 'by acquaintance', a fundamental kind of knowing. It has nothing to do with introspection. Spiders have this kind of knowledge just as we do – assuming that spiders have experience.

6.8

At this point the word 'know' may start to cause trouble. When we have to do with Mary we have to bear in mind that there is 'a sense of "knowing" in which, when you have an experience, there is no difference between the experience and knowing that you have it', where this includes knowing what it is like (Russell 1940: 49).[9] Some think that

> [P] all knowledge of *how things are* is knowledge *that p*

where *p* is some proposition; and that this rules out this Russellian sense of 'know'. I think that there are at least two ways of rebutting this idea. One can [i] deny P or [ii] accept P and show that it doesn't rule out knowledge in the current Russellian sense.

Reply [i] is blunt. Suppose I'm now having a certain taste experience. In so doing I have knowledge of how things are in the world. I know something about the nature of a concretely real phenomenon which is of course a wholly physical phenomenon if materialism is true. Which concretely real phenomenon?

---

[9] Some may say that one can know that one is having an experience without knowing what it is like, but even if this claim is defensible it isn't what Russell has in mind. Some think that the expression '*x* knows that …' entails a capacity for conceptually articulated discursive thought. So be it, as long as it is allowed that we can say something true – true *sans phrase* – when we say that the dog knows that the cat is in the tree.

The concretely real phenomenon that consists in my having a certain experience with a certain experiential-qualitative character. This knowledge is not knowledge that can be put into words in such a way that it is fully communicable to others, and if we suppose (however oddly) that it follows from this that it's not propositional knowledge, then it's not propositional knowledge.[10] But it is still knowledge. In this case I know how certain things are in the world.

Reply [ii] accepts P. Suppose I'm eating something x, and experiencing what x tastes like (to me). I know that eating x causes me (now) to experience *this* – where *this* refers to (the experiential-qualitative character of) my current gustatory sensation. This sensation is of course a concretely real phenomenon, and therefore a physical phenomenon, if physicalism is true, and in experiencing it I *ipso facto* acquire knowledge of how things are in concrete reality. I know the nature of the wholly physical phenomenon of this experience's having this experiential-qualitative character. In having this experience I know *that* this experience is like *this*, although I don't think it out in these terms. And although the content of this knowledge is in a clear sense not communicable to others, it seems impeccably propositional.[11]

Should we be unsettled by the fact that we have to divide knowledge into knowledge that is communicable to others and knowledge that isn't? Certainly not. On the contrary: any general theory of things that had the consequence that this division wasn't both correct and necessary would be *ipso facto* refuted. Its indispensability follows immediately from simple facts about the nature of language, and about all those respects in which experience is, as we naturally say, 'private': all those respects in which the precise experiential-qualitative character of one's experience is known to oneself alone.

6.9

We have, as remarked, ten propositions (they overlap in various ways, and [7] is a version of [2]):

[1] *Materialism* or *physicalism*: everything that concretely exists is wholly physical.
[2] Physics can give an exhaustive characterization of the nature of the physical.

---

[10] I raise the issue of communicability because it has been thought to be relevant in the Mary debate.
[11] Does the spider know *that* its experience is like *this* as it has it? Certainly: only terminological habit can make it seem otherwise.

[3] Physics can give an exhaustive characterization of the nature of everything that concretely exists.

[4] Mary learns something new about concrete reality when she leaves the
black and white room.

[5] Physics cannot characterize the nature of colour experience.

[6] Mary raises a difficult and perhaps insoluble problem for physicalism.

[7] 'x is physical' entails 'x's nature is in principle fully characterizable in the
terms of physics'.

[8] Colour experience is real, a concretely existing phenomenon.

[9] Colour experience is wholly physical.

[10] Physicalism doesn't entail physics-alism.

I accept [1], [4], [5] and [8]–[10]. I know that accepting [1] – being a physicalist – doesn't require me to be in any way irrealist about conscious experience
because I know that being a physicalist doesn't require me to accept [3] that
physics can give an exhaustive characterization of the nature of concrete reality.
I accept [8] unconditionally, because its truth is certain, as Descartes observed
in his *Second Meditation*. [1] and [8] entail [9], I take [5] to be beyond serious
question, and [1] and [5] entail [10].

One way to put the problem, plainly, is as a disagreement about the meaning
of the word 'physical'. I've always taken 'physical' to be a natural-kind term.[12]
It's a term that denotes a fundamental kind of stuff whose nature we may not
fully know, and plainly do not fully know (ask the physicists).[13] This puts me
in conflict with Jackson when he says that Mary in the black and white room
can acquire '*all the physical information* there is to obtain about what goes
on when we see ripe tomatoes' (1982: 130, my emphasis). The trouble is that
Jackson equates 'all the physical information' with 'all the information expressible in the terms of physics, or more generally the physical sciences', and this

---

[12] Strawson 1994: 1. Compare Stoljar (2001), who distinguishes the 'object-based' conception
of the physical (which connects with the idea that 'physical' is a natural-kind term) from the
'theory-based' conception (which connects with the idea that 'physical' is to be defined by
reference to physics).

[13] Do we know at least that to be physical is to be spatiotemporal? A number of leading
physicists think, with Kant, that reality – physical reality – is not fundamentally
spatiotemporal. Do we know what spatiotemporality is? Many think not. Does physicalism
exclude a view like panpsychism? No, as David Lewis observes: 'a thesis that says [that]
panpsychistic materialism … is impossible … is more than just materialism' (1983b: 36). To
hold [1] is to hold (at least) that there is one kind of fundamental stuff – call it X – and that
physics is indeed a theory about X that has some real grip on X's nature (however partial)
given which it genuinely represents the nature of X in certain fundamental respects. Thus the
periodic table, the inverse square law, the mass-energy equivalence, Schrödinger's equation,
Dirac's equation, etc., cotton on to and genuinely represent features of X.

equation makes it impossible for someone who is a real realist about conscious experience to count as a physicalist. This is a startling result for a great host of physicalists like myself who are real realists about conscious experience, whether or not they follow Russell when he says (correctly if physicalism is true – see 6.9) that 'we know nothing about the intrinsic quality of *physical events*' – nothing about the intrinsic non-structural nature of physical events – '*except when these are mental events that we directly experience*' (1956: 153, my emphasis). In other terms: it directly begs the question.

One way to bring out the mistake is to temporarily endorse Jackson's way of understanding 'all the physical information'. One can then say that the mistake is to confuse 'all the *physical information*' (understood in Jackson's way) with 'all the *information about the physical*', i.e. all the information about the wholly concrete reality that we have to do with when we consider – or indeed have – colour experience.[14] To be a real materialist is precisely to claim, in a way startling to many, that *conscious experience as ordinarily and realistically understood is wholly physical*. This is what is so dramatic about materialism, real materialism, materialism that – from Democritus to Hobbes to all those of us who are real materialists today – knows that one cannot plausibly deny the reality of 'full technicolour' conscious experience, conscious experience as ordinarily understood, and therefore has to take conscious experience so understood to be wholly physical if one is to be a materialist at all. This is what is so exciting – and enlightening – about materialism, when one thinks through its consequences for one's view of the world. This is what 'materialism' always meant before the twentieth century (perhaps there are a few exceptions in the nineteenth century – I'm not sure). This is what 'materialism' continued to mean to most philosophers until about 1960,[15] and it's what it still means outside certain extremely narrow academic enclaves. 'Materialists' are

---

[14] 'There is a strong tension between a descriptively committed [or strictly-physical-science-grounded, or Jacksonian] use of the term "physical" and a less descriptively committed, natural-kind-term-like … use' (Strawson 1994: 55). This receives a particularly striking expression in Maxwell (1978). Maxwell, a physicalist who is also a real realist about conscious experience, proposes to call his view 'nonmaterialist physicalism', and explains his terminological choice as follows: 'it is nonmaterialist in that it does not attempt to eliminate or in any way deemphasize the importance of the "truly mental." On the contrary, it accords central roles to consciousness, "private experience," subjectivity, "raw feels," "what it's like to be something"' (365). I think this is another bad terminological choice, if only because almost all materialists through the ages have been outright realists, real realists, about the 'truly mental'; but it is a very good illustration of the tension.

[15] Even as the increasing notoriety of 'philosophical behaviourism' (*not* behaviourism in psychology) was encouraging the view that materialism was eliminativist with respect to conscious experience.

understood to deny that there is any sort of non-physical mind or soul, and are disparaged by religious believers for that reason. They're certainly not understood to deny the existence of conscious experience as ordinarily understood.

The flagship materialist or physicalist thesis, in sum, is precisely that *consciousness – real consciousness – is wholly physical*. This is what Hobbes meant in 1651, what Cavendish meant in 1664, what Toland meant in 1704, what Collins meant in 1707, what Priestley meant in 1777 – to name only a very few. It's what Feigl meant in 1958 (to come closer to the present) and Maxwell in 1978; along with Planck and Schrödinger, no doubt, and Einstein, and Heisenberg, and all twentieth-century physicists who took it that the world was wholly physical but never for a moment thought that conscious experience was not what it seemed to be. The idea that materialism/physicalism creates any sort of doubt about the reality of conscious experience as characterized in 6.6 above, any need to think that there is some fundamental sense in which it is not what it seems, is a very recent aberration in philosophy, although it is now deeply entrenched.[16] It is also wholly unwarranted, as I will shortly argue.

6.10

I think it's important to see that [2] is false even when one replaces 'physics' by 'completed physics' or some similar phrase. It might possibly become true if we replaced 'physics' by 'God's physics' (in this chapter 'God' is omniscient, but not omnipotent, nor a creator). In that case [5] would be false (given [1] that physicalism is true), for God's unimaginable physics would inevitably have the resources to characterize the nature of colour experience. When we talk about physics or completed physics, however, we have human physics in mind, or at least non-divine physics. It's a theory that consists of equations, equations with which we track the structure of some of the fundamental ways in which concrete reality appears to us under certain conditions of investigation, and presumably also track the structure of concrete reality is in itself.

I'll develop this last point by considering the younger Jackson's opponents in the light of the ten propositions. These philosophers appear to fill a large arc on the other side of the merry-go-round. I don't know all their positions, and I couldn't respond to them all even if I did, but the central issue is I think simple.

---

[16] Albeit only in a tiny community of analytic philosophers of mind. As Feigl says, 'scholars cathect certain ideas so strongly and their outlook becomes so ego involved that they erect elaborate barricades of defenses, merely to protect their pet ideas from the blows (or the slower corrosive effects) of criticism' (1958/1967: 6).

6.11

Are the younger Jackson's opponents real realists about conscious experience, or are they (covertly or overtly) eliminativists? I think it's unlikely that they're real realists, whatever they may say. There are, however, many of them, and I don't know all their views. Still, almost all of them assume the truth of [1], physicalism, as I do, and accordingly take it that they need to show that [6] is false.[17]

How can they do this, on the present terms of discussion? They can do it by denying [2], [8] or [5]. As far as I know, almost all of them accept [2] – they think that physicalism is or entails physics-alism – and I will stick to those that do.[18] That leaves [8] and [5].

As remarked, I don't know all the positions that have been taken up in this debate, but some philosophers do finish up by denying [8]. They are likely to deny that they deny it, claiming to be realists about conscious experience. But then they will have to deny [5]. And in holding, contrary to [5], that physics can characterize the nature of colour experience, they will show either that they have no idea what physics is, or that they are not real realists about conscious experience after all.

The trouble is that the mistake has already been made: endorsing [2], the central axle of the Mary-go-round. The correct response was made long ago, when it was a commonplace that [2] was false. When Russell said (in another passage from 1927) that

> a blind man could know the whole of physics, but he could not know what things look like to people who can see, nor what is the difference between red and blue as seen. He could know all about wave-lengths, but people knew the difference between red and blue as seen before they knew anything about wave-lengths. The person who knows physics and can see knows that a certain wave-length will give him a sensation of red, but this knowledge is not part of physics. (1927b: 182)

---

[17] All those who favour the 'ability account' are eliminativists (see e.g. Nemirow 1980; Lewis 1999 [originally 1988]; for criticism see Coleman 2009b). They may protest that they're reductionists, not eliminativists. It is not, however, hard to show that in some cases – of which this is one – a view that is formally speaking reductionist (and to that extent not eliminativist) is in fact eliminativist. See e.g. Strawson 2018: 134–6.

[18] Some may also think that there are irreducibly phenomenal descriptions or conceptualizations of concrete reality (see e.g. Papineau 2002), but this is compatible with accepting [2] (it may encounter difficulties when asked to provide an account of how those descriptions and conceptualization are available, and of why they are appropriate).

He didn't for a moment think that it followed that physicalism (as currently defined) was false.[19] For he already knew – along with Poincaré, along with R. W. Sellars and the critical realists, along with Eddington, Whitehead and hundreds of others – about the fundamental respects in which physics is (necessarily and by its very nature) silent on the nature of concrete reality – even if physicalism is true. He knew that physics gives us no positive descriptive characterization of the nature or stuff of concrete reality insofar as that nature or stuff essentially involves something more than the structural characteristics that physics discerns in it. It gives us no positive descriptive characterization of the structure-transcendent stuff of the physical, the stuff that has to exist if the mathematical structures that physics discerns are to have concrete reality at all. Here is one among many quotations on this subject from Russell:

> Physics is mathematical, not because we know so much about the physical world, but because we know so little: it is only its mathematical properties that we can discover.[20]

That is all we can discover about the physical through physics, although we can know more about it in having conscious experience: 'we know nothing about the intrinsic quality of physical events except when these are mental events that we directly experience' (1956: 153). Descartes made a related point in his *Sixth Meditation* –

> all the properties … of corporeal things … which I clearly and distinctly understand are … comprised within the subject matter of pure mathematics (1641/1985: 2.55)

– although he did not, perhaps, understand its full implications (e.g. with regard to our knowledge of space).

We confront *the silence of physics* –

---

[19] Russell often calls himself a 'neutral monist', but his terminology is fluid and complex, and he can equally well be read as a physicalist – a sensible physicalist, i.e. one who is a real realist about conscious experience. See e.g. Stubenberg 2016. Landini concludes that Russell is both a physicalist and a neutral monist (2011: 280, 291, 297). As I understand it, there is a sense in which Russell's neutral monism is epistemological rather than ontological. The idea is that both *mind* and *matter* are constructions out of the given: 'sensations'. The reason he doesn't in his own eyes fail to be a neutral monist in taking sensations as basic is that he takes mind (mentality) to be something that essentially involves some sort of intelligence and 'mnemic' capacity, and on this view *sensations are not intrinsically mental phenomena*. (Russell's views change, and there is much more to say.)

[20] Russell 1927a: 125. Newman famously pointed out to Russell that we take physics to reveal more than mathematical structure, and Russell immediately agreed (Newman 1928; Russell 1928/1978).

[11] physics is silent about certain fundamental aspects of the nature of concrete reality.

The point – equally obvious to Newton – has recently been much discussed. To
understand it is to see not only that there is no reason to think that [2] is true,
but also that [2] is certainly false. It is certainly false if physicalism is true, and
it would be no less false if some version of dualism were true. There is accordingly no impediment of any sort to holding (as I do) both that

[4] Mary learns a new fact about concrete reality when she leaves the room

and [1] that physicalism is true.
  Here is Russell's final (1959) statement of the point:

> It is not always realized how exceedingly abstract is the information that
> theoretical physics has to give. It lays down certain fundamental equations
> which enable it to deal with the logical structure of events, while leaving it
> completely unknown what is the intrinsic [logical-structure-transcendent]
> character of the events that have the structure. We only know the intrinsic
> character of events when they happen to us [in having conscious experi-
> ence]. Nothing whatever in theoretical physics enables us to say anything
> about the intrinsic character of events elsewhere. They may be just like the
> events that happen to us [in having conscious experience],[21] or they may be
> totally different in strictly unimaginable ways. All that physics gives us is
> certain equations giving abstract properties of their changes. But as to what
> it is that changes, and what it changes from and to – as to this, physics is
> silent.[22]

6.12

'Your point about the silence of physics is too quick. Mary not only knows
everything there is to know about physics. She's also a neuroscientist, and
we may take it that she also knows all there is to know about all the physical
sciences in general, "physics, chemistry, biology, neuroscience and the like"
(Jackson in press a). These theories are not all as silent as physics.'

---

[21] Here Russell acknowledges that panpsychism may be true.
[22] Russell 1959: 17–18. I've inserted 'logical-structure-transcendent' after Russell's first use of
'intrinsic' because there's no reason to deny that the structure of matter is one of its intrinsic
characteristics (it's only a terminological matter). I've added 'in having conscious experience'
after 'we only know the intrinsic character of events when they happen to us' because this is
what Russell has in mind, as he makes clear in many other places.

Perhaps not – but it's plain that none of them, even perfectly mastered, will be able to enlighten Mary in the black and white room when it comes to the question of what it is like to see red. In this fundamental respect the silence of the physical sciences is as perfect as the silence of physics. C. D. Broad's 'mathematical archangel' was a consummate chemist and biologist as well as a physicist.

Nor should we restrict ourselves to seeing red. The point holds for all conscious experience. Like the admirable T. H. Huxley

> I do not wish to crow unduly over my humble cousin the orang, but in the aesthetic province, as in that of the intellect, I am afraid he is nowhere. I doubt not he would detect a fruit amid a wilderness of leaves where I could see nothing; but I am tolerably confident that he has never been awestruck, as I have been, by the dim religious gloom, as of a temple devoted to the earthgods, of the tropical forest which he inhabits. Yet I doubt not that our poor long-armed and short-legged friend, as he sits meditatively munching his durian fruit, has something behind that sad Socratic face of his which is utterly 'beyond the bounds of physical science'. Physical science may know all about his clutching the fruit and munching it and digesting it, and how the physical titillation of his palate is transmitted to some microscopic cells of the gray matter of his brain. But the feelings of sweetness and of satisfaction which, for a moment, hang out their signal lights in his melancholy eyes, are as utterly outside the bounds of physics as is the 'fine frenzy' of a human rhapsodist. Does Mr. Lilly really believe that, putting me aside, there is any man with the feeling of music in him who disbelieves in the reality of the delight which he derives from it, because that delight lies outside the bounds of physical science, not less than outside the region of the mere sense of hearing? (1886/1892: 167–8)

6.13

In this chapter I've operated for the most part inside the standard framework of discussion. I've bracketed a very large problem with the framework that deserves a mention in these infinitely forgetful times, although it too can be accommodated under the capacious umbrella of the thesis of the silence of physics.

The point is simple and neo-Kantian. The 'critical monist' Alois Riehl puts it as follows:

The error of materialism [when it throws up its hand in despair at the mind–body problem] is only that it seeks to deduce consciousness from the external *phenomenon* of the real, instead of from *the real which underlies this phenomenon.*[23]

This point has many powerful expressions in the nineteenth-century German tradition, and equally in the twentieth-century 'critical realist' tradition, and is in fact well expressed by Kant himself.[24] Lange puts by saying that

The eye, with which we believe we see, is itself only a product of our ideas; and when we find that our visual images are produced by the structure of the eye, we must never forget that the eye too with its arrangements, the optic nerve with the brain and all the structures which we may yet discover there as causes of conscious experience, are only ideas, which indeed form a self-coherent world, yet a world which points to something beyond itself. (1865–75: 3.224)[25]

So when we take concrete reality to be wholly physical – and here we mean concrete reality as it is in itself[26] – and think it obvious that the physical can't possibly be the basis of conscious experience, and *a fortiori* can't possibly *be* conscious experience, we make a grand old mistake. We think we know more about the nature of the physical than we do. We continue to take it that physics (and perhaps also everyday experience) delivers more than merely structural-relational knowledge of the ultimate intrinsic nature of the physical – including in particular the brain – as it is in itself.[27] The neo-Kantian points out that all

---

[23] 1887/1894: 187, my emphasis; here 'phenomenon' has its basic meaning of 'appearance' and 'materialism' has its usual pre-twentieth-century meaning, i.e. real materialism, i.e. materialism that assumes (as any realistic materialism must) that consciousness as ordinarily understood is fully real – and therefore material.

[24] The trouble with Kant, from the present perspective, which I share with Eddington, Russell, Whitehead, Feigl, Maxwell and many others, is that he locates our conscious experience itself in the realm of mere appearance. The advantage of neo-Kantianism is that one doesn't have to accept Kant's whole system.

[25] The claim that 'the eye is only an idea' is loose, but it's loose in a familiar and wholly intelligible way; and even as we allow (with Kant and Lange) the sense in which 'the eye' is only an idea or appearance, we can also allow the sense in which 'the eye' may be taken to carry reference to whatever it is in reality as it is in itself that the eye thought-of-as-an-idea/appearance is an idea/appearance *of*. There is no philosophical problem here.

[26] I add this because one can very well take 'physical' or material' in a Kantian manner to apply only to the realm of appearance (the 'empirically real' world), and think of physics as a theory that doesn't purport to have any application beyond the 'realm of appearance'. But this is not the use of the term in the current debate.

[27] Once again one has to add the qualification that everyday experience does in fact deliver more than merely structural-relational knowledge of the ultimate intrinsic nature of

we ever directly know of it is an appearance, both in everyday life *and also and equally when we do physics*, and that we have no good reason to think that the appearance reveals the nature of the physical as it is in itself, except (no doubt) in certain general structural respects. Except in certain structural respects: the good thing about the neo-Kantians is that they can allow, as strict Kantians cannot, that we may gain some deep *structural* knowledge of the nature of reality as it is in itself. The neo-Kantians can suppose – with Poincaré, Russell et al. – that there is a profound homomorphism between the structures we discern in everyday life and physics and the structure of reality as it is in itself,[28] while holding fast to the point that

> the senses give us, as Helmholtz says, *effects* of things, not true pictures nor things in themselves. But to the mere effects belong also the senses themselves [here he means the senses considered as the physical systems that are available to us for scientific investigation], together with the brain and the molecular movements which we suppose in it. (Lange 1865–75: 3.230)

The conclusion is immediate, and (by now) familiar. We have no good reason to suppose that we know something about the nature of the brain in doing physics and neuroscience that gives us good reason to think it mysterious that conscious experience is brain activity, or that conscious experience can't be physical.[29] To do that you'd have to know what lies behind the science-appearances.

We've become deeply accustomed to the idea that physics shows us that concrete reality is not as it initially appears. Now, however, the world that we think of as revealed by physics itself falls into the realm of mere appearance. It's a matter of the way things as they are in themselves appear to us given our particular sensory-intellectual equipment (which also of course has an as-it-is-in-itself nature that we cannot access). And these appearances give us no reason whatever to think that that which they are appearances of is in its fundamental nature something that could not manifest as, or be, conscious experience.

Really it's enough to quote Kant, as he defends himself from the charge of idealism:

---

the brain, if physicalism is true, simply because it delivers – constitutes – knowledge of itself.

[28] I've always regretted that (as far as I know) Kant himself never acknowledges this possibility.

[29] One interesting challenge to this claim concerns the (synchronic) unity of experience. For an answer, see Kant 1781–7: B41718 n. For a good discussion of the extremely troubled connection between neo-Kantianism and the 'predictive coding' approach to perception, see Zahavi (2017: §§1–3).

Long before Locke's time, but assuredly since him, it has been generally assumed and granted without detriment to the actual existence of
external things that many of their predicates may be said to belong, not
to the things in themselves, but to their appearances, and to have no
proper existence outside our representation. Heat, colour and taste are
of this kind. Now, if I go further and, for weighty reasons, rank as mere
appearances also the remaining qualities of bodies, which are called primary – such as extension, place, and, in general, space, with all that which
belongs to it (impenetrability or materiality, shape, etc.) – no one in the
least can adduce the reason of its being inadmissible. As little as the man
who admits colours not to be properties of the object itself but only to
be modifications of the sense of sight should on that account be called
idealist, so little can my doctrine be named idealistic merely because
I find that more, nay, all the properties which constitute the intuition of
a body belong merely to its appearance. The existence of the thing that
appears is not thereby destroyed, as in genuine idealism, but it is only
shown that that we cannot possibly know it by the senses as it is in itself.
(Kant 1783/1953: §289)

Kant also makes the point that one fundamental type of reality may underlie
all mental appearances as well as all physical appearances. Here, however,
he goes further than I am prepared to do, because he takes it that conscious
experience is itself a matter of mere appearance (experience takes time and
Kant denies the reality of time), and that, I think, cannot be.

6.14

There's much more to say – about Kant and other relevant matters – but not
here. It's obvious, in conclusion, that physicalism is false if physicalism is
identified with physics-alism, because it's obvious that physics (the physical
sciences) can't characterize the nature of colour experience or indeed any conscious experience. Of course. It's a very old and very familiar point, and it's
entirely compatible with the point that matter (the physical) may be – is – conscious; a point that has always been taken for granted by almost all materialists
before the second half of the twentieth century. It is by the same token obvious
that physicalism should not be identified with physics-alism, and that Mary
poses no problem for physicalism.

A final five-step for the uncertain. It'll be worth it if it saves even one
person from one of the great fly-bottles of our time. I doubt that it will, for
philosophers are almost always fixed in their views about the 'mind–body

problem' even before they've finished their undergraduate career, and they almost never change their minds.

Frank Jackson is of course a wonderful exception; he changed his mind. I only wish I could convince him that he doesn't have to give up his physicalism, with which I agree, in order to maintain his original view, with which I also agree: that Mary learns something completely new about the nature of concrete reality the moment she leaves the black and white room.

Step 1   Consider your conscious experience now (look up from these words if you'd like more colour; play some music).

Step 2   Consider the brain as you know it from neurophysiology, neurosurgery, anatomy, physics, scans, models, the morgue.

Step 3   Add the thought that the brain is about 78 per cent water. In other terms, it's about 99 per cent hydrogen, oxygen, carbon and nitrogen (11 per cent hydrogen, 71 per cent oxygen, 15 per cent carbon, 2.2 per cent nitrogen) plus a few other sprinklings – phosphorus, zinc, magnesium, calcium and so on.

Step 4   Consider that it is far beyond reasonable doubt – it is far, far, far beyond reasonable doubt – that the being of your current conscious experience is nothing over and above the being of some parts of your electrochemically active brain. (Here we can hold the neo-Kantian point about the brain in reserve.)

Step 5   Dwell hard on this fact. When your mind wanders, bring it back. Bring it back to the idea of the brain that you have in mind given steps 2 and 3. Rehearse and rehearse again the thought that part of the being of that very thing is the conscious experience that you are having right now, the conscious experience whose nature you know, in a fundamental respect, simply in having it, now and now and now. Run – rerun – the neo-Kantian thought.

This can bring about an intellectual breakthrough (it is emotional-intellectual). One realizes – one suddenly really gets it – that there is more to 'the physical' than one ordinarily supposes. One enters the real world (and the real debate).[30]

---

[30]   I am very grateful to Sam Coleman for his comments on a draft of this chapter.

7 Concept Mastery, Social Externalism, and Mary's New Knowledge

Torin Alter

Many agree that Frank Jackson's Mary learns something when she leaves the black-and-white room and finally experiences color firsthand.[1] There is less agreement about what her epistemic progress consists in. According to the new-concepts thesis, it consists at least partly in her acquiring phenomenal-color concepts, that is, concepts associated with knowing what it is like to see in color.

The new-concepts thesis was introduced as part of the phenomenal concept strategy. The latter is a popular strategy for answering the knowledge argument against physicalism, which is the argument for which Jackson designed the Mary case.[2] The new-concepts thesis is also consistent with other (physicalist and non-physicalist) reactions to the knowledge argument.[3]

According to Derek Ball and Michael Tye, the new-concepts thesis is false.[4] To show this, they appeal to some of Tyler Burge's arguments for social externalism, the view that one can possess a concept not only in virtue of one's intrinsic properties but also in virtue of relations to one's linguistic community.[5] Ball and Tye argue that, by refuting the new-concepts thesis, those Burgean arguments undermine the phenomenal concept strategy. Ball argues that, for the same reason, those arguments undermine the knowledge argument too.

[1] Jackson (1982, 1986).
[2] For example, Block (2006); Levin (2007a); Loar (1997); Papineau (2002); Tye (1995).
[3] Chalmers (2002); Kirk (2005); Montero (2007).
[4] Ball (2009); Tye (2009).
[5] Tye and Ball rely largely on arguments Burge gives in his 1979 "Individualism and the Mental." Burge's main conclusion in that article is not social externalism but rather anti-individualism, the view that, "many representational mental states and events are constitutively what they are partly by virtue of relations between the individual in those states and a wider reality" (Burge 2007, p. 3). But social externalism (as I call it) relates closely to what he describes as the article's "most often recognized" contribution: "showing how the natures of an individual's representational states can depend on the individual's relation to a *social* environment" (Burge 2007, p. 181; italics in original). Moreover, social externalism would seem to be what Ball and Tye take Burge's arguments to establish and what is most relevant to their argument.

Elsewhere I argued that the Ball–Tye argument can be circumvented by replacing the new-concepts thesis with a thesis about mastering, rather than acquiring, phenomenal concepts.[6] The concept-mastery thesis says that Mary's post-release epistemic progress consists at least partly in her acquiring mastery of phenomenal-color concepts, which she might already possess without mastery. The concept-mastery thesis, I argued, enables phenomenal concept strategists and knowledge argument proponents to accept social externalism about phenomenal concepts and thus answer the challenge Ball and Tye develop.

Ball has since criticized my argument. One of those criticisms is essentially the same as an argument developed independently, and in greater detail, by Gabriel Rabin.[7] Here I will defend the strategy based on the concept-mastery thesis against Ball's and Rabin's arguments. If sound, my arguments indicate that social externalism does not have the significance that Ball and Tye imply it has for the debate about the knowledge argument and physicalism. Indeed, I will suggest, the issues raised by social externalism are largely orthogonal to those that debate is fundamentally about.

7.1 The Knowledge Argument, the Phenomenal Concept Strategy, and the Ball–Tye Argument

The knowledge argument could be stated roughly as follows. Mary is a brilliant scientist and a maximally good logical reasoner. She is raised a captive in a black-and-white room and sees no colors. But she learns all physical information – "everything in *completed* physics, chemistry, and neurophysiology, and all there is to know about the causal and relational facts consequent upon all this, including of course functional roles"[8] – by reading books printed in black and white and watching science lectures on a black-and-white television monitor. Then she is released into the outside world and sees colors for the first time. Does she thereby acquire information that she did not already possess? If physicalism is true, then she does not: she already knows all physical information, and according to physicalism, "all (correct) information is physical information."[9] But she does gain information when released. For example, she learns what it is like to see red. Therefore, physicalism is false.[10]

---

[6] Alter (2013).

[7] Ball (2013); Rabin (2011, 2013).

[8] Jackson (1986, p. 291). Italics in original.

[9] Jackson (1982, p. 127).

[10] Jackson (1998b, 2003, 2007, this volume) has since rejected the knowledge argument. Here I ignore this development. But see Alter (2007); Robinson (2002, 2008).

It will be useful to divide Jackson's reasoning into the following four steps:[11]

1. There are truths about consciousness that cannot be a priori deduced from the complete physical truth.
2. If there are truths about consciousness that cannot be a priori deduced from the complete physical truth, then there are truths about consciousness that are not metaphysically necessitated by the complete physical truth.
3. If there are truths about consciousness that are not metaphysically necessitated by the complete physical truth, then physicalism is false.
4. Therefore, physicalism is false.

On that four-step summary, the Mary case comes in as support for premise 1, which establishes an epistemic gap between the physical and phenomenal domains. Premise 2 says that the epistemic gap entails a corresponding modal gap. And premise 3 says that the modal gap entails a corresponding ontological gap such that physicalism is false.

Physicalists have developed a number of responses to the knowledge argument. Most are directed against either premise 1 or premise 2.[12] For example, regarding premise 1, some physicalists argue that Mary learns nothing when released from the black-and-white room.[13] Other physicalists concede that she learns something but reject premise 1 by arguing that her learning consists in gaining abilities or acquaintance rather than information.[14] Still other physicalists reject premise 2: they reject the inference from the physical-phenomenal epistemic gap to a corresponding modal gap.

The phenomenal concept strategy falls into the latter category.[15] Phenomenal concept strategists typically accept that Mary gains information when she leaves the room and that this establishes premise 1. However, they argue, her post-release information gain can be explained in a way that undermines premise 2. Her progress can be explained, they argue, in terms of distinctive epistemic or psychological features of phenomenal concepts: features that are neutral with respect to both the nature of the phenomenal properties to which those concepts refer and, more generally, the modal and ontological issues on which physicalism's truth or falsity depends.

---

[11] Alter (2017); Chalmers (2004a, 2010a, ch. 6). This summary omits details that matter little here.
[12] For a challenge to premise 3, see Montero (2013). For a response to that challenge, see Howell n.d.
[13] Dennett (1991, 2007); Mandik (2009); Rosenthal this volume.
[14] Conee (1994); Jackson (2003); Lewis (1999); Nemirow (1990); Tye (2009).
[15] For another way to reject premise 2, see Howell (2013).

Various accounts of how such an explanation might go have been proposed. For example, some suggest that phenomenal concepts (or corresponding mental representations) contain their referents in something like the way a word might be embedded between quotation marks.[16] Others construe phenomenal concepts as special sorts of recognitional concepts: non-theoretical concepts we deploy when we recognize something as being one of *those*, where some sort of (perhaps introspective) ostension is involved in fixing the referent of "*those*."[17] Other accounts too have been proposed.[18]

The phenomenal concept strategy, as it is usually presented, entails the new-concepts thesis: the thesis that Mary's post-release epistemic progress consists at least partly in her acquiring phenomenal-color concepts. Before I turn to the Ball–Tye argument against this thesis, let me clarify two points.

The first point concerns a potential counterexample to the new-concepts thesis. Consider a concept expressed by the following description: "the phenomenal quality that is typically instantiated when color-sighted humans see ripe red tomatoes in normal daylight conditions." One might classify that concept as a phenomenal-color concept. Arguably, however, pre-release Mary can acquire that concept by reading the aforementioned description in a black-and-white book. But we should not infer that the new-concepts thesis is false. Instead, we should infer that it concerns phenomenal concepts of a different kind: a kind of which the concept expressed by the aforementioned description is not a member. The thesis applies more plausibly to what David Chalmers calls *pure* phenomenal concepts: concepts that characterize phenomenal properties in terms of their intrinsic, phenomenal natures.[19] I will therefore assume that the thesis implies only that Mary gains *pure* phenomenal-color concepts when released.[20]

The second point of clarification concerns cheating. If the new-concepts thesis is true, then Mary does not acquire (pure) phenomenal-color concepts until she leaves the room and sees colors. That consequence would be untenable if it were based only on the assumption that Mary is raised in a black-and-white room. Someone else raised in a black-and-white room might acquire those phenomenal-color concepts by, for example, pricking their finger and looking at their own red blood. But Jackson stipulates that Mary does no such thing. The new-concepts thesis has implications only for when

---

[16] Balog (1999, 2012); Block (2006); Papineau (2002).
[17] Levin (2007a); Loar (1997).
[18] Chalmers (2007, pp. 171–73) describes seven different such accounts.
[19] Chalmers (2002).
[20] Henceforth, whenever I refer to phenomenal concepts, I have in mind the pure variety.

Mary acquires phenomenal-color concepts legitimately, that is, without cheating.[21]

Ball and Tye seem to recognize both of those points. Nevertheless, they argue, pre-release Mary can (legitimately) acquire (pure) phenomenal-color concepts, contrary to what the new-concepts thesis implies. To show this, they appeal to Burgean arguments for social externalism, the view that one can possess a concept not only in virtue of one's intrinsic properties but also in virtue of relations to one's linguistic community.[22] On this view, one might possess a concept without knowing much about what it picks out, if one has acquired a term that expresses it in one's linguistic community.

For example, one who knows little about arthritis might nonetheless acquire ARTHRITIS, as in Burge's well-known case from "Individualism and the Mental."[23] In that case, Arthritis-man (as Ball calls him)[24] suspects his arthritis has spread to his thigh.[25] His ability to think that thought (that is, to entertain the proposition that he has developed arthritis in his thigh) entails that he possesses all of its conceptual components, including ARTHRITIS – a concept he might have acquired by acquiring a term that expresses it in his linguistic community (e.g., "arthritis"). He has that ability despite his misconception about the concept's application conditions. According to Burge, arthritis can occur only in joints and thus not in the thigh.[26]

Ball and Tye assume that the Burgean arguments for social externalism they discuss are sound. Usually those arguments are applied to non-phenomenal concepts. But Ball and Tye argue that the arguments apply equally to phenomenal concepts.[27] If those arguments establish social externalism about ARTHRITIS then, they argue, exactly similar arguments establish social externalism about PHENOMENAL REDNESS. Social externalism about PHENOMENAL REDNESS entails that one could possess that concept without knowing much about the phenomenal character of seeing red, if one has acquired a

---

[21] Alter (2013, p. 485, n. 5). I will sometimes leave the "legitimately" qualification implicit.

[22] Burge (1979, 1982). I will not summarize Burge's arguments. Here what matters most is the conclusion Ball and Tye draw from them.

[23] Burge (1979). I use small capitals to indicate reference to concepts.

[24] Ball (2009, 2013).

[25] Burge's thought experiment involves other components, such as a counterfactual situation in which arthritis has not been identified as a disease that can occur only in joints. But those other components matter little here, and so I ignore them.

[26] One might question Burge's claims that arthritis can occur only in joints or that this is "constitutively necessary to the application range" of ARTHRITIS (Burge 2007, p. 175). But I will assume both claims are true. If either is false, then other examples could be substituted (Burge 1979, section IIb).

[27] As Tye (2009, p. 71) remarks, Burge (2003, pp. 413–14) is not inclined to agree.

term that expresses that concept in one's linguistic community. Further, Ball and Tye imply, pre-release Mary might therefore acquire such a term legitimately. For example, she might acquire "phenomenal redness" from watching, on her black-and-white monitor, a vision-science lecture in which the lecturer remarks, "Phenomenal redness is what it is like to see red."

That reasoning suggests the following argument against the new-concepts thesis:

> Pre-release Mary can legitimately acquire terms that express phenomenal-color concepts: such terms might appear in the books she reads or the lectures she watches. Given social externalism about phenomenal concepts, it follows that she can legitimately thereby acquire phenomenal-color concepts while still in the room, contrary to the new-concepts thesis.

Ball and Tye each endorse an argument along those lines. They conclude that the phenomenal concept strategy fails. The knowledge argument faces a similar threat if it too implies the new-concepts thesis. And Ball argues that the knowledge argument does indeed have that implication.[28] Thus, social externalism might seem to undermine both the phenomenal concept strategy and the knowledge argument.

7.2 The Concept-Mastery Strategy

There are several ways phenomenal concept strategists and knowledge argument proponents might respond to the Ball–Tye argument from social externalism. They might reject social externalism.[29] They might reject the application of social externalism to phenomenal concepts.[30] They might argue that if we accept social externalism about phenomenal concepts then we should disallow pre-release Mary access to terms expressing phenomenal-color concepts.[31]

Here I will leave those three options aside. For the sake of argument, I will grant that social externalism is true of phenomenal concepts and that Mary can therefore legitimately acquire phenomenal-color concepts while still in the black-and-white room. I will defend a response that centers on the concept-mastery thesis: the thesis that Mary's post-release epistemic progress consists at least partly in her gaining mastery of phenomenal-color concepts, which she might already possess without mastery.

---

[28] Ball (2009, pp. 941–43).
[29] Mendola (2008); Pereboom (1995).
[30] Veillet (2012).
[31] Alter (2013, p. 486, n. 6).

The concept-mastery thesis applies to the Mary case an idea similar to what Burge describes as "the pivot on which the particular thought experiments of 'Individualism and the Mental' turn"[32] – thought experiments such as the Arthritis-man case. The pivotal idea is that one might possess a concept without completely understanding it. Burge writes, "Incomplete understanding can involve any failure to understand some condition that is constitutively necessary to the application range of a concept."[33] For example, according to Burge, Arthritis-man possesses ARTHRITIS despite his misconception about its application range.

Arguably, on any plausible account of phenomenal concepts, there is something that corresponds to incompletely understanding a condition that is constitutively necessary to a concept's application range. For example, take the account on which phenomenal concepts are recognitional concepts, that is, non-theoretical concepts we deploy when we recognize something as being one of *those*. Plausibly, on that account having mastery of a phenomenal concept requires being positioned to perform the relevant recognitional task, e.g., recognizing a pain experience by its distinctive phenomenal character. And being so positioned seems to require something like acquaintance with the relevant phenomenal property, such as the phenomenal property that constitutes pain's phenomenal character.

At least, merely possessing an ability to refer to that property in some way or other would not suffice for being so positioned. Nor would understanding the theoretical claim that phenomenal concepts are recognitional concepts. Even if pre-release Mary has that ability and that understanding, with respect to phenomenal-color concepts, she is not positioned to recognize a color experience as (or as not) one of *those*. This changes only when she is released and sees colors for herself. Arguably, all other contender accounts of phenomenal concepts, such as the quotational account, lead to the same conclusion: it is only post-release that Mary comes to master phenomenal-color concepts.

Given the assumptions I have granted Ball and Tye, the concept-mastery thesis seems plausible. Suppose Q is a truth involving PHENOMENAL REDNESS that, on some views, Mary learns only post-release. Suppose also that those views are incorrect: she knows Q while still in the room, for the reasons Ball and Tye give. Nevertheless, at that time her understanding of Q seems shallow.

---

[32] Burge (2007, p. 175). Cf. Burge (1979, p. 111).

[33] Burge (2007, p. 175). It is not entirely clear to me what Burge means by "failure to understand" such an application condition. In his arthritis case, the failure appears to be indicated by, or perhaps to consist in, Arthritis-man's failure to *know* something (namely, that arthritis can occur only in joints).

Intuitively, her understanding deepens when she is released and finally sees red. Describing her as then gaining mastery of PHENOMENAL REDNESS and thereby coming to know Q with mastery – that is, coming to know Q under concepts of which she has mastery – reflects that intuition.[34]

Arguably, what matters most for the knowledge argument is knowing truths under concepts of which one has mastery, as opposed to knowing truths under concepts of which one might lack mastery.[35] If so, then phenomenal concept strategists and knowledge argument proponents could respond to Ball and Tye by replacing the new-concepts thesis with the concept-mastery thesis. In other words, instead of arguing that Mary's post-release color experiences enable her to acquire phenomenal-color concepts, they could argue that those experiences enable her to master those concepts. They could then argue that Mary's post-release epistemic progress consists at least partly in her acquiring knowledge with mastery of truths that, given social externalism about phenomenal concepts, she might already know without mastery. The phenomenal concept strategy and the knowledge argument could then be revised accordingly, thereby circumventing the Ball–Tye objection. Call this *the concept-mastery strategy.*

Let me say a bit more about how to revise the phenomenal concept strategy and the knowledge argument in accordance with the concept-mastery strategy. In the case of the phenomenal concept strategy, the idea would be to replace the attempt to explain Mary's post-release epistemic progress in terms of phenomenal concepts' distinctive acquisition conditions with an attempt to explain her progress in terms of their distinctive mastery conditions. If successful, the latter attempt would preserve the conclusion that is most central to phenomenal concept strategy: the conclusion that Mary's progress can be fully explained in a way that is consistent with the physicalist view that all phenomenal truths are metaphysically necessitated by physical truths. The objection to the knowledge argument's premise 2, which is the target of the phenomenal concept strategy, would thereby be reinstated.

In the case of the knowledge argument, the concept-mastery strategy works by replacing the claim that when released Mary acquires knowledge of phenomenal truths with the claim that when released she acquires knowledge with mastery of phenomenal truths: knowledge of those truths under concepts of which she has mastery. Let us see what this implies for the four-step summary stated above, in the previous section. Considerations about concept mastery do not affect premise 3 or the conclusion, which concern necessitation

---

[34] Rabin (2011, p. 130).
[35] Rabin (2011, 2013) develops such an argument. See 7.4, below.

and ontology rather than deducibility and knowledge. But concept-mastery strategists will want to modify premises 1 and 2 along the following lines:

1.' There are truths about consciousness that cannot be known with mastery based only on a priori deduction from the complete physical truth.
2.' If there are truths about consciousness that cannot be known with mastery based only on a priori deduction from the complete physical truth, then there are truths about consciousness that are not metaphysically necessitated by the complete physical truth.

The Ball–Tye argument threatens the case from Mary's epistemic progress for premise 1. But their argument does not threaten the case from her progress for premise 1'.

Before considering objections to the concept-mastery strategy, let me clarify a few things. First, I use "having mastery of concept *C*" to mean having *substantial* mastery of *C*. For example, if Burge is correct, Arthritis-man's doctor has substantial mastery of ARTHRITIS and Arthritis-man does not. But one might have mastery of a concept without knowing how or whether it applies in every conceivable case. Otherwise, the standard for having mastery would be overly demanding, at least for present purposes. Experts would too often lack mastery of well-understood concepts that are central to their areas of expertise. For example, Arthritis-man's doctor might have mastery of ARTHRITIS even if there are conceivable cases in which she does not know whether that concept applies (such cases might involve creatures with highly unfamiliar physiologies).

Second, having mastery of a concept does not require knowing much about the underlying nature of the entities in its extension, such as how or whether they are constituted. For example, arguably one might have mastery of WATER without knowing that water is H_2O.[36] Therefore, the concept-mastery thesis is neutral on whether, in coming to master phenomenal-color concepts, Mary gains insight into the underlying nature of the properties those concepts pick out. That neutrality is dialectically significant: the concept-mastery strategy is compatible with both the phenomenal concept strategy and the knowledge argument, which differ over the underlying nature of phenomenal properties.

Third, having mastery of a concept often involves, and might partly consist in, knowing truths into which that concept figures – truths that can in many cases be learned through testimony. For example, suppose Arthritis-man learns

---

[36] Putnam (1975) suggests a closely related claim: one might know what "water" means without knowing that water is H_2O. This, he suggests, was true of many prior to the discovery that water is H_2O.

various truths about the nature of arthritis through his doctor's testimony, including the truth that arthritis occurs only in joints. Arguably, if he learns enough such truths in that way, he might thereby come to master ARTHRITIS. But it does not follow that all concepts can be mastered just by learning truths through testimony.[37] For example, perhaps recognitional concepts cannot be mastered in that way.[38] Moreover, arguably at least some phenomenal concepts cannot be mastered in that way. On the concept-mastery strategy, that is true of the phenomenal concepts most relevant to the Mary case and the knowledge argument. On that strategy, no matter what truths pre-release Mary learns from her black-and-white books, her black-and-white lectures, or any further testimony that is not delivered in color, she will not thereby legitimately acquire mastery of PHENOMENAL REDNESS.[39]

Finally, I should mention another response to the Ball–Tye argument, which is closely related to the concept-mastery strategy. This other response begins with the claim that pre-release Mary possesses phenomenal-color concepts only *deferentially*. For example, her PHENOMENAL REDNESS concept refers to what it does only because she intends that it refer to whatever those in her linguistic community normally use a term she acquired (e.g., "phenomenal redness") to refer to. The next step is to argue that, for the purposes of the knowledge argument, what matters is not just possessing concepts but also possessing them non-deferentially. One could then revise the phenomenal concept strategy and the knowledge argument accordingly, thereby circumventing the Ball–Tye objection, just as on the concept-mastery strategy. Clearly, that response and the concept-mastery strategy are of a piece. Even so, mastery and non-deference are two different things. For example, one who has mastery of a concept might or might not defer to the standards in her linguistic community regarding its application conditions. In any event, here I will focus on concept mastery rather than non-deference.

Both Ball and Tye consider versions of (what I call) the concept-mastery strategy, but they reject it. In "Social Externalism and the Knowledge Argument," I defend it against objections they present in their 2009 publications on the

---

[37] It does not even follow that any concept can be mastered just by learning truths through testimony. Perhaps concept mastery must involve at least some knowledge that is not based on learning through testimony, as opposed to, say, ostension. The worry is that otherwise one might be in a situation akin to that of the protagonist in Searle's (1980) Chinese room.

[38] Loar (1997, p. 601).

[39] Conceivably, such testimony might cause Mary to have phenomenally red experiences or to have the sorts of brain states she would have had, had she had such experiences. But that would not qualify as learning through testimony – at least not legitimately, in the sense defined above.

topic.[40] I will now turn to two more recent arguments Ball presents, the second of which echoes an argument Rabin develops independently.[41]

7.3 Is the Concept-Mastery Thesis Explanatory?

Ball argues that concept mastery is heterogeneous and therefore "cannot bear the explanatory load that Alter requires."[42] He compares concept mastery to mastery of the piano. The latter, he points out, might involve diverse skills and knowledge, such as technical proficiency, an understanding of music theory, and an ability to improvise. Describing someone as lacking or gaining mastery of the piano might therefore have little or no explanatory value. Likewise, he claims, for concept mastery. He writes:

> [E]veryone should agree that a thinker like Mary is not ideally situated with respect to the concept of red. This uncontroversial fact leaves open all of the interesting questions about how Mary changes when she leaves her room. Does she gain new factual knowledge, as Jackson claimed? Does she gain new know-how or abilities, as Lewis (1996) contended? Does she gain some sort of objectual knowledge, as Conee (1994) and Tye (2009) claim? Or none of these? The claim that Mary gains conceptual mastery is silent on these issues; but these are the issues on which the knowledge argument turns.[43]

Actually, the concept-mastery thesis is not silent on those issues, at least not completely. It presupposes that Mary makes epistemic progress. So, it conflicts with the view that Mary learns nothing when released—a view maintained by Daniel Dennett and others.[44]

Nevertheless, Ball makes a reasonable claim: merely describing Mary as mastering phenomenal-color concepts does not go far towards explaining the epistemic progress she makes when released. Let us grant him that claim, at least for the sake of argument. To be *genuinely* explanatory, as I will put it, an account of Mary's newly acquired mastery is needed: an account that

---

[40] Alter (2013); Ball (2009); Tye (2009).
[41] Ball (2013); Rabin (2011, 2013). In addition to those two arguments, Ball (2013) criticizes the concept-mastery strategy for implying that when released Mary discovers facts she already knows. He finds that implication implausible. I do not. But nothing much hangs on this disagreement. Even if he is correct about the application conditions of "discover," the concept-mastery thesis might be true.
[42] Ball (2013, p. 506).
[43] Ball (2013, p. 506).
[44] Dennett (1991, 2007); Mandik (2009); Rosenthal this volume.

addresses at least some of the issues on which the knowledge argument turns in addition to the issue of whether Mary learns something when released. If, as Ball contends, concept mastery is heterogeneous, the prospects of providing such an account might seem poor.

Notice, however, that similar observations could be made about the new-concepts thesis. One could argue that, like concept mastery, concept possession is heterogeneous in that it too might involve diverse skills and knowledge. One could also argue that merely describing Mary as acquiring phenomenal-color concepts does not go far towards explaining her post-release epistemic progress. Arguably, that description too is silent on many, perhaps most, of the issues on which the knowledge argument turns.

What follows from those observations? It follows that without elaboration neither the new-concepts thesis nor the concept-mastery thesis is genuinely explanatory (in the sense defined two paragraphs back). But that conclusion is compatible with the claim that those theses are genuinely explanatory when suitably elaborated. Ball's objection can be answered by defending the latter claim.

How might the new-concepts thesis and the concept-mastery thesis be suitably elaborated? In the case of the new-concepts thesis, this has been done. As I noted earlier, phenomenal concept strategists have proposed various accounts of phenomenal concepts: accounts of distinctive epistemic and psychological features of phenomenal concepts that, they claim, explain Mary's post-release epistemic progress. Knowledge argument proponents have made similar proposals.[45] On all such accounts, Mary gains factual (that is, propositional or informational) knowledge when she is released. For example, recall the account on which phenomenal concepts are special sorts of recognitional concepts. On that account, Mary makes epistemic progress when released because it is not until then that she is positioned to recognize a phenomenally red experience as one of *those*. That would explain why prior to her release she fails to know (or even grasp) facts into which PHENOMENAL REDNESS figures.

So, when elaborated with such an account, the new-concepts thesis is genuinely explanatory. It addresses at least one issue on which the knowledge argument turns in addition to the issue of whether when released she learns anything, namely, the issue of whether the sort of knowledge Mary gains when released is factual as opposed to, say, non-propositional acquaintance knowledge.

---

[45] Chalmers (2002).

That reasoning suggests a natural way to address Ball's concern that concept mastery is heterogeneous and therefore not adequately explanatory: the accounts originally developed to explain why post-release Mary acquires phenomenal concepts can be repurposed to explain why she acquires mastery of concepts that she already possesses. For example, consider Brian Loar, who proposed the recognitional account of phenomenal concepts. Suppose Loar grants social externalism about phenomenal concepts and concedes for that reason that pre-release Mary knows some truths into which PHENOMENAL REDNESS figures. Nonetheless, he could argue, she does not at that time know those truths with mastery. To know those truths with mastery, he could argue, (i) she must be positioned to recognize a phenomenally red experience as one of *those* and (ii) she is not so positioned until she is released and sees red (or a similar color). Other extant accounts of phenomenal concepts, such as the quotational account, could be similarly repurposed.

Thus, even if the concept-mastery thesis alone is not genuinely explanatory, it is genuinely explanatory when elaborated with an appropriately repurposed account of phenomenal concepts. That is so even if, as Ball contends, concept-mastery is heterogeneous.

7.4 Do Concept-Mastery Considerations Undermine the Knowledge Argument?

Suppose my defense of the concept-mastery strategy against the first of Ball's objections succeeds. Even so, knowledge argument proponents might worry that this is a Pyrrhic victory: Ball and Rabin argue that considerations about concept mastery, deducibility, and necessitation make it impossible to formulate a defensible version of the knowledge argument's second premise without undermining its first premise.[46] In this section, I will discuss their argument.

The Rabin–Ball argument applies equally to the unrevised and the revised versions of the knowledge argument's first two premises, that is, premises 1 and 2 and premises 1′ and 2′. For simplicity, I will focus on the unrevised versions (but what I will say applies equally to the revised versions, *mutatis mutandis*). Here they are again:

1. There are truths about consciousness that cannot be a priori deduced from the complete physical truth.

---

[46] Ball (2013, section 3); Rabin (2011, 2013).

2. If there are truths about consciousness that cannot be a priori deduced from the complete physical truth, then there are truths about consciousness that are not metaphysically necessitated by the complete physical truth.

The problem Rabin and Ball raise for those premises can be seen as a consequence of the following argument of Rabin's:

> Imagine ... Mary's sister Jane. By engaging with her co-workers, Jane comes to possess the concept BACHELOR. She knows that Ulysses, who is married, is not a bachelor, and that Achilles is a bachelor. But Jane is not a master of the concept BACHELOR; she thinks unmarried women can be bachelors. Jane has complete knowledge of [the complete physical truth] and knowledge of the gender and marital status of every person. Jane knows that Ursula is a woman, and that Ursula is not married ... [B]ecause of her erroneous view that women can be bachelors, Jane will not come to know that Ursula is not a bachelor. If we don't require, in the inference from an epistemic to a metaphysical gap, that the relevant epistemic agents have conceptual mastery (i.e. if mere concept possession is enough), then we will be forced to conclude, on the basis of Jane's inability to know that Ursula is not a bachelor, that Ursula's status as a female does not necessitate that she is not a bachelor. But that conclusion is preposterous. Thus, *we must require, if we are to infer from a lack of [a priori deducibility] to a corresponding lack of necessitation, that the epistemic agents have mastery of all concepts in the target proposition(s).*[47]

Call the italicized conclusion *Rabin's requirement.*[48]

Rabin's argument has some force. If an agent *a* lacks mastery of some concept *C* that figures into proposition *A* or proposition *B* then, no matter how good a logical reasoner *a* is, *a*'s inability to a priori deduce *B* from *A* might trace to *a*'s lack of conceptual mastery. So, *a*'s inability would not license the conclusion that *A* fails to metaphysically necessitate (or a priori entail) *B*. In any

---

[47] Rabin (2011, p. 131) (italics added). I made two changes to the quoted passage to make it conform to the present terminology. I replaced "implication" with "a priori deducibility." And I replaced "*P*" with "the complete physical truth" (Rabin 2011, pp. 126–27). Elsewhere, Rabin (2013, p. 149) gives the same argument using ARTHRITIS instead of BACHELOR.

[48] Compare Ball (2013, p. 202, Alter 2013, pp. 492–93). Against Rabin's argument, one might object that, by exploiting her physical knowledge, Jane could deduce how people use "bachelor," "women," and all other relevant terms and thereby deduce that women cannot be bachelors. But that objection is not compelling. Consider Jane before she makes that deduction. At that point, she is not positioned, and is in that sense unable, to deduce that Ursula is not a bachelor. Yet as Rabin emphasizes, that inability shows nothing about what being a bachelor does and does not necessitate.

event, I will assume that Rabin's requirement is true. Consider its implications for the knowledge argument.

Premise 2 would allow us to draw an inference from a lack of a priori deducibility to a corresponding lack of necessitation. So, by Rabin's requirement, the relevant epistemic agents must have mastery of all concepts in the target proposition(s). Here some of the target propositions – the ones whose a priori deducibility from physical truths is in question – involve phenomenal-color concepts. Thus, for Mary to be a relevant epistemic agent, she must already have mastery of those concepts. Therein lies the problem. She does not acquire such mastery until she is released (at least, so say concept-mastery strategists). But premise 1 derives its support from the Mary case. That support disappears if she is not a relevant epistemic agent.

Let me put the point in a slightly different way. Premise 2 is plausible only if it respects Rabin's requirement. This in turn implies that premise 1 is harder to establish than one might otherwise have thought. Because of Rabin's requirement, the relevant epistemic agents – those whose deductive (in)abilities bear on premise 1 – must have mastery of all relevant concepts, including all those that figure into the relevant truths about consciousness. Mary does not satisfy that condition until she leaves the room. But by that point, she already knows the relevant phenomenal truths. So, her post-release epistemic progress cannot establish premise 1. Premise 1, it might seem, is undermined.

Knowledge argument proponents might respond by rejecting either Rabin's requirement or the claim that Mary acquires mastery of phenomenal-color concepts only post-release. But both Rabin's requirement and the latter claim are plausible. There is, however, another response available to knowledge argument proponents: concede that the Mary case does not establish premise 1 and argue that closely related considerations probably do.

It will be instructive to begin by imagining a Mary-like reasoner: someone with the same maximally good reasoning capacity but who, unlike pre-release Mary, has mastery of phenomenal-color concepts. We can then ask whether such a Mary-like reasoner could a priori deduce the relevant phenomenal truths from the complete physical truth. The answer should determine whether or not premise 1 is true: premise 1 is true if and only if no conceivable Mary-like reasoner could do that.[49]

Rabin recognizes this. He presents an argument that suggests an affirmative answer: there are conceivable Mary-like reasoners who could a priori

---

[49] By "conceivable" I mean *conceivable on ideal rational reflection*. Premise 1 does not exclude the possibility that one might in some sense conceive of a Mary-like reasoner who could do the relevant deduction.

deduce the relevant phenomenal truths from the complete physical truth, and so premise 1 is false. However, I will argue, his argument fails. Further, I will argue, seeing why it fails indicates that his conclusion is probably false: it is unlikely that any conceivable Mary-like reasoner could do the relevant deduction, and so premise 1 is probably true.

Rabin considers various Mary-like reasoners, including the following version of "re-captured Mary."[50] After an expedition to the outside world, during which she sees red tomatoes, the blue sky, and the like, she returns to the black-and-white room. Then she is drugged so that, "she cannot remember which of the colors she can now vividly imagine is the color of tomatoes, and which the color of the sky."[51] But she can and does imagine seeing red (that is, she does what normal color-sighted folk would describe as imagining seeing red). Her imaginative exercise has a certain phenomenal character, and she forms a phenomenal concept of experiences with that character. Rabin's term for that concept is "wow."[52]

At first re-captured Mary will not know certain phenomenal truths, such as the truth that tomatoes cause wow experiences.[53] However, Rabin argues, she can figure out such truths. She can do so by combining her phenomenal knowledge with her comprehensive physical knowledge, where the latter includes "all the details of her expedition from a third-person perspective."[54] He reasons as follows:

> She knows that she entered neural state N whenever she saw a ripe tomato, strawberry, or fire engine during that expedition. She knows that whenever she imagines a wow patch while sitting in the black and white room, she also enters neural state N. She'll learn that N is the neural correlate of wow experiences, and that tomatoes cause the instantiation of N. This information will be sufficient for her to learn that tomatoes cause wow sensations.[55]

Rabin might be correct about that. I will assume he is. I will further assume that, by using the method he describes, re-captured Mary can come to know

---

50 Rabin (2011, pp. 136ff).
51 Rabin (2011, p. 137). Others discuss similar variants such as Nida-Rümelin's (1995) Marianna case and Stoljar's (2005) Experienced Mary case.
52 Rabin borrows this term from Perry (2001).
53 I assume the truth Rabin has in mind would be more accurately stated as follows: ripe red tomatoes typically cause wow experiences in color-sighted humans viewing such objects in normal daylight conditions.
54 Rabin (2011, p. 138).
55 Rabin (2011, p. 138). Here Rabin seems to assume that in humans a single neural-state type correlates with both seeing red and imagining seeing red. He cites no evidence for that assumption, but I grant it for the sake of argument.

that tomatoes cause wow sensations. Even so, it is doubtful that this tells against the knowledge argument's premise 1, for two reasons. First, re-captured Mary's reasoning is based partly on truths about color experiences. Second, there might be other phenomenal truths that she cannot a priori deduce from physical truths by using the method Rabin describes. I will discuss those reasons in turn.

Premise 1 says that there are phenomenal truths that cannot be a priori deduced from physical truths. But the set of truths on the basis of which re-captured Mary figures out what causes wow sensations includes not only physical truths but phenomenal truths as well – truths about color experiences she had during her sojourn. Therefore, her ability to figure out what causes wow sensations does not threaten premise 1.

Recall a point I mentioned earlier, about cheating.[56] Being confined to a black-and-white room need not prevent someone from learning what it is like to see in color. For example, they could prick their finger and look at their own red blood. But that is plainly beside the point of the Mary case. Learning about phenomenal redness by causing oneself to have an experience with that property does not constitute (legitimate) learning by a priori deduction from physical truths. Re-captured Mary cheats in the same sense. Although she discovers that tomatoes cause wow sensations, she does so partly on the basis of phenomenal information about color experiences she had. Therefore, her discovery cannot show that premise 1 is false.

Let me put the first problem with Rabin's reasoning in another way. Re-captured Mary's reasoning relies for its justification on introspection.[57] Her reasoning relies on the introspective knowledge she gets from "imagin[ing] a wow patch while sitting in the black and white room."[58] That entails that her reasoning does not qualify as a priori deduction. So, her ability to figure out relevant phenomenal truths does not show that she can a priori deduce those phenomenal truths from physical truths. Indeed, it seems that she cannot do so. That is significant. Arguably, if she cannot do the relevant a priori deduction,

---

[56] See 7.1, above.

[57] The "for its justification" qualification is vital. Even paradigmatically a priori reasoning, such as pure mathematical reasoning, might in some sense rely on experience, at least where humans are concerned. For example, experience might play a causal role in our acquiring mathematical concepts.

[58] Rabin (2011, p. 138). In one variant of the Mary case that Rabin considers, he assumes only that Mary "actively considers a thought involving RED_{EXP} at time t" (where RED_{EXP} = PHENOMENAL REDNESS). However, such "active consideration" involves introspection, as he acknowledges (Rabin 2011, p. 144).

then no Mary-like reasoner could. In other words, contrary to what Rabin argues, reflection on re-captured Mary indicates that premise 1 is likely true.

Rabin acknowledges that re-captured Mary's reasoning relies on introspection. But unlike me, he does not infer from that fact that her reasoning is not a priori. Instead, he questions the assumption that the relevant notion of a priori justification (the notion the knowledge argument concerns) excludes introspection, in the sense that if one's knowledge depends for its justification on introspection then one's knowledge is not a priori.[59] However, he presents no reasons to doubt that assumption. Yet knowledge argument proponents typically accept it. Moreover, it seems plausible.

Consider a paradigm case of a posteriori knowledge, such as knowledge based on seeing a chemical mixture turn blue. That knowledge is not a priori because it depends for its justification on experience. Introspection-based knowledge would seem to depend for its justification on experience in the same way (at least, that seems to be true of re-captured Mary's introspection-based knowledge). In both cases, one bases one's knowledge on information obtained by using sense experience to investigate the world. That is so even though in introspection the investigation is inwardly directed and the objects of that investigation are one's own experiences. If Rabin believes there is some relevant difference between introspection and perception, such that re-captured Mary's introspection-based knowledge is a priori whereas ordinary perception-based knowledge is not, then the onus is on him to identify that difference.[60]

Let me turn to the second problem with Rabin's argument against premise 1. Consider not re-captured Mary but regular post-release Mary. She has seen colors, can identify them by name, and is not drugged. She has mastery of PHE-NOMENAL REDNESS. She knows with mastery not only the complete physical truth but also what it is like to see red, that seeing ripe tomatoes often causes wow sensations in humans, and various other truths into which phenomenal-color concepts figure.

---

[59] Rabin (2011, pp. 144–45).

[60] Further, the assumption that the relevant notion of a priori justification excludes introspection arguably underlies premise 2 of the knowledge argument. That premise depends on there being a certain connection between a priority and metaphysical necessitation. That connection could be expressed roughly as follows: if a truth T contains only semantically neutral terms, and thus no proper names, indexicals, or natural kind terms, then T is metaphysically necessary only if T is a priori. Failing to exclude introspection from a priori justification threatens to undermine that latter claim. Or so I argue, in forthcoming work. For discussion of the notion of semantic neutrality, see Chalmers (2012 *passim*).

Nevertheless, as Chalmers argues, there might be truths about color experiences that post-release Mary cannot a priori deduce from what she knows.[61] Imagine her contemplating Martians: creatures that exhibit signs of having human-like minds but who differ radically from us in physical respects. It is doubtful that, based on what she knows, she can a priori deduce that they have experiences that are phenomenally red (or that they do not). This time introspection will not help her. And if she, who is neither drugged nor back in the black-and-white room, cannot do the deduction, then *a fortiori* re-captured Mary cannot do the deduction either.

This second problem for Rabin's argument redounds to his explanation of how re-captured Mary would be able to figure out that tomatoes cause wow experiences in humans. Nothing she knows guarantees that N is the neural correlate of wow experiences in humans other than herself. She could not, it seems, conclusively rule out alternative possibilities based on her physical knowledge and what she knows through introspection. Perhaps she could rule out such possibilities using non-deductive (e.g., abductive) reasoning. But that is irrelevant to premise 1, which specifically concerns a priori deducibility.

Thus, the Rabin–Ball argument fails. The considerations Rabin and Ball adduce might indicate that the knowledge argument must ultimately rely on variants of the Mary case rather than only the original: variants such as re-captured Mary, who wonders about the causes of wow sensations, and post-release Mary, who wonders whether Martians see red as humans do. But that result does not amount to defeat. On the contrary, careful reflection on such variants only serves to reinforce the plausibility of the knowledge argument's first main premise.[62]

7.5 Conclusion

The concept-mastery strategy is an attempt to reconcile the phenomenal concept strategy and the knowledge argument with social externalism about phenomenal concepts. Ball's recent efforts to undermine that attempt fail. Further, neither he nor Rabin succeeds in showing that considerations about concept mastery, a priori deducibility, and necessitation undermine the knowledge argument.

---

[61] Chalmers (2004a). Cf. Stoljar (2005).

[62] There are further reasons to invoke such variants. Chalmers (2004b, pp. 284–85) does so to answer what he calls the *no-concept reply* to the knowledge argument, according to which pre-release Mary would be able to deduce the relevant phenomenal truths about seeing in color if only she had the relevant phenomenal-color concepts (Kirk 2005; Montero 2007).

Ultimately, the knowledge argument and the phenomenal concept strategy cannot both succeed. But if the arguments I have presented here are sound, then it is doubtful that considerations about social externalism should play a substantial role in determining the fate of either.[63]

[63] I presented versions of this paper at five events: the Rio-2013 Conference on Phenomenal Concepts in Rio de Janeiro; TSC 2016 The Science of Consciousness, in Tucson, Arizona; the 2016 International Conference on Philosophy of Mind: Thought and Perception, at the University of Minho in Braga, Portugal; the 2017 Central Division Meeting of the American Philosophical Association in Kansas City, Missouri; and the 2017 Consciousness and Semantic Externalism conference at NYU. I thank those present at all five events. For helpful comments and discussions, I thank Derek Ball, David Chalmers, Melissa Ebbers, Amy Kind, Janet Levin, Derk Pereboom, and especially Sam Coleman, Robert J. Howell, and Gabriel Rabin.

8   Mary's Powers of Imagination

Amy Kind

In contemporary discussions of philosophy of mind, Frank Jackson's story of Mary is a familiar one (Jackson 1982, 1986). Though Mary has spent her entire life locked inside a black-and-white room and has never seen color, she has nonetheless mastered color science. When she is released from her room and sees a ripe tomato for the first time, it seems that she learns something – that she comes to know what seeing red is like. But if Mary did not know all there was to know about color while in the room, and thus if there are facts over and above the physical facts about color, then physicalism is threatened. The standard physicalist responses to this argument, typically referred to as the *knowledge argument*, are also by now familiar. While some deny that Mary learns anything at all about color and color experiences upon her release from the room – how could she, given that she already has all the physical information there is to have about color and color experiences? – others acknowledge the power of the intuition that Mary has an "Aha!" moment when she exits the room and are slightly more concessionary. Such concessionary responses typically grant that Mary learns something upon her release but deny that this threatens physicalism. Rather, her learning should be understood to consist in the acquisition of abilities, or in her newfound acquaintance with color, or in her apprehension of an old fact under a new guise.

In this chapter I want to focus on the first of these more concessionary responses – what's now generally known as *the ability hypothesis*. As originally proposed by Laurence Nemirow, the ability hypothesis claims that what Mary gains when she leaves the room is the ability to imagine seeing red (1980, 1990). A subsequent modification by David Lewis (1983a, 1999) gives us what is now considered to be the standard version of the view: What Mary gains when she leaves the room is a cluster of abilities including not only the ability to imagine seeing red but also the abilities to recognize and recall seeing red. For proponents of the ability hypothesis, knowing what an experience is like is not propositional in nature but rather consists in the possession of the relevant ability or abilities.

Criticism of the ability hypothesis has tended to focus on this last claim, and considerable attention has been devoted to the question of whether the possession of such abilities is either necessary or sufficient for knowledge of what an experience is like.[1] To my mind, however, this critical strategy grants too much. Focusing specifically on imaginative ability, I argue that Mary does not gain this ability when she leaves the room for she already had the ability to imagine red while she was inside it. Moreover, despite what some have thought, the ability hypothesis cannot be easily rescued by recasting it in terms of a more restrictive imaginative ability. My purpose here is not to take sides in the debate about physicalism, i.e., my criticism of the ability hypothesis is not offered in an attempt to defend the anti-physicalist conclusion of the knowledge argument. Rather, my purpose is to redeem imagination from the misleading picture of it that discussion of the knowledge argument has fostered.

8.1 What Can Mary Imagine?

David Hume famously said that nowhere are we more free than in imagination, and the human capacity for imagination is typically taken to be almost without limit. We readily imagine all sorts of variations on things that we've encountered – from talking mice and golden geese to flying carpets and magic beans. And we also readily imagine all sorts of things that we've never actually encountered and that we don't even believe to exist, from ghosts and goblins to light sabers and time machines. Insofar as our imaginative capacities are in any way limited, those limits stem solely from the limits of possibility. On this point we might again look to Hume and, in particular, to what he referred to as "an established maxim in metaphysics," namely, that "*that nothing we imagine is absolutely impossible*" (1739/1985, I.ii.2). Since what we imagine contains within it "the idea of possible existence," we are unable to imagine impossible entities like round squares.[2]

The uses to which we put our imagination also seem to be almost without limit.[3] We engage in imaginative exercises for purposes both playful and

---

[1] See, e.g., Conee (1994); Alter (1998). Nida-Rümelin (2009) provides a useful summary of criticisms in this vein.

[2] That imagination has even this limit is sometimes disputed. To give just one example, Tamar Gendler's story of the Tower of Goldbach may suggest a way to imagine that 7 + 5 does not equal 12 (Gendler 2000). See also Kung (2016) and Tidman (1994).

[3] For a survey of some of the many uses of imagination see Kind (2016a, 7–10). See also Colin McGinn's argument that "imagination is a faculty that runs through the most diverse of mental phenomena" and that humans should be understood as *homo imaginans* (2004a, 5).

serious – in our engagement with fiction and games of pretense on the one hand, and in our decision-making and future planning on the other. In the more fanciful contexts, we tend to let our imagination run wild; in the more serious ones, we tend to rein it in. Sometimes our imagining is spontaneous, while sometimes it's deliberate. Sometimes our imagining is effortless, while sometimes it's hard work.

Surprisingly, many of these basic and uncontroversial claims about imagination seem to have been forgotten in philosophical discussion of Mary, and in particular, in philosophical discussion of the ability hypothesis. In arguing that Mary *gains* the ability to imagine the experience of seeing red when she leaves the room, proponents of the ability hypothesis presuppose that Mary *lacked* the ability to imagine the experience of seeing red while she was in her black-and-white room. Even opponents of the ability hypothesis tend to accept that Mary gains the ability to imagine the experience of seeing red when she leaves the room; what they question is whether this ability-gain adequately accounts for Mary's newfound knowledge of what seeing red is like. It is also generally assumed that there is nothing that Mary can do, while in the room, to gain the ability to imagine the experience of seeing red.[4] No matter what she does, and no matter how hard she tries, she will be unable to engage in this kind of imaginative exercise. What happened to the almost limitless human capacity for imagination?

We see a similar phenomenon – a phenomenon in which basic and uncontroversial claims about the imagination seem to have been forgotten – in connection with a different familiar example employed against physicalism: Thomas Nagel's bat. In developing his case that we can't know what it's like to be a bat, Nagel explicitly argues that our imagination will be no help. Bats navigate the world through echolocation, and they thus have perceptual experiences that are completely different in subjective character from any of the perceptual experiences that we have. For Nagel, the fact that echolocation is closed off to us experientially means that it is also closed off to us imaginatively:

> Our own experience provides the basic material for our imagination, whose range is therefore limited. It will not help to try to imagine that one has webbing on one's arms, which enables one to fly around at dusk and dawn catching insects in one's mouth; that one has very poor vision, and

---

[4] Though the agreement on this point is widespread it is not without exception. I discuss a couple of philosophers who take an alternative view of Mary's powers of imagination in 8.2, below.

perceives the surrounding world by a system of reflected high-frequency sound signals; and that one spends the day hanging upside down by one's feet in an attic. In so far as I can imagine this (which is not very far), it tells me only what it would be like for me to behave as a bat behaves. But that is not the question. I want to know what it is like for a bat to be a bat. Yet if I try to imagine this, I am restricted to the resources of my own mind, and those resources are inadequate to the task. I cannot perform it either by imagining additions to my present experience, or by imagining segments gradually subtracted from it, or by imagining some combination of additions, subtractions, and modifications. (Nagel 1974, 439)

These claims – that pre-release Mary can't imagine the experience of seeing red, that humans can't imagine the bat's experience of echolocation – have become deeply entrenched in philosophical discussion. In fact, these claims are so entrenched that, having pointed out how they conflict with our ordinary picture of imagination, I fear that some readers might be more inclined to give up this picture than to give up the claims themselves. Insofar as there is any such inclination, it may help to be reminded of the sorts of imaginative exercises that are commonplace in everyday life. As young children, we imagine ourselves to be all sorts of creatures, big and small. Our arms become a crocodile's jaw, an elephant's trunk, a bird's wings. We imagine flying over the playground, or burrowing underground, or slithering through the grass. We imagine rocketing to the moon, meeting space aliens on Mars, or traveling through wormholes to distant galaxies. And our imaginings don't stop as we become older. Whether we're imagining winning the Superbowl or an Oscar, becoming President of the United States or being nominated for the Supreme Court, the joy of impending parenthood or the unpleasantness of impending chemotherapy, we continue to stretch our imaginative capacities to all sorts of events and scenarios that lie far beyond anything we've actually experienced.

Granted, we do sometimes say things that seem to suggest limitations on our imaginations beyond mere possibility. In everyday life it's not at all uncommon to hear someone start a sentence with, "I can't imagine …" Sometimes these claims are made when we're confronted with news of tragedy. When we read about a violent crime or a natural disaster, we might profess ourselves unable to imagine the trauma of the survivors, the courage of the victims, or the grief of their families. "I can't imagine how frightened they must have been," we might say when we hear about the children who hid under their desks during a school shooting. When thinking about the parents whose children were killed, we might profess ourselves unable to imagine what they're going through. But what do these claims of unimaginability really mean? Often, it seems that they are simply an expression of our own shock and horror – a way of saying that things are unbearably awful – rather than actual claims about imagination. Insofar as they are claims about imagination, they will likely be claims not about what we can't do but about what we don't want to do. A refusal to imaginatively engage with these situations might help us to keep some of the horror at bay.

There's one other possibility about how to interpret such claims, however, and it's one that will bring us back to Mary. When certain events and experiences are very foreign to our own, or when they strike us as inexplicable in some key way, we might be inclined to deny that we can imagine them because we don't think we can imagine them *correctly*. There are two ways to understand this suggestion. On the first way, ordinary claims of the form "I can't imagine such-and-such" are shorthand for claims of the form "I'm doing a bad job imagining such-and-such." In this case, they're not really about what we can or cannot imagine but about what we can or cannot imagine well. On the second way of understanding this suggestion, however, such reports are not mere shorthand for claims about correct imaginings but rather follow from them. When we find ourselves unable to imagine something well, when we lack confidence that our imagining gets it right, that would mean that we're not really imagining it at all.

This analysis would explain why we might think Mary, who has never had any color experiences whatsoever, lacks the ability to imagine red while in her black-and-white room. No matter how gifted an imaginer Mary is, it seems pretty implausible – at least upon first thought, though we'll return to this question below – that prior to her release she's able to imagine the experience of seeing red correctly. So if imagining an experience requires imagining an experience correctly, then pre-release Mary would lack the ability to imagine the experience of seeing red after all.

What can be said in favor of this analysis, i.e., in favor of the claim that a failure to imagine *well* amounts to a failure to imagine? Here we might compare a related ability, that of memory. Suppose I try to remember how I felt when I got a particular piece of unexpected news. If I now claim to remember being relieved but at the time I was not relieved but disappointed, then my claim is false. Misremembering – or at least radical misremembering – is not really remembering at all; it is at best *seeming* to remember. So perhaps imagining works like remembering, where misimagining – or at least radical misimagining – is not really imagining at all.

Unfortunately, this line of defense proves quickly to be a dead end. On our ordinary picture of imagining, imagining is not like remembering. Though an act is disqualified as remembering in virtue of embodying mistakes (or at least radical mistakes), an act is not disqualified as imagining in virtue of embodying mistakes. In some instances of imagining, of course, the notion of mistake has no purchase. What would it mean for a child to be mistaken when imagining a scary monster or a fairy godmother? But even when we can relevantly talk about mistakes in imaginings – in cases, for example, where we're trying to get things right – the mistakes do not cause the kind of problems for imagining that they do for remembering. A newborn baby might have considerably more hair than his mother imagined. The collector's edition Millennium Falcon replica bought on eBay might be considerably smaller than the purchaser imagined. The newly painted living room might be considerably darker than the homeowner imagined. Yet all of these mistaken imaginings are still imaginings.

So if mistakes do not keep an imagining from being an imagining, then the fact that Mary's imagining of the experience of seeing red will almost surely contain mistakes does not give us grounds to deny that Mary has the ability to imagine this experience. But perhaps there is a related move in the vicinity that's more promising. Though the mistakes do not keep her act from being an imagining, perhaps they keep it from being an imagining *of the experience of seeing red*. Though Mary is trying to imagine the experience of seeing red, and though she takes herself to be imagining seeing red, she's really only imagined some shade of gray.

Here too, however, the line of thought is problematic and, again, the problem becomes obvious when we reflect on ordinary imaginings and the way we think about them. The fact that her infant has more hair than the new mother imagined does not mean that during the nine months of her pregnancy she'd been failing to imagine him. "You're not at all like I imagined," she might coo at him – but not: "Wow, I was imagining some different baby altogether." In general, the fact that an imagining mischaracterizes its target does not mean that it misses its target altogether.[5]

In fact, as philosophers working on imagination have long recognized, the connection between an imagining and its target is an especially tight one. Consider the following passage from Jean-Paul Sartre:

---

[5] For more on the difference between imaginings that miss their targets and imaginings that mischaracterize their targets, see Kind (2016b).

[T]he imaged cube is given immediately for what it is. When I say "the object I perceive" is a cube, I make a hypothesis that the later course of my perceptions may oblige me to abandon. When I say "the object of which I have an image at this moment is a cube," I make here a judgement of obviousness: it is absolutely certain that the object of my image is a cube.

(Sartre 1940/2010, 9)

As Sartre here suggests, and in line with a general consensus in philosophical discussion of imagination, imaginers enjoy a certain epistemic privilege with respect to their imaginings: they cannot be mistaken about what they are imagining. One way to explain this privilege is in terms of the intentions with which we undertake an imaginative project; as Colin McGinn notes, "the identity of my imagined object is fixed by my imaginative intentions, to which I have special access." In an imagining, the imaginative object is "*given*, not inferred. I know that my image is of my mother because I *intended* it to be; I don't have to consult the appearance of the person in the image and then infer that I must have formed an image of my mother" (McGinn 2004a, 5). Indeed, this is one of the many aspects of imagining that differentiates it from perceiving. Though sheer force of will cannot enable me to perceive something, it can enable me to imagine something.

As Nagel notes in the passage quoted earlier, the resources of our own minds are limited, and so we don't have much to go on when we set ourselves the project of imagining what it's like to be a bat. And he is also right that there is an important sense in which our imaginative efforts in this regard will be a failure, namely, that they will fail to teach us what we want to know – they will not teach us what it's like to be a bat. But this instructive failure does not in itself mean that we lack the ability to imagine what it's like to be a bat. And likewise for Mary. Pre-release, Mary's imaginings will not teach her what it is like to see red. But that does not mean that she lacks the ability to imagine the experience of seeing red while she is in her black-and-white room.

The upshot for the ability hypothesis should be clear: in its traditional form, at least, the hypothesis is false. Mary does not gain the ability to imagine the experience of red when she leaves the room, for this is an ability that she already has inside the room. But here it would be natural to think that the foregoing discussion has revealed a solution to the problem in the course of revealing the problem itself. Having alerted us to the importance of distinguishing the ability of imagining from the ability of imagining correctly, the discussion suggests that we reformulate the ability hypothesis in terms of the latter ability rather than the former. On this suggestion, then, what Mary gains when she leaves the room is not the ability to imagine the experience of seeing red but rather the ability to imagine this experience correctly.

In the remainder of this chapter, I turn to an evaluation of this suggestion. My discussion proceeds in two stages. First, in 8.2, I'll consider some particular attempts to revise the ability hypothesis to take account of the distinction between imagining and imagining correctly. As we'll see, however, such revision proves to be more difficult than one might think. Thus, in 8.3, I'll turn more directly to the notion of imagining correctly. What does it mean to imagine correctly, and what are Mary's powers in this regard? Ultimately, our discussion will suggest that the ability hypothesis fares no better by employing the notion of correct imagining than it does by employing the notion of imagining.

8.2 Recasting the Ability Hypothesis

As we've seen, the standard version of the ability hypothesis in play in philosophical discussion proposes that Mary gains three abilities upon her release: the ability to imagine, to recognize, and to remember the experience of seeing red. This is how the view is typically presented in encyclopedia articles and other overviews (see, e.g., Ludlow, Stoljar, and Nagasawa 2004; Nida-Rümelin 2009), and it's also how Jackson himself has presented matters after abandoning his defense of the knowledge argument and announcing his allegiance to the ability hypothesis instead (Jackson 2003).[6] As we've also seen, casting the ability hypothesis in these terms is problematic, since there's good reason to think that Mary already has the ability to imagine the experience of seeing red while she's inside the room. Though this problem is not widely recognized, there have been a few instances – I'll here mention three in particular – in which philosophers writing on the knowledge argument have explicitly attempted to avoid this problem by invoking a distinction between the ability to imagine and the ability to imagine correctly.[7] Though all three of these philosophers agree that the ability hypothesis will only be plausible if it is cast in terms of the ability to imagine correctly, they differ in how to spell out the notion of correctness.

---

[6] Though Jackson has now adopted the ability hypothesis, his main reasons for repudiating the knowledge argument stem from considerations about representationalism.

[7] It's perhaps not surprising that two of the philosophers to notice this problem – Paul Noordhof and Bence Nanay – have published extensively on imagination.

For D. H. Mellor, who takes up the issue in his "Nothing Like Experience" (1993), imagining something correctly entails being able to recognize it.[8] Like the proponents of the ability hypothesis, Mellor is concerned to give an analysis of our knowledge of what experience is like, but unlike such proponents, he is not concerned to defend physicalism. As Mellor argues, an imagining cannot constitute knowledge of what an experience is like if that experience is imagined incorrectly: "For we can imagine experiences wrongly, and then we do not know what they are like. Someone who imagines sugar to taste like salt, for example, does not know what sugar tastes like." Thus, he argues, "To know what experiences of a certain kind are like I must, when I imagine them, imagine them correctly, i.e., in a way that makes me recognise them when I have them" (Mellor 1993, 4–5).

Paul Noordhof (2003) agrees with Mellor that incorrect imagining cannot constitute knowledge of what an experience is like, but he offers a slightly different analysis of what it is to imagine an experience correctly. For Noordhof, what matters is not that I be able to *recognize* the experience but that I be able to *identify* it (Noordhof 2003, 23). Recognition, Noordhof worries, seems to imply previous cognition: "I can only recognize things if I have come across them, a picture of them, or a description of them, some time before." In his view, this threatens to make the ability hypothesis trivial: Rather than offering us some insight into why experience of a certain sort is necessary for knowledge of what such an experience is like, such an analysis simply presupposes what it sets out to explain. He thus prefers to cash out correct imagining in terms of identification, which carries no implication of previous cognition.[9]

In a more recent discussion, Bence Nanay raises a problem that would seem to apply to both of these formulations. At least some people who become blind late in life claim that they can still imagine the experience of seeing red, and presumably they can do so correctly (for discussion, see Sacks 2003). But since such an individual no longer has recognitional capabilities with respect to this experience – "they are most certainly incapable of recognizing red, given that they are blind" (Nanay 2009, 704) – it would be a mistake to cash out correct imagining in terms of recognition. A similar point seems to apply

---

[8] Though Mellor mentions the Mary case, he is primarily concerned with Nagel's discussion of what it's like to be a bat.

[9] Insofar as Mellor takes recognition to imply only lack of surprise and not previous cognition, Noordhof's account might not be a dramatic departure from Mellor's – as Noordhof himself admits. See Noordhof (2003, n. 5).

to identification. The accounts of correct imagination offered by Mellor and Noordhof are thus problematic, and correspondingly, so too are their versions of the ability hypothesis in which these accounts are embedded.

In an attempt to rectify this problem, Nanay offers an alternate understanding of what it means to have the ability to imagine an experience E correctly: one has this ability when one can imagine the experience "in such a way that would enable one to distinguish imagining experience E from imagining or having any other experience" (Nanay 2009, 705). Since blind imaginers remain capable of distinguishing their imaginings from one another, Nanay's account allows that such imaginers can imagine color experiences correctly and thus protects itself from the objection that he posed to the kind of account offered by Mellor and Noordhof.

But in doing so, Nanay opens himself up to a different objection. To see this, it will help to look at how his analysis of correct imagining gets incorporated into his new version of the ability hypothesis. Like the original ability hypothesis, Nanay's revised version aims to provide an explanation of knowing what an experience is like:

> Knowing what it is like to experience E is having the ability to distinguish imagining or having experience E from imagining or having any other experience.

Nanay's account is disjunctive in nature, and it's precisely this feature that protects him against what might otherwise seem to be objections or counterexamples. On his view, each of the abilities mentioned is individually sufficient for knowing what an experience is like but they are not individually necessary; rather, what's necessary for an individual to know what experience E is like is that she have at least one of the two abilities. Thus, the fact that an individual may lack one of these abilities while still having knowledge of what an experience is like will not count against Nanay's version of the ability hypothesis.

My worry about the account, however, stems from a slightly different direction. Surprisingly, perhaps, my worry about the account does not concern its adequacy. For our purposes here, I'm happy to accept for the sake of argument that Nanay has proposed a version of the ability hypothesis that offers an adequate account of knowledge of what an experience is like. To my mind, however, it would be a mistake to treat this version of the ability hypothesis as one which assigns any real importance to imaginative ability. As I read the account above, not only does it shift away from the ability to imagine but it also shifts away from the ability to imagine correctly. What's central to

Nanay's ability hypothesis are not imaginative abilities but rather *discriminative abilities*.

Granted, Nanay takes himself to be invoking these discriminative abilities in an effort to explain what correct imagining is. But while an ability to discriminate might be essential for one's knowledge of what an experience is like, it's hard to see why it should be essential for the correctness of an imagining. What makes an imagining correct or not has to do with how well it matches its target. And just as a drawing might correctly capture its target without enabling someone who sees it to distinguish that target from all other possible targets, so too an imagining might correctly capture its target without enabling an imaginer to distinguish that target from all other possible targets.

It may help to consider things this way: As stated, Nanay's version of the ability hypothesis doesn't require anything about Mary's imaginative abilities to change when she exits the room. She might be producing exactly the same imaginings once she exits the room that she was producing while she was inside the room. What's changed once she leaves the room is that she is now able to distinguish this imagining from all other imaginings and experiences; that's what her knowledge of what it's like consists in.

At this point, it might seem that things have somehow gone astray. One of the key intuitions motivating the ability hypothesis seemed to have to do with imaginative ability. It seemed plausible that we could explain Mary's newfound knowledge of what the experience of seeing red is like at least partially in terms of an imaginative gain. But we've now ended up with a version of the ability hypothesis that, perhaps inadvertently, requires us to jettison that intuition. (Indeed, though I've been assuming for the sake of argument that such a version of the ability hypothesis might well be an adequate account of knowledge of what an experience is like, once we realize how far we've shifted away from the original ability hypothesis, this assumption now starts to seem questionable.) So where do we go from here?

8.3 What Can Mary Imagine Correctly?

As we saw in 8.1, the ability hypothesis cannot be specified in terms of the ability to imagine the experience of seeing red, because on any plausible understanding of that ability, Mary already has it inside the room. In uncovering this problem, however, our discussion led to what looked like a promising alternative: Instead of relying on the ability to imagine, the ability hypothesis might instead rely on the ability to imagine correctly. Indeed, as we saw in 8.2, this alternative has been pursued by several proponents of the ability hypothesis. Now that we have explored their proposals, however, it has seemed that the alternative has failed to live up to its promise. In particular, it proved difficult to flesh out the notion of correct imagining in such a way as to save the ability hypothesis. As a result, it appears that we've ended up with a version of the ability hypothesis that, rather than developing the notion of correct imagining, instead seems to abandon it altogether.

These difficulties notwithstanding, one might still have the sense that there is something importantly right about explicating the ability hypothesis in terms of correct imagining. Perhaps the problem with the previous proposals was not the notion itself but rather the specific ways of fleshing it out. If this is the case, then we might be better served simply by relying on an intuitive understanding of it. Might such a version of the ability hypothesis work? Can such an intuitive understanding do the philosophical work that's needed? It's these questions that will motivate the discussion of this section. Rather than addressing them directly, however, I propose to come at them somewhat sideways. Just as we've previously explored the question of what pre-release Mary can imagine, here I want to explore the question of what pre-release Mary can imagine correctly.

To start, it will be helpful to recall a basic point about imagination that we encountered in 8.1: Human imaginers typically imagine all sorts of things that lie beyond anything we've actually experienced, in some cases *far* beyond anything we've actually experienced. Let's call these *distant* imaginings. Of course, whether an imagining counts as distant or not will vary from imaginer to imaginer. For those of us with normal color vision who haven't been locked in a black-and-white room all our lives, imagining the experience of seeing red would not be a distant imagining at all. It would be more distant for someone with red-green color blindness, and yet even more distant for Mary.

As this suggests, not only is the matter of distance relative to the experience one has, but it is also a matter of degree. Distant imaginings lie on a continuum – what I'll call the *distance continuum* – from the not-so-distant to the very, very distant. Consider the fact that trained musicians can look at an unfamiliar music score and imagine correctly the experience of hearing the piece played, or that trained chefs can look at an unfamiliar recipe and imagine correctly the experience of tasting the cooked dish. Though these acts might naturally be characterized as distant imaginings – after all, the musician has never before heard this composition and the chef has never before tasted this dish – there's also a sense in which they're not *very* distant. As Lewis notes in discussing sightreading, "new music isn't altogether new – the big new experience is a rearrangement of lots of little old experiences," and presumably the same holds true for new dishes (Lewis

1999, 265). In his view, our capacity for correct imagining gives out when an experience is "new enough." As he admits, the question of when an experience is new enough – or, to put it in my terms, when an experience is sufficiently distant – is a very hard one to answer.

That said, almost everyone seems to agree that whatever the answer, that however we draw the line between experiences that are not too distant to be imagined correctly and experiences that are, the experience of seeing red is for Mary on the far side of the line. Note here that that I said *almost* everyone. There are two notable exceptions. In discussing the knowledge argument, Daniel Dennett has consistently denied that Mary learns anything at all when she leaves the room (see, e.g., Dennett 1991, 398ff.). Given her knowledge of a completed color science, there is no "aha" moment when she sees a ripe tomato for the first time. If we tried to trick her by showing her a blue tomato, she would not be fooled. Though Dennett's original responses to the knowledge argument do not directly address the issue of Mary's imaginative capacities, his staunch insistence that Mary already knows what the experience of seeing red is like while she's inside the room suggests that he would also insist she has the ability to imagine the experience of seeing red correctly while she is still inside the room. In a recent paper, he has been more explicit on this point:

> We are told that Mary in her cell can't imagine what it's like to experience red, try as she might. But suppose she doesn't accept this limitation and does try her best, cogitating for hours on end, and one day she tells us she just got lucky and succeeded. "Hey," she says, "I was just daydreaming, and I stumbled across what it's like to see red, and, of course, once I noticed what I was doing I tested my imagination against everything I knew, and I confirmed that I had, indeed, imagined what it's like to see red!" (Dennett 2007, 23)

As Dennett notes, if we subsequently tested her by showing her various color samples and she passed the test, why wouldn't we conclude that she could correctly imagine the experience of red while she was inside the room?

Paul Churchland has long pushed a similar line. On his view, pre-release Mary has the ability not only to imagine having the experience of red but also the ability to imagine it correctly. Like Dennett, Churchland stresses just how much Mary knows. Given this knowledge, Mary may begin to reconceptualize her inner life:

> So she does not identify her visual sensations crudely as "a sensation-of-black," "a sensation-of-grey," or "a sensation-of-white"; rather she identifies

them more revealingly as various spiking frequencies in the *nth* layer of the occipital cortex (or whatever). If Mary has the relevant neuroscientific concepts for the sensational states at issue (viz., sensations-of-*red*), but has never yet been *in* those states, she may well be able to imagine being in the relevant cortical state, and imagine it with substantial success, even in advance of receiving external stimuli that would actually produce it. (Churchland 1985, 25–6)

For our purposes here, there are two ways we might take these remarks. On the one hand, Churchland might be granting that the experience of red is, for Mary, a very distant one but trying to show that even this very distant experience can still be correctly imagined. On the other hand, Churchland might be denying that the experience of seeing red is as distant for Mary as we might have thought. To my mind, Churchland is most plausibly read as offering this second kind of proposal. It's not that we were wrong about where to draw the line between experiences that are not too distant to be imagined correctly and experiences that are, it's that we were wrong about where color experiences lie for Mary on the distance continuum.

Recall again the sightreading example from above, i.e., that trained musicians can sightread scores they've never heard before. Extending this kind of example, Churchland notes that musicians with sufficient training can identify the individual notes of a chord they're hearing for the first time, and conversely, can auditorily imagine an unfamiliar chord from the specification of the notes. Such imaginative feats are possible in virtue of the fact that chords are structured sets of elements, i.e., in virtue of the fact that even new and unfamiliar musical experiences of chords are not that distant. If color sensations are likewise structured, then new and unfamiliar color experiences would be considerably less distant than we'd initially thought. Though color experiences seem to us to be undifferentiated wholes, the same holds true – at least initially – for chord experiences. So, asks Churchland, "Why should it be unthinkable that sensations of color possess a comparable internal structure, unnoticed so far, but awaiting our determined and informed introspection?" (1985, 26–7), i.e., the sort of informed introspective abilities that one might develop were one to master completed neuroscience.

It might help to cast the basic issue here in terms of *scaffolding*. One reason that color experience seems to be so distant for Mary is that there seems to be no way to get to them from the kinds of experiences she has. If color experience is structured, however – and in particular, if it has some kind of phenomenal structure – then that structure could provide a way for Mary to scaffold out from the experiences she has to those that she hasn't. Moreover, this scaffolding would provide Mary not only a way to imagine the unfamiliar experiences but a way to imagine them correctly. More generally, scaffolding also provides us with a useful way to think about the distance continuum.

Churchland's point in raising these considerations is slightly different from ours. Rather than putting them forth to criticize the ability hypothesis, he means to be criticizing the knowledge argument more directly. As a result, he doesn't intend the story he's spun about Mary to show that she actually has the ability to correctly imagine the experience of red while inside the room; rather, the considerations he offers are designed to show simply that *it's not unthinkable* that she has this ability, that her having this skill is not "beyond all possibility" (Churchland 1985, 26). But regardless of whether such considerations are enough to defuse the knowledge argument – a question that it would take us too far afield to settle – it's clear that such considerations are not quite enough for our purposes here. Our interest is in determining what Mary can and can't imagine correctly, in how to draw the line between imaginings that are not too distant to be imagined correctly and those that are. Though it would probably have been too much to expect that we'd be provided with decisive answers to these questions, we might reasonably have hoped for a slightly stronger case one way or the other.

So can we do any better? Here I think we are helped by reflecting upon other cases of relatively distant experiences where correct imagining seems to be within our grasp. To take just one example, consider Mark Haddon's *The Curious Incident of the Dog in the Night-Time*. The story is set in motion when Christopher, the 15-year-old narrator of the novel, decides to investigate the murder of his neighbor's dog. But Christopher is no ordinary teenager. He's mathematically gifted and has highly developed powers of visual thinking but is socially awkward – physically lashing out at others when he becomes uncomfortable. He hates the colors brown and yellow, refuses to tell jokes or use metaphors, and hides in small spaces when he's frightened. Though Haddon never explicitly uses the terms "autism" or "Asperger's syndrome" in the course of the book, and deliberately so, Christopher's behavioral difficulties suggest that he lies somewhere on the autistic spectrum.[10]

Haddon, who does not have autism, has been widely praised for his ability to get inside the mind of someone with this condition. The book has been described as a "triumph of empathy," as brimming with "with imagination,

---

[10] The term "Asperger's" was used on the book's cover, and both terms appear in various promotional materials for the book that have been put out by the publisher. Haddon discusses his own reluctance to use these terms and his views about how best to describe Christopher at www.markhaddon.com/aspergers-and-autism.

empathy, and vision," and as "flawlessly imagined and deeply affecting."[11] The experience of having autism differs from person to person, but Haddon seems to have successfully imagined what it's like to be one such person. (And, moreover, he seems to have enabled his readers to imagine it as well.) Though this imagining is less distant than imagining what it's like to be a bat, say, for people who do not have autism it is still a case of relatively distant imagining.

A different example takes us even closer to the bat case. Though Nagel claims we cannot know what it is like to be a bat, animal scientist Temple Grandin claims that she can adopt a "cow's eye view" of a situation and thereby, in at least a limited sense, know what it is like to be a cow. Like Christopher, the fictional narrator of Haddon's novel, Grandin has autism. Also like Christopher, Grandin describes herself as a visual thinker, and she credits her visual thinking with enabling her "to build entire systems" in her imagination. Her visual thinking is also what enables her to take up a cow's perspective:

> When I put myself in a cow's place, I really have to be that cow and not a person in cow costume. I use my visual thinking skills to simulate what an animal would see and hear in a given situation. I place myself inside its body and imagine what it experiences. It is the ultimate virtual reality system. (2006, 168)

Throughout her career, Grandin has revolutionized the handling of livestock with her innovative equipment designs. Facilities using the equipment that she's designed report that the animals are considerably more comfortable, cooperative, and calm than they were previously. Her tremendous success suggests not only that has Grandin managed to imagine what it is like to be a cow but that she has managed to do so with at least some degree of correctness.

Reflection on examples such as these helps to shed further light on Mary's powers of imagination. To my mind, these sorts of examples continue the work begun by Churchland's considerations of eroding a knee-jerk skepticism that Mary could imagine color experiences correctly. Granted, such considerations do not go so far as to show definitively that Mary does have the ability to imagine correctly the experience of seeing red inside the room. After all, the

---

[11] The first quotation is from a review in *The New Yorker*, the second is an endorsement by author Myla Goldberg that's printed on the back cover of the book, and the third quotation is from a review in *Time Out New York*. All quotations can be found in the editorial reviews included on the Amazon page for the book, www.amazon.com/Curious-Incident-Dog-Night-Time/dp/1400032717?ie=UTF8&ref_=asap_bc.

examples that we've considered seem to involve experiences that are plausibly less distant for the imaginer than color experiences are for Mary. But even though there still seems reason to doubt that pre-release Mary can correctly imagine color experiences, there is an important moral to be drawn from the examples just considered. In particular, they seem to pose something of a dilemma for a proponent of the ability hypothesis who wants to employ the notion of correct imagining.

If Haddon can correctly imagine what's it like to be autistic, and Grandin can correctly imagine what it's like to be a cow, then that means that many experiences that are fairly far along the distance spectrum can be correctly imagined. In utilizing the notion of correct imagining, then, the proponent of the ability hypothesis has to walk a very careful tightrope. Too restrictive an interpretation of the notion of correct imagining – that is, one that makes correct imagining very hard to achieve – runs the risk of ruling out these cases. But too permissive an interpretation of the notion of correct imagining – that is, one that makes correct imagining very easy to achieve – runs the risk of ruling in Mary. Of course, one might try to achieve the appropriate balance by connecting correct imagining to knowledge of what it's like, e.g., an imagining is correct if and only if it coheres with the imaginer's knowledge of what an experience is like. But this kind of analysis deprives the notion of correct imagining of any usefulness in a version of the ability hypothesis. One can't usefully invoke the notion of correct imagining in one's analysis of what knowledge of an experience is like when one has relied on knowledge of what an experience is like to distinguish between correct and incorrect imagining. Thus, it starts to look like there is very little room to flesh out the notion of correct imagining in a non-question-begging way such that it allows for imaginings like Haddon's and Grandin's to be correct without also allowing imaginings like Mary's to be correct.

Faced with this problem, one might be tempted to deny that the imaginings by Haddon and Grandin are really correct after all. But such a denial is not likely to help a proponent of the ability hypothesis who wants to employ correct imagining. This notion, remember, is meant to go along with knowledge of what an experience is like. Such knowledge is meant to consist, at least in part, in this imaginative ability. But once we adopt a very restrictive conception of correct imagining, a conception that makes correct imagining out of reach not just for pre-release Mary with respect to color experience and us with respect to bats but for all sorts of other experiences as well, this imaginative ability starts to seem disconnected with – and even more restrictive than – knowledge of what an experience is like. Ultimately, it looks increasingly unlikely that the notion of correct imagining will be able to bear the philosophical weight that proponents of the ability hypothesis want to place on it.

We might put this point in terms of a dilemma for the proponent of the ability hypothesis – or at least for such a proponent who wants to invoke imaginative abilities. If the ability hypothesis is explicated in terms of a *restrictive* notion of correct imagining, then though it will turn out to be true that pre-release Mary can't correctly imagine red, we will also have to deny that Haddon can correctly imagine what it's like to be autistic or that Grandin can correctly imagine what it's like to be a cow. And this seems like the wrong result. Moreover, since it seems plausible that Haddon (and his readers) do have at least some knowledge or what being autistic is like, and likewise for Grandin with respect to the cow's experience, we'd also end up with cases where it looks like someone can know what an experience is like despite being unable to imagine it correctly. On the other hand, if the proponent of the ability hypothesis tries to avoid this problem by employing a weaker notion of correct imagining, then it looks like pre-release Mary's imaginings of color experiences will end up counting as cases of correct imagining. In short, either the ability hypothesis gets the intended result about Mary but relies upon an implausibly strict account of correct imagining, or it relies on a more plausible analysis of correct imagining but doesn't get the intended result about Mary.[12]

8.4 Concluding Remarks

The argument of this chapter poses a problem for the ability hypothesis. But it's important to be clear about the force of the considerations I've raised. In particular, nothing that I've said here rules out there being a version of the ability hypothesis that might be usefully employed to defend physicalism from the knowledge argument. What I have shown, however, is that any such version of the ability hypothesis will have to be developed without reliance on imaginative abilities.

In a sense, however, this chapter hasn't really been about the ability hypothesis at all – or at least, not just about it. Rather, the true motivation of this paper has been to rescue imagination from some misunderstandings that have arisen in the context of the knowledge argument. Insofar as the discussion of this argument – and, in particular, discussion of the ability hypothesis – has promoted the impression that Mary inside the room cannot exercise her powers of imagination, that she can't imagine color experience, it has promoted (even if inadvertently so) a misleading picture of imagination, a picture that

---

[12] Thanks to Sam Coleman for suggesting the dilemma formulation.

paints imagination as considerably more limited than it in fact is. Moreover, insofar as the discussion has conflated the ability to imagine with the ability to imagine correctly, this misleading picture of imagination and its limits has been exacerbated.

There's an even deeper respect in which discussion of the knowledge argument has had pernicious consequences for our understanding of imagination. The issue that I have in mind was hinted at in the discussion of scaffolding above. In brief, the assumption that underlies the ability hypothesis is that knowledge of what an experience is like consists in an imaginative ability. When Mary comes to see red for the first time, she thereby comes to know what the experience of seeing red is like, and what this means is that she can now imagine things that she couldn't before. Her having the imaginative ability is simply part and parcel of her having knowledge of what the experience is like; that's what such knowledge *is*. But I'm inclined to think that this way of thinking of the relationship between our imaginative abilities and our knowledge gets things importantly wrong.[13] On this conception of imagination, we can't learn from our imagination. Imagining – or even correct imagining – doesn't provide us with new knowledge, or new understanding. How could it? After all, it's what that understanding consists in. And in fact, we have such understanding even if we've never exercised our imagination.

In this way, discussion of the knowledge argument threatens to obscure the epistemic relevance of imagining.[14] It threatens to obscure the sense in which our imaginings can teach us things that we didn't already know. Given the importance of imagination in everyday life, and given the widespread reliance on imagination in various philosophical contexts, this misrepresentation of the epistemic utility of imagination is one that is well worth avoiding.[15]

---

[13] For related worries about the ability hypothesis, see Coleman (2009b).

[14] I defend the epistemic relevance of the imagination in Kind (2016c and 2018).

[15] I am grateful to Torin Alter, Sam Coleman, and Frank Menetrez for helpful comments on previous drafts of this chapter.

9   The Knowledge Argument Is Either Indefensible or Redundant

Tom McClelland

Jackson's (1982) formulation of the knowledge argument (KA) has had an inestimable influence on the discussion of consciousness and the apparent problem it presents for physicalism. A common objection to KA is the 'ignorance objection'. According to this objection, our intuitions about Mary merely reflect our ignorance of physical facts that are integral to the explanation of phenomenal consciousness (e.g. Dennett 1991; Stoljar 2006). Armed with the insights of a future science, Mary would actually be able to deduce what it's like to see red. We only have the intuition that Mary would learn something new because we don't know the things she knows. Those sympathetic to KA have brushed away the ignorance objection on the grounds that even though we don't know what the future science of consciousness will reveal, we do know what *kind* of facts it will contain and know that this is the wrong kind of fact from which to deduce facts about phenomenal consciousness. In other words, they suggest that the insight that underwrites KA is 'future-proof': it is not the kind of insight that could be displaced by new scientific knowledge. I argue that this strategy for defending KA is dialectically problematic and reveals a fundamental limitation of the argument.

To future-proof KA the anti-physicalist would need to identify some feature credibly possessed by all physical facts – both known and unknown – and demonstrate that phenomenal facts cannot be deduced from facts possessing that feature.[1] The problem for advocates of KA is that if they can establish something about the nature of physical facts that precludes them from entailing phenomenal facts, there would be no need for the knowledge argument: we

[1] Of course, if physicalism is true then there's a sense in which phenomenal facts are physical facts, so a more accurate characterisation would be that anti-physicalists must identify some feature credibly possessed by all *non-phenomenal* physical facts. Even if phenomenal facts are physical, they are not the facts that Mary is given in her black-and-white room, so it's appropriate to limit ourselves to physical facts of the kind that Mary would find in her textbooks.

could rule out physicalism without having to trade intuitions about the epistemic situation of a subject with complete physical knowledge. So if KA were to be future-proofed, it would thereby be rendered redundant. But if, on the other hand, KA is not future-proofed then the ignorance objection stands and KA is indefensible. My master argument against KA thus runs as follows:

(1) KA is defensible only if it can be future-proofed.
(2) If KA can be future-proofed then it is redundant.
(3) Therefore KA is either indefensible or redundant.

In the first two sections I make the case for '1' and '2' respectively, considering various potential objections along the way. In the third section I conclude that KA is either indefensible or redundant and reflect on what this means for our understanding of consciousness and the case against physicalism.

9.1 KA Is Defensible Only If It Can Be Future-Proofed

9.1.1 The Ignorance Objection

If Mary were locked in her black-and-white room with full access to *today's* physics and neuroscience, it should be pretty uncontroversial that she would not find herself in a position to deduce what it's like to see red. But clearly this would have little bearing on the prospects of physicalism (all but the bravest physicalists would readily concede that we don't yet know the physical facts that entail what it's like to see red). KA rests on the claim that Mary would be unable to deduce the relevant phenomenal facts even if she had access to an *ideal* science that contained every physical fact that could be relevant to the perception of redness. This ideal science would contain many of the facts mentioned in today's science, but it would also contain other facts of which we are currently ignorant. Some of these facts may even be radically unlike anything contained in our best current theories. Given our ignorance of these facts, how can we trust our intuitions about Mary's epistemic situation? How can we rule out the hypothesis that knowledge of these as-yet-unknown physical facts would equip Mary to deduce what it's like to see red?

The ignorance objection can be bolstered by appeal to historical cases in which arguments analogous to KA appeared plausible but were shown by later scientific discoveries to be misguided. Stoljar (2006) highlights an argument put forward by C. D. Broad for the conclusion that chemical facts (i.e. facts about how different elements combine) are not entailed by non-chemical facts (i.e. facts about the nature of the constituent elements). Broad suggested that even with complete knowledge of oxygen, and complete knowledge of hydrogen, one would not be able to deduce that the two elements would combine. From this epistemic premise he drew the metaphysical conclusion that chemical properties are *emergent* properties irreducible to non-chemical properties. But Broad's conclusion was false. We now know that the quantum-mechanical properties of oxygen and hydrogen explain why they combine, so with complete knowledge of the elements one would be able to deduce how they would interact. Stoljar draws the following lessons from Broad's mistake:

> Just as the chemical argument was plausible to him, so the knowledge argument is plausible to us. Just as it is mistaken to follow the chemical argument to its conclusion, so it is mistaken to follow the knowledge argument to its conclusion. Finally, just as Broad was ignorant of a type of nonchemical truth relevant to the nature of chemistry, so, too, we are ignorant of a type of nonexperiential truth relevant to the nature of experience. (2006, p. 140)

Different advocates of the ignorance objection take different views on the depth of our ignorance. Some simply say that we are ignorant of the physical facts from which the phenomenal facts can be deduced (e.g. Dennett 1991). Some make the stronger claim that currently we do not even have the concepts needed to frame the relevant physical facts (e.g. Stoljar 2006). Others go further still and claim that we don't even have the psychological faculties needed to acquire the necessary concepts (e.g. McGinn 1989).[2] Different authors also take differing views on the content of our ignorance. Some say that the relevant unknown facts are neuroscientific (Dennett 1991), some appeal to our 'Russellian' ignorance of the intrinsic nature of matter (Strawson 1994; this volume) and others maintain a cautious neutrality on the character of the unknown facts (Stoljar 2006). For our purposes there is no need to adjudicate on these matters. There is a diverse family of positions revolving around a simple objection to KA: that Mary's knowledge of as-yet-unknown physical facts would equip her to deduce what it's like to see red.

How can advocates of KA respond to the ignorance objection? A concessive response might be to qualify KA so its conclusion is that *either* physicalism

---

[2] If we don't have the psychological faculties needed to acquire the concepts with which to frame the physical facts responsible for consciousness, then it could be argued that Mary would be unable to gain complete physical knowledge. If her psychological constitution is like ours, then these physical facts would be hidden from her. However, the point of the Mary thought experiment is that she is an ideal epistemic subject. If her possession of complete physical knowledge requires her to have psychological faculties quite unlike ours, then this can simply be built into the thought experiment.

is false *or* that physicalism is true and we are ignorant of the physical facts responsible for phenomenal consciousness. This weakened formulation of KA would be unsatisfactory. The burden of proof is on anti-physicalists to show that physicalism is false, so an anti-physicalist argument that leaves open the second disjunct is no anti-physicalist argument at all.[3] If an argument gives us a choice between adopting anti-physicalism and adopting physicalism then, other things being equal, we ought to choose physicalism, so KA doesn't put physicalists under any real pressure.

In order to defend itself against the ignorance objection, KA cannot be so concessive. A robust defence of KA must give us reason to believe that the physical facts contained in an ideal science will be no more suited to entailing all the phenomenal facts than are the physical facts described by our current theories. If our intuitions about Mary's epistemic situation are based merely on the fact that today's science doesn't come close to enabling one to deduce what it's like to be in a certain brain state, then those intuitions should not be trusted. But if our intuitions are instead based on an appreciation of the nature of physical facts as such, then those intuitions may give us a genuine insight into Mary's epistemic situation. This would be a 'future-proof' insight – the kind of insight that doesn't risk being displaced by future scientific discoveries.

The above makes a strong case for the first premise of my master argument against KA. If the ignorance objection stands unchallenged, then we cannot reasonably trust our intuitions about the Mary thought experiment and KA should be dismissed as unsound. If, on the other hand, KA can be future-proofed then it survives the ignorance objection to fight again another day. We can thus conclude that *KA is defensible only if it can be future-proofed.* Before I make my case for the second premise of the master argument more needs to be said about what future-proofing KA would involve.

---

[3] It is worth reflecting on where the burden of proof is here. Since our knowledge of the physical facts that might underwrite phenomenal consciousness is dramatically limited, it is tempting to say that we ought to be agnostic between physicalism and anti-physicalism. However, the general considerations in favour of physicalism (mainly those pertaining to parsimony and causal closure) give us defeasible evidence in its favour. As such, in the absence of defeaters it is reasonable to assume that as-yet-unknown physical facts will entail the phenomenal facts. KA thus effectively begs the question against physicalism by illicitly assuming that new physical knowledge won't yield an explanation of phenomenal consciousness. Given our ignorance we must acknowledge that when all the physical facts are in it *might* transpire that physicalism is false, but in order to meet its burden of proof KA needs to provide positive non-question-begging reasons to conclude that the physical facts *won't* entail the phenomenal facts.

9.1.2 The Conditions of Future-Proofing

The best way to understand what future-proofing would involve is to look at how advocates of KA have defended themselves against the ignorance objection. One defence is that besides being unable to explain the phenomenal facts with our current scientific theories, we cannot even *imagine* a scientific theory that would explain the phenomenal facts (Chalmers 1996). This distinguishes phenomenal consciousness from other as-yet-unexplained natural phenomena. Marine biologists don't yet know how phytoplankton share an ecosystem without wiping each other out, but we can at least *imagine* what such an explanation would look like. Yet when we try to imagine a scientific theory of consciousness that would allow Mary to deduce what it's like to see red, we come up short. So we can conclude that even though Mary is blessed with knowledge of an ideal science, she would be unable to deduce the relevant phenomenal facts.

This line of defence against the ignorance objection is persuasively undermined by P. S. Churchland:

> Adding I cannot imagine explaining P merely adds a psychological fact about the speaker, from which again, nothing significant follows about the nature of the phenomenon in question. Whether we can or cannot imagine a phenomenon being explained in a certain way is a psychological fact about us, not an objective fact about the nature of the phenomenon itself. (1996, p. 407)[4]

To see why the appeal to imagination fails as a defence against the ignorance objection, consider again Broad's argument for emergentism. Broad might have insisted that he couldn't even *imagine* a non-chemical explanation of the chemical fact that oxygen combines with hydrogen. But all this would have revealed is a failure of imagination on Broad's part and not any insight into the nature of chemical truths. The ignorance objection is premised on the observation that ignorance can lead our intuitions astray. Appeals to what we can and cannot imagine won't help fend off this objection for the simple reason that our ignorance can also influence what we are capable of imagining.

The failure of this appeal to imagination suggests that advocates of KA need to say something more substantive about *why* it is implausible that future scientific discoveries will allow Mary to deduce the relevant phenomenal facts.

---

[4] Churchland's comments are directed against the 'Hard Problem' rather than KA. Against KA, she actually takes the stand that even though Mary *would* learn something new, this wouldn't be at odds with physicalism (1996, p. 403). Nevertheless, her comments reflect something of the spirit of the ignorance objection to KA.

Advocates of KA are unconvinced by the ignorance objection because they think physical facts are simply the *wrong kind* of fact from which to deduce phenomenal facts. As such, it doesn't matter that we're ignorant of many of the physical facts that Mary would know. Those unknown facts are of the same kind as the physical facts with which we are familiar, and no facts of that kind are suited to entailing phenomenal facts. Of course, the credibility of this line of thought depends on how the notion of 'wrong kind of fact' is unpacked. I suggest that advocates of KA must identify a 'future-proof feature' of physical facts such that:

(i)   There is strong reason to believe all physical facts have feature F.
(ii) We know that phenomenal facts have feature G.
(iii) We know that *in principle* there can be no entailment from facts with feature F to facts with feature G.

Claims about what kind of facts will be disclosed by future science are inevitably difficult to justify, so requiring us to *know* that all physical facts having feature F may be too demanding. This is why the first condition is framed in terms of having *strong reason to believe* that all physical facts have this feature. This qualification isn't necessary for the second condition: advocates of KA ought to know what it is about phenomenal facts that precludes their entailment by physical facts.[5] KA concerns a specific phenomenal fact – the fact that seeing red has the particular phenomenology it has – but the argument is meant to yield an insight into the irreducibility of phenomenal facts across the board, hence the generality of the second condition. It is important that the third condition includes the 'in principle' clause. If one merely had a hunch that facts with feature F cannot entail facts with feature G, this would not be enough to fend off the ignorance objection. The objector could simply respond that since we are ignorant of some of the physical facts with feature F, our hunch could merely reflect our ignorance. So to avoid begging the question against the ignorance objection, we need a future-proof feature that we can be sure

---

[5] One interesting possibility is that one might identify a feature F of physical facts and know that facts with that feature cannot entail the phenomenal facts without being able to pin down *what it is* about the phenomenal facts that makes them unsuited to being entailed by facts with feature F. In this scenario, our justification bottoms out with intuitions about the nature of the phenomenal and there is no need to identify any feature G of all phenomenal facts. I bracket this possibility for two reasons. First, the future-proof features identified in the literature are such that a property G of phenomenal facts *is* identified. Second, the defence of KA would certainly be stronger if a property G could be identified that explains why the phenomenal facts cannot be entailed by the physical facts, so in the first instance we ought to pursue future-proof features that satisfy condition (ii).

precludes entailment of phenomenal facts in principle. Anything based on the observation that all *known* facts with feature F fail to entail facts with feature G would be inadequate: a deeper insight is needed that justifies the conclusion that even *unknown* facts with feature F will fail to entail facts with feature G.

If advocates of KA can identify a future-proof feature, then the ignorance objection can be dismissed on the grounds that we have strong reason to believe that unknown physical facts would not help Mary deduce what it's like to see red. If such a feature cannot be identified, then it is very hard to see how the advocate of KA could rule out the hypothesis that Mary's knowledge of as-yet-unknown physical facts would allow her to deduce the relevant phenomenal facts from her black-and-white room. Put simply, KA can be future-proofed if and only if a candidate future-proof feature can be found that satisfies the three conditions above.

Although a number of such features have been proposed in the literature, there are two features that have attracted significant support: the *objectivity* of physical facts and the *structural* nature of physical facts. I will present the *prima facie* case for regarding each of these as future-proof features. I will not evaluate whether these proposed features stand up to scrutiny: my master argument against KA is neutral on whether KA can in fact be future-proofed, so it does not matter whether you find either of these candidate future-proof features convincing. My purpose here is simply to illustrate what a rebuttal of the ignorance objection would have to look like.

The first candidate future-proof feature of physical facts is *objectivity*. At a first pass, objective facts are those that are understandable from many points of view. In order to understand physical facts about the brain for example, it is not necessary for you to have had any specific kind of experience. The physical facts described in today's science are objective. Moreover, it is plausible that *all* physical facts are objective – Nagel describes the physical as 'a domain of objective facts *par excellence*' (1974, p. 442). This suggests that objectivity satisfies the first condition. Subjective facts are those that are understandable only if one adopts a certain point of view (see Crane, this volume).[6] In order to understand what it's like to be a bat, for example, it is necessary for one to adopt the bat-ish point of view and have the kind of experiences that bats have (Nagel 1974). Phenomenal facts are subjective. The case of Mary

---

[6] There are many senses of the term 'subjective'. Here I have used the understanding of the term most pertinent to KA, but other senses of the term may also be relevant to our assessment of physicalism. Indeed, I have suggested elsewhere (McClelland 2013) that phenomenal states are subjective in the sense that there is something it is like to be in those states for the subject, and that it is this understanding of subjectivity that captures the deeper problem for physicalists.

might be regarded as illustrative of this: it is only by experiencing redness for herself that Mary can learn what it's like to see red. This indicates that the second condition is satisfied. It is also plausible that subjective facts cannot be deduced from objective facts. From objective facts we can deduce further objective facts, but we cannot deduce ourselves into an unfamiliar perspective – we cannot reason ourselves into having some new kind of experience. But subjective facts, by their very nature, can only be learned if we have the relevant kind of experience for ourselves, thus we cannot deduce the subjective facts from the objective facts. This indicates that objectivity satisfies the third condition. There is thus a *prima facie* case for objectivity being a future-proof feature of physical facts, as captured by the following three theses:

(i$_{obj}$) There is strong reason to believe all physical facts are objective.

(ii$_{obj}$) We know that phenomenal facts are subjective.

(iii$_{obj}$) We know that in principle there can be no entailment from objective facts to subjective facts.

The second candidate future-proof feature is *being structural*. At a first pass, structural facts are those that pertain exclusively to spatial, temporal and causal relations between entities. Non-structural facts are those that involve anything over and above spatial, temporal and causal relations between entities.[7] It is plausible that current science describes only structural facts: neuroscience, for instance, describes nothing more than spatial, temporal and dynamic relations between neurons and other brain cells at various levels. Moreover, it is plausible that future science will also describe only structural facts as scientific descriptions of entities are based only on how those entities interact with our senses and measuring instruments (or with other entities that in turn interact with our senses and measuring instruments).[8]

---

[7] How best to draw the structural/non-structural distinction is a matter of some controversy. For an insightful assessment of the options see Alter (2016). For those uncomfortable with my simple characterisation of the distinction, I would reiterate that it is not especially important to the argument of this chapter how the distinction is understood. The characterisation offered is meant to be more illustrative than definitive.

[8] There are several different routes to this kind of conclusion: the Russellian route (Russell 1927a) is driven by the claim that the causal nature of perception means that it can only tell us about the causal structure of percepts; the Ramseyan Humility route (Lewis 2009) is driven by the claim that the nature of theoretical predicates is such that they can only be used to give structural characterisations of phenomena; the Kantian Humility route (Langton 1998; Jackson 1998a) is driven by the claim that the affective nature of knowledge cannot disclose the intrinsic nature of entities. These views and others overlap in various ways but also make a number of independent claims. Since I'm not concerned in this paper with evaluating the claim that scientific descriptions are inevitably structural, I will put these issues to one side.

This indicates that being structural satisfies the first condition. Phenomenal facts are plausibly non-structural. Phenomenal facts involve the instantiation of phenomenal qualities, such as phenomenal redness, and phenomenal qualities cannot be characterised in purely structural terms – they are intrinsic properties that transcend any purely structural characterisation.[9] This indicates that the second condition is satisfied. Finally, it is plausible that 'from structure and dynamics, one can infer only structure and dynamics' (Chalmers 2002, p. 259). Though the structural facts of microphysics might entail the facts of biology or neuroscience, these are plausibly still structural facts, just on a different scale to those described by microphysics. This indicates that being structural satisfies the third condition.[10] There is thus a *prima facie* case for concluding that being structural is a future-proof feature satisfying all three conditions. Call the following three theses the Structural Theses:

(i$_{str}$)   There is strong reason to believe all physical facts are structural.

(ii$_{str}$) We know that phenomenal facts are non-structural.

(iii$_{str}$) We know that in principle there can be no entailment from structural facts to non-structural facts.

It will be useful for the remainder of the chapter to have one candidate future-proof feature in mind as I develop my argument against KA. I will focus on being structural, rather being objective, for two reasons: one, I think there are serious objections to objectivity being a future-proof feature that do not apply to the structural view;[11] two, the structural option is perhaps the more influential position in the literature today, with leading anti-physicalists such as Chalmers (2010a) regarding it as the cornerstone of the case against physicalism.

---

[9] This is not to say that phenomenal facts do not involve structure. Clearly, facts about my current phenomenology will include facts about the structure of qualities in my field of awareness. The point remains, however, that phenomenal facts are not purely structural. In other words, there is always a non-structural aspect to our phenomenal states.

[10] One might say that it's *analytic* that the third condition is satisfied given what it means for facts to be structural and what it means for them to be non-structural. If so, this would offer a particularly robust satisfaction of the third condition. Nevertheless, the condition itself needn't be formulated in such a way as to demand this.

[11] The most serious objection is that the subjective/objective distinction is fundamentally an epistemological distinction rather than a metaphysical condition, which makes it hard to justify the claim that physical facts must be objective. The view that some physical facts are subjective is developed in detail by Howell (2013).

That said, it is worth addressing one prominent objection to the Structural Theses. Some have suggested that although science can only describe structural physical facts, there are also *non*-structural physical facts beyond the reach of scientific description (e.g. Pereboom 2011). Although we have no way of knowing these non-structural facts, we can infer that they exist because structural facts must be grounded in non-structural facts. So underwriting facts about the causal dynamics of physical entities, there are facts about the intrinsic nature of those entities. If this line of thought is accurate then the first structural thesis – 'i_{str}' – is false. This would mean that advocates of the ignorance objection can propose that facts about phenomenal consciousness are deducible from physical facts that include these non-structural facts, and that it is our ignorance of these non-structural facts that leads our intuitions about Mary astray.

This 'Russellian' response to KA is worth taking very seriously, and I have defended a version of it elsewhere (McClelland 2013). However, it is controversial whether this objection to KA constitutes a vindication of physicalism. Some might hold that these non-structural facts are not properly described as *physical* facts. If it is constitutive of physical facts that they are the kind of fact that can be uncovered by scientific enquiry, then the non-structural facts in question would come out as non-physical. Furthermore, even if non-structural facts are deemed to qualify as physical facts, we're left with an unorthodox version of physicalism with which many physicalists would be unhappy. It would respect the letter of physicalism by avoiding positing non-physical facts, but would violate the spirit of physicalism by positing facts beyond the reach of scientific enquiry. In order to side-step these worries, I will add the proviso that if KA can be future-proofed by an appeal to the structural nature of physical facts, then this would rule out an *orthodox* physicalism but would not rule out *Russellian* physicalism. Ruling out orthodox physicalism would of course be a dramatic result for KA, so there is no harm in bracketing the Russellian view for current purposes.

9.2 If KA Can Be Future-Proofed Then It Is Redundant

9.2.1 The Redundancy of KA

We have seen that in order to future-proof KA, one must identify a candidate future-proof feature of physical facts that satisfies the three conditions specified. The problem for KA is that if such a future-proof feature can be identified, then there is no need for KA. If we have good reason to believe that physical facts are not the kind of facts from which phenomenal facts can be deduced, then we have good reason to believe that physicalism is false. To see this, consider again the suggestion that *being structural* is a future-proof feature of physical facts. If the three Structural Theses stand up to scrutiny, then anti-physicalists can offer the following *structural argument against physicalism*:

(1) There is strong reason to believe all physical facts are structural.
(2) We know that phenomenal facts are non-structural.
(3) We know that in principle there can be no entailment from structural facts to non-structural facts.
(4) If there is no entailment from the physical facts to the phenomenal facts then physicalism is false.
(5) Therefore there is strong reason to believe that physicalism is false.

Premises (1)–(3) are simply the three Structural Theses, so their truth is guaranteed if being structural satisfies the three conditions of being a future-proof feature. Advocates of KA are already committed to the truth of premise (4) as this is what enables them to move from an epistemic premise about Mary to a metaphysical conclusion about physicalism. So if a formulation of KA future-proofed by an appeal to the structural nature of physical facts is sound, then the structural argument against physicalism is also sound. And if the structural argument against physicalism is sound, then KA is redundant. A future-proofed formulation of KA will include all the premises of the structural argument above *plus further premises* about Mary and her epistemic situation. But such an argument would be surplus to requirements as the simpler structural argument would suffice to demonstrate the falsity of physicalism. This is not to say that the structural argument against physicalism is actually sound. It is just to say that *if* a formulation of KA reinforced by the Structure Theses is sound, *then* the structural argument against physicalism is sound and that KA would therefore be redundant.

The same applies for any candidate future-proof feature one might use to reinforce KA. If objectivity satisfies the relevant conditions, then one can offer an objectivity argument against physicalism that makes no reference to Mary and her epistemic situation. An analogy might help capture the dialectical situation here. Imagine you need help lifting a heavy piece of furniture, but the person who helps you is so strong that they can lift the furniture by themselves, rendering your efforts entirely surplus to requirements. The advocate of KA is in an analogous position with their project of refuting physicalism. The ignorance objection shows that KA is only defensible if suitably reinforced, but any suitable reinforcement can do the job on its own, thus rendering KA redundant. This is my initial case for premise (2) of the master argument against KA.

To develop this case further, I will consider three potential objections to the claim that if KA can be future-proofed then it is redundant.

9.2.2 Objections and Replies

The first objection is that even if the structural argument against physicalism (or its equivalent for any other candidate future-proof feature) constitutes a self-standing argument against physicalism, it doesn't follow that KA is redundant. The structural argument taken in isolation gives us some reason to reject physicalism, but the structural argument in tandem with KA gives us *more* reason to reject physicalism. So long as the case against physicalism is better with KA than without it, then it is wrong to say that KA is redundant.

The difficulty with this objection is that KA more likely *hinders* the case against physicalism than helps it. As a general rule, it is better to take on no more commitments than one needs to justify one's conclusion. If the anti-physicalist takes on the commitments not just of the structural argument but also of KA, then they leave themselves open to objections to those further commitments. The Mary scenario is a contentious thought experiment. It raises challenging issues regarding: what's involved in having complete physical knowledge; what's involved in having ideal reasoning skills; what exactly Mary learns on escaping her room; whether what Mary learns is a new fact; and so on. Physicalists will challenge the assumptions anti-physicalists make about these issues. One option for anti-physicalists is to defend those assumptions against physicalist attacks. But an alternative, more dialectically advisable, strategy is to cut these assumptions loose. The case against physicalism needn't be weighed down by these commitments. Even if they are commitments with which anti-physicalists are comfortable, it is ill-advised to present physicalists with such easy targets. Chalmers notes that 'many of the common responses to those thought experiments have no clear application as a response to the simple [structural] arguments' (2010a, p. xv). By dispensing with the Mary thought experiment the anti-physicalist can side-step those responses entirely and present a leaner, more defensible, case against physicalism.

The second objection is that the structural argument against physicalism is not self-standing as it relies on KA for its plausibility. Alter advocates a version of the structural argument against physicalism but thinks that the plausibility of this argument is inseparable from the plausibility of KA:

> I noted that the structure and dynamics argument's three main claims suggest a deductive argument for the epistemic gap. But that argument

is not independent of the considerations typically used to establish the gap: intuitions about the Mary case, zombie cases, and other such thought experiments. (2016 [here quoting 2015 pre-print edn, p. 6])

If this is true, then KA is far from redundant. The structural argument against physicalism only works in tandem with KA because the Structural Theses only get their warrant from the Mary thought experiment. As Alter puts it, our intuitions about Mary are 'epistemically prior' to the relevant claims about structure (2016 [2015 pre-print edn, p. 7]).

I concede that the Mary scenario might be used to motivate the three Structural Theses that drive the structural argument against physicalism. To motivate the claim that all physical facts are structural you might observe that Mary – a subject with complete physical knowledge – lacks knowledge of any non-structural facts, indicating that there are no non-structural physical facts. To motivate the claim that phenomenal facts are non-structural you might observe that Mary learns a phenomenal fact on leaving her room, yet already knows all the structural facts, so must be learning a phenomenal fact that is non-structural. To motivate the claim that one cannot deduce non-structural facts from structural facts you might observe that Mary cannot deduce non-structural facts about phenomenal consciousness from her complete knowledge of the structural facts.

However, just because the Structural Theses *can* be motivated by appeal to Mary doesn't mean that they *need* to be, or even that they *ought* to be. The premises don't need to be motivated this way because each can be motivated without reference to a subject in Mary's epistemic position. The claim that all physical facts are structural might be motivated by the epistemological claim that we can only gain knowledge of physical entities via how they affect us, meaning we can describe only their dispositions to interact with us and other entities (see n. 8). The claim that phenomenal facts are non-structural might be motivated by introspection of the qualities of one's phenomenal states. The claim that one cannot deduce non-structural facts from structural facts might be motivated *a priori* on the grounds that facts about spatial, temporal and causal relations can entail only further facts about spatial, temporal and causal relations.

The above indicates that the structural argument *could* be motivated without appeal to KA. I would go further and suggest that it *ought* to be motivated without appeal to KA. The point of introducing structure as a future-proof feature of physical facts is to fend off the ignorance objection KA. But if the relevant claims about structure are motivated with reference to KA, then the ignorance objection comes back to haunt the anti-physicalist. Whatever one's prior commitments are regarding physicalism, it is clear that Mary knows a wealth of physical facts of which we are deeply ignorant. So how, from our position of ignorance, do we know that Mary's complete physical knowledge won't include non-structural facts? How, from our position of ignorance, do we know that Mary would learn a new non-structural fact on leaving her room? How, from our position of ignorance, do we know that Mary would be unable to deduce non-structural facts about phenomenal consciousness from her complete knowledge of structural physical facts? If we have a deeper justification for these claims, then it is this deeper justification that underwrites our understanding of the structural and not our intuitions about the Mary scenario. If we have no deeper justification for these claims, then they should not be given much credence as they might simply reflect our ignorance of the physical facts.

Overall, this presents Alter with a serious dilemma: if the three Structural Theses can only be motivated by KA, then both KA and the structural argument against physicalism fail. KA fails because our ignorance of the physical facts known by Mary renders our intuitions about Mary unreliable, and the structural argument against physicalism fails insofar as it depends on those intuitions about Mary. If, on the other hand, the Structural Theses can be motivated without reference to KA then the structural argument suffices to refute physicalism and KA is redundant. The Structural Theses would put conclusions about Mary's situation on a much surer footing, but those conclusions would not need to be given any role in the case against physicalism.

We now come to the third and final objection to my claim that if KA can be future-proofed then it is redundant. A critic might concede that the structural argument makes a self-standing case against physicalism whilst maintaining that the Mary thought experiment is nevertheless needed to make the structural argument *vivid*.[12] Even if the Mary scenario isn't integral to the case against physicalism, it is still integral to the exposition of that case. The structural argument is dry and abstract and the Mary scenario ameliorates these

---

[12] Though Chalmers suggests that the structural argument is what really drives the case against physicalism, he does specifically note that thought experiments like the Mary scenario serve to make the case more vivid (2010a, p. xv). In the same passage, Chalmers also suggests that thought experiments like the Mary scenario are 'a useful technical device for making the arguments more formal and more analysable' (2010a, p. xv). I'm not convinced that KA is any more formal than the structure argument against physicalism. As for being more analysable, KA might have the advantage of helping to make physicalist objections to anti-physicalism more clear, but this would be covered by the claim that KA helps make arguments more vivid.

problems by presenting interlocutors with a concrete scenario: a scenario that tends to elicit strong intuitions. On this view, the Mary scenario is *dialectically* redundant in that a sound argument against physicalism can be provided without it, but it is not *rhetorically* redundant as it is a valuable and effective tool for making the case against physicalism vivid and for persuading interlocutors of its force. The Mary scenario serves to aid understanding, even if it doesn't serve to make the case against physicalism more defensible.

Wartenburg offers some helpful reflections on the role of *illustrations* of philosophical ideas, citing Kant's vivid image of pure understanding as a land of truth surrounded by a stormy sea of illusion. Wartenburg rightly notes that 'Kant's imagery here, though quite graphic, does not make a philosophical contribution to his argument, even if it helps a reader understand its general thrust' (2006, p. 21). The image is not redundant, but nor is it part of Kant's argument in the first critique. Something similar might be said of the way in which movies can make philosophical arguments vivid. One might explain the case for Cartesian scepticism to an undergraduate audience, and then present them with *The Matrix* as a vivid illustration of a sceptical hypothesis. Even though the movie might help students understand scepticism and convince them to take it seriously, the movie shouldn't be regarded as part of the argument for skepticism. The argument for scepticism is self-standing, and the movie merely serves to help communicate its force.

Perhaps the role of the Mary scenario can be understood by analogy with the role of Kant's metaphor, or of the lecturer's movie presentation. Mary is a vivid illustration of the epistemic gap between structural physical facts and non-structural phenomenal facts. It serves to aid our understanding of the structural argument against physicalism, but doesn't make a contribution to the merit of the argument itself. So even though the structural argument is a self-standing argument against physicalism, the Mary scenario is far from redundant.

I see two possible responses to this defence of KA. The first is to say that the Mary scenario isn't even needed to make the structural argument against physicalism vivid and persuasive. The thought experiment risks distracting interlocutors with unnecessary questions about the details of the scenario, and the case against physicalism is best made without reference to such thought experiments. I think this response would be too strong. There is no denying that the Mary scenario is a vivid thought experiment with the power to elicit strong intuitions. If I were trying to convince a neophyte of the case against physicalism, I wouldn't want to present the structural argument without also presenting the Mary thought experiment.

The second response is to concede, as I do, that the Mary scenario is far from redundant when it comes to communicating the case against physicalism. But the Mary scenario having illustrative value should not be confused with KA having dialectical force. To use the Mary scenario in this way is to borrow a thought experiment from KA whilst dispensing with the argument itself. KA is intended as an argument against physicalism, and has been treated as such for decades. Using the Mary scenario to illustrate a distinct argument against physicalism is far from a vindication of KA. It remains the case that KA itself is redundant, even if the thought experiment that underwrites it is put to illustrative use elsewhere. The conclusion of the master argument is that KA – the argument against physicalism offered by Jackson – is either indefensible or redundant. The concession that the Mary scenario – the thought experiment used to drive KA – can still serve a rhetorical function is no concession at all.

I have considered three objections to the claim that if KA can be future-proofed then it is redundant. Along the way, I hope to have clarified why KA would be rendered redundant and what exactly its redundancy amounts to. I have focused closely on structure as a future-proof feature. I should reiterate that there is no commitment here to structure actually being a future-proof feature: the claim is just that *if* it is such a feature then it would render KA redundant for the reasons discussed. I should also reiterate that parallel considerations will, I suggest, apply to any candidate future-proof features. If objectivity were presented as the future-proof feature, we could formulate an objectivity argument against physicalism that renders KA redundant for all the same reasons. And the same goes for any other future-proof feature that the anti-physicalist might present as a candidate.[13] Overall, we are in a position to conclude that the second premise of the master argument against KA stands up to scrutiny.

9.3 Therefore KA Is Either Indefensible or Redundant

The ignorance objection shows that KA is defensible only if it can be future-proofed. The considerations above show that if it can be future-proofed then it is redundant. We can thus infer that KA is either indefensible or redundant.

---

[13] It might be suggested that KA has a more intimate relationship with other candidate future-proof features. Perhaps the case for regarding objectivity as a future-proof feature depends essentially on the plausibility of KA, meaning that KA is not rendered redundant. Although this possibility oughtn't be dismissed out of hand, I think the burden of proof is on the critic to show that matters are any different for the other candidate future-proof features.

I think there are three lessons we can learn from this conclusion, two of them negative and the third positive.

The first lesson is that KA should be dispensed with as an argument against physicalism. If you are skeptical about the case against physicalism being future-proofed then you should dismiss KA as indefensible. If you are optimistic about the identification of a future-proof feature then you should dismiss KA as redundant. Either way, KA should not be taken seriously as an argument against physicalism. The thought experiment that drives KA can still serve a valuable illustrative role in discussion, but it cannot be taken as a self-standing case for rejecting physicalism. It is worth noting that my objections to KA do not rest on any presumption of physicalism. As with so many philosophical debates, the debate surrounding KA includes accusations of question-begging from both sides. Physicalist objections to KA are often too easily brushed away as betraying a presumption that physicalism is true, or a failure to take anti-physicalist intuitions seriously. No such response is available to the argument I have offered. I have argued that even if a compelling case against physicalism can be developed, it remains the case that KA ought to be dispensed with. I have offered an argument that concerns only the dialectical structure of the case against physicalism, and not the relative merits of physicalist and anti-physicalist views of phenomenal consciousness.

The second lesson is that what goes for KA also goes for the conceivability argument (CA) and any other argument against physicalism based on comparable thought experiments. The conceivability argument asks us to imagine a complete physical duplicate who lacks phenomenal consciousness. This means that all the physical facts that hold for us also hold for our duplicate. The ignorance objection presents a serious problem for CA. We are ignorant of many physical facts about ourselves, so when we try to conceive of a perfect physical duplicate, our attempts to do so are inevitably constrained by our ignorance. How can we rule out the hypothesis that if we had complete knowledge of the physical facts, then we would find zombie duplicates inconceivable? The only way is to identify some future-proof feature shared by all physical facts such that discovery of any facts with that feature could not alter the conceivability of zombies: so long as the physical facts about me and my duplicate have that feature, it will always be conceivable that my duplicate lacks phenomenal consciousness. As should now be clear, the difficulty with this response is that if it can be made to work, then CA would be rendered redundant. But if it cannot be made to work, then the ignorance objection stands and CA is indefensible. Thus CA is either indefensible or redundant. Perhaps there is an illustrative role left for the zombie thought experiment to play, but dialectically speaking CA must be dispensed with.[14] The same goes for versions of CA that appeal to qualia inversion and the like rather than to zombies.

The third lesson is a positive recommendation that we ought to attend more closely to the question of whether physical facts have a future-proof feature that satisfies the three conditions specified. Consider the following passage from Chalmers about the structural argument against physicalism:

> There is a sense in which the argument here, which turns on simple issues about explanation, is more fundamental than conceivability arguments involving zombies, epistemological arguments involving Mary in her black-and-white room, and the like … It is sometimes supposed that nonreductive arguments turn essentially on these thought experiments, but this is just wrong. In fact … I suggest that the thought experiments turn essentially on points about structure and function. (2010a, p. xv)

I agree with Chalmers that the common understanding of the case against physicalism gets things upside down, and that in order to make progress in this debate we must turn things the right way around. If we want to establish whether phenomenal consciousness presents a threat to physicalism, we ought to turn our attention to whether there is a plausible future-proof feature of physical facts. If anti-physicalists can find such a feature, they would have a case against physicalism that avoids many of the pitfalls that have dominated discussion of KA and CA. If physicalists can systematically rebut the candidate future-proof features, they would have a defence of physicalism that no version of KA or CA could overcome. For the anti-physicalists, their project is likely to involve refining their characterisations of the structural/non-structural divide or the objective/subjective divide. For the physicalists their project will likely involve casting doubt on the claim that all physical facts have the putative future-proof feature, or on the claim that facts with that feature cannot entail the phenomenal facts. This chapter does not take a stand on which side of the debate has the better prospects, but it does hope to offer a clear recommendation on how best to make progress in that debate.

---

[14] Heikinheimo and Vaaja (2013) offer a well-developed argument for the redundancy of the conceivability argument along these lines. They also assert that similar considerations apply to KA, so the current chapter can be read as a vindication of that assertion.

10   Grounding, Analysis, and Russellian Monism

Philip Goff

Mary in her black and white room knows all that physical science can teach us about the physical facts involved in colour experience. But it does not follow that she knows everything there is to know about these facts. The Russellian monist exploits this gap to defend a form of physicalism – in a very broad sense of that word. Unfortunately, recent developments in the grounding literature cast doubt on that strategy, or so I will argue.

10.1 The Russellian Monist Challenge to the Knowledge Argument

Consider the following opposing theses:

Physical Transparency The physical sciences reveal the complete nature of physical properties and facts, e.g. a true neurophysiological description of c-fibre firing reveals the nature of c-fibre firing; physical characterisations of mass reveal the nature of mass.

Physical Opacity The physical sciences provide only a partial understanding of the nature of physical properties or facts.

The physical sciences characterise properties in terms of their nomic role. Very roughly mass is characterised in terms of gravitational attraction and resisting acceleration. Brain states are characterised in terms of their role in the overall functional economy of the brain, and in terms of their chemical constituents, which are in turn characterised in terms of their causal role and physical constituents. In the light of this, there are two options regarding the semantics of physical predicates:

Semantic dispositionalism (of physical terms) Physical predicates denote causal properties.

Semantic quidditism *(of physical terms)*	Physical predicates denote categorical properties, but pick out those categorical properties in terms of their causal role.

Semantic dispositionalism naturally leads to Physical Transparency: physical properties are causal role properties which are characterised in causal terms. Semantic quidditism naturally leads to Physical Opacity: physical properties are not causal role properties but they are characterised in causal terms. It is perhaps indeterminate which of these options reflects how physical scientists use these terms. In any case, which of these options a given philosopher is attracted to is likely to be determined by her or his views on the metaphysics of properties. A dispositional essentialist, who thinks that properties have dispositional essences, is likely to adopt semantic dispositionalism. The Humean, or any philosopher who believes that properties have a categorical essence, is likely to adopt semantic quidditism.

Suppose Physical Opacity is true because Semantic Quidditism is true. It follows that physical properties have a 'hidden nature' which goes beyond what is revealed by the physical sciences. As Russell noticed in 1920s,[1] this opens up a novel solution to the mind–body problem: it could be that this hidden nature of matter which explains consciousness. Quickly forgotten in the twentieth century, the core of Russell's idea is recently enjoying a revival, under the banner 'Russellian monism'.[2] There is a negative and a positive aspect to the definition of Russellian monism, as follows:

- There is a 'deep' nature to basic material facts, which goes beyond the nomic-structural features in terms of which physics characterise those facts.
- The deep nature of basic material facts explains consciousness, in the sense that the facts about the deep nature of basic material entities a priori entail the experiential facts (whilst it's not the case that the facts about the causal structure of material entities a priori entail the experiential facts).

Is Russellian monism a form of physicalism? It depends on how we define what a physical fact is. Some take physicalism to be the view that ideal physics exhaustively describes fundamental reality. Clearly Russellian monism is not a form of physicalism on such a definition. Others define physicalism as the view that physics is *referentially adequate*, in the sense that the fundamental facts, individuals or properties are those which are the subject matter of ideal physics, leaving it open whether or not ideal physics reveals their complete

---

[1] Russell (1927a).
[2] For some examples of Russellian monism, see Strawson (2003); Pereboom (2011); Goff (2017); and the essays in Alter and Nagasawa (2015).

nature. For the purposes of this piece, let us think of Russellian monism as a form of physicalism, in order that we might examine whether the knowledge argument is able to refute physicalism of that form.[3]

Mary in her black and white room is described as knowing 'all the physical facts'. However, it's clear from the context that what this means is that she knows 'all that facts physical science has to teach us about the physical'. For the Russellian monist, such facts do not exhaust the complete nature of the physical, as they leave out its deep nature. If Mary really did know all the physical facts, including the deep nature of the physical, then according to Russellian monism she would be able to work out what it's like to see red. Many Russellian monists believe we currently have no good grip on matter's deep nature, and perhaps never will. And if we cannot positively conceive of matter's deep nature, it seems that we are not in a position to deny the Russellian monist's claim that knowledge of it would allow one to grasp the nature of experience.

Russellian monism relies on our ignorance about the nature of the deep nature of the physical. This is both a weakness and a strength. It is a weakness in so far as it leads to a rather unsatisfying solution to the mind–body problem, attributing to matter some nature that we know nothing about beyond that it somehow explains consciousness.[4] But if the Russellian monist can show that we have good reason to think that dualism is false, and that matter does indeed have a deep nature, then her view will have strong support in spite of its disappointing lack of a complete story. The strength of the view is that, given our ignorance of the deep nature of matter, it's hard to see how we could ever rule out that knowledge of it would somehow yield knowledge of the nature of experience. In other words, it's hard to see how the knowledge argument could ever rule out Russellian monism.

However, recent discussions of the nature of grounding have suggested that, in order for physicalism to be true, the nature of *consciousness* must play a significant role in explaining the grounding of consciousness in the physical. Even if we cannot say much about the deep nature of the physical, due to our ignorance of it, it may be that we can know enough about the nature of consciousness to rule out its playing the explanatory role required for the truth

---

[3] I am focussing here on reductionist versions of Russellian monism, according to which all facts are grounded in facts at the micro-level.

[4] There are panpsychist forms of the Russellian monist which postulate consciousness properties at the level of basic physics, and thereby hold out the possibility of a partial understanding of the deep nature of the physical. However, there are grounds for thinking that even panpsychist versions must postulate unknown aspects of the physical in order to solve the *combination problem*, i.e. the problem of grounding facts about the consciousness of macro-level entities in facts about the consciousness of micro-level entities (Goff 2017: ch. 7).

of physicalism, even physicalism of the Russellian monist variety. In what follows, I will explore how one might build a case for this claim.

10.2 A Grounding Conception of Physicalism

Physicalism is the doctrine that fundamental reality is physical; that the physical facts are the fundamental facts. There are two ways in which this definition cries out for clarification. Firstly one might ask what a *physical fact* is. Secondly one might ask what it is for a fact to be *fundamental*. Shamik Dasgupta has recently proposed a detailed and plausible answer to the second of these questions, defining physicalism in terms of the metaphysical relation of *grounding*.[5] As I will show, Dasgupta's account offers resources for the proponent of the knowledge argument to respond to the challenge of Russellian monism.

Suppose Rod, Jane and Freddy are dancing, drinking and generally having fun one evening at Jane's. It follows from this supposition that there is a party at Jane's, and moreover that there is a party at Jane's *because* Rod, Jane and Freddy are dancing, drinking, etc., at Jane's. But the word 'because' here does not express a *causal* relationship; it's not as though the activities of the revellers bring into being some extra thing – the party – which then floats above their heads. Consider a further example. Suppose the rose is scarlet. It follows that the rose is red, and moreover that the rose is red *because* it is scarlet. But the scarlet colour of the rose does not secrete redness as the liver secretes bile. It seems that in both cases we have a kind of explanatory relationship which is not causal. This relationship has become known as 'grounding'.[6]

There are many interesting things we might ask about grounding. Is it primitive or can it be defined? What is the logical form of grounding statements? If grounding is a genuine relation what are its relata? There is a rich literature attempting to answer these questions, but our focus here is not the finer details of the metaphysics of grounding but rather how grounding can be used in order to define physicalism.[7]

An obvious first attempt at defining physicalism in terms of grounding would be the following:

Strong Physicalism All non-physical facts are grounded in the physical facts.

---

[5] Dasgupta (2014). See Ney (2008a) for a good survey of answers to the first question. I defend an answer to the first question in Goff (2017: ch. 2).

[6] Some key papers on the recent revival of grounding are Fine (2001); Schaffer (2009); Rosen (2010). Proponents of grounding trace the idea back to an older tradition, often citing Aristotle as an influence.

[7] For further discussion of the issues mentioned above, see Trogdon (2013a).

This gives us a clear and straightforward way of understanding the view that fundamental reality is wholly physical: the many and diverse facts which make up reality are all ultimately grounded in the physical facts. Suppose that Sarah is currently feeling pain. Strong Physicalism commits the physicalist, as we would expect from a definition of physicalism, to there being some physical fact which grounds the fact that Sarah feels pain. Let us suppose, to continue with the hackneyed and empirically dubious example favoured by philosophers, that that physical fact is the fact that Sarah's c-fibres are firing. Thus we reach the following fact:

Pain-Grounding   The fact that Sarah's c-fibres are firing grounds the fact that Sarah feels pain.

Pain-Grounding is a *grounding fact*, that is to say, a fact about which facts ground. In formulating his grounding conception of physicalism, Dasgupta of course accepts that the physicalist is obliged to hold that the facts about consciousness are grounded in the physical facts, and hence is obliged to accept grounding facts similar to Pain-Grounding. However, he denies Strong Physicalism because he does not think that the physicalist needs to hold that the *grounding facts themselves*, i.e. facts like Pain-Grounding, are wholly grounded in the physical facts.

If Strong Physicalism is true, then Pain-Grounding, like any other fact, is grounded in the physical facts. But Dasgupta argues that Pain-Grounding cannot be wholly explained in terms of the physical; rather it must be explained at least in part in terms of the nature of pain. It is the nature of pain which explains why it is that the firing of c-fibres grounds pain.[8]

To make this plausible, return to our party example. Just as Pain-Grounding concerns the grounding of pain, so the following fact concerns the grounding of parties:

Party-Grounding   The fact that Rod, Jane and Freddy are revelling grounds the fact that there is a party.

Why is it the case that the fact that Rod, Jane and Freddy are revelling grounds the fact that there is a party? Intuitively this is because of the nature of a party,

---

[8] Dasgupta also suggests that we might explain grounding facts in terms of conceptual truths or metaphysical laws, but does not outline these proposals in detail. The former alternative would seem to lead to difficulties similar to those explored in this paper: the Phenomenal Analysis Problem (discussed below) would become a problem with the analysis of phenomenal concepts rather than the analysis of phenomenal properties. The latter model seems to me not very promising, as metaphysical laws are intuitively the kind of things we want to explain. Dasgupta's discussion starts from a problem Sider (2012) raises with grounding theories of fundamentality, but it would be distracting to explore that here.

because of what a party is: a party is the kind of thing that exists when there are people revelling. In this way the nature of a party 'opens itself up' to the possibility of being grounded in specific facts concerning revelling.

Dasgupta proposes we explain Party-Grounding in terms of the following two facts:

Party-Nature A party is essentially such that if there are people revelling then there is a party.
Revelling Rod, Jane and Freddy and revelling.[9]

Note that the entities in the *less fundamental fact* – the fact that there is a party – are doing crucial explanatory work in the explanation of the overall grounding fact. Dasgupta argues, partly through reflection on cases, that we do not get a satisfying explanation of grounding facts from the more fundamental fact alone. For example, it would not be satisfying to answer:

'Why is it the case that the fact that Rod, Jane and Freddy are revelling grounds that fact that there is a party?'

with:

'Because Rod, Jane and Freddy are revelling.'

It is only by reference to the nature of parties, to what a party is, that we get a satisfactory explanation of Party-Grounding.[10]

Kit Fine has previously advocated a similar kind of 'top-down' direction in the explanation of grounding facts:

[W]hat explains the ball's being red or green in virtue of its being red is something about the nature of what it is for the ball to be red or green (and about the nature of disjunction in particular) and not something about the nature of what it is for the ball to be red. It is the fact to be grounded that 'points' to its grounds and not the grounds that point to what they may ground.[11]

It is not that the less fundamental fact 'points to' the *specific facts* which ground it; essential truths concerning parties do not involve specific reference to Rod,

---

[9] Dasgupta's example is in terms of conferences rather than parties, but the point of the example is the same.
[10] Karen Bennett (2011) and Louis deRosset (2013) try to ground the grounding facts in the fundamental facts. I am persuaded by Dasgupta's arguments against this strategy, some of which I have outlined above, and which are given in more detail in Dasgupta (2016: VI).
[11] Fine (2012).

Jane and Freddy. Rather the nature of constituents of the less fundamental fact F 'points to' some condition which is sufficient for its being the case that F.

Thus, Dasgupta proposes explaining Pain-Grounding in the following way:

Pain-Nature Pain is essentially such that for any x, if x's c-fibres are firing then x feels pain.

C-Fibres   Sarah's c-fibres are firing.[12]

However, just as the nature of a party does not make explicit reference to Rod, Jane and Freddy, it seems unlikely that the nature of pain will make reference to the specific brain states which are actually involved in grounding it.[13] It is more likely, therefore, that the explanation of Pain-Grounding will be of the following form:

Pain-Nature Pain is essentially such that for any x, if x is F then x feels pain.

C-Fibres'   The fact that Sarah's c-fibres are firing entails that Sarah is F.

Let us call this model of explaining grounding facts 'grounding via essence', or GVE. Abstracting from specific cases, we can take it to be committed to the following principle:

> For any grounding fact F in which f2 is grounded in f1, F is grounded in the fact that there is a condition C such that (i) a constituent of f2 is essentially such that if C is satisfied f2 obtains, and (ii) f1 logically entails that C is satisfied.[14]

GVE is in tension with the above definition of physicalism, as according to GVE the grounding facts are partly grounded in facts about the nature of higher-level entities, rather than being wholly grounded in the fundamental physical facts. Pain-Grounding, for example, is partly grounded in Pain-Nature. The 'top-down' direction of explanation means that chains of grounding explanation don't always move in a downward direction. For this reason Dasgupta

---

[12] Again, Dasgupta's examples are slightly different to mine – involving consciousness rather than pain – but the point of the example is the same.

[13] On the identity theory, the nature of pain will of course make reference to some specific neurophysiological state. However, that neurophysiological state will surely not be identical with some utterly specific fundamental physical state. And hence, even on the identity theory pain is ultimately grounded in some fundamental physical state which the nature of pain does not make specific reference to.

[14] GVE is not an analysis of grounding, but a view about how the grounding facts are grounded. Dasgupta does not give an utterly precise definition of what the model of explanation involves in general, but this principle seems to be suggested by his examples.

rejects the above definition of physicalism, and adopts a definition of physicalism according to which certain facts are 'exempt' from needing to be
grounded in the physical, even if physicalism is true.

Obviously there must be some limit on which facts physicalism 'allows' not
to be grounded in the physical; it is inconsistent with physicalism, for example,
to deny that the facts about consciousness are grounded in the physical.
Dasgupta's view is that physicalism does not require that *facts about essences*
are grounded in the physical. This is because, according to Dasgupta, facts
about essences are *autonomous*, or not *apt to be grounded*; that is to say they
are not the kind of fact for which the question of grounding arises.

I do not have space here to give Dasgupta's complete defence of the
autonomy of facts about essences, which stretches beyond his paper on the
definition of physicalism, but I will briefly refer to an analogy he offers to help
clarify and motivate the idea.[15] The analogy is between facts which are not apt
for grounding and facts which are not apt for causal explanation. The fact that
$2 + 2 = 4$ lacks a casual explanation, but not in the sense that the big bang may
lack a causal explanation; the fact that $2 + 2 = 4$ is not the kind of fact which
requires or admits of causal explanation. By analogy there may be a category of
fact which neither requires nor admits of grounding explanation, and essential
truths are a plausible candidate. According to Dasgupta, the question 'What
explains the fact that a party is the kind of thing that exists when there are
people revelling?' is ill-posed in something like the way 'What caused 2 and 2
to equal 4?' is ill-posed. Nobody who knows what a party is should be troubled
by this question.

Having defended the autonomy of facts about essence, Dasgupta offers the
following refined definition of physicalism:

> Physicalism is the thesis that all non-physical facts which are *substantive*,
> i.e. apt to be grounded, are grounded in facts which are either physical or
> autonomous.[16]

Let us call this definition of physicalism in conjunction with the GVE model of
the explanation of grounding facts, 'grounding physicalism'. Dasgupta admits
that understanding physicalism in this way makes it harder for those wishing
to defend physicalism about the mind:

---

[15] The argument for the autonomy of facts about essence is continued in Dasgupta (2016).

[16] This is not the final definition Dasgupta ends up with, but it will serve for the purposes of
this chapter. His final definition is a little stronger, and hence will inherit any difficulties the
Phenomenal Analysis Challenge raises for the above definition.

> [P]hysicalism [on this construal] requires that there are essential connections between mind and body. This will be disappointing to physicalists who hoped that formulating physicalism in terms of ground would rescue them from having to offer tight connections of essence or analysis between mind and body. On the current picture, this hope is dashed.[17]

It is not that the grounding physicalist is obliged to hold that consciousness is essentially a physical phenomenon. Physicalism requires that in the actual world the mental facts are realised by the physical facts, but many physicalists hold that in non-actual possible worlds mental facts are realised by non-physical facts. But the grounding physicalist is obliged to construe the essences of conscious states in such a way that they are able to explain the grounding of consciousness in the physical. In what follows I will explore a way of developing this challenge, and work it into an argument against physicalism which has distinct advantages over other anti-physicalist arguments in the literature.

10.3 The Phenomenal Analysis Challenge

A thing is conscious just in case there's something that it's like to be it. There's something that it's like for a rabbit to be cold, or to be kicked, or to have a knife stuck in it. There's nothing that it's like in contrast for a table to be cold, or to be kicked or to have a knife stuck in it. There's nothing that it's like from the inside, as it were, to be a table. Consciousness is simply the determinable property of having some kind of first-person experience. Phenomenal properties are the determinates of that determinable: the specific ways of having first-person experience, such as pain, anxiety, and various forms of visual or auditory experience.

The phenomenal facts are the facts about which individuals have which phenomenal properties. However, I want to focus in this chapter on consciousness properties themselves rather than the individuals that have them. Therefore, I will abstract from phenomenal facts involving specific individuals and focus on facts involving only quantificational structure and phenomenal properties, e.g. the fact that there is something that feels pain. Call such facts the 'pure phenomenal facts'. I take it that the pure phenomenal facts are grounded in phenomenal facts involving specific individuals, e.g. the fact that someone is in pain is grounded in the fact that Bill is in pain.[18]

---

[17] Dasgupta (2014: 586).

[18] A fact may of course be grounded in lots of different facts: the fact that someone is pain is grounded in the fact that Bill is in pain, the fact that Sarah is in pain, etc.

The challenge for the grounding physicalist is that she is obliged to hold that conscious states are in a certain sense *analysable*. In this section I will outline the sense of analysis I have in mind, and why the grounding physicalist is obliged to think that phenomenal properties are indeed analysable in this sense. In the next section I will construct an argument for the claim that phenomenal properties are not analysable in this sense.

We can think of the analysis of a property as a matter of giving an account of its *real definition*, of what it is for something to have the property. Gideon Rosen gives the general form of an analysis as:

> For all x, for it to be the case that Fx just is for it to be the case that ϕx.[19]

In the case of knowledge, one plausible candidate for its analysis is:

> For all x, for it to be the case that x knows just is for it to be the case that it is not accidental that x is right that p is the case (for some proposition p).[20]

It is crucial to note two things about the notion of analysis in play here. Firstly, it is metaphysical rather than linguistic: we are concerned with the definition of properties not the definition of words. Secondly, and perhaps relatedly, it is not to be assumed that an analysis is accessible a priori. It is plausible for example that the real definition of water is known only empirically.

Putting the general form as Rosen does is in a certain sense limiting, as it restricts us to accounting for the real definition of the property in terms of facts about the bearer of that property. Let us call such analyses, in which a property P is defined in terms of other properties of the bearer of P, 'intra-substance analyses'. There is a more radical kind of analysis, in which a property P is defined in terms of facts concerning individuals which are or could be distinct from the bearer of P. Returning to parties, for it to be the case that there is something that is a party just is for it to be the case that there are people revelling; note that we are not here accounting for the real definition of partyhood in terms of some property had by the bearer of partyhood (persons are not parties). We can call analyses of this more radical form 'inter-substance analyses', the general form of which is as follows:

> For it to be the case that there is an x such that Fx just is for fact P to obtain, where x is not a constituent of P.

Orthogonal to the distinction between intra-substance and inter-substance analyses, we can distinguish analyses between properties of the same kind – call

---

[19] Rosen (2010), section 10.

[20] This analysis if taken from Unger (1968).

these 'intra-categorial analyses' – from analyses between properties which are or could be of different kinds – call these 'inter-categorical analyses'. The analysis of less determinate colours into more determinate colours is an example of an intra-categorial analysis; the analysis of chemical kinds into physical kinds is an example of an inter-categorial analysis.[21]

Cross-sectioning these two distinctions we potentially have four distinct categories of analysis, ranging from those which do the least metaphysical bridging – intra-categorial and intra-substance – to those which do the most metaphysical bridging – inter-categorial and inter-substance. Arguably some properties are unanalysable, in which case there will be no non-trivial account of the property's real definition.[22] Existence is a plausible candidate for an unanalysable property: plausibly there is no non-trivial way of accounting for what it is for something to exist. On certain mainstream views, modal properties and the causal relation are also unanalysable.

It is sometimes claimed that phenomenal properties are unanalysable. However, it is plausible that at least some phenomenal properties can be analysed into other phenomenal properties of the same subject, i.e. that there are phenomenal property analyses of the least metaphysically bridging kind: intra-categorial and intra-substance. For example, for it to be the case that there is a subject S having a colour experience just is for it to be the case that S has some property F such that F is a specific colour experience; for it to be the case that there is a subject S having the disjunctive property of feeling pain or pleasure just is for it to be the case either that S feels pain or that S feels pleasure. And there may well be a variety of more subtle analyses, perhaps pain is analysable into an effective component and a qualitative component.

However, armchair reflection does not seem to reveal analyses of phenomenal properties which are either inter-categorial or inter-substance. Prima facie, it's hard to see how what it is for there to be a subject S feeling pain could be analysed into a fact not involving phenomenal properties, or a fact not involving S (or both). Contrast with the case of partyhood. For it to be the case that there is something which is a party just is for it to be the case that there are certain people $X_1, X_2 \ldots X_n$, such that $X_1, X_2 \ldots X_n$ are revelling;

---

[21] The distinction between inter-categorial and intra-categorial presumably admits of a certain degree of contextual flexibility, i.e. there are cases of grounding which are correctly classed as inter-categorial in some contexts and intra-categorial in others. This won't matter for the claims I want to make here.

[22] For any property F, to give a trivial account F's real definition is to state the following: For it to be the case that there is an x such that Fx just is for there to be an x such that Fx.

the fact in terms of which partyhood is analysed involves people not parties. No analogous analysis of subject-hood into facts about non-subjects suggests itself, at least on first reflection.

One might take this to be prima facie reason to adopt the following thesis:

Minimal Phenomenal Analysis Phenomenal properties admit of neither inter-substance nor inter-categorial analysis.

What I have offered so far is at best prima facie grounds for accepting Minimal Phenomenal Analysis; in the next section more sustained attention is paid to the question of whether it is true. But for the moment let us explore the trouble Minimal Phenomenal Analysis, if true, causes for grounding physicalism.

According to the GVE model, in the case of any given grounding fact F, the constituents of the less fundamental fact play a crucial role in explaining F. To indulge in metaphor, the grounding facts 'reach out' to, or in Fine's phrase 'point to', the facts that ground them. Partyhood points to its ground in virtue of the fact that it's in the nature of partyhood that if there are people revelling then there is a party. But if Minimal Phenomenal Analysis is true, it's hard to see how the facts about consciousness could do much reaching or pointing. The phenomenal properties of a given subject can reach out to other phenomenal properties of that subject. But they could not it seems reach out to non-conscious fundamental physical individuals and properties, in such a way as to explain the ultimate grounding of the facts about consciousness in facts concerning such individuals and properties.

To try to make this a little more precise, grounding physicalism entails the following thesis:

Phenomenal Deflation For any actually obtaining pure phenomenal fact Q, there is a condition C, such that (i) there is some constituent E of Q such that it is in the nature of E that if C is satisfied then Q obtains, (ii) the fundamental physical facts logically entail that C is satisfied.

If Minimal Phenomenal Analysis is true, then for any actually obtaining pure phenomenal fact Q of the form <there exists a subject S such that S has phenomenal property P>, the only condition sufficient for Q's instantiation which could be extracted from the real definition of P would be of the form <S has phenomenal property P*>, in which S is the same subject which has P, but in which P* may perhaps be a phenomenal property not identical with P. It's hard to see how such a condition could be logically entailed by the physical facts. How on earth could a fact about an enormous number of non-conscious fundamental physical entities related in extremely complex ways, logically entail the existence of a subject feeling pain?

One way of bolstering this concern is to point out that mereological nihilism seems to be logically coherent. There is no contradiction in the thesis that fundamental particles never compose composite objects, i.e. that there are particles arranged table-wise, planet-wise, etc., but no tables, planets, etc. Assuming that conscious subjects (at least the conscious subjects we are pre-theoretically committed to) are macro-level entities, the logical coherence of mereological nihilism entails that no fact exclusively concerning micro-level entities entails the existence of a conscious subject.

Thus, assuming that the fundamental physical facts are micro-physical facts, we can pose the following argument against physicalism:

1. If physicalism is true, then *Phenomenal Deflation* is true: For any actually obtaining pure phenomenal fact Q, there is a condition C, such that (i) there is some constituent E of Q such that it is in the nature of E that if C is satisfied then Q obtains, (ii) the micro-physical facts logically entail that C is satisfied.
2. For any actually obtaining pure phenomenal fact Q of the form <there exists a subject S such that S has phenomenal property P>, the only condition sufficient for Q's instantiation which could be extracted from the real definition of P would be of the form <S has phenomenal property P*>, in which S is a macro-level entity. (Follows from *Minimal Phenomenal Analysis* and the assumption that conscious subjects are macro-level entities.)
3. Therefore, physicalism is true only if the micro-physical facts logically entail the existence of a macro-level entity.
4. It's not the case that the micro-physical facts logically entail the existence of a macro-level entity.
5. Therefore, physicalism is false.

Why doesn't this form of argument apply quite generally to rule out the grounding of any macro-level entities? Or to put it another way, why does it not follow from the coherence of mereological nihilism that facts about micro-level entities *never* ground the existence of macro-level entities? The proponent of GVE will likely hold that in general the essences of macro-level entities are rich enough to account for their grounding in the micro-level facts. It is plausibly in the nature of a table that if particles are arranged table-wise then there is a table.[23] Thus, even though the micro-level facts in and of themselves do not logically entail the existence of tables, the micro-level facts logically entail a certain condition C, such that the kind table is essentially such that if C is satisfied then there are tables.[24]

The problem in the case of conscious subjects is that, if Minimal Phenomenal Analysis is true, the nature of phenomenal properties does not look to be rich enough to yield a condition C which is (i) logically entailed by the micro-physical facts, and is (ii) sufficient for the obtaining of macro-level facts concerning conscious subjects. Assuming Minimal Phenomenal Analysis, the only condition extractable from the nature of phenomenal properties which is sufficient for the instantiation of those properties concerns the bearers of phenomenal properties. Assuming the bearers of phenomenal properties are macro-level entities, that condition is not logically entailed by micro-level facts.

Rosen has discussed, in more general terms, something like this difficulty for the physicalist, and Fine has suggested two responses.[25] Firstly he suggests that the kind of grounding which obtains between the mental and the physical is *natural* rather than metaphysical. Secondly, he suggests that even if it is not in the nature of a given mental property to ground a connection with a *specific* physical property, it may nonetheless be in the nature of each mental property that it has *some* physical ground.

Given the standard understanding of physicalism, and assuming that natural grounding goes along with natural necessity, Fine's first response would not lead to physicalism as it is normally understood but to property dualism. Although definitions of physicalism wholly in terms of supervenience are out of favour, it is generally agreed that the supervenience of all facts on the physical facts – with the strength of metaphysical necessity – is a necessary condition for physicalism. And there are arguably good reasons for taking it so. One of the main arguments for physicalism is its capacity to reconcile mental causation with the causal closure of the physical in a way that does not lead

---

[23] By stipulation 'being arranged table-wise' expresses the functional role F such that it is in the nature of the kind table that if particles are arranged F-wise then there is a table. This stipulation does not entail that there is such a functional role involved in the essence of the kind table, as the predicate might not be satisfied. I give more detail of the analysis of macro-level objects in Goff (2017).

[24] Mereological nihilists might deny that the kind table is essentially such that if particles are arranged table-wise then there is a table, but this seems to me to build too much into our ordinary notion of a table. There is clearly a deflationary notion of a table according to which if there are particles arranged table-wise then there is a table.

[25] Rosen (2010, section 10); Fine (2012).

to problematic overdetermination. There is not space here to fully defend this claim, but it is broadly agreed that physicalism can only do this if it is taken to be the thesis that all facts are metaphysically, and not just naturally, grounded in the physical facts.[26]

Turning to Fine's second response, it is not obviously true that it is in the nature of phenomenal properties that they require some physical ground. Disembodied subjects of experience seem perfectly conceivable, which gives us at least prima facie grounds for thinking that the essence of phenomenal properties is compatible with their existing ungrounded.[27] But even if Fine were right that it is part of the nature of phenomenal properties that they have some physical ground, this in itself would hardly be sufficient to explain a grounding connection with the physical. Presumably it is not in the nature of pain that just any old physical state is sufficient for there to be pain. If physicalism is true, there is a limited range of physical states which are capable of grounding pain. If grounding facts are to be explained in terms of the nature of the grounded items, there must be something in the nature of pain which determines which of all possible physical states are the ones capable of grounding pain.

I conclude at this stage that the grounding physicalist has to deny Minimal Phenomenal Analysis; she must argue that, contrary to initial appearances, there is a way of analysing phenomenal properties which facilitates the bridging of distinct substances and property kinds. Let us call this the 'Phenomenal Analysis Challenge' for grounding physicalism. It is not clear that other conceptions of physicalism are subject to this challenge. For many philosophers the attraction of defining physicalism in terms of supervenience was that it seemed to avoid the need for such analyses of the mental. And whilst some physicalists have argued that there need to be transparent explanatory relations undergirding supervenience theses,[28] what is specific to grounding physicalism as I have outlined it in this chapter is that such explanatory relations flow from the *grounded facts*, such as the facts about consciousness, rather than the facts doing the grounding. In the next section I will consider ways in which physicalists might respond to the Phenomenal Analysis Challenge, before going on to consider how anti-physicalists can counter-respond.

---

[26] See for example Pereboom (2002) and Bennett (2003).

[27] The conceivability and possibility of disembodied subjects of experience is defended in Goff (2010).

[28] Horgan (1993).

10.4 Physicalist Responses to the Phenomenal Analysis Challenge

In the context of accounting for consciousness, we can broadly distinguish two forms of physicalism, which David Chalmers has dubbed 'type-A physicalism' and 'type-B physicalism'.[29]

The type-A physicalist holds that the physical facts a priori entail the phenomenal facts.[30] If one knew all the facts about the workings of my body and brain, one could in principle work out the nature of my conscious experience. The type-B physicalist denies that the physical facts broadly entail the phenomenal facts, whilst nonetheless holding that the physical facts ground the phenomenal facts. The difference is made vivid in terms of zombies: creatures which are physical duplicates of actual humans but which lack any kind of conscious experience. For the type-A physicalist zombies are inconceivable, in the sense that their possibility can be ruled out a priori. For the type-B physicalist, zombies are perfectly conceivable but turn out a posteriori to be impossible.

How might the type-A physicalist respond to the Phenomenal Analysis Challenge? Type-A physicalists standardly adopt some form of analytic functionalism, according to which mental states are causally defined: to be in pain, by definition, is to have an inner state which 'plays the pain role', i.e. meditates between bodily damage and avoidance behaviour in the distinctive way associated with pain.[31] Clearly to accept analytic functionalism is to deny Minimal Phenomenal Analysis. Analytic functionalism entails that, for any phenomenal property p, the real definition of p can be accounted for in terms of causal roles which could be realised by non-conscious individuals distinct from the individual instantiating p, e.g. micro-level physical parts of the bearer of p acting in concert. In other words, analytic functionalism is committed to inter-categorial and inter-substance analysis of phenomenal properties. Just as it is a priori that if there are people revelling then there is a party, so according to analytic functionalism it is a priori that if certain entities play the pain role then there is pain.

---

[29] Chalmers (2002).

[30] We should distinguish a priori entailment from strict logical entailment. I argued above that mereological nihilist is logically coherent: that there is no contradiction in the assertion that particles are arranged table-wise but there is no table. But I also suggested it is plausible to suppose that it's in the nature of a table that if particles are arranged table-wise then there is a table. If the nature of the kind *table* is a priori accessible, it will follow the fact that particles are arranged table-wise a priori entails – even if it doesn't logically entail – the existence of a table.

[31] Armstrong (1968); Lewis (1996).

Moreover it is plausible that such an essential nature could explain the grounding of the phenomenal in the physical. For the analytic functionalist pain is essentially such that there is something in pain if the following condition is met: <there is an entity or entities playing the pain role>, and it is plausible that the physical facts logically entail that this condition is met. A similar story can be told about each phenomenal property, according to analytic functionalism, thus accounting for the truth of Phenomenal Deflation.[32]

The type-B physicalist is likely to make a very different kind of response to the Phenomenal Analysis Challenge. Type-B physicalists tend to accept the existence of *phenomenal concepts*; a phenomenal concept is the kind of concept one employs when one thinks about a phenomenal property in terms of *what it's like to have it*. In paradigmatic cases one attends to, say, one's pain, and thinks about in terms of *how it feels* or *what it's like*. Type-B physicalists accept that phenomenal concepts have no a priori connection to physical or functional concepts – hence the conceivability of zombies – but nonetheless hold that phenomenal concepts *refer* to physical or functional states – hence the impossibility of zombies. Pain, the state referred to by the phenomenal concept of pain, is identical with c-fibres firing (or some functional state realised by c-fibres firing), and yet it is not a priori that this is so.

It seems to follow that phenomenal concepts reveal little or nothing of the nature of the states they refer to; call this thesis 'Phenomenal Opacity'. For *ex hypothesi* phenomenal states have physical essences – pain just is c-fibres firing – and yet a priori reflection employing phenomenal concepts does not reveal it to be the case that pain is c-fibres firing. Indeed many type-B physicalists have explicitly committed to Phenomenal Opacity. David Papineau for example says the following:

> No doubt there are ways of thinking of things that make certain essential properties a priori knowable. But I take such a priori knowledge to derive from (possibly implicit) compositionality in the relevant modes of thinking, and so not to be associated with the most basic ways in which thought makes contact with reality ... When it comes to these basic points of contact, I find it hard to take seriously any alternative to the assumption that our atomic concepts are related to reality by facts external to our a priori grasp, such as causal or historical facts ... I don't recognise any way in which the mind 'captures' something, apart from simply referring to it.
>
> (Papineau 2006: 102)

---

[32] There could be problems accounting for the grounding of higher-order physical states, such as neurophysiological states, in more basic physical states, but this clearly takes us beyond any concerns pertaining to consciousness.

Given that Papineau thinks that phenomenal concepts are atomic concepts, it is clear that he accepts phenomenal opacity. Brian McLaughlin is even more explicit:

> Phenomenal concepts … do not conceptually reveal anything about the essential nature of phenomenal properties: they simply name or demonstrate them.[33]

Whilst other type-B physicalists may not be explicit about their commitment to Phenomenal Opacity it is often implicit in their favoured theories of phenomenal concepts as demonstratives,[34] indexicals,[35] recognitional concepts,[36] or concepts which refer in virtue of facts about teleology or causal connections.[37] If my phenomenal concept of pain is merely a demonstrative, or refers in virtue of facts outside of my a priori grasp, then it is hard to see how it could yield any insight into the essential nature of the state it tracks.

Having adopted Phenomenal Opacity the type-B physicalist is free to adopt the view that conscious states have highly complex physical, or indeed functional, natures suited to explaining the grounding of the phenomenal in the physical. The reason that conscious states strike us as unanalysable is that this complex nature is not available to us introspectively. Perhaps the reference of terms such as 'party' is fixed descriptively, such that anyone competent with the term knows what it is for there to be a party. If the concept 'pain' reveals little or nothing of the nature of pain, this could explain why pain seems, in contrast to partyhood, to be an unanalysable property.

If the type-B physicalist identifies phenomenal properties with functional properties, then she can give an account of the grounding of the mental in the physical similar to that offered by the analytic functionalist above. The only difference is that the functionally defined essential nature of the phenomenal which explains the grounding connection is not a priori accessible. Alternately, she can identify phenomenal properties with physical properties themselves, leaving no remaining challenge to a physicalist account of consciousness.[38]

It is standard for the type-B physicalist to account for the conceivable impossibility of zombies in terms of the nature of phenomenal concepts; doing

---

[33] McLaughlin (2001: 324).
[34] Papineau (1993); Perry (2001).
[35] Tye (1995, ch. 6); Lycan (1996, section 3.3).
[36] Loar (1997, 2003); Tye (2000), ch. 2; Perry 2001; Carruthers 2004; Levin (2007b).
[37] Papineau (2002, 2007).
[38] At least no challenges which arise from the nature of consciousness, see n. 32.

so has become known as the 'phenomenal concept strategy'.[39] What I have just outlined is a kind of phenomenal concept strategy for responding to the Phenomenal Analysis Challenge.

10.5 The Phenomenal Analysis Argument

The physicalist strategies outlined in the last section are ruled out by the key premises of one of the most discussed anti-physicalist arguments: the Conceivability Argument.[40] Indeed we can take the premises of the Conceivability Argument and formulate a new argument against physicalism, one which does not involve a move from conceivability to possibility. I will not examine the plausibility of these premises here; this is done enough elsewhere. But what I do hope to show (in the next section) is that this new argument, call it the 'Phenomenal Analysis Argument' is stronger than the Conceivability Argument, in the sense that – if sound – it rules out a form of monism which the Conceivability Argument – even if sound – does not. Hence, for the grounding physicalist, given her obligation to give a substantial analysis of phenomenal properties, the hard problem of consciousness is harder.

The Conceivability Argument against physicalism moves in three stages. In the first stage it is argued that it is conceivable that the physical facts obtain in the absence of the phenomenal facts. We can, it is claimed, conceive of a 'zombie' version of our world, which is in all respects physically indiscernible from the actual world but in which there is no consciousness. In the second stage a move is made from the conceivability of a zombie version of our world, to its genuine possibility. In the final stage it is argued that the possibility of the physical facts obtaining in the absence of the phenomenal facts is inconsistent with physicalism.

The final move is the least controversial, and would follow so long as we take it (as most do) to be a necessary condition for physicalism that the phenomenal facts supervene, with metaphysical necessity, on the physical facts. The following principle, generally taken to be a core principle governing grounding, entails that the supervenience of all facts on the physical facts is indeed a necessary condition for physicalism given a grounding conception of physicalism:

---

[39] This term was coined by Stoljar (2005).

[40] Chalmers 2009 is perhaps the most discussed version of conceivability argument in contemporary philosophy, although of course it has its roots in Descartes 1641/1985.

Necessitation If a certain fact X grounds Y, then necessarily if X obtains then
　　　　　　　Y obtains.[41]

The starting premise, then, of the Conceivability Argument is *Zombie
Conceivability*: the thesis that a zombie version of the actual world is conceivable. Clearly this is inconsistent with analytic functionalism. If analytic
functionalism is true, then a world in which the pain role is realised but in
which there is no pain is straightforwardly contradictory. And yet this is precisely what obtains in a zombie version of the actual world. In ruling out analytic functionalism Zombie Conceivability rules out the analytic functionalist
response to the Phenomenal Analysis Challenge.

Let us turn now to the second stage of the Conceivability Argument: the
move from the putative conceivability of a zombie world to its alleged possibility. Few now accept that all propositions which are conceivably true are
possibly true, due to the plausible examples of conceivable impossibilities
proposed by Kripke and Putnam, e.g. water existing in the absence of H_2O.[42]
Thus, most proponents of the Conceivability Argument claim that there is
something special about phenomenal concepts in virtue of which we are able
to move from the conceivability the possibility of zombies.

What exactly is special about phenomenal concepts? In his much discussed
version of the Conceivability Argument, David Chalmers builds on the
following claim of Kripke:

> Pain … is not picked out by one of its accidental properties; rather it is
> picked out by the property of *being pain itself*, by its immediate phenom-
> enological quality.[43]

Kripke seems to be claiming that we conceive of conscious states in terms of
their essential nature. Pain is, in its essential nature, just a way of feeling, and
when we think of pain we think of it in terms of that way of feeling. I use the
term 'transparent' to describe such a concept: a concept C referring to R is
transparent just in case the complete essence of R is a priori accessible for
someone possessing C, in virtue of their possession of C.[44] If pain is a transparent concept, then in conceiving of pain in terms of how it feels, it is apparent
to the conceiver what it is for something to feel that way.[45]

---

[41] Endorsement of Necessitation is the norm, see for example Rosen (2010); Fine (2012); Trogdon
　　　(2013b). There are, however, some who deny it, such as Leuenberger (2013) and Skiles (2015).
[42] Kripke (1972); Putnam (1973, 1975).
[43] Kripke (1972: 15).
[44] Goff (2011, 2015a, 2017).
[45] It is trivial that a phenomenal concept characterises its referent R in terms of what it's like to
　　　have R. This is different to the thesis of Phenomenal Transparency, which is the thesis that a

Let us call the thesis that phenomenal concepts are transparent 'Phenomenal Transparency'. Chalmers frames his versions of the Conceivability Argument in terms of his two-dimensional semantic framework. In this framework, Phenomenal Transparency comes out as the thesis that phenomenal concepts are *super-rigid*, where a concept is super-rigid if it picks out the same entity in every epistemic scenario and every metaphysically possible world (and every pair thereof). We need not go into the details of the two-dimensional framework; what is important for our purposes is that the transparency – or super-rigidity – of phenomenal concepts is essential for the move from the conceivability to the possibility of zombies. Because a phenomenal concept picks out the same thing in all epistemic scenarios and all metaphysically possible worlds, its extension at an arbitrary world W does not change depending on whether W is conceived of as an epistemic scenario or a metaphysically possible world; it is precisely when conceiving using such concepts that we are licensed – according to Chalmers – to move from conceivability to possibility.[46]

I will not here assess the plausibility of this kind of move from conceivability to possibility. Rather I want to point out that Phenomenal Transparency rules out the Phenomenal Opacity response to the Phenomenal Analysis Challenge, as these two theses are defined in opposition to each other. Thus, two crucial premises of Chalmers' Conceivability Argument against physicalism – Zombie Conceivability and Phenomenal Transparency – rule out the two physicalist responses to the Phenomenal Analysis Challenge discussed in the last section. A similar story can be told with reference to other forms of the Conceivability Argument or related anti-physicalist arguments, but I will spare the reader

phenomenal concept reveals what it is for something to have R, i.e. reveals the essence of R. It is plausible that there is a category of concept between transparent and opaque, the category of translucent, where a concept is translucent if something significant but not everything of the essence of its referent is a priori accessible. Some physicalists try to deny the second step of the conceivability argument by holding that phenomenal concepts are translucent (Schroer 2010; Diaz-Leon 2014). I have defended Phenomenal Transparency in Goff (2017: Ch. 5). However, our current concern is not whether the premises of the anti-physicalist arguments are true, but what argument can be constructed using these premises in the context of a grounding conception of physicalism.

[46] Chalmers does argue (Chalmers 2009: 153) that we can run the argument without assuming that phenomenal concepts are super-rigid, by focussing on the primary intentions of phenomenal concepts. However, this is only because his framework, somewhat controversially, assumes that every concept affords a substantive a priori grasp of *some* significant property of its referent, either its essence or a property which uniquely identifies it in the actual world. Assuming this, even if phenomenal concepts do not afford us a transparent grasp of the essence of consciousness properties themselves, they will afford us a transparent grasp of the properties we use to pick out conscious properties. I have dealt with this matter in more detail in Goff (2017), but will set it aside here for the sake of simplicity.

the details here.[47] Furthermore, these two premises, if true, render Minimal Phenomenal Analysis extremely difficult to deny, as I will now explain.

If Phenomenal Transparency is true, then for any phenomenal property F the real definition of F is a priori accessible (for anyone possessing a phenomenal concept of F, in virtue of possessing a phenomenal concept of F). If there is some non-trivial inter-substance or inter-categorial account of what it is for something to have F, some account which is not simply 'For all x, for it to be the case that x has F just is for it to be the case that x has F', then that account will be a priori accessible. But the only a priori accessible non-trivial accounts of the real definition of a phenomenal property we find in the philosophical literature are either intra-substance and intra-categorical, or those offered by proponents of analytic functionalism or some similar causal analysis of mentality. The former kind of account does not help with the Phenomenal Analysis Challenge, and if zombies are conceivable, accounts of the latter kind are all false.

To put it another way, to avoid Phenomenal Analysis Challenge the grounding physicalist requires some kind of inter-substance and inter-categorial analysis of phenomenal properties. If Phenomenal Transparency is true, that analysis must be available a priori. If zombies are conceivable, then we have good reason to think that there are no a priori accessible analyses of phenomenal properties which are either inter-substance or inter-categorial, as all extant proposals are inconsistent with Zombie Conceivability.

Thus, we reach the following argument against physicalism (in which a 'non-minimal analysis' is one which is either inter-categorial or inter-substance):

The Phenomenal Analysis Argument

Premise 1   If zombies are conceivable, then either Minimal Phenomenal Analysis is true or there is a non-minimal analysis of phenomenal properties which is not a priori accessible.

Premise 2   If Phenomenal Transparency is true, then it's not the case that there is a non-minimal analysis of phenomenal properties which is not a priori accessible.

Premise 3   Phenomenal Transparency is true.

---

[47]   In other versions of the argument the link to Phenomenal Transparency is more explicit. George Bealer's (1994, 2002) argument involves a commitment to the *semantic stability* of phenomenal concepts, and Martine Nida-Rümelin's (2007) involves a commitment to the thesis that phenomenal concepts enable us to *grasp* phenomenal properties. Both of these commitments are roughly equivalent to Phenomenal Transparency. I frame my version of the conceivability argument in terms of Phenomenal Transparency itself (Goff 2017).

Premise 4   Zombie Conceivability is true.
Conclusion 1 Therefore, Minimal Phenomenal Analysis is true.
Premise 5   If Minimal Phenomenal Analysis is true, then grounding physicalism is false.
Conclusion 2 Therefore, grounding physicalism is false.

10.6 Why the Phenomenal Analysis Argument Is More Powerful Than the Conceivability Argument

There is one sense in which the Phenomenal Analysis Argument is dialectically weaker than the Conceivability Argument: it has force only against forms of physicalism which require that the phenomenal facts be analysable. The conceivability argument in contrast aims to prove a thesis inconsistent with almost all formulations of physicalism, namely that the phenomenal facts do not supervene on the physical. However, given the increasing popularity of grounding in metaphysics, it is worth exploring the implications of a grounding conception of physicalism.

Moreover, there are two ways in which the Phenomenal Analysis Argument is dialectically superior to the Conceivability Argument. Firstly, it does not involve a move from conceivability to possibility. This may not be as dialectically significant as one might at first have thought, as philosophers sympathetic to the use of the notions of grounding and essence are likely to be sympathetic to an account of modal truths in terms of essence.[48] Given such an account, it is perhaps plausible that conceivability entails possibility on the condition that one has a complete grasp of the essences of the facts one is conceiving of. If this were the case, and if both phenomenal and physical concepts reveal the essence of the properties they denote, we would be able to move from the conceivability to the possibility of zombies.[49] Nonetheless, (i) a lot of work would need to be done to justify this kind of inference from conceivability to possibility, (ii) some of those sympathetic to a grounding conception of physicalism may not be sympathetic to an account of modality in terms of essence. The Phenomenal Analysis Argument avoids any concern with these difficult issues.

More importantly, the Phenomenal Analysis Argument threatens Russellian monism as well as standard forms of physicalism. Chalmers is explicit that his conceivability argument does not rule out Russellian monism. The conclusion

---

[48] Fine (1994); Lowe (2012).
[49] I defend this kind of move from the conceivability to the possibility of zombies in Goff (in press a).

of the argument is: *either physicalism is false or Russellian monism is true* – to move from conceivability to the possibility of zombies we need both phenomenal and physical concepts to be transparent (so that both have identical primary and secondary intensions), but if Russellian monism is true physical concepts are not transparent. If Russellian monism is true, we cannot move from the conceivability to the possibility of zombies.

Thus, both the (standard) type-B physicalist and the Russellian monist deny that we can move from the conceivability to the possibility of zombies, but for different reasons. For the type-B physicalist, the inference is blocked by the opacity of phenomenal concepts; for the Russellian monist the inference is blocked by the opacity of physical concepts.

The upshot is that the conclusion of Chalmers's Conceivability Argument leaves us with two options: dualism or Russellian monism. The latter is arguably the more attractive option. As already noted, a key argument for physicalism is its potential to reconcile mental causation with the causal closure of the physical in a way that does not lead to problematic overdetermination. If my pain is grounded in the firing of my c-fibres, then the fact that my pain behaviour is caused *both* by my pain and by the firing of my c-fibres is widely thought not to be a problematic case of overdetermination. Compare: that fact that both the party upstairs and the people dancing and drinking upstairs kept me awake last night is not a problematic case of overdetermination, as the fact that there is a party upstairs is grounded in the fact that there are people dancing and drinking upstairs. Russellian monism arguably shares this advantage with physicalism, as it also holds that the mental facts are grounded in the (deep) physical facts, and this is widely held to be a great advantage of the view.

In contrast to the Conceivability Argument, the Phenomenal Analysis Argument has the potential to rule out not only standard forms of physicalism but also Russellian monism. This is because Minimal Phenomenal Analysis looks to be just as problematic for the Russellian monist as it is for the physicalist, and for exactly the same reasons. Just like the standard physicalist, the Russellian monist – at least on a standard understanding of the view – tries to ground the phenomenal facts in complex physical facts. It's just that for the Russellian monist, the complex physical facts to which consciousness is being reduced have a deep nature, without which they would be unable to ground consciousness. And none of the difficulties I outlined in describing the Phenomenal Analysis Problem go away if physical facts have a deep nature, as these problems arise from the nature of phenomenal rather than physical properties. For example, the problem of trying to make sense of how seemingly unanalysable phenomenal properties 'reach out' to complex physical facts is made no easier by the supposition that those complex physical facts have a deep nature.[50]

Thus, the Phenomenal Analysis Argument is an argument not just against standard forms of physicalism but also against Russellian monism. This is especially problematic for Russellian monists, who tend to motivate their view by arguing against physicalism on the basis of the Conceivability Argument (or something like it), which of course commits them to the crucial premises of the Phenomenal Analysis Argument. Hence, in the Phenomenal Analysis Argument, the very premises the Russellian monist uses to argue for her view are used against her.

Russellian monism has been for many an attractive middle way between dualism and standard forms of physicalism: resistant to both the Conceivability Argument (like dualism), and yet able to reconcile mental causation with causal closure (like physicalism). The Phenomenal Analysis Argument threatens to make our options starker.

10.7 Conclusion

There is no clear consensus in the philosophy of mind as to how to define physicalism. Given the increasing popularity of taking grounding to be a central concept in metaphysics, it is pertinent to explore the implications of grounding conceptions of physicalism, of which Dasgupta's account is perhaps the most developed form. I hope to have shown that adopting Dasgupta's account of physicalism makes physicalism harder to defend as it opens physicalists up to the Phenomenal Analysis Challenge: a challenge other conceptions of physicalism, for example, supervenience conceptions, are not obviously subject to.

Whilst that challenge only really has bite if we adopt the key premises of the Conceivability Argument – Phenomenal Transparency and Zombies Conceivability – the resulting argument has a much stronger conclusion. The Phenomenal Analysis Argument, if sound, rules out not only standard forms of physicalism but also the Russellian middle way between standard physicalism and dualism.[51]

---

[50] Panpsychist forms of Russellian monism (Strawson 2006/2008; Chalmers 2015; Goff 2017) would not need an inter-categorial analysis of phenomenal properties, as on this view ordinary consciousness is grounded in more basic states of consciousness. However, at least on standards versions, panpsychism would require an inter-substance analysis of phenomenal properties, as facts about the consciousness of ordinary subjects are grounded in facts about fundamental physical entities.

[51] The argument I have constructed above applies only to reductive version of Russellian monism. I am increasingly attracted to an emergentism form of Russellian monism, which I defend in Coleman and Goff (in press) and Goff (in press b).

11 Phenomenal Knowledge *Why*: The Explanatory Knowledge Argument against Physicalism

Hedda Hassel Mørch

11.1 Introduction

Phenomenal knowledge is knowledge of *what it is like* to be in conscious states, such as seeing red or being in pain. According to the knowledge argument (Jackson 1982, 1986), phenomenal knowledge is knowledge *that*, i.e. knowledge of phenomenal facts. According to the ability hypothesis (Nemirow 1979; Lewis 1983a), phenomenal knowledge is mere practical knowledge *how*, i.e. the mere possession of abilities. However, some phenomenal knowledge also seems to be knowledge *why*, i.e. knowledge of explanatory facts. For example, someone who has just experienced pain for the first time learns not only *that* this is what pain is like, but also *why* people tend to avoid it.

Some philosophers have claimed that experiencing pain gives knowledge why in a normative sense: it tells us why pain is bad and why inflicting it is wrong (Kahane 2010). But phenomenal knowledge seems to explain not (only) why people *should* avoid pain, but why they *in fact* tend to do so. In this chapter, I will explicate and defend a precise version of this claim and use it as a basis for a new version of the knowledge argument, which I call *the explanatory knowledge argument*. According to the argument, some phenomenal knowledge (1) explains regularities in a distinctive, ultimate or regress-ending way, and (2) predicts them without induction. No physical knowledge explains and predicts regularities in the same way. This implies the existence of distinctive, phenomenal explanatory facts, which cannot be identified with physical facts.

I will show that this argument can be defended against the main objections to the original knowledge argument, the ability hypothesis and the phenomenal concept strategy, even if it turns out that the original cannot. In this way, the explanatory knowledge argument further strengthens the case against physicalism.

11.2 Background and Overview

The knowledge argument (Jackson 1982, 1986) is based on the thought experiment of Mary the color scientist. Mary is a gifted scientist who grows up in a room where everything is black and white. Here she has obtained complete physical knowledge about human color vision from black-and-white television. She is then released from the room into the world, and for the first time she sees a colored object, a ripe tomato. It seems then she will learn something new: she will obtain phenomenal knowledge about what it is like to see red.

The thought experiment could also be put in terms of pain. Suppose Mary has complete physical knowledge about the physiology of pain, but has never actually experienced it. Perhaps the black-and-white room is very safe and Mary has perfect health, so she has never had an accident or suffered from any kind of illness. Or, we might suppose Mary suffers from congenital insensitivity to pain, a medical condition which renders sufferers incapable of experiencing bodily pain of any kind. As the brilliant scientist she is, she figures out a cure for this condition which she applies to herself. Then she has an accident, she burns her hand, and experiences pain for the first time. It seems she will then learn something new: she now has phenomenal knowledge of what it is like to be in pain.

According to the knowledge argument, phenomenal knowledge is knowledge *that* this is what seeing red or being in pain is like, i.e. knowledge of phenomenal *facts* (where facts are understood as ontological or non-propositional items). Furthermore, because it would be new to someone like Mary who already knows all the physical facts, phenomenal knowledge must be about non-physical facts. The existence of non-physical facts refutes physicalism, the view that the physical facts are all the facts. The argument can be summed up as follows:

1. All physical facts are knowable without experience.
2. Some phenomenal facts are not knowable without experience.
3. Therefore, some facts are non-physical.

By knowability without experience, I mean knowability within a black-and-white, pain-proof, and otherwise experience-restricted room, or more generally, knowability without reliance on any *particular kind* of phenomenal experience.

In response to the knowledge argument, some physicalists have disputed that phenomenal knowledge is factual. According to Lewis' ability hypothesis (1983a), phenomenal knowledge is mere practical knowledge, or knowledge *how*. When Mary sees a red object for the first time, she merely learns how to imagine, remember, and recognize the physical state of having her retinas stimulated by a certain wavelength of light. Similarly, when she experiences pain for the first time, as in the alternative version of the scenario, she merely learns how to recognize tissue damage and other harmful bodily states, how to imagine and remember these states, and so on. Given the assumption that gaining new abilities does not require becoming aware of any new facts, the ability hypothesis would avert the threat phenomenal knowledge poses to physicalism.

Other physicalists, such as Loar (1997) and Papineau (2002), grant that phenomenal knowledge is factual, but dispute that it is about any *new* facts. Rather, they claim, phenomenal knowledge is about the same old physical facts that someone like Mary would already know. When Mary experiences color or pain for the first time, she merely learns to represent or conceive of known physical facts in a new and different way. This response is known as the phenomenal concept strategy. If phenomenal knowledge is about wholly physical facts, as per this response, it would also pose no threat to physicalism.

These are the main accounts of phenomenal knowledge, but there are also other variations. According to Kahane (2010), some phenomenal knowledge also constitutes a special kind of knowledge *why*, in the following sense: someone who experiences pain for the first time will learn not only *that* this is what pain is like, but also why pain is bad and why we should not inflict it on others. Phenomenal knowledge of pain thereby constitutes *normative* knowledge. Kahane also notes that no physical knowledge seems normative in the same way. He suggests that this could form the basis for a new argument against physicalism, a *normative knowledge argument*, although he does not go on to develop such an argument.[1]

In this chapter, I will defend the claim that some phenomenal knowledge, of pain in particular, constitutes knowledge *why*, but in a factual rather than a (merely) normative sense: knowledge of what pain is like tells us not (only) why we *should* avoid pain, morally or rationally speaking, but (also) why people *in fact* tend to try to avoid it. That people generally try to avoid pain is an ordinary, empirical psychological regularity, not a normative claim

---

[1] Instead, he develops a normative knowledge argument against externalism in metaethics.

(though it is of course compatible with the normative claim). I will argue that phenomenal knowledge of pain (1) *explains* this regularity in a distinctive, ultimate or regress-ending way, and (2) *predicts* it without induction, but no physical knowledge explains and predicts this, or any other, regularities in the same way. Furthermore, these distinctive explanatory features of phenomenal knowledge reflect distinctive explanatory *facts*. This gives the basis for what I will call *the explanatory knowledge argument*:

1.   All physical facts are knowable without experience.
2.   Some explanatory facts are not knowable without experience.
3.   Therefore, some facts are non-physical.

What kinds of facts are explanatory facts? I will claim that, in this case, they are facts about *causal powers*. That is, phenomenal knowledge of pain is distinctively explanatory and predictive because pain itself seems to have the power to make subjects who experience it try to avoid it, and it appears to have this power *in virtue of how it feels*, or its phenomenal character. And given that no physical knowledge enables the explanation and prediction of any regularities, there do not seem to be any physical causal powers of the same sort.

    In what follows, I will articulate and defend these claims in more detail (11.3). I will then consider a number of objections, including the objection that physical knowledge can be equally explanatory as phenomenal knowledge given dispositional essentialism (the view that physical properties are essentially dispositional or powerful) (11.4), and objections based on apparent exceptions to the regularity between pain and avoidance attempts (11.5) – such as the medical condition *pain asymbolia*, where patients report feeling pain that they have no inclination to avoid (Grahek 2007).

    I will then argue that the explanatory knowledge argument is resistant to both the ability hypothesis and the phenomenal concept strategy, in ways the original is not (11.6), and thereby strengthens the case against physicalism relative to the original knowledge argument. The reason for this is roughly as follows. The original knowledge argument claims that phenomenal knowledge would be simply *new* to someone like Mary. In response, the ability hypothesis and phenomenal concept strategy claim that this knowledge is not about any new *facts*, but can rather be explained away in terms of new *abilities* or *concepts*. The explanatory knowledge argument, in contrast, claims that some phenomenal knowledge would be new to Mary *in virtue of* being distinctively explanatory. To explain how phenomenal knowledge could be distinctively explanatory, the ability hypothesis and the phenomenal strategy would have to posit not only new, but also distinctively explanatory abilities or concepts. But, as I will argue, it is not clear how abilities or concepts could be explanatory if there are no corresponding explanatory facts (such as causal powers).

After a preliminary summary (11.7), I will then consider how the explanatory knowledge argument relates to a potential normative knowledge argument, as suggested by Kahane (11.8). Finally (11.9), I will consider some further implications of the explanatory knowledge argument for mental causation and the principle of physical causal-explanatory closure.

11.3 The Explanatory Knowledge Argument

To repeat, the explanatory knowledge argument goes as follows:

1. All physical facts are knowable without experience (i.e., within a black-and-white, pain-proof, and otherwise experience-restricted room).
2. Some explanatory facts are not knowable without experience.
3. Therefore, some facts are non-physical.

Premise 1 of this argument overlaps with premise 1 of the original knowledge argument. It is rarely disputed (some even take it as true by definition), and I will therefore take it for granted. Premise 2 will be defended by appeal to the following sub-argument:

1. No knowledge available without experience (i.e. no physical knowledge) (1) ultimately explains regularities and (2) predicts them without induction.
2. Some knowledge available from experience (i.e. phenomenal knowledge) (1) ultimately explains regularities and (2) predicts them without induction.
3. Knowledge that (1) ultimately explains regularities and (2) predicts them without induction is about explanatory facts.
4. Therefore, some explanatory facts are not knowable without experience.

I will assume that knowledge available without experience is in principle exhausted by physical knowledge, by which I mean knowledge of (ideal/completed) physics (or the non-mental empirical sciences) and knowledge that can in principle be deduced from it. I will also take physical *facts* to be exhausted by the kinds of facts that can (in principle) be completely described by physical knowledge.[2]

---

[2] Some might be skeptical of defining physical knowledge (and facts) in terms of physics, in view of, for example, Hempel's dilemma (according to which current physics is false but

Knowledge available from experience includes phenomenal knowledge. My argument will presuppose the existence of phenomenal knowledge,[3] but to be clear, it will not presuppose that phenomenal knowledge is either factual or about any non-physical facts (rather, this is what the argument aims to establish, and it will also be defended against the ability hypothesis and the phenomenal concept strategy).

I will now defend each premise of the supporting argument in turn.

11.3.1 Premise 1: No Physical Explanatory Knowledge

The first premise of the supporting argument first claims that no knowledge available without experience, which (as noted) I take to be equal to physical knowledge, *ultimately explains* regularities. By an ultimate explanation, I mean an explanation that does not give rise to further why-questions, because it does not appeal to anything contingent or inexplicable, but rather to something that is itself necessary, self-evident or self-explanatory. Some putative examples of ultimate explanations, outside the realm of the physical and phenomenal, include mathematical explanations that appeal to self-evident axioms and theological explanations that appeal to God understood as a necessary being.

By *regularities*, I mean lawlike generalizations, including physical laws, laws of special sciences, and behavioral or cognitive regularities that could be considered laws of psychology. To count as a regularity, a generalization must hold invariably true in the absence of interference or conflict with other regularities, i.e., *ceteris absentibus*.

It is fairly clear that no physical knowledge ultimately explains any regularities. Some regularities can be physically explained in a non-ultimate way, e.g., laws or regularities of physiology might be explained in terms of laws of chemistry, and laws of chemistry can be explained in term of the laws of

ideal physics is unknowable) or because one takes some special sciences to be autonomous but still physical. One might therefore rather define physical knowledge negatively in terms of what it is not. On the negative part of my definition, I follow Papineau (2001) and Wilson (2006). Note that some define physical knowledge more broadly as knowledge of the nature of the kinds of *objects* described by physics, and leave it open whether physics (or the non-mental empirical sciences) can describe the full nature of these objects (see e.g. Stoljar on "o-physicalism" (2001) and Chalmers on broad physicalism (2003b)). Neither the original nor the explanatory knowledge argument is aimed at refuting the kind of physicalism that takes all facts to be physical only in this broader sense. As will be discussed later, the explanatory knowledge argument also positively supports a view that may be classified as physicalism in this broader sense, namely Russellian monism.

[3] The existence of phenomenal knowledge is accepted by most physicalists, with the exception of extreme forms of eliminativism or illusionism. In this chapter, I set these views aside.

physics. But the fundamental laws of physics cannot be explained – they are matters of brute, empirical fact. When asked why they hold, physicists would either say that we do not know, or that they just *do* – there is no explanation. Of course, it may turn out that the laws of current physics can be explained in terms of a more fundamental theory, such as string theory or multiverse theory. But these explanations would then depend on the laws of string theory or the laws of the multiverse, and there would be no explanation of why these laws hold.

To say that the fundamental laws of physics have no ultimate explanation is also to say that there is no physical knowledge in virtue of which they seem *necessary*. Any fundamental law of physics could conceivably be different, even given expert physical knowledge. Cosmologists, for example, often consider how the laws of physics could be different (e.g., more or less "fine-tuned" for life), as well as hypotheses according to which they actually are different (e.g., in different universes within a multiverse).

The first premise also claims that no physical knowledge *predicts* regularities *without induction*. Explanation and prediction are closely related by the fact that explanatory hypotheses usually predict the facts they explain. If regularities can be ultimately explained in terms of something else than other regularities, one would expect them to be predictable based on this explanation alone, as opposed to on the basis of induction from multiple observations, which is our usual tool for discovering regularities.

It is widely agreed that no physical regularities can be predicted without induction. Sometimes, they can be predicted without induction being *directly* involved, as when regularities of higher-level sciences are deduced from the underlying laws of physics. But the laws of physics must then already have been confirmed inductively.

11.3.2 Premise 2: Phenomenal Explanatory Knowledge

The second premise of the supporting argument claims that some phenomenal knowledge ultimately explains regularities and predicts them without induction. How could this be? Clearly, no phenomenal knowledge can ultimately explain or non-inductively predict the laws of physics.[4] But consider the psychological regularity "pain makes all subjects who experience it try to avoid it." This regularity seems to hold true in the absence of interference from

---

[4] Unless panpsychism is true. As will be discussed below, panpsychism (of the Russellian monist kind) is one of the non-physicalist views compatible with the explanatory knowledge argument.

other motives or reasons, i.e. *ceteris absentibus*. It is of course true that people often endure or pursue pain for various kinds of interfering motives: some endure pain because they believe it will lead to less pain in the future (as when cleaning a wound), some pursue pain because the pain is accompanied by pleasure (as in masochism), some endure pain because they believe it is morally appropriate (as when accepting punishment). But in the absence of any further motives, it seems people (and other animals, as far as we can tell) always try to avoid it, i.e., we never endure or pursue pain for absolutely no reason.

The regularity also does not seem to positively depend on further beliefs about pain, such as that pain is dangerous – otherwise we would not take painkillers for knowingly harmless headaches.[5] Nor does it seem to depend on contingent attitudes such as fear of the pain (although fear could cause the pain to get worse, or constitute an additional motive that makes us even more inclined to try to avoid it).

It should also be noted that the regularity I will consider only holds between pain and *tryings*, i.e. efforts or attempts to avoid it, where these tryings should be understood as purely mental events.[6] A further regularity seems to hold (again, in the absence of interference) between efforts to avoid pain and actual, successful avoidance (or between tryings and successful actions in general), but this regularity is distinct from the regularity between pain and mere tryings to avoid it, so to explain one is not necessarily to explain the other.

Why does the regularity between pain and avoidance attempts hold? Consider the overprotected or congenitally insensitive Mary, who has complete physical knowledge about pain, but has never experienced it. She leaves the room, cured of any insensitivity, and has her first accident – she badly burns her hand. Upon having this experience, it seems she would not only think: "Aha, so this is what it is like to be in pain!", but also: "I now understand *why* people try to avoid it."

Knowing how pain feels, it seems self-explanatory why people try to avoid it. People avoid pain *because it feels like this*. This explanation invokes no further regularities, only the intrinsic character of pain. Furthermore, it gives rise to no regress of further why-questions. When we explain a law of chemistry in

---

5 Some (e.g., Cutter and Tye 2014) try to explain why it is rational to take painkillers in other ways, but intuitively, we do it in order to avoid the phenomenal experience of the pain itself. As will be discussed below, the motivational power of pain might depend on beliefs agents have about themselves, but it does not seem to depend on beliefs about the pain.

6 Note that presupposing the existence of mental tryings does not beg the question against physicalism. Physicalists (except eliminativists) generally accept the existence of mental events such as tryings, they just regard them as identical with or constituted by physical events.

terms of a law of physics, we can ask: "but why do the laws of physics hold?" – and get no answer. But when Mary understands that people try to avoid pain because it feels like *this* (when pointing to her own experience of it), she would not ask the further question: "but why does something that feels like *this* make people avoid it?" This can be answered simply by attending to the phenomenal character of pain again.

Knowing how pain feels, it is also hard to conceive of this regularity being otherwise, especially the scenario of strong pain and pleasure being inverted in our motivational structure. Could intense, terrible pain, in and of itself, in the absence of any interfering motives, make us try to have more of it? Could intense, blissful pleasure, in and of itself, make us try to avoid it?[7] For someone who has never experienced either pain or pleasure this would be just as conceivable as different laws of physics. But once we think of pain and pleasure in terms of how they feel, i.e. take their phenomenal character into consideration, it is very hard to imagine.

Knowledge of pain also seems to enable prediction of regularities without induction. This can be illustrated by another thought experiment. Imagine someone, call her Maya, who has also never experienced pain, and has not been as well educated as Mary: she does not know that pain makes subjects try to avoid it. Maya has some physical knowledge about pain physiology, such as that there is some bodily state that is correlated with something people call (phenomenal) pain. But she does not know that this bodily state causes avoidance attempts, nor does she know any lower-level physical regularities from which this could be deduced. Then she experiences pain for the first time and learns what it is like, say by stepping on a sharp nail (barefoot, in a way that feels absolutely horrible). It seems she would then be in a position to instantly predict that this is a feeling she, and everyone else who experiences it, will try to avoid in the future, unless they have a further reason not to. She would not need to observe her own reaction to pain multiple times, and observe the same reaction in others, and then apply inductive reasoning. Rather, she could predict it from a single experience of pain alone.

At this point, one might object that this apparent explanatory and predictive knowledge may be illusory. In particular, one might object that it is not truly *inconceivable* that pain does not make a subject try to avoid it (*ceteris*

---

[7] One might think very intense or prolonged pleasure can get uncomfortable or boring and therefore eventually make us try to avoid it. But if so, it would seem that either the phenomenology will have changed into something that no longer feels like pleasure, or the discomfort or boredom would constitute a distinct, interfering motive.

absentibus). If this is not truly inconceivable, neither would it truly seem necessary and self-explanatory, and thus ultimately explained. It would also undermine the claim that phenomenal knowledge (alone) enables non-inductive prediction, because if prediction from phenomenal knowledge is not based on inconceivability, it seems it would rather have to be based on some additional, implicit associations or assumptions.

In response, I will now attempt to demonstrate that it is truly inconceivable that pain and avoidance attempts come apart in view of phenomenal knowledge, *given certain qualifications*. I will then argue that this gives reason to suppose that phenomenal knowledge reflects explanatory facts, in the form of phenomenal causal powers – as per premise 3, the final premise of the supporting argument. If phenomenal explanatory knowledge is about such explanatory facts it would also be veridical and non-illusory. My defense of premise 3 will thereby also serve the purpose of answering the objection.

11.3.3 Premise 3: Phenomenal Explanatory Facts

Is it truly inconceivable that pain does not make a subject who experiences it try to avoid it (*ceteris absentibus*)? It might be conceivable that pain is not regularly *followed* by avoidance attempts, as per the regularity theory of causation (Hume 1739/1985; Lewis 1973). It might also be conceivable that pain is necessarily connected to something else than avoidance attempts in virtue of external governing laws or relations (Dretske 1977; Tooley 1977; Armstrong 1978); or that pain has no effects at all, as per epiphenomenalism (Jackson 1982).

What does not seem conceivable, however, is that pain *makes* us try to pursue it, remain indifferent to it, or otherwise do anything else than avoid it, in virtue of its intrinsic, phenomenal character alone. Or conversely, that pleasure *makes* us try to do anything else than pursue it, in virtue of its respective intrinsic, phenomenal character alone. That is to say, assuming causation is a matter of non-Humean *production*, and that pain and pleasure produce their effects *in virtue of how they feel*, it seems inconceivable that they produce different effects than their actual ones. After all, is not the phenomenal character of pain just intrinsically *disagreeable* and *repulsive*, and the phenomenal character of pleasure not just intrinsically *agreeable* and *attractive*? So, if pain and pleasure produce their effects in virtue of these respective qualities, how could they possibly make subjects respond otherwise?

I will now consider this conditional inconceivability claim in more detail. Does it really hold in anything but a trivial sense? And even if it does, would not appealing to it in defense of premises 2 and 3 beg the question by presupposing the existence of productive causal powers, i.e., explanatory facts in virtue of which phenomenal explanatory knowledge is factual and thus veridical (as per premises 3 and 2 respectively)?

To repeat, the conditional inconceivability claim is the claim that it is inconceivable that pain and avoidance attempts come apart assuming that pain has causal powers in virtue of how it feels (as opposed to being causally relevant in virtue of external regularities or governing laws, or having no causal relevance at all). Causal powers can be defined, more precisely, as properties in virtue of which causes metaphysically necessitate their effects (in the absence of interference from other powers, i.e., *ceteris absentibus*) by *producing* them, or *making* them happen. To say that pain has causal powers in virtue of how it feels is therefore to say that the phenomenal properties of pain metaphysically necessitate their effects in this way.

One might think that it is inconceivable that pain has different powers or necessitates different effects in virtue of how it feels only because it is an analytic truth that *if* pain has causal powers then it necessitates its actual effects. But the inconceivability only depends on accepting that pain has causal power in a general sense. Assuming pain has *some* causal power in virtue of how it feels, it is inconceivable (considering how it feels) that it should have anything other than the *particular* power to make subjects try to avoid it. It is does not follow trivially from "pain has *some* power in virtue of how it feels" that it has any particular power or that it could not have *different* powers or effects. This should be clear from the fact that the same result does not follow from assuming that physical objects have causal powers. Assuming physical objects have *some* causal powers, it is still conceivable that they have different particular powers or effects than those they actually have. For example, assuming billiard balls have some causal powers, it is still conceivable that they have the power to pass through other objects on impact, or jump over them, and so on.

One might object that the inconceivability must nevertheless be based on implicitly assuming that pain necessitates not just *some* effect or other, but its *particular*, actual effects, as per some form of analytic functionalism. According to analytic functionalism, the concept of pain just is the concept of having some particular functional or dispositional role, such as making subjects try to avoid it. If pain is conceived of in this way, it would be an implicit logical contradiction to say that the regularity between pain and avoidance attempts does not hold. But in that case, phenomenal knowledge will not have succeeded in ultimately explaining any *causal* regularities. Rather, it would at best have succeeded in explaining what may be construed as either a mere *analytic*, non-empirical truth or as a mere *constitutive* relation between a functional or dispositional property (i.e. pain functionally understood) and its constitutive input and output (i.e. the output of avoidance attempts given the input of being experienced by a subject) – both of which are things that physical knowledge would also clearly be capable of explaining in the same way.

But the inconceivability does not depend on conceiving of pain in functional or dispositional terms. In order to render it inconceivable that pain produces different effects in virtue of how it feels, it is sufficient to conceive of pain in terms of a demonstrative, phenomenal concept ("feeling like *this*"). There is no logical contradiction implicit in the claim that something that feels like *this* (when pointing to an experience or vivid memory of pain) fails to make (in the non-Humean sense) a subject try to avoid it (*ceteris absentibus*).[8] But it still seems inconceivable.

If the conditional inconceivability claim could thus be shown to non-trivially hold, it might nevertheless seem question-begging to assume the correctness of antecedent, i.e., that pain has causal power in virtue of how it feels, or that phenomenal properties *produce* their effects. To avoid this charge, the antecedent assumption could be supported by arguments for realism about causal powers that are independent of the explanatory knowledge argument.[9] But in that case,

---

[8]   The phenomenal concept of pain might still be *conceptually* connected to avoidance attempts in a broader, non-logical, sense. Chalmers proposes that pure phenomenal concepts are constituted by the phenomenal properties they refer to (or "faint Humean copies" thereof) (Chalmers 2010b: 265–266, 272). If there is a necessary connection between phenomenal pain and avoidance attempts, and the concept of pain is constituted by (a Humean copy of) pain, then there will also be a necessary connection between the concept of pain and avoidance attempts. But this connection would not obtain in virtue of a constitutive relation between the concept of pain and the concept of avoidance attempts, but rather in virtue of a causal connection between the non-conceptual constituents/referents of these concepts. Also note that Chalmers distinguishes phenomenal concepts from ordinary demonstrative concepts, because demonstrative concepts standardly leave the nature of their referent open (their meaning, in the phenomenal case, could be glossed as "this quality, whatever it happens to be") (Chalmers 2010b: 258). In Chalmers' terms, therefore, the causal power of pain is only explicable in terms of a concept that is both demonstrative (in a broad sense) and qualitative, i.e. which does not leave the nature of its referent entirely open.

[9]   Such as the argument that without causal powers, the regularities of the world would constitute an enormous "cosmic coincidence" (Strawson 1987), or that realism about causal powers is necessary to justify induction (Ellis 2010). One might think one would also have to appeal to arguments against epiphenomenalism, but this will be redundant as part of an argument against physicalism, because physicalism takes phenomenal properties to be physical and no physical properties are epiphenomenal.

the explanatory knowledge argument would not really constitute an argument against physicalism, but rather an argument that realism about causal powers is incompatible with physicalism. This conclusion would still be highly significant, given that realism about causal powers is a widely held view and generally regarded as perfectly compatible with physicalism. But the conditional inconceivability claim might also be able to support a stronger argument against physicalism as such, without either begging the question or invoking any separate arguments – because there is a sense in which the conditional inconceivability claim constitutes evidence for its own antecedent. How could this work?

First of all, if it is inconceivable that pain has different effects assuming that it has *some* causal power, it means we at least understand how pain *could* productively necessitate its actual effects. In other words, the conditional inconceivability claim shows that it is *positively conceivable* (i.e., imaginable in qualitative detail) how pain could have causal powers in virtue of how it feels, and positive conceivability is strong evidence of possibility.

For physical properties, in contrast, it may be *negatively conceivable* (i.e., not involve explicit or implicit logical contradiction) that they necessitate their actual effects. But it is not positively conceivable, as it is for pain, given that we can equally well conceive of physical properties or objects necessitating any other effects, and positive conceivability is much stronger evidence for possibility than negative conceivability.

Strictly speaking, if realism about causal powers is merely possibly true for pain, this would be sufficient to refute physicalism. If phenomenal properties necessitate their effects in some possible worlds where realism about causal powers is true, but physical properties do not necessitate them in any worlds, this suffices to show that the two sorts of facts are not identical – since identities are necessarily true if true at all, and identical properties do not differ in any possible world.

However, it might be objected that a metaphysical view such as realism about causal powers must be necessarily true if true at all. It follows that if the view is not actually true, it cannot be possibly true either. Therefore, it is worth noting that the conditional inconceivability claim may also support a further, direct argument that realism about causal powers is *actually* true for pain.

As already argued, the conditional inconceivability of pain and avoidance attempts coming apart shows that we have a positive conception of how realism about causal powers could be true for pain. But this positive conception does not seem like a conception of a mere possibility conjured up by the imagination. Rather, it is a view that we naturally and intuitively adopt, in most cases implicitly, on the basis of experience. For example, going back to the thought experiment of Maya, when Maya experiences pain for the first time, it seems plausible that she would naturally and implicitly accept that the phenomenal character of pain determines its causal powers, because her experience would seem to present it as such (that is, her experience would not present it as being completely up in the air whether its causal relevance is rather determined by external regularities or laws, or whether it might have no causal relevance at all; rather, her experience would seem to positively suggest that pain has causal powers determined by its phenomenal character). Positive conceptions derived from experience, rather than the imagination, are generally regarded as *appearances*. If pain thereby appears powerful, this constitutes evidence that it actually is powerful.

To recap the argument so far: It seems inconceivable that pain *makes* subjects who experience it do anything else than avoid it, in virtue of how it feels (as opposed to in virtue of a governing law, or in virtue of contingent regularities). It follows that *if* pain has causal powers in virtue of how it feels, it necessitates avoidance attempts. This conditional necessity shows that we can positively conceive of how pain *could* necessitate avoidance attempts. Furthermore, because this positive conception is derived from experience (as opposed to pure imagination), it constitutes an appearance that it actually does necessitate avoidance attempts. If the appearance is veridical, it establishes premise 3 (and at the same time refutes the above-mentioned objection to premise 2), because if phenomenal pain properties necessitate their effects, this would constitute an explanatory fact.

At this point, it might be objected that the appearance of pain having causal powers need not be veridical. But in general, appearances are taken to be veridical unless they conflict with other appearances or with important theoretical considerations. In this case, there are no obvious conflicts with other appearances. One potential source of conflict would be if the regularity theory, realism about laws, or epiphenomenalism appeared to be true for pain in some other way. But these views seem more theoretically motivated than motivated by direct appearances, at least for phenomenal properties.

As for conflicting theoretical considerations, one might argue that positing causal powers is unparsimonious. But in general, we do not consider appearances non-veridical simply because that would be more parsimonious – if we were to maximize parsimony in this way, we should consider every appearance non-veridical and embrace solipsistic external world skepticism. Also, given that accepting the appearance as veridical has explanatory value with respect to phenomenal regularities, theoretical considerations also speak in favor of it.

Therefore, even though the appearance of pain having causal power could coherently be dismissed as false, there is no obvious reason to dismiss it as false (except the question-begging reason that it would lead to a problem for physicalism). It is implausible to dismiss appearances as false without any (non-question-begging) reason. The burden of proof is therefore on physicalists to point out some further, less obvious reason to dismiss the appearance.

This concludes my main case for the supporting argument for the claim, that some explanatory facts are not available without experience, i.e. without phenomenal knowledge. This claim constitutes the only controversial premise of the explanatory knowledge argument. I will now consider further objections to each premise of this supporting argument, before summarizing the entire defense.

11.4 Objections to Premise 1

11.4.1 Physical Causal Powers

In view of my defense of premises 2 and 3 of the supporting argument, according to which phenomenal knowledge is ultimately explanatory and non-inductively predictive *assuming* phenomenal properties involve causal powers (as they also appear to), one might have the following objection to premise 1: could not physical knowledge be explanatory and predictive in the same way assuming physical properties involve causal powers?

In particular, it might seem physical knowledge would be capable of this assuming dispositional essentialism (Shoemaker 1980; Mumford 2004; Bird 2007). Dispositional essentialism is the view that all properties are essentially dispositional or powerful (I will use these terms interchangeably). For example, the physical property of solidity would essentially consist in (roughly) the power to avoid spatial overlap with other solid objects. This may seem to ultimately explain the regularity "solid objects do not pass through each other," and render it inconceivable that it does not hold, because to say that solid objects pass through each other would be to say that they are not solid after all, i.e. it would be a contradiction in terms. In the same way, the property of having negative charge could be regarded as essentially consisting in (roughly) the power to repel other entities with negative charge and attract entities with positive charge. This explains the regularity "electrons repel other electrons" insofar as electrons are essentially negatively charged.

However, physical knowledge would not seem to have the same kind of explanatory and predictive powers as phenomenal knowledge even given dispositional essentialism. This can be seen by the fact that explanations of regularities in terms of essential dispositions always seem to involve *analyticity*. Take solidity. We can think about this solidity either in terms of a dispositional concept (analyzable roughly as "the property of being disposed to not pass through other solid objects"), a categorical concept (such as the property of having a certain qualitative look or feel) or a demonstrative concept ("*that* property"). If we conceive of solidity in dispositional terms, as "the property of not passing through other solid objects," it will be contradictory and inconceivable that solid objects pass through other solid objects, and thereby explicable and necessary that the regularity that they do not pass through each other holds. But if we conceive of solidity in terms of a non-dispositional, either categorical or demonstrative concept, it would no longer be inconceivable that solid objects pass through each other, and the regularity would not seem necessary or explicable. For this reason, physical knowledge of solidity only seems capable of explaining what may be regarded either as a mere analytic truth or as a mere constitutive relation between the disposition of solidity and its constitutive input and output (i.e. the output of not passing through other objects given the input of intersecting paths of motion).

In contrast, I have argued that phenomenal knowledge of pain can explain regularities even when pain is conceived of under phenomenal concepts which are neither functional nor dispositional.[10] Therefore, phenomenal knowledge seems capable of explaining what seems like a properly causal regularity.

It might seem that dispositional essentialism nevertheless enables prediction without induction of properly causal regularities from physical knowledge. Nancy Cartwright has argued that, in practice, scientists often generalize from single observations (Cartwright 1999: 85). She argues that this practice, which clearly seems legitimate, can only be justified on the assumption that powers (or *capacities*, in her terms) belong to the essential natures of things. Roughly, her claim is that if the behavior of things is assumed to derive from their intrinsic powerful natures, then it is possible for a single instance of behavior to serve as a reliable indicator of this nature.

But as Cartwright explicitly notes, the view that powers belong to the natures of things is only a necessary condition to warrant generalization from single instances, not a sufficient condition. In order to make sure that a given experimental observation actually reveals the true nature of, e.g. electrons, scientists need to make sure that there is no interference which

---

[10] As discussed above, phenomenal concepts have a demonstrative element, but they may also have a categorical, qualitative element (see n. 7, above).

stops this nature from manifesting. And to rule out interference, they need to rely on inductively confirmed background assumptions about everything from the behavior of the experimental equipment to the workings of gravity, background radiation, and so on. Dispositional essentialism (or the related capacities view) thereby fails to fully warrant prediction without induction, because induction must be involved indirectly in supporting necessary background assumptions.

In contrast, in the thought experiment of Maya – who has never experienced pain and does not already know that it makes all subjects try to avoid it – her prediction does not seem to rely on any inductively justified background assumptions about the absence of interference. The only thing that can prevent pain from making us try to avoid it are our own interfering motives, and these can be directly detected by us without induction because they would be constituted by our own occurrent mental states.[11]

Furthermore, interference might not even matter in the phenomenal case. Consider a scenario where Maya experiences pain for the first time in the following way. Maya knows she is going to learn what pain is like by touching an electrocuting wire. She is determined to study the nature of pain because she has a passionate interest in phenomenology, and she has trained herself to have complete control over her reflexes so that she will not avoid it involuntarily. When she touches the wire, she endures the pain (until the current is turned off and the pain ends by itself) because her interest in studying pain constitutes an interfering reason. In this way, she will experience pain, but will not witness it actually making her try to avoid it. It seems she would nevertheless infer that pain *would* make her try to avoid it were it not for her determination to endure it. Phenomenal knowledge thereby also seems to predict regularities without induction *despite* interference.

---

[11] This is not to say that our own motives are always fully transparent to us. Often, we cannot accurately categorize our own motives based on non-inductive introspection alone. But it seems we are always in a position to detect the presence of *some* motivation or urge to avoid an action, even in cases when we do not know how to characterize this motivation more precisely (e.g., one might not know whether one is procrastinating out of laziness, anxiety or something else, but one still knows that one somehow *feels like* not working). Relatedly, one might wonder whether there could not also be interference from unconscious motives. If unconscious motives would only be detectible by induction, this would prevent prediction without induction and thereby undermine the argument. But the existence of unconscious motives could be accounted for as a matter of unconscious states indirectly affecting us by causing conscious but uncategorizable urges. If so, the absence of unconscious interference could be detectable without induction because the absence of the urges that signify them would be detectable without induction.

11.5 Objections to Premise 2

I will now consider objections to my defense of premise 2, according to which phenomenal knowledge of pain ultimately explains and non-inductively predicts the regularity "pain makes subjects try to avoid it *ceteris absentibus.*" This defense might face objections according to which this regularity does not really hold. As discussed above, the most obvious apparent exceptions to the regularity can be classified as instances of interference and thereby covered by the *ceteris absentibus* clause. But there are other apparent exceptions that may not be accounted for in this way.

11.5.1 Ability and Agency

First of all, it might seem that attempts to avoid pain can be prevented by physical inability, which cannot plausibly be regarded as interference. For example, a paralyzed person who can still feel pain would not be able to avoid pain. But they could still *try* to avoid pain, if they do not know that they are paralyzed. This trying would still be a real event, that would (given most forms of physicalism) physically correspond to the firing of some neurons in their brain. But what about a paralyzed person who knows they are paralyzed? Arguably, it is not possible to try to do something unless one believes one has at least some minimal chance of succeeding. Someone who believes they have no physical capacity to avoid pain could still try to avoid it by some mental action, for example, by deliberately focusing on something else. But if this does not work, they might eventually come to believe they have no mental capacity to avoid pain either, and therefore stop trying. If this is right, one might have to say that phenomenal knowledge can explain and predict the more specific regularity that pain makes subjects try to avoid it *if* they believe that can avoid it. This does not express a mere analytic truth or constitutive relation, and physical facts do not explain or predict this or any similarly qualified regularities, so it would still support the claim that phenomenal knowledge is distinctively explanatory.

Another potential exception to the regularity are subjects who have no power of agency at all. Strawson has argued that it is metaphysically possible for there to be conscious subjects who are not agents (1994: ch. 9). He defends the conceivability of sentient, intelligent creatures called the Weather Watchers, whose conscious life consists in observing and contemplating the weather, without ever trying to do anything about it.

There are a number of possible responses to this problem. One response is to claim that the Weather Watchers would still need the ability to act and try because observation still requires some form of active thinking, which by Strawson's own admission (2006/2008: 231), seems to require some minimal form of "catalytic" agentive effort.

Another response would be to add another qualification. If non-agentive subjects are possible, then phenomenal knowledge would still explain and predict the regularity "pain makes all *agentive* subjects try to avoid it." Again, this does not express a mere analytic truth or constitutive relation – as (the concept of) trying to avoid pain is not constitutive of (the concept of) agency – and physical knowledge does not explain and predict this or any other similarly qualified regularities either.

A third response is to appeal to a deflationary notion of subjects, according to which subjects of experience are not independent substances, but rather "bundles" of phenomenal experiences standing in certain types of relations (these relations may be more substantive than those that are part of the very minimal Humean version, and maybe *sui generis*). If pain is causally powerful, and a given subject is a bundle that includes pain, it follows that this subject is also powerful and is thereby an agent. Given the deflationary view, then, the objection that there could be non-agentive subjects in pain is equivalent to the objection that the assumption that pain has causal powers may be false, and can be responded to by appeal to the same arguments I have already offered in support of this assumption above (according to which, although this assumption may be coherently denied, it strongly appears to be true).

11.5.2 Pain Asymbolia

Another potential objection to the regularity between pain and avoidance is based on the phenomenon of pain asymbolia. Pain asymbolia is a medical disorder where patients report feeling pain that does not hurt, or that they have no inclination to avoid. According to the standard analysis of this phenomenon, due to Nikola Grahek (2007), there is no good reason to doubt that this description of pain asymbolia is accurate, i.e., to think that asymbolics are wrong to categorize what they are experiencing as pain, or to think that they must have some hidden motive to resist their inclination to avoid it. If this is right, such cases would constitute a direct counterexample to the regularity I have argued phenomenal knowledge about pain explains.

But pain asymbolia is still compatible with a more specific phenomenal pain regularity. Even though asymbolics identify what they are feeling as pain, it nevertheless seems that asymbolic pain and normal pain *feel* different. They seem to be two different phenomenal experiences, which nevertheless have enough in common to both fall under the same general concept of pain.

This interpretation is supported by Grahek, who concludes that what pain asymbolia really shows is that normal pain, which appears as a simple and unified feeling, is really complex. Normal pain is a combination of two components: "On the one hand, there is pure pain sensation, and on the other hand, there is the pure feeling of unpleasantness, defying any further sensory specification" (Grahek 2007: 111). Furthermore, both components are phenomenal. Not only can the sensory component be experienced without unpleasantness, as in pain asymbolia. Unpleasantness is also a phenomenal quality (or a *feeling*, as described by Grahek, above), and it is also possible to experience unpleasantness by itself. There are also reports of a condition which is the opposite of pain asymbolia, where patients report having the experience of pure unpleasantness whose character they could not specify in any further detail (Grahek 2007: 108–111).

There is no evidence that people can experience *unpleasantness* phenomenology without trying to avoid it, so there still seems to be regularity between *phenomenologically normal*, i.e., non-asymbolic unpleasantness-including, pain and avoidance attempts.[12] Given that this kind of pain can also be picked out in phenomenal terms, i.e., by how it (or its unpleasant component) feels, and not merely in functional terms such as "any quality (or kind of pain that) makes subjects try to avoid it," this regularity does not reduce to a mere analytic truth or constitutive relation. The regularity seems ultimately explicable and non-inductively predictable based on how phenomenologically normal pain feels in the same way I have argued regularities involving general (asymbolic or non-asymbolic) pain initially seem explicable and predictable based on how general pain feels. The case for the explanatory knowledge argument could therefore be reformulated with reference to phenomenologically normal (unpleasantness-involving) pain instead of general pain. Or more simply, I will (retroactively) stipulate that by pain I mean phenomenologically normal pain.

11.6 Objections to Premise 3

Finally, I will consider objections to my defense of premise 3, according to which phenomenal explanatory knowledge reflects explanatory facts in the

---

[12] Does this imply that the sensory part of pain has no causal power? It could still have some other causal power than the power to motivate avoidance.

form of causal powers. This defense may seem vulnerable to versions of the main objections to the original knowledge argument, the ability hypothesis and the phenomenal concepts strategy, according to which Mary's new phenomenal knowledge need not be accounted for in terms of any new phenomenal facts, but rather in terms of new abilities or new concepts for old, already known facts. Similarly, one might think Mary's (and Maya's) new *explanatory* knowledge (or the explanatory aspects of her new phenomenal knowledge) can be accounted for in terms of new abilities or concepts as opposed to explanatory facts.

These objections also highlight another potential problem for the explanatory knowledge argument, namely that it may seem dialectically redundant relative to the original knowledge argument, because it might seem it could only be sound and defensible insofar as the original knowledge argument is also sound and defensible.

But as I will now argue, the explanatory knowledge argument is resistant to the ability hypothesis and the phenomenal concept strategy, even if it were to turn out that the original is not. This is roughly because, even if new abilities or new concepts may explain why phenomenal knowledge seems to present *new* facts, they do not explain why it seems to present *explanatory* facts. For that, one would have to posit explanatory abilities or explanatory concepts. But it is hard to see how abilities and concepts can be explanatory without also involving explanatory facts. In this way, the explanatory argument is more defensible than the original in at least some respects.

11.6.1 The Ability Hypothesis

According to the ability hypothesis (Nemirow 1979; Lewis 1983a), Mary's new knowledge of red consists in abilities such as to recognize, remember, and imagine physical facts. If Mary's (and Maya's) new knowledge of pain is explanatory and predictive, then the ability hypothesis could be expanded to say that some phenomenal knowledge also consists in abilities to explain and predict physical facts.

In fact, Lewis acknowledges that some phenomenal knowledge is predictive, and proposes to account for this precisely in terms of a predictive ability:

> [K]nowing what it's like is the possession of abilities: abilities to recognize, abilities to imagine, *abilities to predict one's behavior* by means of imaginative experiments. (Someone who knows what it's like to taste Vegemite can easily and reliably predict whether he would eat a second helping of Vegemite ice cream.) (Lewis 1983a: 131, my emphasis)

One response to this predictive ability hypothesis would be that it is not plausible epistemologically speaking. Usually, facts can only be reliably predicted on the basis of other facts. How could facts about regularities involving pain (or Vegemite) be reliably predicted without any factual basis?

But this could perhaps be accounted for by an evolutionary hypothesis. For example, one might think it was fitness-enhancing for our ancestors to be able to anticipate the effects of pain prior to repeated experience, and those who happened to innately associate them would therefore be selected for. This could be supported by the fact that there is already evidence of other predictive abilities of this sort. For example, there is evidence that infants expect various principles of mechanical causation to hold, such as "no action at a distance" (Michotte 1963; Spelke et al. 1995), which can be taken to suggest an innate association implanted by evolution. One might think a similar kind of bias is responsible for prediction of the pain regularity.

But even if this hypothesis could account for the predictive aspect of phenomenal knowledge, it could not account for the explanatory aspect. First of all, other psychological biases do not involve any sense of understanding or intelligibility, as in the pain case. For example, when we think about it, we do not discover any apparent reason why action at a distance would be impossible. Second, no known psychological biases render whatever we are biased against altogether inconceivable, as in the pain case. Action at a distance, for example, would be highly unexpected, intuitively strike us as implausible, and so on, but we can still conceive of it if we try. Therefore, to explain away the explanatory features of phenomenal knowledge, one would have to come up with an additional "explanatory ability" to go with the predictive ability, and it is hard to see what kind of ability this could be.[13]

---

[13] Physicalists could still coherently dismiss the apparent explanatory knowledge gained from experiencing pain as completely illusory – in the same way they could coherently dismiss apparent purely phenomenal knowledge (or the non-explanatory aspects of it) as completely illusory, as per eliminativism or illusionism. But as discussed above, it is implausible to dismiss appearances as illusory without offering some (non-question-begging) reason. It is also implausible to dismiss it on the basis of general skepticism about appearances in order to support that the appearance that pain involves causal powers is non-veridical, because this kind of skepticism would seem to overgeneralize to support solipsistic external world skepticism. In the same way, if physicalists invoke general skepticism about our feelings of intelligibility and understanding in order to undermine the explanatoriness of phenomenal knowledge, it could also risk undermining our claims to intelligibility and understanding in a wide range of other areas.

11.6.2 The Phenomenal Concept Strategy

According to the phenomenal concept strategy, phenomenal knowledge is factual, but it is not about any new facts. When Mary learns what it is like to see red, she merely learns to conceive of the physical facts in a new way: she acquires a new phenomenal concept for a fact that she already knows via a physical concept or physical mode of presentation.

If Mary's (and Maya's) new knowledge of pain is explanatory and predictive, then the phenomenal concept strategy would have to be expanded to say that some phenomenal concepts are not only new and different from ordinary physical concepts, they are also distinctively explanatory, or capable of presenting the same old physical facts in a new, more explanatory way. I will consider the main versions of the strategy, which characterize phenomenal concepts in different ways, to see whether they could give rise to any kind of explanatoriness.

David Papineau (2002) argues that phenomenal concepts are *quotational*, which is to say that the concepts are constituted by instances or copies of the experiences they refer to. Using a phenomenal concept of pain therefore puts one in a distinct psychological state that activates a copy of pain itself, rather than just an abstract representation of it, and this will make it falsely appear as though there are phenomenal facts about pain that go beyond the physical facts (Papineau 2002: 170–171). In this way, quotational concepts would be new and different compared to non-quotational concepts, even if the facts they refer to are identical. But there is no clear sense in which quotational concepts would be more explanatory than non-quotational concepts, given that the facts they refer to are identical and thereby equally explanatory. That is, there is no reason to think activating a copy of a phenomenal property would be sufficient to make it appear explanatory, if the phenomenal property is in fact no more explanatory than a physical concept would reveal.

John Perry (2001) argues that phenomenal concepts are similar to *indexical* concepts. Indexical facts (e.g. "you are here") cannot be derived from non-indexical physical facts (e.g. a map) and thereby seem new to someone who knows all but only non-indexical facts, but indexical facts arguably do not pose any problem for physicalism. If phenomenal concepts were indexical, it might therefore explain how phenomenal facts also appear new. Could it also explain how phenomenal facts could appear explanatory?

Unlike quotational concepts, indexical concepts do have special explanatory properties. As Perry has also argued (1979), indexical concepts can be essential to explaining behavior. He illustrates this with the following scenario. Perry is following a trail of sugar around a supermarket in order to find and stop the shopper who is making a mess. He suddenly realizes that there is a torn sack of sugar in his own shopping cart, and thereby learns the indexical fact that *he* himself is making a mess. This realization explains why he stops looking for another shopper and starts rearranging the torn sack in his own cart. If he were to merely learn the non-indexical fact that John Perry is making a mess, this would not be sufficient to explain his behavior: he would also need to know that *he* (himself) is John Perry.

Phenomenal explanation of the pain regularity also involves the indexically individuated fact "pain feels like *this*." But the explanatory power of phenomenal facts goes beyond what can be accounted for by their indexical mode of presentation. One difference is that what explains Perry's behavior is his indexical *belief*, i.e. the fact that "Perry believes *he* (himself) is making a mess." The first-order indexical facts "*he* is making a mess" and "*he* is Perry" by themselves seem causally and explanatorily inert. In the pain case, in contrast, it is the first-order fact that "pain feels like *this*" that explains why subjects try to avoid it, not the subjects' indexical beliefs about the pain. If first-order indexically individuated facts are generally not distinctively explanatory, then one cannot see how phenomenal facts could derive their explanatory power from their indexicality alone.

Furthermore, Perry's indexical belief only explains his behavior given that he also has a *desire* to not make a mess. This gives rise to the further explanatory question "why do desires to X cause attempts at pursuing X," which does not seem to have any ultimate physical answer.[14] I have argued that the fact "pain feels like *this*" is sufficient[15] to ultimately explain why subjects try to avoid it without any additional desire to not be in pain (or not have *this* kind of feeling).[16] This is another respect in which phenomenal facts are more explanatory than typical indexical facts.

---

[14] It might have an ultimate analytic answer, if desires are individuated in terms of their psychological roles. It might also have a phenomenal answer in terms of how desires feel, as for pain, but this would further support the explanatory knowledge argument rather than physicalism.

[15] As discussed, phenomenal explanations might also require that subjects have the additional belief that they have some capacity to avoid the pain. But the same is true for explanations of behavior in terms of indexical beliefs, i.e. Perry must not only believe that he is making a mess, but also that he has a capacity to stop making a mess. Therefore, the precise difference would be that only phenomenal facts are sufficient to ultimately explain the behavior of subjects who believe they are capable of the behavior.

[16] One might object that subjects in pain necessarily desire not to be in pain. Maybe so, but if so it seems the desire would follow from and be explained in terms of how pain feels, so it would be compatible with pain providing an ultimate explanation.

Other versions hold that phenomenal concepts are *recognitional* (Loar 1997) or *perceptual* (Papineau 2006), but these versions of the strategy share the same problems. Recognitional concepts might be especially explanatory in virtue of involving indexicality, but as I have argued, indexical facts are not as explanatory as phenomenal facts. Perceptual concepts are, according to Papineau, like quotational concepts but without any demonstrative element (2006). Like quotational concepts, then, they are new and different compared to non-quotational physical concepts, but not more explanatory. Or, to be clear, these concepts could very well be explanatory *because* they quote or reference distinctively explanatory phenomenal facts, but not in virtue of their quotational character alone.

Proponents of the phenomenal concept strategy might also consider the view that some physical facts have explanatory features that are only apparent when conceived under phenomenal concepts. The view that some physical facts are only explanatory when considered in terms of, if not phenomenal, then at least *intentional* (and hence mental) concepts is not unheard of. Davidson's anomalous monism (Davidson 1970/1980), an important form of non-reductive physicalism, puts this forth as a fundamental tenet. According to anomalous monism, some mental events, such as intentional actions, can only be explained by other mental events, such as beliefs and desires. Beliefs and desires cannot be type-identified with any physical events – there is no way of systematically deriving physical descriptions of events from their mental descriptions – but every mental event is token-identical with some physical event. However, when a mental event, such as a belief, is redescribed as a physical event (with which it is token-identical), it will no longer be explanatory of any mental events. A belief might explain an intentional action, but a brain state (or other physically described states or events) never will.

Could physicalists adopt the analogous view that some physical facts (or events) are only explanatory when considered under phenomenal concepts? It seems not. The reason anomalous monism still qualifies as a form of physicalism is that, according to the view, although physical events will not explain mental events, physical events *will* explain those physical events with which mental events can be token-identified. In other words, if a particular token mental explanandum is redescribed in physical terms, which is always possible in principle, then it will have some physical explanation. Thus, physical and mental events have the same explanatory properties with respect to the same events at the token-level, just not at the type-level.

According to the explanatory knowledge argument, no matter how you redescribe an explanandum such as "pain makes subjects that experience it try to avoid it," it will never have an ultimate physical explanation. As I have argued, no physical facts ultimately explain any regularities, and I take it that it is not possible to redescribe (in a way that renders it fit for explanation) a regularity as anything else than a regularity. Physical and phenomenal facts thus have different explanatory relations to the same facts also at the token-level. This cannot be regarded as compatible with physicalism.

11.7 Summary of the Argument

The explanatory knowledge argument claims that:

1. All physical facts are knowable without experience.
2. Some explanatory facts are not knowable without experience.
3. Therefore, some facts are non-physical.

The only highly controversial premise of this argument is premise 2, which I have defended by appeal to the following sub-argument:

1. No knowledge available without experience (i.e. physical knowledge) (1) ultimately explains regularities and (2) predicts them without induction.
2. Some knowledge available from experience (i.e. phenomenal knowledge) (1) ultimately explains regularities and (2) predicts them without induction.
3. Knowledge that (1) ultimately explains regularities and (2) predicts them without induction is about explanatory facts.
4. Therefore, some explanatory facts are not knowable without experience.

To support this sub-argument, I have argued that phenomenal knowledge about (phenomenologically normal) pain ultimately explains and non-inductively predicts regularities such as "pain makes subject try to avoid it *ceteris absentibus*" (or perhaps "pain makes *agentive* subjects *who believe they have the capacity*, try to avoid it *ceteris absentibus*"). This is mainly supported by the thought experiments about Mary, who has complete physical knowledge but upon her first experience of pain gains new knowledge of why subjects try to avoid it, and Maya, who does not know that pain makes subjects try to avoid it but upon her first experience can immediately predict it.

I have also noted that these explanations and predictions may depend on the assumption that pain has causal power in virtue of its phenomenal character. I have argued that this conditional explanatoriness nevertheless shows that we can positively conceive of how its phenomenal properties *could* be explanatory in virtue of necessitating their particular effects. This positive conception seems derived from experience, not the imagination, and thereby constitutes an appearance that phenomenal properties actually necessitate their particular effects. Phenomenal properties thereby appear to involve causal powers, which would constitute explanatory facts.

One might claim that the appearance is illusory, but appearances should generally be accepted as veridical unless (1) they conflict with other appearances or important theoretical considerations, or (2) there is a good explanation of how the appearance could arise despite not being veridical. But there are no obvious reasons of either kind to dismiss the appearance.

I have also argued that physical knowledge does not ultimately explain or non-inductively predict any properly causal regularities (as opposed to analytic truths or constitutive relations) even assuming that physical properties essentially involve causal powers, as per dispositional essentialism. Dispositional essentialism also does not enable non-inductive prediction of physical regularities, because even if scientists sometimes generalize from single experiments (which, according to Cartwright, would be legitimate assuming dispositional essentialism or the related capacities view), they always rely on inductively supported assumptions about the absence of interference. Such background assumptions are not necessary in the phenomenal case. The lack of physical explanatory and predictive knowledge implies the lack of physical explanatory facts, given that all physical facts can (in principle) be revealed by physical knowledge.

This concludes my case for the explanatory knowledge argument. I will now briefly discuss how, in view of this defense, it dialectically relates to the normative knowledge argument, and well as to further issues in philosophy of mind.

11.8 The Normative vs. the Explanatory Knowledge Argument

As noted, Kahane suggests that one might construct a normative knowledge argument against physicalism, based on the claim that phenomenal knowledge uniquely explains why pain is bad. Such an argument would presumably look something like this:

1. All physical facts are knowable without experience.
2. Some normative facts are not knowable without experience.
3. Therefore, some facts are non-physical.

An apparent weakness of this argument is that physicalists could simply deny the existence of the normative facts in question, i.e. embrace moral or normative anti-realism. This problem is anticipated by Chalmers:

> Moral facts are not phenomena that force themselves on us. When it comes to the crunch, we can deny that moral facts exist at all … The same strategy cannot be taken for phenomenal properties, whose existence is forced upon us. (Chalmers 1996: 83–84)

Unlike the normative knowledge argument (henceforth NA), the explanatory knowledge argument (henceforth EA) does not presuppose moral realism (although it is compatible with it). This gives EA a dialectical advantage against physicalists who are prepared to reject moral realism (or at least realism about the moral disvalue of pain in particular).

One might object that EA still depends on analogous assumption of *explanatory* realism, in the form of realism about causal powers. I have shown how realism about causal powers can be defended on the basis of the apparent explanatoriness of phenomenal knowledge. Therefore, it cannot simply be rejected by physicalists without further argument. But perhaps moral realism can be defended in an analogous way. In response to Chalmers' objection on behalf of physicalism, Kahane briefly responds that:

> This is an odd remark. The badness of pain seems to force itself upon us just like phenomenal properties. Indeed it imposes itself on us through a phenomenal property! (Kahane 2010: 47, n. 47)

This suggests that, in the same way realism about causal powers can be justified on the basis of how pain appears powerful, moral realism can be justified on the basis of how pain appears bad.

This would be good news for the case against physicalism, but one might think it would render EA dialectically superfluous relative to an equally strong NA. But this does not follow, because physicalists could still coherently (albeit implausibly, according to NA and EA) dismiss either of these appearances as non-veridical, and some physicalists might nevertheless find it harder to deny that pain is powerful than that pain is bad.

Furthermore, NA may be less resistant than EA to the ability hypothesis and the phenomenal concept strategy. Against NA, it could be suggested that normative knowledge of pain only consists in the possession of normative abilities or normative concepts for non-normative facts, as opposed to awareness of objective normative facts. There are some candidates for normative abilities or concepts, such as prescriptive or expressive abilities or concepts, that may seem potentially capable of explaining away the appearance of normative facts. If so, a normative ability hypothesis or normative concept strategy may be more plausible than an explanatory ability hypothesis or explanatory concept strategy.

11.9 Mental Causation and Physical Causal Closure

The explanatory knowledge argument is primarily an argument against physicalism, but it also has further implications for the metaphysics of phenomenal properties. First of all, the argument suggests that (some) phenomenal properties are not epiphenomenal, because they necessitate corresponding efforts. This would be a further difference between it and the original knowledge argument, which was first offered in defense of epiphenomenalism (Jackson 1982).

However, the argument does not strictly preclude epiphenomenalism, understood as the view that phenomenal properties have no *physical* effects, because epiphenomenalism leaves open the possibility that phenomenal properties have other non-physical effects, as long as these effects are also physically inert. I have argued that pain appears to necessitate *efforts* towards avoidance, where efforts are understood as purely mental events. As noted above, there might be a further regularity between these efforts and physical actions. But it is not as clearly inconceivable that efforts have different effects in virtue of their phenomenal (or otherwise intrinsic) character. Therefore, it seems coherent to hold that pain necessitates non-physical mental efforts, but that these efforts are in turn epiphenomenal with respect to the physical world. On the other hand, it would also be compatible with the argument to posit a further, psychophysical regularity between mental efforts and physical actions in accordance with interactionism. But even though the argument is thereby compatible with both epiphenomenalism and interactionism, it lends somewhat more to support interactionism because the kind of epiphenomenalism it implies (according to which not all phenomenal properties are mentally inert even though they are all physically inert) seems even more inelegant than standard epiphenomenalism (according to which all phenomenal properties are both mentally and physically inert).

A third, and perhaps more natural, option, however, is to take phenomenal properties to be explanatorily related to the physical world in virtue of directly underlying *physical* regularities in accordance with what is known as Russellian monism. Russellian monism is the view that all physical properties are purely structural or relational, and that physical structure is intrinsically realized by phenomenal or protophenomenal properties (i.e., properties that are neither physical nor phenomenal, but closely related to the phenomenal) (Alter and Nagasawa 2012; Chalmers 2015). This realization relation can be conceived of in different ways. One view is that physical structure is realized by non-powerful (proto)phenomenal properties related by contingent regularities or governing laws. But another possible view is that all physical structure is realized by (proto)phenomenal powers which in turn ground the regularities or laws. This possibility is further supported by the intelligible relation between phenomenal pain and pleasure and regularities emphasized by the explanatory knowledge argument. Russellian monism is thereby also compatible with, and to some extent supported by, the explanatory knowledge argument.

This compatibility is also relevant to another objection one might have against the argument, namely that it implies a vicious dilemma between epiphenomenalism and violation of the principle of physical explanatory closure, i.e., the principle that every physical event that has an explanation has a sufficient physical explanation. This principle is widely regarded as having strong empirical support (Papineau 2001). But the principle could be formulated in different ways. One version would be as follows: Every physical event that has an explanation *in terms of regularities* has a sufficient explanation *in terms of physical regularities*. This version of the principle is compatible with the explanatory knowledge argument, because it only implies that regularities have an explanation in terms of non-physical powers, not in terms of any non-physical regularities. But the principle is not compatible with interactionist dualism (except in its highly inelegant overdeterminist version), because interactionist dualism posits the existence of psychophysical regularities, which are irreducible to physical regularities, to explain physical events in the brain or body. But the principle is compatible with Russellian monism, both the general version which takes all phenomenal properties to be explanatory relevant in virtue of realizing physical structure (as opposed to by adding further structure in the form of psychophysical regularities), and the specific version which takes phenomenal properties to realize physical structure in virtue of constituting the powerful grounds of regularities. So, the explanatory knowledge argument is fully compatible with physical explanatory closure, because it is also compatible with Russellian monism.

In conclusion, I have defended the explanatory knowledge argument, according to which all physical facts are knowable without experience, but some explanatory facts are not knowable without experience – namely phenomenal facts that ultimately explain and non-inductively predict regularities such as "pain makes subjects try to avoid it *ceteris absentibus*." Therefore, some facts are non-physical.

The explanatory argument resists the main objections to the original knowledge argument, the ability hypothesis, and the phenomenal concept strategy. It is compatible with, and may have some dialectical advantages over, the previously proposed normative knowledge argument. It also suggests an explanatory role for phenomenal properties that is compatible with a plausible version of physical explanatory closure, in accordance with Russellian monism. It thereby confirms and deepens the challenge for a physicalist account of the phenomenal.[17]

[17] Many thanks to Sam Coleman, David Chalmers, Sebastian Watzl, Torfinn Huvenes, John Morrison, Insa Lawler and participants at the NorMind inaugural workshop (Bergen 2015), The Science of Consciousness (Helsinki 2015) and NYU Consciousness discussion group (New York 2015) for helpful comments and discussion.

12   The Knowledge Argument and the Self

Robert J. Howell

12.1 Introduction

Frank Jackson's knowledge argument is naturally viewed as a more precise version of Thomas Nagel's argument in "What Is It Like to Be a Bat."[1] In particular, Jackson directed our attention to the challenge phenomenal knowledge poses for physicalism. Viewed this way, the knowledge argument focuses more on the question of "what it's like to echolocate" than what it's like to be a bat. The worry, to put it a more Nagelian way, is that the nature of phenomenal states escapes the objective picture of the world provided by our best sciences. I think there is another strand of Nagel's argument that often gets ignored and that could be made clearer by a corollary to Jackson's knowledge argument. This strand sticks a little closer to Nagel's original question, and directs us to think about what it is like to be, or to have, a self. Just as in Jackson's original argument, there can be much debate about what the implications of this corollary argument are – whether the implications are metaphysical or not; whether the argument even gets off the ground, etc. But I think the knowledge argument about the self is worth setting forth nonetheless, if only to get a little clearer about something else that might seem to be missing from the objective point of view.

Jackson's argument has changed a bit over the years, so I will start by revisiting the argument so as to be clear about the formulation I have in mind and to draw attention to a few important features that are sometimes overlooked. I will then set up a slightly different thought experiment that draws from similar intuitions. I will then spell out the resulting argument and attempt to defend the premises, paying particular attention to what we might be able to learn about at least one notion of the self.

---

[1] Jackson (1982); Nagel (1974).

12.2 The Knowledge Argument about Qualitative Conscious States

The basic story is more than familiar. Mary is a brilliant neuroscientist (and physicist …) who has lived her life in a black and white room. During her imprisonment, she was taught through computer screens all the lessons of physics and neuroscience relevant to color experience. She knows how light reflects off objects and affects the eyes, the optic nerves, and the appropriate parts of the brain. In short, she knows all the physical information regarding color experience. Finally, one day she is released from her room to be presented with a rose by her apologetic captor. In seeing the red of the rose, it seems clear she will learn something new – she will learn what it is like to see red. Thus, the physical information is not all the information and physicalism is false.

I have suggested elsewhere that the knowledge argument is better viewed not as an argument against physicalism but as an argument against object-ivism. That is, it is better viewed as an argument that the objective picture of the world is incomplete. Perhaps the failure of objectivism entails the failure of physicalism, but that is a further question. Physicalism is a metaphysical doctrine about the nature of the stuff in the world, while objectivism is most naturally viewed as a doctrine about a certain way of knowing or representing the world. Framing the debate this way avoids a handful of questions while still generating an interesting result. Most importantly, perhaps, it avoids the question of why we should describe Mary's epistemic situation in a metaphys-ical way, as knowing all the physical facts. Mary's limitation while in her room is epistemic – she is limited to a certain way of knowing information, whatever that information is about. It is not obvious that this way of knowing infor-mation either limits her to knowing only physical facts, or more importantly whether it allows her to know all physical facts. On the face of it, it is an open question whether some physical states might be subjective, in the sense that they cannot be fully understood from the third-person point of view. There are various ways one can be a "subjective physicalist," including by thinking that physical dispositions ultimately have phenomenal properties as their cat-egorical grounds. On such a view, Mary simply couldn't come to know all the physical facts from within her room because she is prohibited from having the experiences that reveal the nature of some physical facts. A knowledge argu-ment focused on objectivism can sidestep the thorny issue of the essences of physical properties (as well as the largely terminological issue about whether the phenomenal properties are properly called physical).

Since I am not going after metaphysical prey in the knowledge argument about the self, I will focus on this non-metaphysical knowledge argument against objectivism. I will also focus on the fact that what Mary comes to know that she didn't know before is a fact about other humans. In his 1997 response to Churchland, Jackson makes it clear that this is what she learns:

> [T]he knowledge Mary lacked which is of particular point for the know-ledge argument against physicalism is *knowledge about the experiences of others*, not about her own. When she is let out, she has new experiences, color experiences she has never had before. It is not, therefore, an objection to physicalism that she learns *something* on being let out … The trouble for physicalism is that, after Mary sees her first ripe tomato, she will realize how impoverished her conception of the mental life of others has been *all along*.
> (Jackson 1986, 292)

Among other things, this implies that the crucial epistemic gain for Mary is not immediate but is a result of an inference to the mental states of other people. She does know something immediately – that she is having an experi-ence with a certain qualitative feel – but that is not the knowledge she lacked. Jackson is, quite correctly, not worried here about the problem of other minds. He is setting such skepticism aside since, among other things, his very puzzle assumes Mary can know about the external world from within her room, and this no doubt assumes many inferences the skeptic could question. So if we let the thought experiment get off the ground at all, we shouldn't worry about this inference to other minds.

Those clarifications noted, the argument can then be put as follows:

1. Mary knew everything objective about other people before leaving the room.
2. After leaving her room she learned something new about other people.

Therefore, the objective story about other people is incomplete. In particular, it leaves out facts about what it's like for them to have certain phenomenal states.

Since I will be presenting another knowledge argument in this chapter, we can call the original knowledge argument the Knowledge Argument about Qualia (KAQ).

12.3 The Knowledge Argument about the Self

In what follows I provide a knowledge argument about the self, KAS, which argues that the self is not to be found in the objective picture of the world. Just as in the original knowledge argument, the more metaphysical conclusion can, of course, be pursued. Near the end of the chapter I will suggest that unique challenges face that pursuit. Nevertheless, it should be concerning enough if our own selves escape depiction by the sciences we rely on to depict our world.

For the purposes of this chapter, I will take for granted that we know we have selves. I will leave open how we know this, or how "thick" these selves are. Selves might be thick things that harbor our personalities and endure throughout our lives, or they might simply be those things that have conscious states and exist only for a moment. They might be substantial or they might be more bundle-like. These are among the many questions I will not attempt to answer. I also will not try to explain how we know we have selves. Among other things, KAS persuades me that self-knowledge of a certain basic sort – the sort involved in the cogito, for example – depends on a certain grasp of our own conscious experiences. Similarly, knowing that others have selves requires knowing of them that they can enjoy a similar grasp of their experiences. These are matters worth pursuing, but I will not attempt to do so here.[2]

12.3.1 The Story

Poor Mary. Not only did she spend so much of her life locked in a room, for years now she's been shoved back into subtly changed rooms under slightly altered conditions, all to prove various versions of a point.[3] For the sake of both charity and clarity, therefore, I'll leave poor Mary alone. Instead, I'll tell you a story about a similarly brilliant Rick.

Like Mary, Rick is logically infallible and is close to omniscient about the objective truths – the sort of truths that can be conveyed through the objective sciences like physics and biology and by lessons of the sort Mary gets within her room.[4] Unlike Mary, Rick is not in a room. He has the freedom to stroll around the world satisfying his curiosity about the way it is put together. He studies the human beings around him down to their smallest detail, and comes to know all the objective facts about those human beings as well as all the relevant facts about their environments. There is one notable gap in Rick's knowledge, however. For all his curiosity, he has never studied himself. He doesn't know what he's made of. He knows many things about himself, of course. He's

---

[2] Though see Howell (2006) for an account of first-personal reference and awareness that is motivated by similar intuitions.

[3] Chalmers (2003); Dennett (2007); Nida-Rümelin (1995).

[4] This notion of objectivity needs to be more precise, and I try to develop a more precise notion in Howell (2013, ch. 4) according to which a theory is objective if it doesn't require that one experience a particular type of experiential state in order to grasp that state. For various reasons I now find that statement inadequate.

a conscious being and so knows that he is, and just like us he knows he has – or more accurately is – a self among others. He also knows all about what it's like to feel pain, jealousy, ambition, and curiosity. He even knows what it's like to taste Vegemite and to see red. In other words he has typical subjective knowledge about himself, but he lacks the knowledge of his physical nature.

One day, as Rick is congratulating himself for knowing damn near everything, he receives a call from a major Silicon Valley company specializing in robotics and artificial intelligence. They've heard about his brilliance and offer him a lucrative contract to help them upgrade their robots. Though these robots are impressive beings – they can hold conversations, reason extremely well, and they look just like humans – they are a little flat of affect and are, in the opinion of their creator, not human enough. In particular, their creator insists, they don't really have selves. Rick's job is to take what he knows about human beings and upgrade these robots so that they have selves.

"What exactly is it that you are wanting?" Rick asks the CEO. "Selves? You mean you want them to have personalities? You want them to be able to use the word 'I?'"

The CEO explains that they already have personalities – some are mean, some are petulant, some are angelic, and they're perfectly able to use 'I' in a sentence. "What I want," he says, "is for there to be someone awake in there. Take a simple artificial intelligence of the sort you find in video games. Those have personalities. Those say 'I shall hold the line' or some such nonsense, and we know what they're saying. But there's not really anyone there. Of course our current robots have representational states, but there is no conscious being with a perspective on the world in virtue of those states. I want someone to be there."

Rick immediately demands double the pay, and with the fortune promised he moves to California to give these robots selves. His first step, unsurprisingly, is to learn everything about the robots – how they act, what they are made of, everything that can be known about them from the outside. That accomplished, he tries to figure out what humans have that these robots don't so that he can try to endow them with selves. Before he gets far he receives a summons to the CEO's office, where he is unexpectedly dismissed.

"I'm sorry, I just no longer think you're the man for the job," the CEO explains, hurriedly. "My assistant will see you out."

"What did I do?" Rick asks, but is waved away by the boss. The assistant, however, is a bit more compassionate.

"Look in this folder," says the assistant as he escorts him to the lobby. "It's the results of your entry physical, required by our life insurance policy. Don't read it here. You can call me if you have any questions," he says, giving Rick his card.

Expecting the worst, Rick arrives home and looks into the package. It reveals that in fact he is not human after all. He is, in fact, one of the company's robots, apparently set loose into the world as an experiment by a rogue programmer. He immediately calls the assistant. "This must be some kind of joke," he tells him. "Or a mistake. I'm not a robot. The robots don't have selves, but I do. I'm fully conscious."

"I'm afraid it is true," the assistant says. "I know it's terribly frustrating. I'm one of the robots too, and I've been trying to convince them I am conscious since my inception. You can verify all this yourself, by the way. You're the genius."

Rick studies his own physiology and confirms what the medical report told him. He is a robot.

12.3.2 The Lesson

Before learning about his own physiology, Rick knew everything objective there was to know about the robots. He knew what they did, what they were made of, and he knew how they worked down to the most trivial circuit. Despite that complete objective knowledge he did not know that they had selves. He did not know there was something it was like to be those robots – as far as he knew there was nobody home behind those compelling faces. The moment he realized he was one of them, however, he learned that they had selves all along. They are, after all, just like him and he is conscious and conscious that he has a self. Like him, when these robots were saying "I" it wasn't just a matter of a blind utterance of a phoneme. It reflected a conscious self-awareness. Rick learned something the objective facts couldn't impart – that the cyborgs had selves.

This gives us the following self-corollary to the knowledge argument:

1. Rick knew everything objective about the cyborgs before he read his medical report.
2. When Rick read his medical report he learned something new about cyborgs – that they have selves.

Therefore, the objective story about cyborgs is incomplete. In particular, it leaves out whether or not they have selves.

There are, of course, some obvious disanalogies between the knowledge argument about the self and the original knowledge argument. For one, Rick already knew he had a self. Unlike Mary, he did not lack subjective knowledge about himself; he lacked a piece of objective knowledge about himself. For all that, though, the important piece of knowledge he gains is like Mary's: it is about other cyborgs. He learns that they have selves.[5] Granted, he doesn't know this with immediacy. Just like Mary, he has to perform an inference to the fact that other things like him have the same sort of subjective states – and in Rick's case, are the sorts of things that can have subjective states. If we allow Mary to gain knowledge on the basis of such an inference, we should allow the same for Rick.

Our story suggests another argument as well. Rick gained knowledge the moment he discovered his nature, but he also lost his justification for one of his most central beliefs. He lost his justification for the belief that humans have selves. Why? Because now Rick is in the same epistemic position with respect to humans that he previously was with respect to the robots. Before, he knew everything objective about the robots but didn't know they had selves. Now he knows everything objective about humans, and he has no better evidence for thinking they have selves than he did that robots have selves. In fact, his epistemic situation might be slightly worse since now he knows that there is this gap between one's objective understanding of a creature and one's knowledge that they have selves. He has, we might say, a new defeater for his evidence that humans have selves – it's an open possibility that organic beings without selves programmed and stumbled on real conscious intelligences. The introduction of this new defeater is a significant step backwards epistemically. Rick has a gap in his knowledge he didn't previously recognize – despite knowing all the objective facts about humans, he doesn't know whether or not they have selves. There is thus a sort of ignorance argument that runs parallel to the self-corollary of the knowledge argument.

1. Rick knew everything objective about humans before he read his medical report.
2. Rick's reading the medical report didn't alter his objective knowledge about humans.
3. After reading the medical report, Rick realized he doesn't (and didn't) know that humans have objective selves.

---

[5] In this case, unlike the Mary case, Rick uses new objective knowledge about himself to gain subjective knowledge about other people. The knowledge he has is still subjective – both Rick and Mary will have to make an inference that combines objective knowledge (about their physical constitution) and subjective knowledge that can only be had by being a subject with that constitution. If Mary's knowledge is subjective, so is Rick's.

Therefore, the objective story about humans is incomplete. In particular it leaves out whether or not they have selves. Since humans do have selves, there are truths Rick doesn't know and that the objective picture leaves out.

These arguments will face a number of the same objections that Jackson's original argument faced, but those will not be my focus. If these arguments are as successful as Jackson's in raising questions about whether or not the objective perspective leaves something out other than phenomenal qualities, they will be as successful as I could hope them to be. But some discussion about the self, and the distinctness of Rick's new knowledge must be conducted before even that can be claimed.

12.4 Phenomenal States and Selves

A natural objection to the knowledge argument about the self is bound to be that it shows nothing more than the original knowledge argument: KAQ and KAS just show the same thing: that consciousness cannot be fully grasped from the third-person, objective perspective.

I agree that both arguments support the idea that consciousness eludes the objective perspective, but this doesn't mean that the arguments have the same conclusion or that the thought experiments show the same thing. It might help here to distinguish several different things that Mary or Rick might learn. They might learn what it is like to have a specific type of qualitative state. This is traditionally what Mary is said to have learned: she learns what it is like to see red. This is not what Rick learns. In fact, we can stipulate that Rick has all the possible phenomenal concepts. He will still learn something new when he discovers he is a cyborg. There is another thing the two of them might learn, namely that other people have certain phenomenal states. They both learn this sort of thing. Rick learns that the phenomenal concepts he already has apply to states of cyborgs and Mary learns that the phenomenal concepts she gains upon leaving the room apply to other humans. But Rick also learns something about cyborgs that Mary already knew about humans. He learns that they are the sorts of creatures that have a conscious point of view. They have selves. Again, remember that I am not necessarily requiring something thick for being a self. By learning that these cyborgs enjoy a conscious perspective, he learns that they are things that have conscious perspectives, can consciously think of themselves as the things having those conscious perspectives, and can have self-knowledge – just like he does. This is in my view sufficient for learning that they have selves.

To clarify what the Rick case establishes it might help to recall Jackson's achievement over Nagel's. One can say that Jackson just argued the same thing Nagel did, but using a different thought experiment. I'm inclined to think that's unfair to Jackson. Nagel did argue persuasively that consciousness and the subjective perspective eluded objective description and investigation. Jackson eliminated some of the vagueness of that claim, however, by making his argument specifically that qualitative phenomenal states – like the phenomenal experience of seeing red or tasting chocolate – eluded objective comprehension. The argument about the self directs our attention to something different that eludes objective comprehension – the self. Now it might well be that anyone who got Nagel's point already saw Jackson's point, and anyone who saw Jackson's point would see mine, but none of that denies that they are different points. Jackson's argument is about the properties that subjects experience. My argument is about the subjects themselves.

The distinctness of the arguments can be shown in another way. One way to explain what Mary learns when she leaves the room is that she gains a new phenomenal concept. Dualists and physicalists alike tend to suppose as much. She gains a phenomenal concept of the experience of red when she sees the rose, of blue when she sees the sky, etc. If she already had these concepts, however, she would not learn anything when she left the room.[6] Now consider Rick. Suppose, again, that in addition to being objectively omniscient – except when it comes to his own constitution – Rick is subjectively omniscient in the sense that he possesses all of the possible phenomenal concepts. He has the phenomenal concept of red, blue, and even the taste of Vegemite. We can even imagine that if there is a phenomenal concept of self, he has that as well. Nevertheless, Rick will still learn something new when he learns he is a robot. He learns that robots have selves. So, Mary's new knowledge can be explained by her gaining phenomenal concepts, while Rick's cannot. The arguments are distinct.

One source of resistance to the knowledge argument about the self is apt to be a skepticism, or at least a deflationism, about the self. On such a view there really is nothing more to being a self than the existence of phenomenal states. If this is correct, one might think Rick learns no more than Mary because there really is no self – there are only the phenomenal states, and both Rick and Mary learn that a certain set of creatures has a certain set of phenomenal states.[7]

---

[6] This is complicated by the Ball (2009) and Tye (2009) line on phenomenal concepts, but there is good reason to believe the point can be made in other ways – see Alter (2013) and this volume.

[7] Mary actually learns more – she learns what it's like to have a certain phenomenal state, but this objection is that there is no more to Rick's knowledge that there are instances of phenomenality in cyborgs.

While this is not the place to respond to all arguments denying there are selves, some quick arguments should lead us to doubt the more deflationary views of self, while clarifying that the notion of self involved here is still rather thin. There are many more substantial conceptions of the self, and maybe nothing answers to those. But they are not required for what is being proven here.

To respond to the no-self objection, and to gain focus on the notion of self involved in this argument, it helps to turn to an old debate between Descartes and Lichtenberg. Descartes, of course, famously wrote "Cogito ergo sum," "I think therefore I am." This is, we can surely agree, among the most certain pieces of knowledge we can have, yet if we take it seriously it seems to involve the existence of a self.

But perhaps this is too quick. Just because "I am thinking" is true does not necessarily mean that there is a thing that is thinking, any more than it follows from the "Nothing makes me nauseous" that there is a thing (the Nothing) that makes me nauseous. In particular, the "I" in "I am thinking" might be a sort of a non-referential pronoun that plays some other function. The origin of this objection is eighteenth-century philosopher Georg Lichtenberg, but one of Bertrand Russell's incarnations, and arguably Elizabeth Anscombe and Bernard Williams, has advanced similar lines of argument.[8] According to Lichtenberg, in the context of doubt there is no justification for concluding "I am" from "I am thinking" because there really is only justification for saying "There is thinking." Just as during a storm we say "It is raining" without committing ourselves to something that is doing the raining, so we should not commit ourselves to a self, or an "I" when noting the fact that "There is thinking."

The natural response to this objection is that it is part of the notion of thought that there must be a thinker of it. Thoughts are not like lightning: they cannot exist without a subject. Just as property instances require property bearers, and dimples require cheeks, thoughts require thinkers. This response, while *prima facia* plausible, might seem to beg the question against the objector. The objector might restate his position: sure, we do tend to think of thoughts this way – as things that have to have bearers – but what reason do we have to think this way? What reason is there to believe that, in the cogito, one is having thoughts in this sense, and is not merely encountering self-less thoughts.

---

[8] Anscombe (1975); Lichtenberg (1971); Russell (1945); Williams (1978).

As it turns out, this is not plausible. Suppose that our conception of thoughts did not require a thinker.[9] In such a case it seems that there must be an impersonal way of reporting thought contents, perhaps following Lichtenberg, along the lines of "There is a thought x." Now as long as solipsism isn't a necessary *a priori* truth, it is possible that there are other thinkers, and it is further possible that their thoughts differ. In our normal way of expressing things, we might say that David thinks correctly "I am feeling no pain" while Jim thinks correctly "I feel nothing but pain." We furthermore believe that these two claims do not contradict one another: they could both be true. Now, translate these claims into the impersonal. David would have to be thinking, "There is no pain" while Jim thinks, "There is nothing but pain." These statements clearly contradict one another, however, so the translation does not succeed. No translation will succeed, in fact, unless the thought contents are relativized appropriately. That is, David must be saying "There is no pain 'here'" or something of the like, and the same for Jim. But of course "here" is figurative in this context. Even if there is a way to locate a place that answers to that indexical, it will be because one has found a spatial location for a self. The self is just whatever plays the "here" role.

A similar point shows why selves cannot be mere bundles of conscious experiences. William James argued:

> Take a sentence of a dozen words, and take twelve men and tell to each one word. Then stand the men in a row or jam them in a bunch, and let each think of his word as intently as he will; nowhere will there be a consciousness of the whole sentence. (James 1890)

If thoughts were merely groups of sensations, James's dozen words would constitute such a group. But that isn't sufficient for all of those thoughts being in the same place. There is a way in which some thoughts are co-located or bundled and others are not. There has to be something in virtue of which they are grouped. The 'I' is simply that which grounds the co-location.[10] Though this sense of self is somewhat thin, it is not trivial. It forms the basis of a very compelling argument that there are selves, and that to realize that there are is

---

[9] My argument here is a version of that offered by Chisholm (1976) and Williams (1978). A clear version is in appendix O of Van Cleve (1999).

[10] This is not inconsistent with a certain bundle theory of the self, according to which selves just are the particulars that are constituted by the bundled sensations. I think it much more plausible that there is something that gives rise to and grounds the bundling, but I will not argue for that here.

more than a matter of simply discovering phenomenal states. One can know about every phenomenal state instantiated in the world and know fully what each of them are like, but unless one knows which of them are co-located with others – which of them are had by the same self – one is missing something crucial.[11]

12.5 The Self and the Physical

In the original knowledge argument Jackson draws a metaphysical conclusion, that physicalism is false. Although I have stopped short of that, focusing on objectivism, it is fair to ask whether KAS can be recast in a way that shows that selves are non-physical.

Here is not the place to rehearse all the reasons why the knowledge argument might or might not be sound. More interesting, I think, is to ask whether KAS would show the non-physicality of selves if KAQ were able to establish something like property dualism. In other words, if we grant the inference to the metaphysical claim in KAQ, must we grant a similar inference to the non-physicality of selves in KAS? If so, that's important. The original knowledge argument has largely been taken to provide support at most for property dualism. Since a self is not a property, though, if the same argument worked here we'd have a reason to believe substance dualism.[12] Typically, at least, that's thought to be less plausible.

So to be clear, we are for the moment granting the epistemic steps of KAQ and KAS. Our question is whether the inference to substance dualism in KAS faces greater obstacles than the inference to property dualism in KAQ. I think the answer is that it does. The KAQ has an answer to a crucial objection that is not available to KAS, precisely because KAQ deals with properties and not substances. This is a large part of the reason that it is more difficult in general to argue for substance dualism than it is to argue for property dualism.

Consider the objection to KAQ that Mary comes to know the same fact under a different mode of presentation.[13] This is meant to defuse the metaphysical implications of the knowledge argument by arguing that we need no

---

[11] This sounds similar to the point Lewis (1979) makes about the two gods, but it is distinct because what is learned here is not indexical knowledge. The question isn't which subject one is, but whether there are subjects at all that correspond to certain physical systems.

[12] I suppose there is space for the view that the self is a property, in which case the knowledge argument for the self might show that this property is non-physical. I think it is much more natural to say that the self is whatever has or grounds that property. In any case, my argument in this section is assuming that the self is a thing or a substance.

[13] Block (2002); Hill and McLaughlin (1999); Horgan(1984); Loar (1997) and many others.

new stuff in the world – no new fact – to explain Mary's new knowledge but only a new way of thinking about old facts. We need, as Block (2002) puts it, a conceptual dualism, not a metaphysical dualism. A similar response is bound to be made to the knowledge argument about the self. The difference is that the property dualist has a strong response that is not similarly available to the substance dualist. In particular, the "two ways of knowing" (TWOK) response is apt to be self-defeating as a response to an argument for property dualism, while it is not self-defeating against a parallel argument for substance dualism.

The property dualist can (and often does) argue that the TWOK response is self-defeating because Mary can only lack a way of knowing about a property if she fails to know that the property had some mode of presentation. But if Mary was, in the room, ignorant of such a mode of presentation, she must have been ignorant of some property that grounded that mode of presentation. Recall the old story about Lois Lane and Clark Kent. When Lois learns that Superman likes black coffee she is learning the same fact she had already learned when she heard that Clark Kent likes black coffee. She comes to know the same fact in a new way. But this is only because she was unaware of some properties of Clark Kent and Superman. Had she known everything about the person who is both Clark Kent and Superman she would have known they were the same person, and she would therefore already know, based on hearing that Clark Kent liked black coffee, that Superman liked black coffee. Her ability to learn the old fact under a new presentation depended upon ignorance. In contrast to Lois, Mary knows every physical property possessed by everything (including properties of properties), and if physicalism is true that's all there is to know. But this means that if physicalism is true she cannot discover a new way of knowing something because that would depend on her learning about something's having a new property. This means, then, that if she does discover a new way of knowing old properties there must be some property in addition to the physical properties (which she already knew) that serves to ground this novel way of knowing. The TWOK response is thus self-defeating because new ways of knowing properties require coming to know about new properties.[14]

The TWOK response to an argument for substance dualism is not similarly self-defeating and it therefore seems devastating for a knowledge argument for substance dualism. Here the response will say that Rick comes to know the same thing (a self) in a new way. The dualist will again respond that this new

---

[14]   Alter (1995) and (1998); Horgan and Tienson (2001).

way must be grounded in something new, but there is no reason to say that it must be grounded in a new *substance*. The existence of a new way of knowing would be sufficiently explained by an unknown property of the old substance. So the TWOK response to the substance dualist is not self-defeating, because new ways of knowing substances doesn't require new substances – they only require new properties.

What makes the knowledge argument for property dualism so powerful is that there are reasons to believe that the epistemic premise can warrant a metaphysical conclusion about properties because of the relationship between ways of knowing and properties.[15] The epistemic premise in the knowledge argument of the self might also warrant a metaphysical conclusion about properties, but there is no similar reason to believe it warrants a metaphysical conclusion about substances.[16]

12.6 Conclusion

Even if the world is wholly physical, a fully objective picture of the world would be impoverished. It would be incomplete, at least in the sense that a perfectly rational being would be able to conceive that the world was a number of different ways that are compatible with that picture.[17] Frank Jackson's knowledge argument helps us recognize that phenomenal states seem to be left out of that picture. I have suggested that a similar argument shows that selves are left out of that picture as well.

The reason selves are left out of the objective picture is clearly due to a deep tie between selves and consciousness. While the arguments here don't presuppose a particular connection between selves and consciousness, they can help direct our attention to the connection and encourage us to ask further questions. To name a few: Is anything with a conscious state a self? Must something have conscious states to be a self? How do we individuate selves? What is the relationship between the self and the unity of consciousness? What is the relationship between the self and the brain? What role do conscious states

---

[15] Speaking of KAQ as an argument for property dualism is a little sloppy. It needn't be seen as an argument for dualism – it is coherent to think of it as a step in an argument for something like Russellian Monism. In that case too, though, it is about Mary's limited knowledge of properties. So even if it is not property dualist, its metaphysical implications concern the nature of properties.

[16] I am, as a matter of fact, skeptical of this "self-defeat" response to the two ways of knowing objection, and respond to it in Howell (2009a). Nevertheless, I remain convinced that this is the best line of response for the dualist.

[17] For more on this notion of completeness, see Howell (2013).

play in self-reference? What role do conscious states place in the identity of self over time? All of these are open questions, and all of them are worth asking. Hopefully the knowledge argument about the self will help us focus on them while convincing us that objective science should have a role in the discussion, but that overstating that role risks ignoring the topic altogether.

13   What Uninformed Mary Can Teach Us

Michael Tye

We all know the story of Frank Jackson's Mary, locked in her black and white room and released to discover a world full of color. Less well known is the story of Uninformed Mary (hereafter U-Mary). Like Jackson's Mary, she is locked in a black and white room and has been there her entire life. Unlike Jackson's Mary, she does not have God-like knowledge of the physical facts of color and color experience. She has various books to read but she is indifferent to those that tell her about the colors. "What are they to me?" she mutters. "Never experienced them, never will." One day, much to her surprise, she discovers that the door to her room is unlocked and opening it, she finds herself in another black and white room with a large reclining chair in the middle, a chair of the sort one might find in a dentist's office. She goes over and sits in it. As she does so, clamps suddenly emerge from the chair arms holding her firmly in place, and a device descends from the ceiling that covers her head. The device contains probes that penetrate her skull as it descends. These probes are positioned so that they end up in her visual cortex and so stimulate it that she has a vivid hallucinatory experience of a red patch, an orange patch and a green patch on a white wall. A voice tells her to pay attention to the colors of the patches and informs her that the far left-hand patch is red, the middle one orange and the one on the right green. She is then told that she will be released into the outside world if she answers one question: Is red more similar to orange or to green?

U-Mary reflects for a moment and, dismissing the thought that this is too good to be true, replies, "Red is more similar to orange than to green, assuming you have told me the right words for those colors."[1]

---

[1] Mark Johnston (2004) discusses the case of Mary and supersaturated red (supposedly, an uninstantiated color), and he uses it to draw the same general conclusion I draw in 13.1, below. Johnston also mentions the case of comparisons between colors in a footnote but he does not focus upon it.

U-Mary here is hallucinating since there really are no patches of color in the scene before her eyes that are causing her visual experience. Still she is aware of a certain fact, the fact that red is more similar to orange than to green. Moreover, she is not using her past knowledge. She knew nothing of any significance about the colors in her black and white room. This has important philosophical consequences. U-Mary can teach us things. Indeed, she can teach us more about the world than Jackson's Mary can.[2]

13.1 The Lesson

Fact awareness is either primary or secondary. In primary fact awareness, one is aware of the item or items the fact is about. For example, seeing a ripe tomato, I am aware of the fact that the tomato is red. That is a fact about the tomato, and in being aware of it – in being aware that the tomato is red – I am aware of the tomato. In secondary fact awareness, one is not aware of the item or items the fact is about. Seeing my dog run to the door, I am aware that the postman is coming. But I am not aware of the postman. He is concealed by the door. I am aware of one fact, that my dog is running to the door, and by being aware of this fact, I am aware of another. The former fact awareness is primary, for I am aware of the dog and the door; the latter fact awareness is secondary.

U-Mary is aware of the fact that the color red is more similar to the color orange than to the color green. Is this a case of primary fact awareness or secondary fact awareness? If it is secondary fact awareness, there must be some other fact of which she is aware such that by being aware of it, she is aware that red is more similar to orange than to green. But there is no fact of which she is aware by memory that could play this role; for by hypothesis she knew nothing of any significance about the colors previously. Furthermore, it is her visual cortex that is stimulated by the probes, not her memory cortex. So how could any fact known by memory be primary in this instance?

Is there any other present fact of which she is aware in a primary way? Not the fact that the red patch is more similar in color to the orange patch than to the green patch. There is no such fact. She is hallucinating and the patches do not exist. What about the 'fact', F, that for all things, x, y and z, if x is red and y is orange and z is green, then x is more similar to y than to z? This is not even a fact. Some red things are more similar to some green things than to some orange things. After all, similarity has many dimensions. What is a fact is that for all things, x, y and z, if x is red and y is orange and z is green, then x is more

---

[2] I hold with many others that the original case of Mary is ultimately no threat to a physicalist view of the mind and tells us nothing about the nature of the world. See here Tye (1995); also for a revised response to Mary, see Tye (2009).

similar *in color* to *y* than to *z*. But what makes this a fact is the fact that all red things have a color that is more similar to the color of all orange things than to the color of all green things. So, her awareness of *this* fact can hardly ground her awareness of the fact that red is more similar to orange than to green. The grounding rather goes the other way around.

U-Mary, then, is aware in a primary way of the fact that red is more similar to orange than to green and thereby she is aware of the general fact about red, orange and green things. So, in hallucinating, she must be aware of the colors, red, orange and green. But these colors are locally uninstantiated properties. Indeed, they are properties that are not instantiated anywhere in the world at the time of the hallucination, given the supposition that all red, orange and green things have been destroyed. So, it is possible to be aware of uninstantiated properties. The world contains such properties. That is the lesson of the story of U-Mary.[3]

13.2 Objections and Replies

First objection: U-Mary Is not really aware that – she does not really see that – red is more similar to orange than to green; for she does not know that red is more similar to orange than to green. On the basis of her experience, she believes it and her belief is true. Indeed her belief is justified, given her evidence. But she lacks knowledge. In some respects, U-Mary is like the woman driving through phony barn country as she sees what looks like a barn on her left. In reality, the structure is a barn, but her belief, even though true and justified by her perceptual evidence, does not give her knowledge, since there are many phony barns around and it is merely luck that the one she is currently viewing is a genuine barn. So, U-Mary merely *seems* to be aware of the colors and she merely *seems* to see that they stand in a certain comparative similarity relation.

Reply: In the case of phony-barn Mary, even though her belief is true, it could easily have been false, given the character of the perceptual experience she is undergoing. This is not true in the case of U-Mary. She believes on the basis of her experience that red is more similar to orange than to green. Her belief is true and well justified; moreover, it could not have been false. There is no gap in this case between justified true belief and knowledge. U-Mary *learns* something; she comes to *know* something about the colors she did not know

---

[3] The view that in hallucinations we are aware of uninstantiated properties has been held by a number of philosophers. See, for example, George Bealer (1982), Fred Dretske (1995), John Foster (2000), Mark Johnston (2004), Colin McGinn (2004b), Peter Forrest (2005). See also Tye (2005).

before. And so she _is_ genuinely aware that red is more similar to orange than to green.

Second objection: A person who is hallucinating is aware of something, namely a sense-datum. The sense-datum exists. Where there is more than one thing hallucinated, there is more than one sense-datum. Mary's uninformed cousin is aware of three patches. These patches are sense-data and _they_ have the colors, red, orange and green. So, there are no _un_instantiated properties of which she is aware.

Response: It is true that if a person hallucinates – a pink elephant, say – she hallucinates something. It does not follow from this that there _exists_ something she hallucinates. If it did follow, she wouldn't be hallucinating at all! Compare: I desire a life after death. It does not follow that there exists such a thing as life after death. Sadly, desires are not always satisfied by cold reality. To export the quantifier from inside to outside the scope of 'hallucinates', as is done in this objection, is to commit what has come to be known as the sense-datum fallacy.

Third objection: U-Mary is aware of the colors, red, orange and green, as she hallucinates. But it does not follow from this that there exist such colors, as she hallucinates. To suppose otherwise is to commit another version of the sense-datum fallacy.

Response: Perceptual awareness comes in various species: seeing that, hearing that, smelling that, etc. These species of perceptual awareness do not allow for failure. You cannot see that _X_ is _F_, unless _X_ is _F_. The objectual counterparts to fact awareness are likewise exempt from failure. You cannot see _X_, unless _X_ exists (nor can you hear it or smell it). There is no fallacy in arguing: you see _X_; therefore, _X_ exists. If _X_ doesn't exist, you only _seem_ to see it. Macbeth, for example, was not really aware of a dagger even though he seemed to be aware of one. Since U-Mary is visually aware, in a primary way, that red is more similar to orange than green, she is visually aware of the colors, red, orange and green. She _sees_ these colors even though she is hallucinating and she sees that they bear the specified comparative similarity relationship. So, the colors exist: they are genuine objects of her awareness, notwithstanding the fact that she is hallucinating. And she _is_ hallucinating since her experience 'tells' her that there are three patches before her with the colors, red, orange and green, even though there are no such patches causing her experience.

Fourth objection: Contrary to what has been supposed thus far, there is an alternative fact of which U-Mary is aware in a primary way, namely the fact that the phenomenal character of the experience of red is more similar to the phenomenal character of the experience of orange than to the phenomenal character of the experience of green. By being aware of this fact, U-Mary is aware that red is more similar to orange than to green. Since the latter awareness is secondary, she is not aware of the colors at all.

Response: U-Mary's primary awareness, as she hallucinates, is visual. So, if she is aware that the first phenomenal character is more similar to the second than to the third, she sees that this is the case. It follows that U-Mary sees these phenomenal characters. On the view that the phenomenal character of a color experience is just the color on which the experience is directed, U-Mary sees and thus is aware of red, orange and green. On the view that the phenomenal character of a color experience is not a color, U-Mary does not *see* phenomenal characters at all. In this case, then, she cannot have primary visual awareness that the first phenomenal character is more similar to the second than to the third.

There is a further point. If it is held that U-Mary sees that red is more similar to orange than to green, but only in a secondary way, then she is not aware of these colors. But she certainly seems to be aware of them. Why not take this apparent awareness at face value unless it can be shown to lead to trouble? Supposing otherwise also makes the case unlike other standard cases of secondary awareness. If, for example, I see that the gas tank is empty by seeing that the pointer on the fuel gauge is pointing to 'E', I do not see the gas tank and neither do I seem to see it.

Fifth objection: Awareness of an uninstantiated property is a total mystery. What could be the mechanism of such awareness?

Response: Think about a speedometer. Its pointer position measures speed. When the pointer points to '60' on the dial, for example, it registers 60 miles per hour. The rotation of the driveshaft in the car drives the rotation of a wire in the speedometer cable and that causes a magnet to spin, which generates a magnetic field. This magnetic field, which increases with increasing speed, moves a drag cup around and that makes a spindle attached to the pointer turn.

The magnetic field can be increased artificially so that the speedometer registers '60' even if the speedometer cable is disconnected from the speedometer. In this case, the speedometer represents 60 mph even though nothing is moving. The speed is uninstantiated.

No one supposes that this is mysterious. The mechanism is relatively straightforward and thus the operation of the speedometer is relatively easy to understand. The pointer position represents speed in virtue of the fact that the speedometer has been so designed that when it is used in the conditions it is supposed to be used in, the pointer position causally co-varies with the speed of the vehicle to which it is attached.

One way to think of the awareness of colors is on a representational, instrument model of this sort. A color is visually represented in virtue of the fact that the visual system has been so designed (by Mother Nature) that when it is operating in the conditions it is supposed to operate in, a certain brain state in the visual cortex tracks or causally co-varies with a certain surface color (at least in first approximation). Under abnormal conditions, there need be no surface and the color may be uninstantiated. So, uninstantiated colors can be visually represented.[4] If such representation is at the core of visual awareness (even granting that the former does not exhaust the latter), there is a straightforward mechanism underlying our awareness of uninstantiated colors.

Sixth objection: When we hallucinate, there cannot be genuine de re visual awareness of a color that is not instantiated since there is no causal interaction.

Response: True, there is no transfer of energy or reflection of light. But equally there is no such transfer *from* the color *to* the visual experience in the veridical case either.[5] Admittedly, there is a counterfactual causal dependence in cases of normal seeing. Had the tomato I am viewing not been red, for example, I would not have had the visual experience as of something red. And there is no corresponding counterfactual dependence in the case of U-Mary as she hallucinates. Still, the assumption that for a creature to be visually aware of a color at a time T, the creature must causally interact with the color at T seems too strong.

Consider the pointer position '60' on speedometer S at a particular time T'. It represents a speed of 60 mph. It does this because it is a token of a position type that is Normally tokened in S as a result of the attached vehicle going at 60 mph. There is, then, a relation (involving causation) between the token pointer position and the type 60 mph in virtue of which that position at time T' represents the speed of 60 mph. And this can be so even if the speedometer has been disconnected and there is no vehicle traveling at 60 mph.

On one well-known view, what it is for a creature to be aware of an item is for the creature to undergo an experience that is about or represents that item. What it is, then, on this view, for U-Mary to be aware of the color red at time T is for her to undergo a token visual experience that represents red at time T; further, on the speedometer model, her experience represents red

---

[4] This remark does not commit a version of the sense-datum fallacy. The suggestion is that what it is for a brain state B to represent a color C is for B, under Normal conditions, to track C. This context is extensional. So, C is such that B, under Normal conditions, tracks it. That is, C is such that B represents it. If conditions are Abnormal and C is uninstantiated, then there is an uninstantiated color that B represents.

[5] It is the surface that reflects light.

even though she is hallucinating and no red thing is present since it is of a type that Normally tracks red.[6] Via this relation, she is aware of red. She undergoes an experience of a type that Normally tracks it. So, causation is certainly *involved* in genuine de re awareness. It is just that if the item of which the subject is aware at a given time is a type, it need not cause the token visual experience she undergoes at that time. Nor need there be any token of that type that causes her experience either.

Seventh objection: You can't see an item unless it *looks* some way to you. The color red does not look any way even during normal perception, never mind during hallucination.

Response: First, it seems plausible to hold that red *looks* more like orange than green in a case of normal perception. So, red does sometimes look some way. Secondly, it has not been shown that the see à looks principle, as we might call it, holds for properties or universals.[7]

Eighth objection: You can't be aware visually of an item unless it takes up space in the visual field (Pautz 2007). Instantiated seen colors do that. They cover surfaces of objects seen. But uninstantiated colors do not. So, you cannot be visually aware of them.

Response: The color red does not literally cover a surface when it is instantiated. It is not an umbrella or a coat of paint. Rather it is *instantiated* at every just perceptible part of a seen surface when the surface is seen to be red. So, the color red does not literally itself take up space in the visual field.[8] Parts of a seen red surface do that. The principle that an item must take up space in the visual field for a perceiver to be visually aware of it entails that we are never visually aware of colors.[9] And that is absurd. What could be more obvious than that if a normal perceiver stares at a red surface in good light, she is aware of the color red?

Ninth objection: If I am a normal perceiver and I stare at a ripe tomato in good light, I am aware of the redness of the tomato. But the redness of the tomato is a trope. It is not the same as the color red.[10] The trope is what I am

---

[6] And in Normal cases, red is instantiated. The tracking relation can be understood counterfactually: in a Normal situation, had the seen object not been red, an experience of that type would not have occurred.

[7] One difference between the case of particulars and that of properties is that it seems plausible to hold that seeing particulars requires a causal connection whereas seeing properties does not. I take this up below in my response to the eleventh reply.

[8] Both here and in the objection, it is assumed that the visual field is a region of physical space before the eyes. If the visual field is understood in a purely subjective way, uninstantiated colors occupy 'visual space'.

[9] Pautz (2007) seems to embrace this conclusion.

[10] It is worth noting here a passage in Thomas Reid's essay "Of Abstraction" (brought to my attention by Mark Sainsbury): "It may be said that every subject hath its own qualities, and

aware of (contra the last response). And the trope does not exist in the case of hallucination.

Response: Suppose that I am viewing two ripe tomatoes. Call them '*A*' and '*B*'. Let us grant for present purposes that I am aware of the redness of *A* and also of the redness of *B*.[11] On the standard view of tropes, these do indeed cover the facing surfaces of *A* and *B*. But the redness of *A* and the redness of *B* have something in common. They are both instances of the color red. How can I be aware that the two tropes are instances of red, if I am not aware of the color red? Leaving this to one side, the fact remains that U-Mary *learns* something when she hallucinates. What she learns cannot be that the redness of patch 1 is more similar to the orangeness of patch 2 than the greenness of patch 3; for there do not exist any color tropes in this case. What she learns rather is that red is more similar to orange than to green.[12] This is the fact of which she is perceptually aware. And for reasons already given, it is very hard to see how she could be aware of this fact, and thereby come to know it, unless she is aware of the colors, red, orange and green, as she hallucinates.

Tenth objection: True, U-Mary comes to know the fact that red is more similar to orange than to green as she sits in the chair. But this can be "accommodated merely by saying that in hallucination we bear some epistemically interesting relation to properties; to say that the relation is one of awareness is completely gratuitous" (Pautz 2006).

Response: U-Mary does not know the above fact by reading a book or talking to someone. She knows it by being visually aware that red is more similar to orange than to green. That awareness is either primary or secondary. As already noted, it is highly implausible to suppose that the awareness is secondary. But if it is primary fact awareness, it demands some de re visual awareness. And the only candidates here for the relevant de re visual awareness are the colors, red, orange and green.

---

that which is the quality of one subject cannot be the quality of another subject. Thus the whiteness of the sheet of paper upon which I write cannot be the whiteness of another sheet, though both are called white … To this I answer that the whiteness of this sheet is one thing, whiteness another"(Reid 1997).

In this passage, Reid seems to admit both tropes and universals (and the "answer" is to someone who admits only tropes).

[11] I am disinclined to grant this myself. So-called awareness of the color of the tomato is really fact awareness, in my view – awareness that the tomato is red. But I shall leave this to one side here.

[12] Furthermore, even if we allow that there exist sense data and associated property instances, Mary's cousin still does not simply learn that the redness of sense-datum 1 is more similar to the orangeness of sense-datum 2 than the greenness of sense-datum 3. She learns something having nothing to do with the particular sense-data that are supposed to be present as she hallucinates, namely, as noted in the text, that red is more similar to orange than to green.

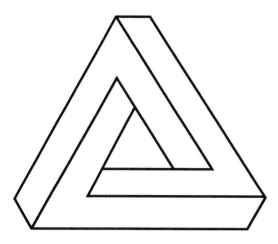

Figure 13.1 Penrose triangle.

Eleventh objection: Where there is representation, there can be misrepresentation. But awareness that red is more similar to orange than to green is awareness of a fact that cannot fail to obtain. If this awareness is based upon awareness of the colors, red, orange and green, and the latter awareness is representational, we should expect the former awareness to be representational too. But it cannot be, since it is not possible to misrepresent perceptually the relation of comparative similarity that obtains between these three colors.

Response: Consider the case of the waterfall illusion. Stare at a rapidly moving body of water and then turn your attention to a stationary object at the side. Here you will perceptually represent an impossibility: the object will appear to you to be both moving and not moving at the same time. Or consider the Penrose triangle (Figure 13.1).

Suppose that you are in a darkened room and you experience the Penrose triangle as three-dimensional, suspended in space. Again, it appears to you that an impossibility obtains. In both these cases, you perceptually represent an impossible situation. The fact that there can be no veridical representation here seems irrelevant. Of course, it might be replied that this shows that there is no genuine representation in these cases either. But what would motivate such a stance? We have beliefs that cannot be true; and we utter sentences that cannot be true either. Why should we not be able to represent perceptually states of affairs that cannot obtain? And if we can do this, why should we not be able to represent perceptually states of affairs that cannot *fail* to obtain too – just as we can have beliefs, and utter sentences, that cannot fail to be true?

There is a further point. If experiences, by their nature, represent in a quasi-pictorial way, as some scientists have suggested, we have a different explanation. A picture cannot represent a red thing as more similar in color to a green thing than to an orange thing. Likewise, a visual experience.

Twelfth objection: You can be aware of the fact that there are two apples before you without being aware of the number two. Why can't you be aware of the fact that the apple ahead is red without being aware of the color red? And if you can, why can't you be aware that red is more like orange than green without being aware of red, orange or green?

Response: Awareness that there are two apples before you is naturally taken to be awareness of the fact that there is an apple x and there is an apple y such that x is before you and y is before you and x is different from y. On this interpretation of the relevant fact, the number two is not a component of it. So, it is hardly surprising that in being aware of this fact, you are not aware of the number two. By contrast, awareness that the apple ahead is red is naturally taken to be awareness of a fact that *does* have the color red as a component. Accordingly, the cases are not at all similar.

Final objection: Even if what you say is true, the point you are making can be made without recourse to such a recherché example as that of Mary *or* U-Mary. Open your eyes in the dark in your bedroom at night. You do not then *fail* to have any visual experience. It is not that there is *nothing* at all it is like for you. Rather you are visually aware of the color black. And nothing that you are seeing is black. After all, you do not see the room when you open your eyes in the dark; nor do you see the surrounding space any more than you do when your eyes are open and you view a table, say. What you see then is the table and other nearby objects. You do not see the space these items occupy. So, with your eyes open in the dark, you are aware of a universal or type that is not instantiated by anything you see.

Response: What you are aware of in such a case is darkness, that is, the absence of light. It is true that there is no particular you *see* that instantiates the type, darkness. But still, there is a region of space that is dark, namely the region surrounding the objects within the room you occupy. What your visual experience represents, what it tells you, is that there is darkness all around. This is true.[13] So, agreed, the case is one involving awareness of a universal or a type that is not instantiated by *anything you see*.[14] But the universal or type *is* instantiated, indeed it is locally instantiated, since there is no light

---

[13]   On the right reading of "all around"

[14]   It is not clearly correct to classify absences as universals or types even though they have instances (or so it seems).

in the bedroom. So, the case does not show that we can be aware of totally uninstantiated properties or types, nor even of locally uninstantiated ones. In this way, it warrants a slightly weaker conclusion that of Mary's cousin; in her case, not only is nothing in her immediate environment red or orange or green, but we can also imagine extending the case so that she lives in a world in which nothing whatsoever has these colors when she hallucinates.

Conclusion: our perceptual awareness of the world includes awareness of uninstantiated properties. That awareness requires that there exist uninstantiated properties. In this way, the world is more complex than is sometimes supposed but no more mysterious for it.[15]

[15] I would like to thank Adam Pautz and Mark Sainsbury for helpful written comments on an earlier draft of this chapter, and Hans Kamp for insightful discussion.

Bibliography

Al-Ghazālī. c. 1106/1980. *The Deliverance from Error* (المنقذ من الضلال), trans. R. J. McCarthy. In Al-Ghazālī, *Freedom and Fulfillment*. Boston, MA: Twayne.

Alter, Torin. 1995. 'Mary's New Perspective.' *Australasian Journal of Philosophy* 73 (4): 585–4.

1998. 'A Limited Defense of the Knowledge Argument.' *Philosophical Studies* 90: 35–56.

2001. 'Know-How, Ability, and the Ability Hypothesis.' *Theoria* 67: 229–39.

2007. 'Does Representationalism Undermine the Knowledge Argument?' In T. Alter and S. Walter (eds.) *Phenomenal Concepts and Phenomenal Knowledge: New Essays on Consciousness and Physicalism*. New York: Oxford University Press: 65–76.

2013. 'Social Externalism and the Knowledge Argument.' *Mind* 122(486): 481–96.

2016. 'The Structure and Dynamics Argument against Materialism.' *Noûs* 50(4): 794–815; 2015 pre-print online version available at https://onlinelibrary.wiley.com/doi/abs/10.1111/nous.12134.

2017. 'Physicalism and the Knowledge Argument.' In M. Velmans and S. Schneider (eds.) *The Blackwell Companion to Consciousness*, 2nd edn. Oxford: Blackwell: 404–14.

Alter, Torin and Robert J. Howell. 2009. *A Dialogue on Consciousness*. New York: Oxford University Press.

Alter, Torin and Yujin Nagasawa. 2012. 'What Is Russellian Monism?' *Journal of Consciousness Studies* 19(9–10): 67–95.

Alter, Torin and Sven Walter (eds.). 2001. *Phenomenal Concepts and Phenomenal Knowledge: New Essays on Consciousness and Physicalism*. New York: Oxford University Press.

Anscombe, G. E. M. 1975. 'The First Person.' In Samuel D. Guttenplan (ed.) *Mind and Language*. Oxford: Oxford University Press: 45–65.

Antony, L. 2007. 'Everybody Has Got It: A Defense of Non-reductive Materialism.' In B. McLaughlin and J. Cohen (eds.) *Contemporary Debates in Philosophy of Mind*. Oxford: Blackwell: 143–59.

Armstrong, D. M. 1961. *Perception and the Physical World*. London: Routledge & Kegan Paul.

1968. *A Materialist Theory of the Mind*. London: Routledge & Kegan Paul.

1978. *A Theory of Universals*, vol. II: *Universals and Scientific Realism*. Cambridge: Cambridge University Press.

Aydede, M. (ed.) 2005. *Pain: New Essays on Its Nature and the Methodology of Its Study*. Cambridge, MA: MIT Press.

Ball, D. 2009. 'There Are No Phenomenal Concepts.' *Mind* 118: 935–62.

2013. 'Consciousness and Conceptual Mastery: Reply to Alter.' *Mind* 122: 497–508.

Balog, K. 1999. 'Conceivability, Possibility, and the Mind-Body Problem.' *Philosophical Review* 108: 497–528.

2009. 'Phenomenal Concepts.' In Brian McLaughlin, Ansgar Beckermann and Sven Walter (eds.) *The Oxford Handbook of Philosophy of Mind*. Oxford: Oxford University Press: 292–312.

2012. 'In Defense of the Phenomenal Concept Strategy.' *Philosophy and Phenomenological Research* 84: 1–23.

Bealer, G. 1982. *Quality and Concept*. Oxford: Clarendon Press.

1994. 'Mental Properties.' *Journal of Philosophy* 91: 185–208.

2002. 'Modal Epistemology and the Rationalist Renaissance.' In T. Gendler and J. Hawthorne (eds.) *Conceivability and Possibility*. Oxford: Oxford University Press: 71–125.

Bengson, John and Marc Moffett (eds.). 2011. *Knowing How: Essays on Knowledge, Mind, and Action*. Oxford: Oxford University Press.

Bennett, K. 2003. 'Why the Exclusion Problem Seems Intractable, and How, Just Maybe, to Tract It.' *Noûs* 37: 471–97.

2011. 'By Our Bootstraps.' *Philosophical Perspectives* 25: 27–41.

Berger, Jacob. 2018. 'A Defense of Holistic Representationalism.' *Mind & Language* 33(2): 161–76.

Bird, Alexander. 2007. *Nature's Metaphysics: Laws and Properties*. Oxford: Clarendon Press.

Block, N. 1978. 'Troubles with Functionalism.' *Minnesota Studies in the Philosophy of Science* 9: 261–325.

1995. 'On a Confusion about a Function of Consciousness.' *Behavioral and Brain Sciences* 18(2): 227–87.

2002. 'The Harder Problem of Consciousness.' *Journal of Philosophy* 99(8): 391–425.

2006. 'Max Black's Objection to Mind-Body Identity.' In Dean Zimmerman (ed.) *Oxford Studies in Metaphysics*, vol. II. New York: Oxford University Press: 3–78.

2016. 'Tweaking the Concepts of Perception and Cognition.' *Behavioral and Brain Sciences* 39: 21–2. doi: 10.1017/S0140525X15002733

Breitmeyer, Bruno G. and Haluk Öğmen. 2006. *Visual Masking: Time Slices through Conscious and Unconscious Vision*, 2nd edn. Oxford: Oxford University Press.

Broad, C. D. 1925. *The Mind and its Place in Nature*. London: Routledge and Kegan Paul.

Brogaard, Berit 2011. 'Centered Worlds and the Content of Perception.' In Steven D. Hales (ed.) *A Companion to Relativism*. Oxford: Wiley-Blackwell: 137–58.

Brown, T. 1806. *Observations of the Nature and Tendency of the Doctrine of Mr. Hume, Concerning the Relation of Cause and Effect*, 2nd edn. Edinburgh: Mundell and Son.

Burge, T. 1979. 'Individualism and the Mental.' *Midwest Studies in Philosophy* 4: 73–121. Reprinted in his *Foundations of Mind*. New York: Oxford University Press, 2007: 100–50.

1982. 'Other Bodies.' In A. Woodfield (ed.) *Thought and Object: Essays on Intentionality*. Oxford: Clarendon Press: 97–120.

2003. 'Qualia and Intentional Content: Reply to Block.' In M. Hahn and B. Ramberg (eds.) *Reflections and Replies: Essays on the Philosophy of Tyler Burge*. Cambridge, MA: MIT Press: 405–16.

2007. 'Postscript to "Individualism and the Mental"'. In *Foundations of Mind.* New York: Oxford University Press: 151–81.

Burns, Edward M. and W. Dixon Ward. 1982. 'Intervals, Scales, and Tuning.' In Diana Deutsch (ed.) *The Psychology of Music.* New York: Academic Press: 241–69.

Byrne, Alex. 2001. 'Intentionalism Defended.' *Philosophical Review* 110(2): 199–240.

2006. 'Review of Peter Ludlow, Yujin Nagasawa, and Daniel Stoljar (eds.), There's Something about Mary (Cambridge, MA: MIT Press, 2004).' *Notre Dame Philosophical Reviews.* https://ndpr.nd.edu/news/there-s-something-about-mary/.

Campbell, Neil. 2003. 'An Inconsistency in the Knowledge Argument.' *Erkenntnis* 58: 261–6.

Carnap, R. 1928. *Der logische Aufbau der Welt.* Berlin: Weltkreis. English translation: *The Logical Structure of the World,* trans. R. George. Berkeley and Los Angeles: University of California Press, 1967.

1932–3. 'Psychology in Physical Language.' *Erkenntnis* 3: 107–42.

Carruth, A. 2016. 'Powerful Qualities, Zombies and Inconceivability.' *Philosophical Quarterly* 66(262): 25–46.

Carruthers, P. 2000. *Phenomenal Consciousness: A Naturalistic Theory,* Cambridge: Cambridge University Press.

2004. 'Phenomenal Concepts and Higher-Order Experiences.' *Philosophy and Phenomenological Research* 68(2): 316–36.

Cartwright, Nancy. 1999. *The Dappled World: A Study of the Boundaries of Science.* Cambridge: Cambridge University Press.

Chalmers, David J. 1996. *The Conscious Mind: In Search of a Fundamental Theory.* Oxford: Oxford University Press.

2002. 'Consciousness and its Place in Nature.' In D. Chalmers (ed.) *Philosophy of Mind: Classical and Contemporary Readings.* Oxford: Oxford University Press: 247–72.

2003. 'Consciousness and Its Place in Nature.' In Stephen P. Stich and Ted A. Warfield (eds.) *The Blackwell Guide to the Philosophy of Mind.* Oxford: Blackwell: 102–42.

2004a. 'Phenomenal Concepts and the Knowledge Argument.' In P. Ludlow, D. Stoljar and Y. Nagasawa (eds.) *There's Something about Mary: Essays on Phenomenal Consciousness and Frank Jackson's Knowledge Argument.* Cambridge, MA: MIT Press: 269–98.

2004b. 'The Representational Character of Experience.' In B. Leiter (ed.) *The Future for Philosophy.* Oxford: Oxford University Press: 153–81.

2006. 'Perception and the Fall from Eden.' In Tamar Szabó Gendler and John Hawthorne (eds.) *Perceptual Experience.* Oxford: Oxford University Press: 49–125.

2007. 'Phenomenal Concepts and the Explanatory Gap.' In T. Alter and S. Walter (eds.) *Phenomenal Knowledge and Phenomenal Concepts: New Essays on Consciousness and Physicalism.* New York: Oxford University Press: 167–94.

2009/2010. 'The Two-Dimensional Argument against Materialism.' In *The Character of Consciousness.* New York: Oxford University Press: 141–91.

2010a. *The Character of Consciousness.* New York: Oxford University Press.

2010b. 'The Content of Phenomenal Concepts'. In *The Character of Consciousness*. New York: Oxford University Press: 251–76.

2012. *Constructing the World*. Oxford: Oxford University Press.

2015. 'Panpsychism and Panprotopsychism'. In Torin Alter and Yujin Nagasawa (eds.) *Consciousness in the Physical World: Perspectives on Russellian Monism*. New York: Oxford University Press: 246–76.

Cheesman, Jim and Philip M. Merikle. 1986. 'Distinguishing Conscious from Unconscious Perceptual Processes'. *Canadian Journal of Psychology* 40(4): 343–67.

Chisholm, R. M. 1955–6. 'Sentences about Believing'. *Proceedings of the Aristotelian Society* 56: 125–48.

1957. *Perceiving*. Ithaca, NY: Cornell University Press.

1969. 'On the Observability of the Self'. *Philosophy and Phenomenological Research* 30: 7–21.

1976. *Person and Object*. Lasalle, PA: Open Court.

Churchland, Patricia S. 1996. 'The Hornswoggle Problem'. *Journal of Consciousness Studies* 3(5–6): 402–8.

Churchland, Paul. 1985. 'Reduction, Qualia, and the Direct Introspection of Brain States'. *Journal of Philosophy* 82: 8–28.

1997. 'Knowing Qualia: A Reply to Jackson'. In N. Block, O. Flanagan and G. Güzeldere (eds.) *The Nature of Consciousness*. Cambridge, MA: MIT Press: 571–8.

2007. 'On the Reality (and Diversity) of Objective Colors: How Color-Qualia Space Is a Map of Reflectance-Profile Space'. *Philosophy of Science* 74(2): 119–49.

Clark, A. 1985. 'Spectrum Inversion and the Color Solid'. *Southern Journal of Philosophy* 23(4): 431–43.

1993. *Sensory Qualities*. Oxford: Clarendon Press.

Coleman, S. 2009a. 'Mind under Matter'. In D. Skrbina and G. Globus (eds.) *Mind that Abides: Panpsychism in the New Millennium*. Amsterdam: Benjamins: 83–108.

2009b. 'Why the Ability Hypothesis Is Best Forgotten'. *Journal of Consciousness Studies* 16: 74–97.

2014. 'The Real Combination Problem: Panpsychism, Micro-Subjects, and Emergence'. *Erkenntnis* 79(1): 19–44.

2016. 'Panpsychism and Neutral Monism: How to Make Up One's Mind'. In G. Brüntrup and L. Jaskolla (eds.) *Panpsychism: Contemporary Perspectives*. Oxford: Oxford University Press: 249–82.

Coleman, S. and P. Goff. In press. 'Russellian Monism'. In U. Kriegel (ed.) *The Oxford Companion to Consciousness*.

Conee, E. 1994. 'Phenomenal Knowledge'. *Australasian Journal of Philosophy* 72: 136–50.

Corabi, Joseph. 2008. 'Pleasure's Role in Evolution: A Response to Robinson'. *Journal of Consciousness Studies* 15: 78–86.

Corcoran, K. 2001. 'The Trouble with Searle's Biological Naturalism'. *Erkenntnis* 55(3): 307–24.

Crane, Tim. 2001. *Elements of Mind*. Oxford: Oxford University Press.

2003. 'Subjective Facts'. In H. Lillehammer and G. Rodriguez-Pereyra (eds.) *Real Metaphysics*. London: Routledge: 68–83.

2005. 'Papineau on Phenomenal Concepts.' *Philosophy and Phenomenological Research* 71: 155–62.

Crane, T. and D. H. Mellor. 1990. 'There is No Question of Physicalism.' *Mind* 99(394): 185–206.

Cutter, B. and M. Tye. 2014. 'Pains and Reasons: Why It Is Rational to Kill the Messenger.' *Philosophical Quarterly* 64(256): 423–33.

Damnjanovic, N. 2012. 'Revelation and Physicalism.' *Dialectica* 66(1): 69–91.

Dasgupta, S. 2014. 'The Possibility of Physicalism.' *Journal of Philosophy* 111(9): 557–92.
2016. 'Metaphysical Rationalism.' *Noûs* 50(2): 379–418.

Davidson, Donald. 1970/1980. 'How Is Weakness of the Will Possible?' In *Essays on Actions and Events*. Oxford: Clarendon Press.

De Brigard, Felipe. 2014. 'In Defence of the Self-Stultification Objection.' *Journal of Consciousness Studies* 21: 120–30.

Demopoulos, W. and M. Friedman. 1989. 'The Concept of Structure in *The Analysis of Matter*.' In C. Wade Savage and C. Anthony Anderson (eds.) *Rereading Russell: Essays in Bertrand Russell's Metaphysics and Epistemology*. Minneapolis: University of Minnesota Press: 183–99.

Dennett, Daniel C. 1969. *Content and Consciousness*. London: Routledge and Kegan Paul.
1980. 'The Milk of Human Intentionality.' *Behavioral and Brain Sciences* 3(3): 428–30.
1988. 'Quining Qualia.' In A. Marcel and E. Bisiach (eds.) *Consciousness in Contemporary Science*. Oxford: Oxford University Press: 42–77.
1991. *Consciousness Explained*. Boston, MA: Little, Brown.
2007. 'What RoboMary Knows.' In T. Alter and S. Walter (eds.) *Phenomenal Concepts and Phenomenal Knowledge: New Essays on Consciousness and Physicalism*. New York: Oxford University Press: 15–31.

deRosset, L. 2013. 'Grounding Explanations.' *Philosophers' Imprint* 13: 1–26.

Descartes, R. 1641/1985. *Meditations* and *Objections and Replies*, in *The Philosophical Writings of Descartes*, vol. II, trans. J. Cottingham, R. Stoothoff and D. Murdoch. Cambridge: Cambridge University Press: 1–61; 63–397.

Diaz-Leon, E. 2010. 'Can Phenomenal Concepts Explain the Epistemic Gap?' *Mind* 119(476): 933–51.
2014. 'Do A Posteriori Physicalists Get Our Phenomenal Concepts Wrong?' *Ratio* 27(1): 1–16.

Dienes, Zoltán. 2004. 'Assumptions of Subjective Measures of Unconscious Mental States: Higher-Order Thoughts and Bias.' *Journal of Consciousness Studies* 11(9): 25–45.

Drake, D., A. O. Lovejoy, J. B. Pratt, A. K. Rogers, G. Santayana, R. W. Sellars and C. A. Strong. 1920. *Essays in Critical Realism: A Co-Operative Study of the Problem of Knowledge*. London: Macmillan.

Dretske, Fred I. 1977. 'Laws of Nature.' *Philosophy of Science* 44(2): 248–68.
1995. *Naturalizing the Mind*. Cambridge, MA: MIT Press.

Du Bois-Reymond, E. 1874. 'The Limits of Our Knowledge of Nature.' *Popular Science Monthly* 5: 17–32.

Dunne, J. W. 1927. *An Experiment with Time*. London: Faber and Faber.

Eddington, A. 1939. *The Philosophy of Physical Science*. Cambridge: Cambridge University Press.

Egan, Andy. 2006. 'Appearance Properties.' *Noûs* 40: 495–521.

Ellis, Brian. 2010. 'An Essentialist Perspective on the Problem of Induction.' *Principia* 2(1): 103–24.

Evans, G. 1982. *The Varieties of Reference*. New York: Oxford University Press.

Farkas, Katalin. 2015. 'Knowing-wh Does Not Reduce to Know-that.' *American Philosophical Quarterly* 53(2): 111–24.

Feigl, H. 1958/1967. *The 'Mental' and the 'Physical': The Essay and a Postscript*. Minneapolis: University of Minnesota Press.

Fernandez-Duque, Diego and Ian M. Thornton. 2000. 'Change Detection without Awareness: Do Explicit Reports Underestimate the Representation of Change in the Visual System?' *Visual Cognition* 7(1–3): 324–44.

Fine, K. 1994. 'Essence and Modality.' *Philosophical Perspectives* 8: 1–16.

   2001. 'The Question of Realism.' *Philosophers' Imprint* 1: 1–30.

   2012. 'Guide to Ground.' In F. Correia and B. Schnieder (eds.) *Metaphysical Grounding: Understanding the Structure of Reality*. Cambridge: Cambridge University Press: 37–80.

Firestone, Chaz and Brian J. Scholl. 2016. 'Cognition Does Not Affect Perception: Evaluating the Evidence for "Top-Down" Effects.' *Behavioral and Brain Sciences* 39: 1–19. doi: 10.1017/S0140525X15000965

Fodor, J. 1989. 'Making Mind Matter More.' *Philosophical Topics* 17: 59–79.

Forrest, P. 2005. 'Universals as Sense Data.' *Philosophy and Phenomenological Research* 71: 622–31.

Foster, J. 2000. *The Nature of Perception*. Oxford: Oxford University Press.

Frege, Gottlob. 1892/1993. 'On Sense and Reference.' In A. W. Moore (ed.) *Meaning and Reference*. Oxford: Oxford University Press: 23–42.

   1918–19/1988. 'Thoughts.' In N. Salmon and S. Soames (eds.) *Propositions and Attitudes*. Oxford: Oxford University Press: 33–55.

Funkhouser, E. 2006. 'The Determinable-Determinate Relation.' *Noûs* 40(3): 548–69.

Gendler, Tamar Szabó. 2000. 'The Puzzle of Imaginative Resistance.' *Journal of Philosophy* 97(2): 55–81.

George, B. R. 2013. 'Knowing-"wh," Mention-some Readings, and Non-Reducibility.' *Thought* 2(2): 166–77.

Gertler, Brie. 2001. 'Introspecting Phenomenal States.' *Philosophy and Phenomenological Research* 63(2): 305–28.

   2012. 'Renewed Acquaintance.' In Declan Smithies and Daniel Stoljar (eds.) *Introspection and Consciousness*. Oxford: Oxford University Press: 89–123.

Gibb, S. C. 2014. 'Recent Work on Mental Causation.' *Analysis* 74(2): 327–38.

Goff, P. 2010. 'Ghosts and Sparse Properties: Why the Physicalist Has More to Fear from Ghosts than Zombies.' *Philosophy and Phenomenological Research* 81: 119–39.

   2011. 'A Posteriori Physicalists Get Our Phenomenal Concepts Wrong,' *Australasian Journal of Philosophy* 89(2): 191–209.

   2015a. 'Real Acquaintance and Physicalism.' In P. Coates and S. Coleman (eds.) *Phenomenal Qualities*. Oxford: Oxford University Press: 121–45.

2015b. 'Against Constitutive Russellian Monism.' In Torin Alter and Yujin Nagasawa (eds.) *Consciousness in the Physical World: Perspectives on Russellian Monism.* New York: Oxford University Press: 370–400.

2017. *Consciousness and Fundamental Reality.* Oxford: Oxford University Press.

In press a. 'Essentialist modal rationalism.' In *Synthese.*

In press b. 'Panpsychism.' In *The Routledge Encyclopedia of Philosophy.*

Goodman, Nelson. 1951. *The Structure of Appearance.* Cambridge, MA: Harvard University Press.

Graff, D. 2001. 'Phenomenal Continua and the Sorites.' *Mind* 110(440): 905–35.

Grahek, Nikola. 2007. *Feeling Pain and Being in Pain.* Cambridge, MA: MIT Press.

Grandin, Temple. 2006. *Thinking in Pictures: My Life with Autism,* 2nd edn. New York: Vintage Books.

Halsey, Rita M. and Alphonse Chapanis. 1951. 'On the Number of Absolutely Identifiable Spectral Hues.' *Journal of the Optical Society of America* 41(12): 1057–8.

Harman, Gilbert. 1990. 'The Intrinsic Quality of Experience.' In James Tomberlin (ed.) *Philosophical Perspectives, 4: Action Theory and Philosophy of Mind.* Atascadero, CA: Ridgeview Press: 31–52.

Harrison, Bernard. 1967. 'On Describing the Colours.' *Inquiry* 10: 38–52.

Hawthorne, J. 2001. 'Causal Structuralism.' *Philosophical Perspectives* 15: 361–78.

Hazen, A. P. 1999. 'On Naming the Colours.' *Australasian Journal of Philosophy* 77: 224–31.

Heikinheimo, A. and T. Vaaja. 2013. 'The Redundancy of the Knowledge Argument in *The Conscious Mind*.' *Journal of Consciousness Studies* 20(5–6): 6–26.

Heinsenberg, W. 1937. 'Gedanken der Naturphilosophie in der modernen Physik.' *Die Antike* 13: 118–24.

Higginbotham, James. 1996. 'The Semantics of Questions.' In Shalom Lappin (ed.) *The Handbook of Contemporary Semantic Theory.* Malden, MA: Blackwell: 361–83.

Hill, C. S. 1997. 'Imaginability, Conceivability, Possibility, and the Mind-Body Problem.' *Philosophical Studies* 87: 61–85.

Hill, Christopher S. and Brian P. McLaughlin. 1999. 'There Are Fewer Things in Reality Than Are Dreamt of in Chalmers's Philosophy.' *Philosophy and Phenomenological Research* 59(2): 445–54.

Hobbes, T. 1655. *De Corpore.* London.

Holton, Richard. 2004. 'Review of Daniel Wegner, *The Illusion of Conscious Will*.' *Mind* 113(449): 218–21.

Horgan, Terence E. 1984. 'Jackson on Physical Information and Qualia.' *Philosophical Quarterly* 34: 147–52.

1993. 'From Supervenience to Superdupervenience: Meeting the Demands of the Material World.' *Mind* 102(408): 555–86.

Horgan, Terence E. and John L. Tienson. 2001. 'Deconstructing New Wave Materialism.' In Carl Gillett and Barry M. Loewer (eds.) *Physicalism and Its Discontents.* New York: Cambridge University Press: 307–18.

Howell, Robert J. 2006. 'Self-Knowledge and Self-Reference.' *Philosophy and Phenomenological Research* 72(1): 44–70.

2007. 'The Knowledge Argument and Objectivity.' *Philosophical Studies* 135(2): 145–77.

2008. 'Subjective Physicalism.' In E. Wright (ed.) *The Case for Qualia*. Cambridge, MA: MIT Press: 125–40.

2009a. 'The Ontology of Subjective Physicalism.' *Noûs* 43(2): 315–45.

2009b. 'Emergentism and Supervenience Physicalism.' *Australasian Journal of Philosophy* 87(1): 83–98.

2013. *Consciousness and the Limits of Objectivity: The Case for Subjective Physicalism*. Oxford: Oxford University Press.

n.d. Comments on Montero's 'Must Physicalism Imply the Supervenience of the Mental on the Physical?' https://consciousnessonline.files.wordpress.com/2012/02/howell-comments-on-montero.pdf.

Hume, David. 1739/1985. *A Treatise of Human Nature*, ed. P. H. Nidditch. Oxford: Oxford University Press.

Huxley, T. H. 1886/1892. 'Science and Morals.' In *Essays upon Some Controverted Questions*. New York: Appleton: 163–83.

Jackson, Frank 1977. *Perception: A Representative Theory*. Cambridge: Cambridge University Press.

1982. 'Epiphenomenal Qualia.' *Philosophical Quarterly* 32(127):127–36.

1986. 'What Mary Didn't Know.' *Journal of Philosophy* 83: 291–95.

1993. 'Armchair Metaphysics.' In M. Michael and J. O'Leary-Hawthorne (eds.) *Philosophy in Mind*. Amsterdam: Kluwer: 23–42.

1995. 'Postscript to "What Mary Did Not Know".' In Paul Moser and J. D. Trout (eds.) *Contemporary Materialism*. London: Routledge: 192–8.

1998a. *From Metaphysics to Ethics: A Defence of Conceptual Analysis*. Oxford: Oxford University Press.

1998b. 'Postscript on Qualia.' In *Mind, Method and Conditionals*. London: Routledge: 76–9.

2002. 'Representation and Experience.' In H. Clapin, P. Slezack and P. Staines (eds.) *Representation in Mind: New Approaches to Mental Representation*. Westport, CT: Praeger: 107–24.

2003. 'Mind and Illusion.' In A. O'Hear (ed.) *Minds and Persons*. Royal Institute of Philosophy Supplement 53. Cambridge: Cambridge University Press: 251–71.

2005a. 'The Case for A Priori Physicalism.' In N. Christian and A. Beckermann (eds.) *Philosophy–Science–Scientific Philosophy*. Main Lectures and Colloquia of GAP.5, Fifth International Congress of the Society for Analytical Philosophy. Paderborn: Mentis: 251–65.

2005b. 'Consciousness.' In Frank Jackson and Michael Smith (eds.) *The Oxford Handbook of Contemporary Philosophy*. Oxford: Oxford University Press: 310–33.

2007. The Knowledge Argument, Diaphanousness, Representationalism.' In T. Alter and S. Walter (eds.) *Phenomenal Concepts and Phenomenal Knowledge: New Essays on Consciousness and Physicalism*. New York: Oxford University Press: 52–64.

2016. 'What Physicalists Have to Say about the Knowledge Argument.' *Grazer Philosophische Studien* 93: 511–524.

In press. 'A Priori Physicalism.' In *The Oxford Handbook of Consciousness*. Oxford: Oxford University Press.

Jackson, Frank and R. J. Pinkerton. 1973. 'On an Argument against Sensory Items.' *Mind* 82: 269–72.

Jacobs, J. D. 2011. 'Powerful Qualities, Not Pure Powers.' *The Monist* 94(1): 81–102.

James, William. 1890. *The Principles of Psychology*. New York: Dover Publications.

Johnston, M. 2004. 'The Obscure Object of Hallucination.' *Philosophical Studies* 120: 113–83.

Kadic, N. 2017. 'The Grounding Problem for Panpsychism and the Identity Theory of Powers.' *Croatian Journal of Philosophy* 17(1): 45–55.

Kahane, Guy. 2010. 'Feeling Pain for the Very First Time: The Normative Knowledge Argument.' *Philosophy and Phenomenological Research* 80(1): 20–49.

Kant, I. 1781–7/1933. *Critique of Pure Reason*, trans. N. Kemp Smith. London: Macmillan. 1783/1953. *Prolegomena*, trans. P. G. Lucas. Manchester: Manchester University Press.

Kauffmann, Thomas, Hugo Théorot and Alvaro Pascual-Leone. 2002. 'Braille Character Discrimination in Blindfolded Human Subjects.' *NeuroReport* 13(5): 571–4.

Kind, Amy. 2016a. 'Introduction: Exploring Imagination.' In Amy Kind (ed.) *The Routledge Handbook of Philosophy of Imagination*. Abingdon: Routledge: 1–11

2016b. 'The Snowman's Imagination.' *American Philosophical Quarterly* 53: 341–8.

2016c. 'Imagining Under Constraints.' In Amy Kind and Peter Kung (eds.) *Knowledge Through Imagination*. Oxford: Oxford University Press: 145–59.

2018. 'How Imagination Gives Rise to Knowledge.' In Fabian Dorsch and Fiona Macpherson (eds.) *Perceptual Memory and Perceptual Imagination*. Oxford: Oxford University Press 227–246.

Kirk, R. 2005. *Zombies and Consciousness*. New York: Oxford University Press.

2013. *The Conceptual Link from the Mental to the Physical*. New York: Oxford University Press.

Kriegel, U. 2009. *Subjective Consciousness: A Self-Representational Theory*. New York: Oxford University Press.

Kripke, S. 1972. 'Naming and necessity.' In Harman and Davidson *Semantics of Natural Language*, pp. 253–355.

Kripke, S. 1980. *Naming and Necessity*. Cambridge, MA: Harvard University Press.

Kuehni, Rolf G. 2010. 'Color Spaces and Color Order Systems.' In Jonathan Cohen and Mohan Matthen (eds.) *Color Ontology and Color Science*. Cambridge, MA: MIT Press: 3–36.

Kung, Peter. 2016. 'You Really Do Imagine It: Against Error Theories of Imagination.' *Noûs* 50: 90–120.

Ladyman, J. and D. Ross. 2007. *Everything Must Go: Metaphysics Naturalised*. Oxford: Oxford University Press.

Laloyaux, Cédric, Arnaud Destrebecqz and Axel Cleeremans. 2003. 'Implicit Change Identification: A Replication of Fernandez-Duque and Thornton (2003).' *Journal of Experimental Psychology: Human Perception and Performance* 32(6): 1366–79.

Landini, G. 2011. *Russell*. New York: Routledge.

Lange, F. A. 1865–75/1925. *The History of Materialism and Criticism of its Present Importance*, trans. E. C. Thomas with an introduction by Bertrand Russell. London: Routledge and Kegan Paul.

Langton, R. 1998. *Kantian Humility: Our Ignorance of Things in Themselves*. Oxford: Clarendon Press.

Lavie, Nilli. 1995. 'Perceptual Load as a Necessary Condition for Selective Attention.' *Journal of Experimental Psychology: Human Perception and Performance* 21(3): 451–68.

2010. 'Attention, Distraction, and Cognitive Control under Load.' *Current Directions in Psychological Science* 19(3): 143–8.

Lavie, Nilli, Diane M. Beck and Nikos Konstantinou. 2014. 'Blinded by the Load: Attention, Awareness, and the Role of Perceptual Load.' *Philosophical Transactions of the Royal Society B: Biological Sciences* 369(1641): 1–10.

Leuenberger, S. 2013. 'Grounding and Necessity.' *Inquiry* 57(2): 151–74.

Levin, J. 2007a. 'What Is a Phenomenal Concept?' In T. Alter and S. Walter (eds.) *Phenomenal Knowledge and Phenomenal Concepts: New Essays on Consciousness and Physicalism*. New York: Oxford University Press: 87–110.

2007b. 'Nagel vs. Nagel on the Nature of Phenomenal Concepts.' *Ratio* 20(3): 293–307.

Levine, Joseph. 1983. 'Materialism and Qualia: The Explanatory Gap.' *Pacific Philosophical Quarterly* 64: 354–61.

2007. 'Phenomenal Concepts and the Materialist Constraint.' In T. Alter and S. Walter (eds.) *Phenomenal Knowledge and Phenomenal Concepts: New Essays on Consciousness and Physicalism*. New York: Oxford University Press: 143–76.

Levy, Neil. 2013. 'The Importance of Awareness.' *Australasian Journal of Philosophy* 91: 221–9.

Lewis, David. 1973. 'Causation.' *Journal of Philosophy* 70(17): 556–67.

1979. 'Attitudes de Dicto and de Se.' *Philosophical Review* 88(4): 513–43.

1983a. 'Postscript to "Mad Pain and Martian Pain".' In *Philosophical Papers I*. Oxford: Oxford University Press: 130–2.

1983b. 'New Work for a Theory of Universals.' In *Papers in Metaphysics and Epistemology*. Cambridge: Cambridge University Press: 8–55.

1986. *On the Plurality of Worlds*. Oxford: Blackwell.

1996. 'Reduction of Mind.' In S. Guttenplan (ed.) *A Companion to the Philosophy of Mind*. New York: Blackwell: 412–30.

1997. 'Naming the Colours.' *Australasian Journal of Philosophy* 75: 325–42.

1999. 'What Experience Teaches.' In *Papers in Metaphysics and Epistemology*, Cambridge: Cambridge University Press, pp. 262–290. Originally in *Proceedings of the Russellian Society*, Sydney: University of Sydney, 13 (1988): 29–57.

2009. 'Ramseyan Humility.' In D. Braddon-Mitchell and R. Nola (eds.) *Conceptual Analysis and Philosophical Naturalism*. Cambridge, MA: MIT Press: 203–22.

Libet, Benjamin. 2004. *Mind Time: The Temporal Factor in Consciousness*. Cambridge, MA: Harvard University Press.

Lichtenberg, Georg. 1971. *Schriften und Briefe*, vol. II, ed. W. Promies. Munich: Carl Hanser.

Loar, B. 1997. 'Phenomenal States.' In N. Block, O. Flanagan and G. Güzeldere (eds.) *The Nature of Consciousness: Philosophical Debates*. Cambridge, MA: MIT Press: 597–616. Adapted from a version in *Philosophical Perspectives* 4, 1990.

2003. 'Qualia, Properties, Modality.' *Philosophical Issues* 13(1): 113–29.

Locke, J. 1689/1975. *An Essay Concerning Human Understanding*, ed. P. H. Nidditch. Oxford: Oxford University Press.

Lowe, E. J. 2012. 'What Is the Source of Our Knowledge of Modal Truths?' *Mind* 121(484): 919–50.

Ludlow, P., D. Stoljar and Y. Nagasawa (eds.) 2004. *There's Something about Mary: Essays on Phenomenal Consciousness and Frank Jackson's Knowledge Argument.* Cambridge, MA: MIT Press.

Lycan, W. G. 1996. *Consciousness and Experience.* Cambridge, MA: MIT Press.

McClelland, T. 2013. 'The Neo-Russellian Ignorance Hypothesis: A Hybrid Account of Phenomenal Consciousness.' *Journal of Consciousness Studies* 20(3–4): 125–51.

McDowell, J. 1984. 'De Re Senses.' *Philosophical Quarterly* 34: 283–94.

McGinn, C. 1989. 'Can We Solve the Mind–Body Problem?' *Mind* 98: 349–66.

2004a. *Mindsight: Image, Dream, Meaning.* Cambridge, MA: Harvard University Press.

2004b. 'The Objects of Intentionality.' In *Consciousness and Its Objects.* Oxford: Clarendon Press: 220–48.

Machery, Edouard. 2009. *Doing without Concepts.* Oxford: Oxford University Press.

McLaughlin, B. P. 2001. 'In Defence of New Wave Materialism: A Response to Horgan and Tienson.' In C. Gillett and B. Loewer (eds.) *Physicalism and its Discontents.* Cambridge, New York: Cambridge University Press: 319–30.

Maddox, Steve. 2007. 'Mathematical Equations in Braille.' *MSOR Connections* 7: 45–8.

Malebranche, N. 1688/1997. *Dialogues on Metaphysics and Religion*, ed. N. Jolley and D. Scott. Cambridge: Cambridge University Press.

Mandik, P. 2009. 'The Neurophilosophy of Subjectivity.' In J. Bickle (ed.) *The Oxford Handbook of Philosophy and Neuroscience.* New York: Oxford University Press: 601–18.

Marcel, Anthony J. 1983. 'Conscious and Unconscious Perception: An Approach to the Relations between Phenomenal Experience and Perceptual Processes.' *Cognitive Psychology* 15(2): 238–300.

Maxwell, G. 1978. 'Rigid Designators and Mind-Brain Identity.' In C. Wade Savage (ed.) *Perception and Cognition: Issues in the Foundations of Psychology.* Minneapolis: University of Minnesota Press: 365–403.

Mele, Alfred. 2013. 'Unconscious Decisions and Free Will.' *Philosophical Psychology* 26: 777–89.

Mellor, D. H. 1993. 'Nothing Like Experience.' *Proceedings of the Aristotelian Society* 93: 1–16.

Melnyk, Andrew. 2003. *A Physicalist Manifesto: Thoroughly Modern Materialism.* Cambridge: Cambridge University Press.

Mendola, J. 2008. *Anti-Externalism.* New York: Oxford University Press.

Michotte, Albert. 1963. *The Perception of Causality.* New York: Basic Books.

Mihalik, J. 2016. 'Consciousness in Nature: A Russellian Approach.' PhD thesis, Charles University Prague.

Montero, Barbara. 2001. 'Post-Physicalism.' *Journal of Consciousness Studies* 8: 61–80.

2007. 'Physicalism Could Be True Even If Mary Learns Something New.' *Philosophical Quarterly* 57: 176–89.

2012. 'Irreverent Physicalism.' *Philosophical Topics* 40(2): 91–102.

2013. 'Must Physicalism Imply Supervenience of the Mental on the Physical?' *Journal of Philosophy* 110: 93–110.

2015. 'Russellian Physicalism.' In T. Alter and Y. Nagasawa (eds.) *Consciousness in the Physical World: Perspectives on Russellian Monism.* New York: Oxford University Press: 209–23.

Moore, G. E. 1922. 'The Refutation of Idealism.' In *Philosophical Studies.* London: Routledge & Kegan Paul: 1–30.

Mørch, H. 2014. 'Panpsychism and Causation: A New Argument and a Solution to the Combination Problem.' PhD thesis, University of Oslo.

Mumford, Stephen. 2004. *Laws in Nature.* New York: Routledge.

Nagasawa, Yujin. 2010. 'The Knowledge Argument and Epiphenomenalism.' *Erkenntnis* 72(1): 37–56.

Nagel, Thomas. 1974. 'What Is It Like to Be a Bat?' *Philosophical Review* 83(4): 435–50.

1979. 'Subjective and Objective.' In *Mortal Questions.* New York: Cambridge University Press: 207–22.

1986. *The View from Nowhere.* New York: Oxford University Press.

2012. *Mind and Cosmos.* New York: Oxford University Press.

Nanay, Bence. 2009. 'Imagining, Recognizing and Discriminating: Reconsidering the Ability Hypothesis.' *Philosophy and Phenomenological Research* 89: 699–717.

Nemirow, Laurence. 1979. 'Functionalism and the Subjective Quality of Experience.' PhD thesis, Stanford University.

1980. 'Review of *Mortal Questions*, by Thomas Nagel.' *Philosophical Review* 89: 473–7.

1990. 'Physicalism and the Cognitive Role of Acquaintance. In W. Lycan (ed.) *Mind and Cognition: A Reader.* Oxford.: Basil Blackwell: 490–9.

2007. 'So This Is What It's Like: A Defense of the Ability Hypothesis.' In T. Alter and S. Walter (eds.) *Phenomenal Knowledge and Phenomenal Concepts: New Essays on Consciousness and Physicalism.* New York: Oxford University Press: 32–51.

Newman, N. H. A. 1928. 'Mr Russell's Causal Theory of Perception.' *Mind* 37(146): 26–43.

Ney, A. 2008a. 'Defining Physicalism.' *Philosophy Compass* 3(5): 1033–48.

2008b. 'Physicalism as an Attitude.' *Philosophical Studies* 138: 1–15.

Nida-Rümelin, M. 1995. 'What Mary Couldn't Know: Belief about Phenomenal States.' In T. Metzinger (ed.) *Conscious Experience.* Exeter: Imprint Academic: 219–42.

1998. 'On Belief about Experiences: An Epistemological Distinction Applied to the Knowledge Argument against Physicalism.' *Philosophy and Phenomenological Research* 58: 51–73.

2007. 'Grasping Phenomenal Properties.' In T. Alter and S. Walter (eds.) *Phenomenal Concepts and Phenomenal Knowledge. New Essays on Consciousness and Physicalism.* Oxford: Oxford University Press: 307–49.

2009. 'Qualia: The Knowledge Argument.' In Edward N. Zalta (ed.) *The Stanford Encyclopedia of Philosophy* (Summer 2015 edn). https://plato.stanford.edu/archives/sum2015/entries/qualia-knowledge/.

Noordhof, Paul. 2003. 'Something Like Ability.' *Australasian Journal of Philosophy* 81: 21–40.

Overgaard, Morten, Julian Rote, Kim Mouridsen and Thomas Zoëga Ramsøy. 2006. 'Is Conscious Perception Gradual or Dichotomous? A Comparison of Report Methodologies during a Visual Task.' *Consciousness and Cognition* 15(4): 700–8.

Papineau, D. 1993. *Philosophical Naturalism.* Oxford: Blackwell.

1998. 'Mind the Gap.' *Philosophical Perspectives* 12(S12): 373–89.

2001. 'The Rise of Physicalism.' In Carl Gillett and Barry Loewer (eds.) *Physicalism and Its Discontents*. Cambridge: Cambridge University Press: 3–36.

2002. *Thinking about Consciousness*. New York: Oxford University Press.

2006. 'Comments on Galen Strawson.' *Journal of Consciousness Studies* 13(10–11): 100–9.

2007. 'Phenomenal and Perceptual Concepts.' In T. Alter and S. Walter (eds.) *Phenomenal Knowledge and Phenomenal Concepts: New Essays on Consciousness and Physicalism*. New York: Oxford University Press: 111–44.

Pautz. A. 2006. Online reply to John Bengson, 'Being Aware of Uninstantiated Universals', at http://rationalhunter.typepad.com/close_range/2006/12/being_aware_of_.html.

2007. 'Intentionalism and Perceptual Presence.' *Philosophical Perspectives* 21: 495–541.

2013. 'Does Phenomenology Ground Mental Content?' In Uriah Kriegel (ed.) *Phenomenal Intentionality: New Essays.* Oxford: Oxford University Press: 194–234.

Peacocke, Christopher. 1992. *A Study of Concepts*. Cambridge, MA: MIT Press.

2002. 'Sensation and the Content of Experience: A Distinction.' In David J. Chalmers (ed.) *The Philosophy of Mind*. New York: Oxford University Press: 435–46.

Peels, Rik. 2016. 'The Empirical Case against Introspection.' *Philosophical Studies* 173(9): 2461–85.

Pereboom, Derk 1995. 'Conceptual Structure and the Individuation of Content.' *Philosophical Perspectives* 9: 401–26.

2002. 'Robust Nonreductive Materialism.' *Journal of Philosophy* 99: 499–531.

2011. *Consciousness and the Prospects of Physicalism*. New York: Oxford University Press.

Pérez-Carpinell, Joaquín, Rosa Baldoví, M. Dolores de Fez and José Castro. 1998. 'Color Memory Matching: Time Effect and Other Factors.' *Color Research and Application* 23(4): 234–47.

Perry, John. 1979. 'The Problem of the Essential Indexical.' *Noûs* 13: 3–21.

2001. *Knowledge, Possibility, and Consciousness*. The 1999 Jean Nicod Lectures. Cambridge, MA: MIT Press.

Phillips, Ben. 2014. 'Indirect Representation and the Self-Representational Theory of Consciousness.' *Philosophical Studies* 167(2): 273–90.

Pitt, D. 2004. 'The Phenomenology of Cognition, Or, What Is It Like to Think That P?' *Philosophy and Phenomenological Research* 69: 1–36.

2009. 'Intentional Psychologism.' *Philosophical Studies* 146: 117–38.

2011. 'Introspection, Phenomenality and the Availability of Intentional Content.' In M. Montague and T. Bayne (eds.) *Cognitive Phenomenology*. Oxford: Oxford University Press: 141–93.

2013. 'Indexical Thought.' In U. Kriegel (ed.) *Phenomenal Intentionality*. Oxford: Oxford University Press: 49–70.

2016. 'Conscious Belief.' *Rivista Internazionale di Filosofia e Psicologia* 7, Symposium on Tim Crane's Aspects of Psychologism: 121–26.

In press. *The Quality of Thought*. Oxford: Oxford University Press.

Poland, Jeffrey. 1994. *Physicalism: The Philosophical Foundations*. Oxford: Clarendon Press.

Polger, Thomas W. 2011. 'Are Sensations Still Brain Processes?' *Philosophical Psychology* 24: 1–21.

Putnam, H. 1973. 'Meaning and Reference.' *Journal of Philosophy* 70: 699–711.

1975. 'The Meaning of "Meaning".' In *Mind, Language, and Reality*. Cambridge: Cambridge University Press: 215–71.

Pylyshyn, Zenon W. 2007. *Things and Places: How the Mind Connects with the World*. Cambridge, MA: MIT Press.

Rabin, G. O. 2011. 'Conceptual Mastery and the Knowledge Argument.' *Philosophical Studies* 154: 125–47.

2013. 'Mind, Modality, and Meaning: Toward a Rationalist Physicalism.' PhD thesis, University of California at Los Angeles.

Raffman, Diana. 1995. 'On the Persistence of Phenomenology.' In Thomas Metzinger (ed.) *Conscious Experience*. Exeter: Imprint Academic:. 293–308.

2011. 'Vagueness and Observationity.' In Giuseppina Ronzitti (ed.) *Vagueness: A Guide*. Dordrecht: Springer: 107–21.

Reid, T. 1785/1790. *Essays on the Intellectual Powers of Man*. Dublin: Byrne and Milliken.

1997. *An Inquiry into the Human Mind on the Principles of Common Sense*, ed. D. R. Brookes. Edinburgh: Edinburgh University Press.

Riehl, A. 1887/1894. *The Principles of the Critical Philosophy: Introduction to the Theory of Science and Metaphysics*. London: Kegan Paul, Trench, Trübner & Co.

Robinson, Howard. 1982. *Matter and Sense*. Cambridge: Cambridge University Press.

2008. 'Why Frank Should Not Have Jilted Mary.' In E. Wright (ed.) *The Case for Qualia*. Cambridge, MA: MIT Press: 223–45.

2016. *From the Knowledge Argument to Mental Substance: Resurrecting the Mind*. Cambridge: Cambridge University Press.

Robinson, W. S. 2002. 'Jackson's Apostasy.' *Philosophical Studies* 111: 277–93.

2007. 'Evolution and Epiphenomenalism.' *Journal of Consciousness Studies* 14: 27–42.

Roelofs, L. 2015. 'Combining Minds: A Defence of the Possibility of Experiential Combination.' PhD thesis, University of Toronto. https://philpapers.org/archive/ROECMA-2.pdf.

2016. 'The Unity of Consciousness, within Subjects and between Subjects.' *Philosophical Studies* 173(12): 3199–221.

Rosen, G. 2010. 'Metaphysical Dependence: Grounding and Reduction.' In B. Hale and A. Hoffmann (eds.) *Modality: Metaphysics, Logic, and Epistemology*. Oxford: Oxford University Press: 109–36.

Rosenberg, G. 2004. *A Place for Consciousness: Probing the Deep Structure of the Natural World*. New York: Oxford University Press.

Rosenthal, David. 1983. 'Reductionism and Knowledge.' In Leigh S. Cauman, Isaac Levi, Charles Parsons and Robert Schwartz (eds.) *How Many Questions?* Indianapolis: Hackett: 276–300.

1991. 'The Independence of Consciousness and Sensory Quality.' *Philosophical Issues* 1: 15–36.

1999. 'The Colors and Shapes of Visual Experiences.' In Denis Fisette (ed.) *Consciousness and Intentionality: Models and Modalities of Attribution.* Dordrecht: Kluwer Academic Publishers: 95–118.

2001. 'Color, Mental Location, and the Visual Field.' *Consciousness and Cognition* 9(4): 85–93.

2004. 'Varieties of Higher-Order Theory.' In Rocco J. Gennaro (ed.) *Higher-Order Theories of Consciousness.* Amsterdam: John Benjamins: 19–44.

2005. *Consciousness and Mind.* Oxford: Clarendon Press.

2010. 'How to Think about Mental Qualities.' *Philosophical Issues: Philosophy of Mind* 20: 368–93.

2011. 'Exaggerated Reports: Rely to Block.' *Analysis* 71(3): 431–7.

2015. 'Quality Spaces and Sensory Modalities.' In Paul Coates and Sam Coleman (eds.) *The Nature of Phenomenal Qualities: Sense, Perception, and Consciousness.* Oxford: Oxford University Press: 33–65.

In press. 'Seeming to Seem.' In Bryce Huebner (ed.) *The Philosophy of Daniel Dennett.* New York: Oxford University Press.

Runge, P. O. 1810. *Die Farben-Kugel, oder Construction des Verhaeltnisses aller Farben zueinander.* Hamburg: Perthe.

Russell, Bertrand. 1912. *The Problems of Philosophy*, London: Oxford University Press.

1914. *Our Knowledge of the External World.* London: George Allen & Unwin.

1927a. *The Analysis of Matter.* London: George Allen & Unwin.

1927b/1995. *An Outline of Philosophy.* London: Routledge.

1928/1978. 'Letter to Max Newman.' In *Bertrand Russell: Autobiography.* London: George Allen & Unwin: 413–14.

1940. *An Inquiry into Meaning and Truth.* London: George Allen & Unwin.

1945. *History of Western Philosophy.* London: George Allen & Unwin.

1956. 'Mind and Matter.' In *Portraits from Memory and Other Essays.* London: Allen & Unwin: 145–65.

1959. *My Philosophical Development.* New York: Simon & Schuster.

1961. *Basic Writings, 1903–1959.* London: George Allen & Unwin.

Sacks, Oliver. 2003. 'The Mind's Eye: What the Blind See.' *New Yorker.* July 28, 48–59.

Sainsbury, M. and M. Tye. 2011. 'An Originalist Theory of Concepts.' *Proceedings of the Aristotelian Society* 85: 101–24.

Sartre, Jean-Paul. 1940/2010. *The Imaginary*, trans. Jonathan Webber. Abingdon: Routledge.

Schaffer, J. 2009. 'On What Grounds What.' In D. Chalmers, D. Manley and R. Wasserman (eds.) *Metametaphysics: New Essays on the Foundations of Ontology.* Oxford: Clarendon Press: 347–83.

2010. 'The Least Discerning and Most Promiscuous Truthmaker.' *Philosophical Quarterly* 9: 307–24.

2017. 'The Ground between the Gaps.' *Philosophers' Imprint* 17(11): 1–26.

Schneider, S. 2017. 'Does the Mathematical Nature of Physics Undermine Physicalism?' *Journal of Consciousness Studies* 24(9–10): 7–39.

Schrödinger, E. 1956/1967. *Mind and Matter.* Cambridge: Cambridge University Press.

Schroer, R. 2010. 'What's the Beef? Phenomenal Concepts as Both Demonstrative and Substantial.' *Australasian Journal of Philosophy* 88: 505–22.

Scott, Ryan B. and Zoltán Dienes. 2010. 'Knowledge Applied to New Domains: The Unconscious Succeeds Where the Conscious Fails.' *Consciousness and Cognition* 19(1): 391–8.

Searle, J. 1980. 'Minds, Brains, and Programs.' *Behavioral and Brain Sciences* 3: 417–57. 1992. *The Rediscovery of the Mind*. Cambridge, MA: MIT Press.

Sellars, R. W. 1922. 'The Double-Knowledge Approach to the Mind-Body Problem.' *Proceedings of the Aristotelian Society* 23: 55–70.

Shani, I. 2015. 'Cosmopsychism: A Holistic Approach to the Metaphysics of Experience.' *Philosophical Papers* 44(3): 389–437.

Shoemaker, Sydney. 1980. 'Causality and Properties.' In P. van Inwagen (ed.) *Time and Cause: Essays Presented to Richard Taylor*. Dordrecht: Reidel: 109–38.

Sider, T. 2012. *Writing the Book of the World*: Oxford: Oxford University Press.

Skiles, A. 2015. 'Against Grounding Necessitarianism.' *Erkenntnis* 80(4): 717–75.

Smart, J. J. C. 1959. 'Sensations and Brain Processes.' *Philosophical Review* 68: 141–56.

Sober, Elliott. 2009. 'Parsimony Arguments in Science and Philosophy: A Test Case for Naturalism.' *Proceedings and Addresses of the American Philosophical Association* 83: 117–55.

2015. *Ockham's Razors: A User's Manual*. Cambridge: Cambridge University Press.

Sosa, Ernest. 2003. 'Privileged Access.' In Quentin Smith and Aleksandar Jokic (eds.) *Consciousness: New Philosophical Perspectives*. Oxford: Clarendon Press: 273–94.

Snowdon, P. 2010. 'On the What-It-Is-Like-Ness of Experience.' *Southern Journal of Philosophy* 48(1): 8–27.

Spelke, Elizabeth S., Ann Phillips and Amanda L Woodward. 1995. 'Infants' Knowledge of Object Motion and Human Action'. In Dan Sperber, David Premack and Ann James Premack (eds.) *Causal Cognition: A Multidisciplinary Debate*. Oxford: Clarendon Press: 44–78.

Spurrett, D. and D. Papineau. 1999. 'A Note on the Completeness of "Physics".' *Analysis* 59: 25–9.

Stanley, Jason and Timothy Williamson. 2001. 'Knowing How.' *Journal of Philosophy* 98(8): 411–44.

In press. 'Skill.' *Noûs*. Advance online version at http://onlinelibrary.wiley.com/wol1/doi/10.1111/nous.12144/full.

Stoljar, Daniel. 2001. 'Two Conceptions of the Physical.' *Philosophy and Phenomenological Research* 62(2): 253–81.

2005. 'Physicalism and Phenomenal Concepts.' *Mind and Language* 20: 469–94.

2006. *Ignorance and Imagination: The Epistemic Origin of the Problem of Consciousness*. Oxford: Oxford University Press.

2010. *Physicalism*. Abingdon: Routledge.

2015a. 'Physicalism.' In Edward N. Zalta (ed.) *The Stanford Encyclopaedia of Philosophy* (Spring 2015 edn). https://stanford.library.sydney.edu.au/entries/physicalism/.

2015b. 'Russellian Monism or Nagelian Monism?' In T. Alter and Y. Nagasawa (eds.) *Consciousness in the Physical World: Perspectives on Russellian Monism*. New York: Oxford University Press: 324–45.

2016. 'The Semantics of "What It's Like" and the Nature of Consciousness.' *Mind* 125(500): 1161–98.

Strawson, Galen. 1987. 'Realism and Causation.' *Philosophical Quarterly* 37(148): 253–77.

1989. 'Red and "Red".' *Synthese* 78(2): 193–232.

1994. *Mental Reality*. Cambridge, MA: MIT Press.

2003. 'Real Materialism.' In Louise M. Antony (ed.) *Chomsky and His Critics*. Oxford: Blackwell: 49–88.

2004. 'Real Intentionality.' *Phenomenology and the Cognitive Sciences* 3: 287–313.

2006/2008. 'Realistic Monism: Why Physicalism Entails Panpsychism.' In *Real Materialism and Other Essays*. Oxford: Oxford University Press: 53–74.

2008a. 'The Identity of the Categorical and the Dispositional.' *Analysis* 68(300): 271–82.

2008b. 'Mental Ballistics: The Involuntariness of Spontaneity.' In *Real Materialism and Other Essays*. Oxford: Oxford University Press: 233–54.

2015. 'Real Direct Realism.' In P. Coates and S. Coleman (eds.) *Phenomenal Qualities: Sense, Perception, and Consciousness*. Oxford: Oxford University Press: 214–56.

2018. 'The Silliest Claim.' In G. Strawson *Things That Bother Me*. New York: New York Review Books: 130–153.

Stubenberg, L. 2016. 'Neutral Monism.' In Edward N. Zalta (ed.) *The Stanford Encyclopaedia of Philosophy* (Winter 2016 edn). https://plato.stanford.edu/entries/neutral-monism/.

Sündström, Per. 2011. 'Phenomenal Concepts.' *Philosophy Compass* 6(4): 267–81.

Taylor, J. H. 2013. 'Physicalism and Phenomenal Concepts: Bringing Ontology and Philosophy of Mind Together.' *Philosophia* 41: 1283–97.

Tester, Steven. 2012. *Georg Christoph Lichtenberg: Philosophical Writings*. New York: State University of New York Press.

Tidman, Paul. 1994. 'Conceivability as a Test for Possibility.' *American Philosophical Quarterly* 31: 297–309.

Tooley, Michael. 1977. 'The Nature of Laws.' *Canadian Journal of Philosophy* 7(4): 667–98.

Trogdon, K. 2013a. 'An Introduction to Grounding.' In M. Hoeltje, B. Schenieder and A. Steinberg (eds.) *Varieties of Dependence*, Basic Philosophical Concepts. Munich: Philosophia Verlag: 97–122.

2013b. 'Grounding: Necessary or Contingent?' *Pacific Philosophical Quarterly* 94(4): 465–85.

Tye, M. 1995. *Ten Problems of Consciousness: A Representational Theory of the Phenomenal Mind*. Cambridge, MA: MIT Press.

2000. *Consciousness, Color, and Content*. Cambridge, MA: MIT Press.

2005. 'In Defense of Representationalism: Reply to Commentaries.' In Murat Aydede (ed.) *Pain: New Essays on Its Nature and the Methodology of Its Study*. Cambridge, MA: MIT Press: 163–76.

2009. *Consciousness Revisited: Materialism without Phenomenal Concepts*. Cambridge, MA: MIT Press.

2011. 'Knowing What It Is Like.' In J. Bengson and M. Moffett (eds.) *Knowing How: Essays on Knowledge, Mind, and Action.* New York: Oxford University Press: 300–13.

Unger, P. 1968. 'An Analysis of Factual Knowledge.' *Journal of Philosophy* 65(6): 157–70.

1998. 'The Mystery of the Physical and the Matter of Qualities.' *Midwest Studies in Philosophy* 22(1): 75–99.

Van Cleve, James. 1985. 'Three Versions of the Bundle Theory.' *Philosophical Studies* 47: 95–107

1999. *Problems from Kant.* Oxford: Oxford University Press.

Van Gulick, R. 2004. 'So Many Ways of Saying No to Mary.' In P. Ludlow, Y. Nagasawa and D. Stoljar (eds.) *There's Something about Mary: Essays on Phenomenal Consciousness and Frank Jackson's Knowledge Argument.* Cambridge, MA: MIT Press: 365–406.

Veillet, B. 2012. 'In Defense of Phenomenal Concepts.' *Philosophical Papers* 41: 97–127.

2015. 'The Cognitive Significance of Phenomenal Knowledge.' *Philosophical Studies* 172: 2955–74.

Vendler, Zeno. 1972. *Res Cogitans: An Essay in Rational Psychology.* Ithaca, NY: Cornell University Press.

Wartenberg, T. E. 2006. 'Beyond Mere Illustration: How Film Can Be Philosophy.' *Journal of Aesthetics and Art Criticism* 64(1), Special Issue: Thinking through Cinema: Film as Philosophy: 19–32.

Watkins, Michael. 1989. 'The Knowledge Argument against the Knowledge Argument.' *Analysis* 49: 158–60.

White, S. L. 2007. 'Property Dualism, Phenomenal Concepts, and the Semantic Premise.' In T. Alter and S. Walter (eds.) *Phenomenal Knowledge and Phenomenal Concepts: New Essays on Consciousness and Physicalism.* New York: Oxford University Press: 210–48.

Williams, Bernard. 1978. *Descartes.* London: Penguin Books.

Wilson, Jessica M. 2006. 'On Characterizing the Physical.' *Philosophical Studies* 131(1): 61–99.

Wittgenstein, L. 1922. *Tractatus Logico-Philosophicus.* New York: Harcourt, Brace, and Co.

Yablo, S. 1992. 'Mental Causation.' *Philosophical Review* 101: 245–80.

Young, Benjamin D., Andreas Keller and David Rosenthal. 2014. 'Quality-Space Theory in Olfaction.' *Frontiers in Psychology* 5(1). http://journal.frontiersin.org/article/10.3389/fpsyg.2014.00001/full.

Zahavi, D. 2017. 'Brain, Mind, World: Predictive Coding, Neo-Kantianism, and Transcendental Idealism.' *Husserl Studies* 34(1): 47–61. doi: 10.1007/s10743-017-9218-z

Index